LOWER MISSISSIPPI

Books *by* Hodding Carter

CIVILIAN DEFENSE OF THE UNITED STATES
(With Colonel R. Ernest Dupuy, G.S.C.)
LOWER MISSISSIPPI

Rivers of America Books already published are:

KENNEBEC by Robert P. Tristram Coffin
UPPER MISSISSIPPI by Walter Havighurst
SUWANNEE RIVER by Cecile Hulse Matschat
POWDER RIVER by Struthers Burt
THE JAMES by Blair Niles
THE HUDSON by Carl Carmer
THE SACRAMENTO by Julian Dana
THE WABASH by William E. Wilson
THE ARKANSAS by Clyde Brion Davis
THE DELAWARE by Harry Emerson Wildes
THE ILLINOIS by James Gray
THE KAW by Floyd Benjamin Streeter
THE BRANDYWINE by Henry Seidel Canby
THE CHARLES by Arthur B. Tourtellot
THE KENTUCKY by T. D. Clark
THE SANGAMON by Edgar Lee Masters
THE ALLEGHENY by Frederick Way, Jr.
THE WISCONSIN by August Derleth

THE RIVERS OF AMERICA

Edited by
STEPHEN VINCENT BENÉT and CARL CARMER
As Planned and Started by CONSTANCE LINDSAY SKINNER
Art Editor RUTH E. ANDERSON

LOWER MISSISSIPPI

by *Hodding Carter*

HODDING CARTER

Illustrated by JOHN MCCRADY

FARRAR & RINEHART

INCORPORATED

New York   *Toronto*

To
My Father
and the Memory of
My Mother

Contents

PART FOUR: *Years of the Locust*

PART FIVE: *Unsolved River*

The River

A CONTINENT once ended where the Lower Mississippi begins. Fifty thousand years ago a great inland sea covered what are now the pleasant prairies of Illinois, Indiana, Missouri, and Iowa; a sea that was level with and linked to Lake Michigan. Persistently seeking an outlet to the south it lapped for centuries at a spur of the Ozarks stretching from St. Louis to Cairo. Just as persistently the Ohio River hacked away at the Allegheny foothills of Kentucky.

Eventually they conquered and became allies. The course which the Mississippi now takes from river-girt Cairo to its ever-extending mouth we call the Lower Mississippi. If it shows periodically too proprietary an interest in the valley through which it twists, the lower river is acting within its legal rights, for this immense alluvial plain is of its own making. When the rocky barriers had been worn away the Mississippi sought the long arm of the sea below, and with the aid of the exploratory waters of the Ohio began an endless land boom. The sediment the rivers carried became in time the banks of a doomed estuary and the uncertain earth of an encroaching valley; and the estuary retreated as the lengthening river pushed and built southward for more than twelve hundred miles. Today, where the forked tongues of the Mississippi's mouth jut into the blue Gulf of Mexico, the process is still going on. It always will.

So developed the most important river of the North American continent. In evaluating its relation to the vassal earth you forget the geologist and grope for superlatives to describe the wealth potential of its plain, the misery and promise it has impartially dealt. From the colonization of the valley to the close of the Civil War, control of the

3

Mississippi was the most important single objective in American military strategy. In its four hundred recorded years more men have died defending or conquering or exploiting this river than any other in North America.

Unfriendly observers have named the Mississippi the Great Sewer and the Slimy Monster. The songs and poems and doggerel which have been written about it do not dwell upon its dreaminess or complaisance, for it has neither of these attributes. Nor is its beauty readily discernible. You look at the Mississippi and you are immediately aware of only three things: that its shores are far apart, that its current is fearfully swift, that its color is an unpleasant mud-yellow. Save for the infrequent bluffs against which it swirls on its shifting passage to the gulf, the Mississippi's banks seem a monotonous extension of tangled flatness, above which at a respectful distance from the river thread the watchful levees.

But the Mississippi makes up to the geographer, the engineer, the historian, and the economist what it lacks for the casual poet. Like a crooked, fluid spine, it gives support and direction to the nation's body. Forty tributaries from thirty-one states and Canada, all navigable at least in part, join nervewise with the Mississippi to create fifteen thousand miles of inland waterways and an annual outlet for more than three-quarters of a billion cubic yards of sea-destined water. Held in solution until their discharge at the river's end, a half billion tons of sediment give body and color and creative purpose to the Mississippi; black earth of Illinois, disintegrating rock of Ohio and West Virginia, clay of Kentucky, top soil of the prairies and brook-borne petrification of the hills, torn from the desolated land.

The river's statistical aspects are as unending as its fight against the men who have tried to tame it. We might tabulate them until figures and distances would become dizzily and uselessly jumbled, but these are facts to be readily

found in encyclopedia and textbook. As easily available are
the chartings of the Lower Mississippi's course, and the proof
that the Mississippi Valley can nourish and clothe the continent. All these matters will have a related place in this
story.

But not a primary place. For the real history of the
Lower Mississippi is a history of an American challenge;
a challenge to a wilderness and unpredictable devastation,
to savagery and plague and disorder, to blighting war and
the yet unriddled contradictions of democracy.

If in the telling the skeptic can also be persuaded that
there is beauty and poetry to the Lower Mississippi, that
will be good. Opinions differ. Some say that beauty ends
where the blueness of the Ohio is drowned at Cairo in the
green and yellow and brown of its merging. But have they
seen the Mississippi at Natchez, tawny in the sunset, its
river sky of crimson and indigo and gold plummeting from
the bluffs to the flat green land beyond its western banks?
Have they watched from the levee the lights of barge and
showboat, so yellow in the thick, whispering night? In the
fury of a storm in the South Pass, the whitecaps rise so
high that you cannot see the reedy rim of land across the
river; only angry water and a gray sky from which the
heron and pelican have vanished. And there is humbling
beauty in this unity of wild water and wild heaven. In
the fall we hunt the deer in the swampy forests between
the river and the levees. Go quietly at dawn into those
brakes of cypress and cane and cottonwood and water oak.
Paddle beside the banks of the Lower Mississippi's bayous
and false lakes which once were part of its channel. You
will find something of what the Spaniard, the Frenchman,
and the Englishman swore and marveled at: the disordered
lavishness of a wilderness sprung from the earth droppings
of a river's uncounted years.

But it is not only you or I who will travel here beneath

the clay cliffs, the caving red banks, the man-made bastions of the river, reacting in our own ways to its threats and treachery and riches. This journey is four hundred years long. It is made by copper-skinned men and women who offered sacrifice to the sun and by men and women who are alive today. And from the beginning to the end of these four hundred years runs a purposeful link.

I thought the story would be easy to tell, for most of my life had been spent on the river or within an hour's drive of it. I needed only to remember a little and read a little and revisit a little, and the story would tell itself.

So, first, I remembered.

The gray river shrimp would nibble our naked bodies. They weren't so bold in the deep channel, but in the beginning you didn't swim that far. Later, when you were fourteen or so, you would dare the river, with a rowboat near you and your heart loudly cold, until the current and your heavy arms had pulled you across and a mile below. And, until another lad had disappeared in the choppy white wake of the ferry's paddle wheel, you dived that summer from the automobile deck. Your foolhardiness frightened the travelers and you too, and you were glad when the captain ended it, but grieved and sobered for the reason.

But the story of the Lower Mississippi can't be put together from the memories of a boy's summers at his grandmother's home, where the rowboat was moored to a back-yard chinaberry tree, and the last of the packets hooted beyond the levee. It isn't found in the dusty riding through mortgaged cotton fields with an old man who couldn't hold his land against the river. These things are part of the story, and they help in understanding, but they do not make a book.

So, next, I read.

This is depressing, because so many have written about

the river: LaSalle and Audubon, Mark Twain, and Zadok Cramer the navigator, and Lyle Saxon, and Raven-Hart, the bearded Englishman who canoed past our town three years ago, and scores of others. I have read what most have written, and without them I could not add another book to the list. Yet when you leave them you are still confused, for their eyes saw different things and at different times. The navigator tells his story and the explorer his, and the historian and the planter, the naturalist and the pilot and the soldier. The river is in all of them. But if you try to use them piecemeal, you find a patternless puzzle.

So, lastly, I traveled—from Cairo at the southern tip of Illinois, to the Gulf.

For time so long as to be uncomprehended, the Lower Mississippi has deposited, overrun, and again invigorated this uneasy silt; but though it has thus brought identification and meaning to the valley and its people, the river has not given uniformity. If you follow the Mississippi from its turbulent confluence with the Ohio to the jetties at its dissolving mouth you will learn that cultures and livelihoods lose kinship each two hundred miles or less. You cannot say: "This is the Lower Mississippi and these its homogeneous people." Memphis is a robust, booming American city into which Midwesterners fit easily, and Tory Natchez has come to life again because of its old homes and new factories, and New Orleans is still languidly beautiful and wanton. The trappers of the passes and the planters of the Yazoo-Mississippi Delta are as alien to each other as are both to an Arkansas share-cropper or a patois-speaking Negro below Baton Rouge. Their dissimilarities give no unification to the story of the river.

This lack of a pattern troubled me until I discovered one from the sum of what I had read and remembered and seen again. It is this. The Lower Mississippi's valley is a precarious Eden, which the river has fashioned and caused to be populated because of its promise. It is a promise beset by ordeal and still only partly fulfilled.

Against the fertility of the valley are weighed four hundred years of uncertainty and conflict. The people of the river have been tested in the recurrent ravages of flood, and in the bloodier, man-directed violence they met or created. Their survival is a triumph over the Choctaw and Chickasaw, the swift and terrible yellow fever, the slow malaria, the cholera and the loathsome bubonic plague which was a by-product of their commerce overseas. Their lives have been cheap to the hair-trigger dandies, the river pirates, and the swaggering bullies of the ports. Indigo and cane, cotton and commerce came as gifts from the river and its rich earth, but the wealth which grew with each could not be maintained uninterruptedly against the changing demands and products and inventiveness of a newer civilization. In the War Between the States, the blockade and the torch, the river gunboat and the armies of occupation desolated and impoverished the Lower Mississippi from New Madrid to New Orleans. And in the river counties of Arkansas and Mississippi and Louisiana, vengeful Reconstruction delayed almost beyond mending the slow recovery and the slower understanding of the broken, outnumbered white man and the free black.

Yet always the people of the Lower Mississippi Valley have fought their way upward. Yellow fever has been conquered and malaria checked, and the bubonic plague has disappeared. The United States Army engineers have bridled, though not tamed, the river with higher and higher levees; cutoffs and spillways. The valley still breeds gun-reaching hotheads, but the accepted violence of the old days has gone with the code duello and the flatboat bucko. Cotton is no longer king, but the green fields behind the levees are more richly diversified than when the stacked bales on the steamboat decks held the valley's only hope of prosperity.

Eden's threat is less primal today, its promise nearer fulfillment.

This is to be the story of the people of this valley, a long time ago and now, and of the river that has nourished and tempted and troubled them.

PART ONE

Stepchildren of Empire

CHAPTER I

De Soto Found No Gold

HERNANDO DE SOTO, who came first, contributed nothing to the river he crossed. He saw the Mississippi only as an obstacle to further search for gold, and the men who survived him knew it only as an avenue of escape from vengeful tribesmen.

Yet today, four hundred years after the battered Spaniards came upon and doggedly crossed the Mississippi, De Soto is remembered. Historians of two states, Tennessee and Mississippi, quarrel over the location of his crossing. And they are much less certain of where the weighted body of De Soto was dropped overboard secretly by night so that the Indians would believe that the conqueror had merely whisked his immortal presence to his home in the sun. Nevertheless, De Soto, the cavalier legend, has given his name to counties and towns, and even to automobiles and hotels. Scholars have produced for the Congress of the United States a painstaking, documentary account of his travels and travail. Oddly, no instrument of terror—dynamite or bomber or even a simple six-shooter—bears his name, though that would have been the most proper tribute of all. For intrepid, persistent, enduring as they were, Hernando De Soto and his men were first of all destroyers. They ravaged, stole, raped, and murdered across the South and Southwest for four years, and no one profited from their bloody failure, least of all themselves.

But in their own time they were honorable. The Span-

ish horsemen in America were the last of the knights of
Europe, the vanishing mounted men in armor who feared
their own God, if strangely, served the king and their own
ambition, and met death with a thrusting sword. The records of their successes and failures were written for other
adventurers to read. Frenchmen and Englishmen, more adept
at trade and colonization, followed and superseded them
throughout North America and especially on the river which
balked and then saved the men of De Soto. And if there
were nothing else worth remembering, the heroism of the
Indians of the lower valley whose bare bodies darted between De Soto and conquest provides a stirring beginning
to this story of the Mississippi.

❦   ❦

It is 1492, and the bright blades of Spain are restless
in their sheaths. The last Moor has been driven from
Granada, Saracen citadel in Europe for eight hundred years.
Castile and Leon are at peace with Aragon. Spain is united.
Spain is ascendant.

It is 1492, and Christopher Columbus has stumbled
upon an outlet for the energies of men who know only
how to make war. No need now to proffer the mercenary
sword and crossbow. No need to plot civil strife. Across
the conquered Atlantic lies El Dorado.

The fighting men of Spain sweep westward. By 1498
Santo Domingo bows to their greed and cruelty, their endurance and valor. Twenty-two years later, and Cuba has
been conquered, Panama settled, and Cortez rides trium-
phantly into Mexico City. Peru falls to Pizarro in 1532.
The resisting Indian writhes on the dipping lance or, enslaved, dies in the mines of Mexico and Ecuador and Chile.
The gaudy galleons lurch homeward, their holds heavy with
the gold and silver of the Indies; and in Asturias, and

Estremadura and Andalusia the hidalgo and the peasant grow, lightheaded with golden dreams.

Now the conquistadors of South America turn to the great continent to the north. Coronado strikes from Mexico into the deserts of the Southwest, seeking the seven treasure cities of Ciboli. Pineda has skirted the Gulf of Mexico, and Panfilo de Narváez and three hundred men have died beneath the palms and cypresses of the coastal plain or on the bleak refuge of the Texas coast. And safe again in Spain, Cabeza de Vaca, one of the four survivors of the de Narvaez expedition, stirs by meaningful silence the court of Charles. Surely Florida and the green death traps to the north and west hide riches to rival Peru, they whisper. Provocative de Vaca must be closemouthed for a purpose. He shares his secret only with the king.

So reasons Hernando De Soto, favorite of Pizarro and the king, home from Peru with wealth enough from slave-taking and gold to satisfy any man but himself. So destiny begins to draw a doomed adventurer westward again to a great river which is to be his monument and his tomb.

❦　❦

In the harbor of Havana, the five ships, the two cara-vels and the pair of tiny pinnaces of Hernando De Soto make ready to weigh anchor. A brave sight they are in the spring sunlight, a sight to banish the premonitions of the Doña Isabella, his wife, and the other wives who are to remain in Cuba while their husbands sail with the new adelantado of Florida.

For a year, since the king appointed him governor of Florida in 1538, De Soto has prepared for this venture. His captains are his friends, tested in Peru, loyal, fearless, hard-bitten. And under them serves many another knight and gentleman of Portugal and Spain, drawn by the Peruvian fame of the bronzed, hawk-eyed 38-year-old governor and his promise of treasure for the winning.

De Soto has poured his cruzados into the selection of men, equipment, and supplies such as the New World has never seen. The foot soldiers are hand-picked men, veterans for the most part of the Isthmian and Peruvian campaigns, expert bowmen and swordsmen, seasoned to 30-mile marches, to cold and rain and heat. And with them are enrolled skilled craftsmen aplenty; Ruiz the stocking maker, Algalin the shoemaker, the swordcutler Rodon from Aragon, Balthasar the notary, the tailors Carrion and Sayago, de Lera, Salamanca and Carrosco, Perez, the farrier, Bernaldo the calker; honest fellows from Seville and De Soto's own hills of Badajoz, and Toledo and Villanueva. Most of the army are Spanish or Portuguese, but among the seven hundred mingle a handful of aliens, men from Genoa and Sardinia and the Levant, three Negroes, and an Englishman who sticks to his longbow. Two women sail with them, and one is to return. And for the glory of God, the good Franciscans and Dominicans have furnished eight priests and four brothers.

Admiringly a ship's officer writes to the king of De Soto's equipment:

"He carries 237 horses, besides some of relief, 300 footmen as well as those mounted, in all 513 men without the sailors. With these go more abundant subsistence than could have been got out of Spain for an armada. There are three thousand loads of cacabi; 2,500 shoulders of bacon and 2,500 homegas of maize; moreover, there are beasts on hoof for the settlement, and for the butchery to be in readiness on the return of the vessels in which we are to receive large supplies . . . much iron, steel, irons for saddlebows, spades, mattocks, panniers, ropes and baskets, things very necessary for settlement."

The supplies so necessary for a settlement were useless,

for no more is to be heard of colonization. The spades will dig nothing but graves. The lettuce, radish, and other garden seed will rot forgotten. De Soto's ships carry three kinds of domestic animals to the Florida mainland—horses, dogs, and hogs. But the horses are war steeds, the dogs are ravenous bloodhounds brought to track down and tear to pieces the recalcitrant guides and runaway slaves. Only the hogs serve the same purpose as in a land of peace. The multiplying, foraging herd of three hundred swine accompanies the expedition for nearly two years, increasing in numbers until one red night when most of them are burned to death in a surprise attack.

De Soto and his seven hundred knights and men at arms and craftsmen make a good enough beginning. At Tampa Bay they take possession of Florida for the king of Spain on June 3, 1539. Seven horsemen canter inland, and meet ten Indians. Two Indians and two horses are slain. De Soto is vexed. Horses are more important than men. The expedition will shortly learn that the Indians laugh at slow-moving foot soldiers.

"These people are so warlike and so quick that they make no account of foot soldiers," chronicled the unidentified Gentleman of Elvas, supposedly a Portuguese survivor of the expedition. "For if these go to them, they flee and when their adversaries turn their backs they are immediately upon them. The farthest they flee is the distance of an arrow shot. They are never quiet but always running and crossing from one side to another, so that the crossbows or the arquebuses cannot be aimed at them, and before a crossbowman can fire a shot an Indian can shoot three or four arrows; and very seldom does he miss what he shoots at."

The Gentleman of Elvas also notes, innocent of double meaning, that "because the Indians had not heard of the Christians they were careless." For four years the arrows of ever more careful Indians will pierce De Soto's horses, so that only 26 of the 237 survive to the journey's end; and with the horses will die two-thirds of the army. But now this lies in the unascertained future. The first tribe met on the Florida coast is inclined to be friendly after the initial encounter. They make peace with De Soto and are liberally rewarded. Cloaks, coats, doublets, breeches, stockings, armor, pikes, lances and helmets—gifts to marvel at—enrich and adorn grotesquely the Mococo chief and his men.

In return, the chief sends De Soto a scarecrow figure of a man, who is to become the most valuable member of the army. He is Juan Ortiz, forgotten survivor of the de Narvaez failure, who for nine years has lived under the protection of the chief. Ortiz is versed in the tongues of many tribes, and so like an Indian in appearance that he is nearly shot by the Spaniards before he haltingly shouts his identity.

The march inland, unparalleled for the cruelty and fortitude of its participants, begins. For four years the men of De Soto cross rivers, climb mountains, struggle through swamps seeking a golden will-o'-the-wisp. For four years they butcher and are in turn butchered. Florida is a rebellious nightmare, and a chain of burned villages. Indian guides, leading the Spaniards astray, are torn to shreds by the bloodhounds. Indian women who are reluctant to obey also are thrown to the dogs. Other Indian women, the comely ones, are purchased for looking glasses and knives, for a shirt apiece, or taken forcibly to gratify the Spaniards. The governor's quota is usually two women, carefully selected from each conquered or pacifically acquired village.

Northward through Florida, west to Apalachee, and north again into Georgia the army marches in the winter of 1539-40 against almost unremittingly hostile Indians. The Apalachees, the Mavila, the Chickasaws, those southern branches of the great Muskhogean stock, give ground but rarely homage, and die in battle or by torture for their temerity. Indian slaves, taken for burden bearers, drop dead in their chains in the bitter winter. The hands of hog stealers are roped to fallen logs and hacked off with rusting Biscayan axes. And even those tribes which meet De Soto in peace have but one idea, to send the white men packing with stories of gold in distant lands.

The Spaniards find no gold. In the spring of 1540 they are heartened in Georgia by a rumor of treasure to the northeast. So northeast they plunge. And in Georgia occurs the one romantic episode of the journey. They are welcomed by the beautiful chieftainess, the Lady of Cafitachequi, who gives to De Soto two hundred pounds of pearls and receives from him a ruby ring. But the avaricious Spaniards ransack the temple for more pearls, and force the Lady of Cafitachequi to accompany them. She escapes shortly afterward by asking with proper modesty to be allowed to answer the call of nature in wooded seclusion. And one story is that there disappeared with her one of the Negroes of the army, perhaps to rule with her in a land happily quit of the invaders.

The ranks of the army are thinning. Some have died of arrow wounds, others of cold and starvation. The Spaniards are not woodsmen. In Florida they have learned to eat corn and corn meal, and have kept their larders stocked with the pumpkins, beans, and dried plums supplied by the Indians. But unless the tribesmen bring these and game, the Spaniards are nearly helpless. Indian dogs are eaten to break the monotony of pork, but men cry for salt and a more varied diet. The forests are full of rabbits and partridge and deer, but they are not successful at hunting them.

On through South and North Carolina, then westward into Tennessee and northern Alabama and Mississippi the dwindling army moves. The Indians who face them now

are better warriors. In southern Alabama, Mavila tribesmen
kill twenty Spaniards, wound many others, and cause ir-
reparable loss among the horses. The Mavila are all but
decimated, the Spaniards estimating the Indian dead at from
2,500 to 11,000 warriors and others. But such victories are
costly for an army that cannot gain recruits.

In the spring of 1541 De Soto suffers his greatest disaster. Camped in a Chickasaw village in what is now Tallahatchie County, Mississippi, and lulled by apparent friend-
liness, the army is surprised by night and the village set
afire. Twelve soldiers and fifty to sixty horses are slain.
Three hundred hogs die in the flames, and most of the
army's clothing is lost. And here, heavy with child, dies
Francisca Henetrosa, one of the two women who accompanied their husbands. A rain halts the Indian attack, or
De Soto and his soldiers might have been wiped out.

The Indians are driven off, and the Spaniards, better
armsmiths than naturalists, manufacture bellows of bearskin
to retemper their fire-dulled swords. New lances are fashioned from ash trees, and wooden saddle frames carved.
Westward again they march, nearer to the great river of
whose existence they now know. At Fort Alibamo, in western
Mississippi, they fight again against "many armed men,
daubed over with red ochre and with their bodies, legs and
arms painted black, white, yellow and red, in the manner
of stripes which made them look as though they were in
breeches and doublet." The painted, beplumed Alibaman
hold off the Spaniards; even make a sortie from their fortified
village and kill fifteen men, most of them foot soldiers
who have been drawn up protectively before horses more
valuable now than themselves. Then the Spaniards attack,
and the fort is taken, its defenders slain or routed.

Now on May 8, 1541, a Sunday, scarcely half the resplendent seven hundred of Havana reach the Mississippi. They travel slowly, for many are wounded, and less than a hundred of their cavalrymen have horses to ride. They are ragged, scarred, emaciated. Beneath their bucklers hang tattered Indian blankets or long shirts fashioned of skin and pliable bark. Many are hatless and barefooted, and few share their leader's conviction that a fortune in gold and jewels awaits them somewhere beyond the river. The more despondent do not believe they can keep going another six months. Not even the most hardy would predict that they will continue the unfruitful wanderings, at the last leaderless, for two more years.

If De Soto or any of his men sensed that there was any unusual significance to this juncture with the Mississippi it was not recorded. The surviving Franciscan chanted no Te Deums in honor of its discovery. The Mississippi, which they called the Rio Grande, was just another river to cross, distinguished only because it was wider, swifter, muddier than the others. Here is no encouraging vision of an empire whose wealth the great river would bear to the sea. Here is only the reality of a difficult passage and the foreboding sight of waiting Indians on the opposite shore.

De Soto scouts ahead.

"He went to see the river and found there was an abundance of timber near it from which piraguas could be constructed, and an excellently situated land for establishing the camp," noted the Gentleman of Elvas. "It was nearly a half league wide, and if a man stood still on the other side one could not tell whether he were a man or something else. It was of great depth, and of very strong current. Its waters were always turgid and continually many trees and wood came down it, borne along by the force of the current. . . . It had abundance of fish of various kinds and most of them different from those of the fresh waters of Spain."

Today the civic-spirited citizens of Memphis will tell you that the discovery was made at the Chickasaw Bluffs just below their city; while Mississippi historians are convinced that the Spaniards came upon the river in Tunica County, some forty miles below. Had you lived in either place at the time you would have thanked your tribal gods if the honor had gone to the other fellow. It makes no difference to most of us now, and it made no difference to De Soto, for he was unaware that it was for this principally that history would identify him.

🌿 🌿

Of what were you aware, Hernando De Soto? What did you muse upon as your ragged men went down with their horses to drink the yellow waters? There beneath the tangled black oak and water maple, as you singled out the straightest trees for the barge building, did you think of the olive trees of Spain? Did the bloom of the dogwood and the triumph of the passion flower and the trumpet vine remind you of the ordered gardens of Badajoz? Or had you forgotten Spain? You placed your sentries at dusk beyond the clearing at the river's edge. You listened absently to the moans of wounded, fitful men. Did the endless months of vigil seem futile now, or did the golden motes of the western sun quicken again your stubborn dream? Or can men beset think beyond the necessities of the hour?

We would like to know more about you, Hernando De Soto, as you stare across the river that will give you burial and immortality. We know your lance was the most skillful in the New World, that in a cruel day you were less cruel than most. We know that men followed you in cold and hunger and screaming death with no thought of mutiny

or retreat. But you are as dim as the shadow you cast between the campfire and a river four hundred years ago.

You will struggle for another year, pursuing a mocking
nothingness across Arkansas and into Texas, and back again
to the river. And somewhere along the Lower Mississippi,
you will die of fever a year from the discovery. They will
bury you by night, then disinter your body and consign
it to the river. And they will tell the questioning cacique
that you have gone to the sky as you have often done before;
for the Indians' belief in your godlike immortality is the
most powerful weapon of all. They will sell at auction your
two men and two women slaves, your three horses. And
in March, 1543, nearly four years from that gay departure,
they will build boats and fight their way downstream under
your friend and successor, Luis de Moscosco. The bowmen
of the Natchez, the Caddo spearmen, and the riverwise
lesser tribes will harry them to the river's mouth. At the
end they will find haven at Panuco, on the Mexican coast,
strange, forlorn tatterdemalions dressed in skins, for whom
the flesh of those last sturdy horses has almost meant life
itself.

But we will leave you here, in the twilight of a day
four hundred years ago, when you came upon the Mississippi.
On it you put your bloody, tenacious stamp, and its history
for four hundred years after you will be written in tenacity
and blood.

CHAPTER 2

Bienville Remembers

THE RIVER and its wilderness closed in upon the relics of De Soto. The brittle leaves of autumn decayed above the rusted cuirass and the broken lance; the spring rains washed away the loose-packed earth of Spanish graves, and the river in spring flood buried more deeply the bones of Spain beneath the thick silt of its deposit.

In the rare villages to which De Soto had come in friendship, tribesmen handed down moldy remnants of gift cloth, discolored trinkets and awkward wargear from warrior to warrior's son. And among the inheritors were young braves on whose adolescent cheeks sprouted a dark, downy reminder of the white horsemen's casual lust. These were called the Bearded Ones. And this was all that remained of the venture of De Soto.

Spain had struck from the south and her failure discouraged her emulators for a hundred and thirty years. Then France descended from her strong northern seigneuries of Canada to conquer the Mississippi. From Quebec, Joliet the trader and Marquette the monk journeyed to the upper Mississippi and floated down it as far as the Arkansas. Returning to Quebec, they gained honor and official recognition of the value of the waterway whose rendezvous with the Gulf of Mexico they had ascertained. But they were not immediately followed. Not until seven years after their peaceful odyssey did René Robert Cavelier, Sieur de la Salle and the Chevalier de Tonti and their priests and soldiers open the Mississippi for France.

La Salle, the heroic visionary, was murdered in Texas by disaffected followers, but not before his epic fifteen years of exploration had won a new empire for France. Faithful, adventurous Tonti survived him to join the succession of great explorers whose exploits preserved for eighty years the river kingdom that a stupid Bourbon would abandon. It is difficult to gloss over the saga of La Salle and Tonti; but the eighty-year history of French domination of the Mississippi is more significantly told in the story of Jean Baptiste Le Moyne, Sieur de Bienville. Almost exactly was his lifetime bracketed by the flowering and withering of the fleur-de-lis on the banks of the river.

Now in 1765, at the close of that heartbreaking period, Jean Baptiste Le Moyne is nearly eighty-six years old. The white-haired Norman Canadian will not live much longer. His death is being hastened by the last effort he is making to save France's valley, his valley, in the New World.

In his obscure Paris lodgings, Bienville is entertaining a visitor from Louisiana. It has been nearly twenty-five years since the imperious old man quit the colony in grief and under a cloud. But he remembers dimly this merchant of New Orleans, Jean Milhet, who now consults him. And Milhet, emissary from a distraught colony, remembers Bienville and his greatness. Because of this vanished fame, because the old man's voice might move Louis XV to reconsider the abandonment of Louisiana, Milhet has crossed the Atlantic to seek him out.

The Louisianians are desperate. A few months ago they have belatedly learned that Louis has secretly given the colony to Spain, and that Spain and England have agreed upon boundaries from which France is completely excluded. The deal is a great gain for victorious England; and the transfer of Louisiana is an unexpected windfall for Spain.

But to the Louisianans it is catastrophe. The colony, the river, the people are French. They want none of Spain. They desire only to remain loyal, stubborn, forgotten Frenchmen. *We implore your Majesty.* . . .

Bienville and Milhet rehearse their audience with the king's prime minister, the Duc de Choiseul. In their hearts they know their appeal will fail, for de Choiseul himself has advised the king to cede the colony to his cousin of Spain. The minister has only disgust for the expense and the precariousness of Louisiana, and prefers that it should go as a gift to an ally rather than perhaps later to an enemy through conquest.

In the parlor of Bienville's hotel, so unlike the first shelters he built in Louisiana, Bienville and Milhet drink unhappily to their homeland. Perhaps the brandy overcomes the respectful hesitancy of the younger man and the bitter reticence of the old. Perhaps Jean Milhet questions Jean Baptiste Le Moyne. It could have been so.

Of what does an old man dream, Sieur de Bienville?

Among the Norman townsfolk of Dieppe who sailed for Canada in 1541, one was a fifteen-year-old lad who was to be the father of Bienville. This boy, Charles Le Moyne, turned to the Jesuits of Canada for employment, and as their agent he lived among the Hurons, learning the dialects, the customs, and commercial predilections of the northern tribes. In a few years, Charles Le Moyne, now trader, soldier, and interpreter, counted the peltries and gold that his apprenticeship had taught him to earn. And later, at the exposed post of Montreal, he fought the Iroquois for France, and won the adopted girl, Catherine Tierry, as his bride. From their marriage came fourteen sons and daughters; and from Charles Le Moyne's shrewdness and service to his king came wealth and letters of nobility.

Was there another such family sired in America?

From the fortresslike Chateau of Longueil, nine of the twelve sons of the emigrant from Dieppe went out to serve France in the Old World and the New. Seven would become provincial governors. Three would die in battle. And now, Bienville, the old Parisian exile who was perhaps the greatest of these, dreams of the guardrooms, the watchtower and church spire of Canadian Longueil, and of the bold brothers with the courage and fortunes of grand seigneurs.

Especially does he dream of Iberville, the elder brother whose destiny guided his own; Iberville, the naval genius who defeated the British in icy Hudson's Bay, and who bound the ensign Bienville's first wound. He dreams of Iberville, long dead, to whom France gave the commission sixty-seven years earlier to discover and possess the mouth of the Mississippi, and who took with him the eighteen-year-old brother whose life was thenceforth to be identified almost wholly with its brown torment.

What quickens an old man's blood, Sieur de Bienville?

The little frigates, *Badine* and *Marin,* and the two Norman fishing boats which were transports, stand out from Brest on October 24, 1698, under the brothers Le Moyne. Their holds and decks are crowded with filibustering Canadians, Frenchmen, and Spanish deserters from Mexico, recruited to beat the English in a peacetime race for the river's mouth. When they reach Santo Domingo six weeks later many have died of the fever of Siam and spoiled food, but they still number enough for the task ahead.

In Santo Domingo, flour is kneaded into biscuit, water casks are refilled, and the longboats mounted. Although fever is still aboard the expedition prepares hurriedly, for English vessels are sighted on the last day of the old year. They set sail again, skirting the coast of Cuba and thence to the channel of Yucatan and into the Gulf of Mexico. Through the warm blue waters where the flying fish leap before their bows and the gray gulls swoop in their wake, they sail for twenty-three days. At the end of the twenty-third day red flames along the horizon, perhaps the fires of Indian hunters, tell them that land lies ahead. Then through the dusk they make out the flat white sand, the low-lying forest and burning prairies of Apalachicola Bay.

There are Spaniards here, but France and Spain are at peace. The officers of the Spanish garrison are nervously friendly and nearly as hungry as their three hundred mutinous men. The Frenchmen do not linger, for the river's mouth is still westward.

Driven violently by shifting gales, the expedition approaches Mobile Bay under a black sky rent by lightning. Iberville and Bienville reconnoiter the channel, and spend three drenched days and nights ashore. Between the gulf and the bay lies an island, awesomely heaped with human skulls and bones, and they name it Massacre Island. But the great river's mouth does not open upon this coast.

Farther westward they sail. They discover and name Horn and Chandeleur islands, Ship Island and Cat Island, miscalled because of the unfamiliar raccoons. At Ship Island they find anchorage, and the sea-weary voyagers go ashore to fish and bathe and rest. At a distance frightened natives watch the white men who have come across an old lame Indian and an aged squaw. The French woo the pair with food and tobacco, and though the crippled tribesman burns to death when left too near a campfire, the befriended old woman makes known the kindness of the white strangers. The Indians come to them, rubbing their stomachs in greeting, and they eat sagamité together and exchange presents.

Bienville and two Canadian woodsmen are left ashore as hostages for three warriors who are taken aboard the flagship for an eye-opening reception. While Iberville regales

his guests with cannon fire, presents and brandy, Bienville
hunts buffalo and turkey. On the hunt he meets opportunely
some visiting chiefs and warriors of the Mongoulaches and
Bayogoulas, who tell him they live beside the big river. After
a final feast to celebrate an alliance, the Indians depart without giving notice. But, although their hoped-for guides have
gone, the Frenchmen are confident now that the river's
mouth is within easy reach of their barges.

On February 27, 1699, Iberville and Bienville load two
barges with arms, ammunition and provisions for twenty-five
days. Attached in tow are canoes which they know will
be needed later. With fifty men selected for endurance,
they set out. The fleet is left behind at Ship Island, with
orders to return to France in six weeks if the expedition has
not returned.

They move slowly along the tortuous coast. They are
shrouded in fog, tossed by a violent storm, nearly frozen
by wet, penetrating cold. On their right is the hardly discernible mainland, a strip of woodless sand. They skirt interminable islets, sand bars and reefs, suddenly jutting points
of land, and strange mud heaps rising from the gulf. They
huddle at night upon a platform of logs and rushes, built
upon quivering land which lies half a foot underwater.

For two days they push on despite the fury of the
storm. The coastal breakers nearly swamp the barges. Finally,
in the afternoon, they sight what must be the gaping mouth
of the Mississippi. But it is guarded, or so it seems, by a
barrier of rocks. For three hours they hover uncertainly
off the river's mouth. Then, in desperation, Iberville drives
his barge against the jagged reefs. The barrier gives way
before the impact. It is only a composite of driftwood, slime
and sediment.

The brothers Le Moyne have entered the Mississippi.

But they do not pause to rejoice, for this mating bed
of river and gulf is not a safe place for celebration. They

push upstream, away from the inrushing whitecaps of the gulf and the tentacles of inundated weedy growths, until firmer, higher ground is reached. Here they pitch camp, cut long grasses for dry beds, and eat porridge ravenously. Not until Mardi gras, the feast Tuesday of the next day, do they chant the Te Deum and raise the cross of the church before proceeding upriver. As they drive their paddles, the rushes and sedge change to willows and cane, and then to thick cypress forests. They sight duck, bustards, a wolf, and opossums aplenty, and on the banks they find the tracks of deer. This is the beginning of the promise of the lower river, the beginning of the unrealized vision of Jean Baptiste Le Moyne.

The brothers explore far upstream. Iberville makes the short portage from where New Orleans now stands to Lake Ponchartrain. Later, from Baton Rouge, he descends the Amite into Lake Maurepas and Lake Pontchartrain, and thence into the Gulf of Mexico. Bienville, with most of the party, pushes on upriver for four weeks, meeting and making friends of the Mongoulaches, the Bayogoulas, and the Houmas whose domain is marked by the red stick, the baton rouge. Mosquitoes and alligators plague the Canadians, and they are afflicted with dysentery. Constant recourse to brandy makes them quarrelsome. But Bienville is learning the river and its people, and he is in high spirits when he is reunited with Iberville at Ship Island.

Shortly Iberville sails away. He will return later with sixty Canadian coureurs de bois, a priest, a royal commissary, a geologist, and notable associates: his brother, Antoine Le Moyne, the Sieur de Boisbriant, and the gallant explorer, Juchereau Saint-Denis. The expedition, a colony now, settles at Biloxi on the gulf, plants corn and peas and erects a fort and barracks. The veteran Tonti comes from his post on the Arkansas to give advice and aid. And the Frenchmen chuckle at an exploit of the young Bienville while returning downriver from another exploratory trip. On this journey,

Bienville met an English ship coming upstream. He caused its Captain Banks to turn tail with a story that his was but an advance party of a large force of Frenchmen. Ever since, the place of this encounter has been called English Turn.

Iberville returns, and the brothers establish a fort at Natchez, with Bienville in command, among those handsome, suicidal sun worshipers whose beauty and culture the French admire. Iberville, striving to persuade France of the colony's value, sails again to France to argue in vain for a chain of forts along the river.

He returns from his second trip in December, 1701, with another brother, Le Moyne de Serigny, to find the men at Biloxi ill of fever and dissatisfied with their surroundings. So Bienville is sent to establish a permanent capital, early in 1702, at Fort St. Louis de la Mobile. The youngster, threatened by English inroads—for the War of the Spanish Succession is having its repercussions in the New World— makes allies of the Choctaws and Chickasaws and leads them in a bloody, scalp-taking war against the Alibamans, friends of the English.

By 1704 the colony seems assured of survival. Ships arrive, though with ominous infrequency, bringing livestock, food, and more clergy. And in 1704 the *Pelican* lands twenty-three young girls "reared in piety, drawn from sources above suspicion, and who know how to work."

But the *Pelican* also carries the fever. Two-thirds of the colonists become ill, many fatally. Among the dead are the irreplaceable Tonti, a priest, thirty soldiers, and half the crew of the *Pelican*. This disaster is only a harbinger of what is to come. Inevitably the neglected colonials quarrel and plot against one another. A terrible loss is sustained with the death of Iberville in Havana, in 1706; and shortly Bienville, target of a cabal resentful of the brothers Le Moyne, is accused of malversion, peculation, illicit trade in skins, and interception of letters. He is vindicated by Diron d'Artaguette, the new commissary sent from France. But a shadow has fallen upon the colony and upon his spirit, and only occasionally in the next fifty years will it lift. This is to be Bienville's tragedy, and the tragedy of France's blindness.

What makes an old man brood, Sieur de Bienville?

By 1712 Louisiana is paying a bitter price for a decade of neglect, colonial intrigue, and exploitation. No one in France knows what to do with the untended possession. No one except, perhaps, Sieur Antoine de Crozat, the great merchant capitalist and favorite of the king; and it has taken two years to persuade even Crozat to accept the colony in return for all the profits which he might make. A selfish monopolist, Crozat's idea is to bleed Louisiana dry by control of price and by trading its products with the Spanish. But through the Peace of Utrecht, England—ever the Nemesis —causes the Spaniards to close their ports to French trade. Crozat, already hampered by colonial smuggling, is doomed.

Seemingly doomed too is Louisiana. Wholesale desertions to the English have become common among the soldiery. The unimpeachable young women of the *Pelican,* and those who come out later, have succumbed to enervating hopelessness. The unmarried men, frolicking with the native women, are nearly as savage as their woodland consorts. And Bienville, reduced to the command of Fort Rosalie at Natchez and the Mississippi district, is supplanted by a new governor, Antoine de la Mothe Cadillac. This successor is a shrewd, facile and tireless Gascon, with twenty years' experience in Canada. Yet he does not know how to take advice, and he fails to get along with the colonists, and especially with Bienville.

Moreover, Cadillac becomes discouraged early. Reporting upon the colony he ridicules the infertile Gulf coast which was "the Paradise, the Pomona, the Fortunate Isles of the Relations—Pure Fables." As for the people, they are "the dregs of Canada, who had no respect for religion or government and were addicted to Indian women." The soldiers are badly disciplined and a hundred more troops are needed, as well as Canadian woodsmen, sailors, laborers, masons, stonecutters, millers, and carpenters. He accuses Bienville, and Duclos, the latest commissary who is pleading for free trade, of being in league against him. He concedes, however, that Bienville is skilled in managing the Indians, who are troubling him with increased demands.

The relationship between the deposed leader and his successor grows worse. Cadillac continues to inveigh against Bienville, twice disciplines him for "lying." He metes out harsh punishment to soldiers who demand more food. The colonists also are clamoring because staple prices are fifty per cent higher than in France, and because the Crozat regime has forbidden them to trade or to own boats. To punish their leaders, Cadillac forbids sword-bearing to all but the handful of nobility; certainly no way to win over these independent, warlike men.

Bienville is completely discouraged. Writing in 1713 to his brother, the Baron de Longeuil, he says that Cadillac has put the country in consternation, and that he himself has had to sell his slaves and furniture to buy flour, shirts and other clothing at Crozat's unreasonable prices. After seven years the men have received only one coat and two shirts, and they are eating bad flour. The trappers are being mulcted out of their skins. He is worried too over their brother, Saint-Hélène, now settled in the colony. Saint-Hélène smokes and drinks a great deal, "the only one in the family who does so." He never sticks to anything, and on a visit to Vera Cruz he spent 5,000 livres in nine months. Bienville does not believe Crozat can hold Louisiana; as for himself, he hopes to be replaced as commander of the Mississippi district. The letter also gives the only glimpse of any love affair in his life. He admits that he would like to marry Cadillac's daughter, but would hate him for a father-in-law. Neither that match nor any other is ever made.

Meanwhile the English are taking advantage of the colony's plight. Their traders swarm through the valley in defiance of France's suzerainty, trading even along the river and almost under Cadillac's nose with the Natchez, the Yazoos, the Choctaws and the Chickasaws. Bienville is the only one who can win back the Indians, and he does so with treaty and threat. The English are driven out, but the Le Moynes pay heavily. The spendthrift brother, Saint-Hélène, loses his life in a Chickasaw village when, mistaken for an Englishman, he is shot while lighting his pipe in a cabin.

In 1715, Cadillac goes upriver to the Illinois district after hearing that valuable ore is to be found there. He returns disappointed and wrathful. Meanwhile, the Natchez have risen because Cadillac has slighted their calumet. They have slain five Frenchmen, and pillaged Crozat's Natchez warehouse. So Cadillac, probably laughing behind his hand, sends Bienville against them in 1716 with only 49 men.

By a ruse defensible only because of the disparity of the opposing forces, Bienville traps the Great Sun and two lesser Sun chiefs of the Natchez and forces them to name and surrender the ringleaders of the uprising. The guilty are put to death. The Natchez are compelled to return the warehouse merchandise, and to supply 2,500 pieces of acacia wood and bark from 3,000 cypress trees to build a stronger fort. Bienville returns in July, only to be censured by Cadillac for his drastic action.

Happily, Cadillac is recalled in 1717, but Bienville, expecting the governorship himself, is again disappointed. He is awarded only unprofitable Horn Island in soccage and decorated with the Cross of St. Louis. Nor is he able to get along with the new governor, de l'Epinay, any better than he had with Cadillac.

De l'Epinay's regime is short, for in the same year Crozat washes his hands of Louisiana. And now the colony is to become the center of wild, catastrophic exploitation. For in France, John Law, the Scot money juggler, has gained the ear of Louis XV, who succeeded the Grand Monarch in 1715. John Law's Company of the West is about to begin the blowing of the Mississippi Bubble. Noble and shopkeeper pour their money into his hands and the New World's first boom is under way.

What does an old man regret, Sieur de Bienville?

The Company of the West took over the Crozat grant, and received the Canadian fur trade rights as well, both for twenty-five years. In financing the company, Law promised that the shares would advance rapidly. Selling them at 300 francs he placed a 500-franc par value on them. Then the incredible financier obtained the East Indies Company and an African trade franchise, and merged the three into an immense operation known as the Indian Company. The shares of this mammoth holding company had a par value of 500 francs. Its principal lure was that it held exclusive rights to French trade in Asia, Africa, and America, besides virtual ownership of the Mississippi Valley.

But to own shares in the Indian Company, the purchaser had to pay par plus a 50-franc premium, and also had to own four shares in the old Company of the West for one share in the new venture. The resultant wild scramble for the old shares provided the air for the bubble.

The last astounding step in Law's scheme was to substitute the Indian Company for the government itself in financial matters. The French treasury was all but empty. The public debt stood at about 1,600,000,000 francs. So

Law proposed to lend the government the 1,600,000,000 francs, which the company would raise through selling the shares. The government would pay three per cent interest on the loan, which would cut its previous interest rate almost in half. And the company would collect all French revenues and taxes for the customary service fees and commissions.

Law's scheme might have worked for a long time had there not ensued such a headlong rush to get in on the Indian Company's ground floor. The 500-franc shares soared to 8,000 francs before the unloading began.

What did this mean to Louisiana? Law was primarily a promoter. As a promoter he saw that to make the American section of the company's three-continent monopoly pay, he must develop the valley. And such development required settlers.

So, throughout Europe there circulated the story of Louisiana's fertility, of the wealth which settlers could gain with little work, of the resources beneath its soil. The company's seal was in the rash spirit of its promises. It pictured an old river-god leaning upon a cornucopia from which poured golden coins.

The small, troubled German states were ripe for Law's prospectuses. By the thousands the sober German peasants and little merchants and landowners answered his call to the land so blessed—on paper—with gold, silver, copper, lead, and agricultural ease. After the famines, the despotism, the constant wars of the duchies, this would be heaven on earth. By the thousands they started, mostly afoot, for the French ports of embarkation. Fewer thousands reached those ports. Of the estimated five thousand who embarked on the pest ships, less than two thousand set foot on Louisiana.

Even these were too many for a colony unable to care for so sudden a multitude. Emigrants died horribly where they landed, of fever, hunger, and exposure. Biloxi, Mobile,

Ship Island, and Dauphin Island could hardly bury the dead, much less care for the living. But some of these sturdy men and women and children of the Palatinate survived; the Vogels to become Fauquels by association with the French; the Troxlers, Trosclairs; the Hubers, Oubres; the Ziriacs, Sirjacques. From the beginning these German emigrants gave a greater agricultural stability, and a sounder earthiness than the colony had ever known. Many went as far upriver as Law's own personal grant in what is now southeast Arkansas. But they wouldn't remain in this isolated region. Returning to New Orleans, which Bienville had founded as soon as he had reassumed command, they settled a short distance above the new town. There they engaged in truck farming, poultry raising and horticulture. And today this region is still known as the German Coast.

But not all the settlers were of their caliber. Law's ships brought also the outcasts of the asylums, the hospitals, and the reformatories of France. And a few who rose to Law's lure were adventurous scions of the French nobility and aristocratic officers.

When Law took control of Louisiana, Bienville had been appointed to direct the affairs of the colony with the title of commandant-general. For fifteen years he had begged France to send settlers and supplies. Now he faced the super-human task of giving sustenance and then putting to good use this deluge of paupers, prostitutes from the Salpêtrière, black sheep of good families, honest emigrants, and the infirm so quickly dumped upon barren Dauphin Island. He did the best he could to help the dregs which came first and then the later, higher type of colonists attracted by the company's propaganda. But the assimilation and rehabilitation were tragically slow.

In 1720 Biloxi was renamed the capital of the colony. This was an unfortunate selection. Luckily, a drunken ser-

geant's pipe started a fire which destroyed the then unhealthy little coastal town, and led to the establishment of the colony's seat of government in New Orleans in 1722. In that year its first census recorded 72 civilians, 44 soldiers, 11 officers, 22 ship captains and sailors, 28 European laborers, 177 Negro slaves, and 22 Indians. Sixty-five of the civilians, officers, and ship captains were married, and there were 38 children.

The short-lived bubble burst though the company hung on until 1731. Bienville was left with the floundering colony, once more the unwanted stepchild of France. And worse for his own future, he had strong, treacherous enemies. As commandant, his will was not supreme. Under the Company of the West, the powers of the first councilor were almost as great as his own, and the Superior Council and the resident directors of the company frequently acted independently of his orders.

Moreover, the bishop of Canada had assigned the Capuchins to minister to the colony's spiritual needs. Bienville, close friend to the Jesuits who in Canada had aided his father, disliked the Capuchins heartily. When the Jesuits came in 1721 to work among the Indians, he befriended them. Thenceforth, he was hated by the Capuchin priests. Malice, temporal and clerical, thrived upon the disorder and uncertainty into which Louisiana was plunged.

Continual complaints and accusations against Bienville went to France. Finally, an accusation charging him with misconduct in office was signed by Raguet, the commissary, and Father Raphael, superior of the Capuchins. Bienville was summoned to France to answer the charges, and this after twenty-five years of unrelieved service to the colony. For the next seven years he lived in the Rue Champfleury, a side street in Paris, almost destitute. Although an investigation in Louisiana brought personal vindication, his enemies were sufficiently believed to prevent his return.

Then in 1731 the Company of the West petitioned the crown to relieve it of its Louisiana charter. Grudgingly Louis XV acceded. Convinced that none but Bienville could keep the colony alive, the government ordered him to return to Louisiana in 1733.

The years of his absence had been dark ones for the colonists. In 1727 the Natchez had risen against Chepart, a stupid, land-grabbing commandant at Fort Rosalie. In the bloodiest vengeance ever exacted by Indians in the history of the valley, they slaughtered some 290 men and women, sparing among the men only the Negro slaves and a French teamster and tailor. They butchered pregnant women and those with infants, and made prisoners of 80 or more women and 150 children.

Retaliatory campaigns under Perier, who had succeeded Bienville, were only partly successful. The Natchez released their prisoners and secretly withdrew from their fortress towns along the river. Some found refuge among the Chickasaws; others fled westward across the river. A later expedition, reinforced with fresh troops from France, located the largest concentration of the fugitive Natchez in the Black and Ouachita river country west of the Mississippi. The Frenchmen laid siege, then persuaded the Great Sun and another chief to come out from their defenses under a flag of truce. The chiefs expressed contriteness, and asked for peace. But Perier, violating the flag of truce, made them his prisoners. About 35 braves and most of the women and children then surrendered, but a dogged handful of 70 warriors and their families escaped in a heavy, three-day rainstorm. They made a heroic flight eastward again, recrossed the Mississippi, and joined their brethren under the protection of the fierce Chickasaws.

Bienville's principal mission on returning to the colony was to punish the Chickasaws and the remaining Natchez whom they harbored. But his old fire was lacking. In his defense it is recorded that the officers and troops of the colony were in poor state, inadequately quartered, haphazardly paid, and equipped with rusted weapons. Of the 800 troops in the colony, an unacclimated two-thirds were ill with fever, dysentery, and other complaints. France's old allies, the Choctaws and the Illinois, seemed ready to follow the Chickasaws and the Alibamans into the camp of the English.

However valid these explanations, Bienville's ambitiously planned pincers movement from the Illinois country and New Orleans against the Chickasaws failed miserably. Early in the campaign 47 French soldiers were captured and tortured to death. Of the total of 3,600 regulars, militia, and Indians in Bienville's armies, hundreds died of disease. And finally, instead of exacting stern vengeance, the French merely secured a treaty of peace and friendship with the Chickasaws.

The end of the extended Chickasaw campaign in 1740 preceded by just two years the final retirement of Jean Baptiste Le Moyne. He was an aging man, past sixty. Except for his few years of exile he had devoted his life, since he was eighteen, to Louisiana. He knew the river, the colony, and the Indians as no other man in its history had. Strong willed, unable to tolerate leadership other than his own, he had nevertheless demonstrated that only under his direction had there been any progress at all.

Bienville founded a city that was to be his lasting monument; but he ended his services to Louisiana with a conviction of failure. His petition for release from his duties ended with the wish that "the officer who will be chosen to succeed me will be happier than I."

He returned to France neither a wealthy man nor a penniless one. The sale of his personal property and slaves, and his savings from his yearly salary of 12,000 livres during his last term, were sufficient to maintain him comfortably

for the rest of his life. Only two governors, de Vaudreuil
and Kerlerec, were to follow him before Louisiana passed
to Spain. Under them also, the story of France's valley was
to be one of disappointment, neglect, and painfully slow
growth. And at last an old man and a merchant of New
Orleans would talk hopelessly together in Paris of turning
the king from his decision.

In what does an old man glory, Sieur de Bienville?

The river was the highway of the valley. The commerce of all of Louisiana must move upon it. Even in 1700,
a year after the first settlement, the hardy Canadians had
begun their river traffic in furs and produce. They brought
their furs to Biloxi by way of the Mississippi, the Amite,
and Manchac Bayou channel which was called the Iberville
River, into Lakes Maurepas and Pontchartrain, and thus
into the Gulf of Mexico. The last phases of the journey, after
they left the Mississippi, entailed increased labor and time.

So, reasoned Bienville, a receiving depot on the banks
of the Mississippi itself was a sounder proposition than a
capital in distant Biloxi.

The proponents of Biloxi and Mobile were strong enough
to delay for eighteen years the realization of Bienville's plans
for a river city near the lakes. Finally, John Law's company
agreed with Bienville. A river settlement was approved.
Natchez had its supporters, and other men argued for the
high lands just below the present city of Baton Rouge, and
with easy access to the Amite and the lakes.

But Bienville held out for the place of his own choosing.
It lay in a crescent curve of the Mississippi, five miles from
Lake Pontchartrain. Here the cypress-locked earth rose a
little higher than the surrounding marshes. Here river and
lake came the closest together, with a short bayou almost
joining them. The river's mouth was but a hundred miles

below the site, and Bienville believed that one of its three forks could be made navigable the year round for seagoing vessels.

And in 1717, he had his way, despite the protests of Le Blond de la Tour, the colony's chief engineer, who wanted Biloxi as the capital. Bienville was supported by the assistant engineer, Adrien de Pauger, who made surveys and soundings at the mouth, and whose favorable report convinced the company.

A few carpenters and about eighty illicit saltmakers who had been banished to Louisiana, accompanied Bienville to the site to clear the underbrush. They were rebellious and disinclined to work. In the first year, only the space of four city blocks was cleared, and a parapet and defensive ditch constructed. Not until 1720 was de Pauger able to lay out the original city, a modest eleven blocks along the river and six blocks deep, with a Place d'Armes on the river front. Even then, soldiers had to do most of the work, for the recalcitrant saltmakers fled to the woods.

Bienville named his riverside clearing Nouvelle Orléans, in honor of rakehelly Louis Philippe, Duc d'Orléans and prince regent of France. Some of the streets of his muddy, unbuilt city received names as noble: Conti, Chartres, Toulouse, Du Maine, Bourbon, Burgundy, Orleans. Others were christened with religious designations: St. Louis, St. Philip, St. Ann, St. Peter. Fine names for a swamp clearing.

When New Orleans became the capital of Louisiana in 1722, its future was not discernible in its present. Yet it set some to dreaming. A few months before, Father Charlevoix, the Jesuit missionary, had visited the settlement.

"This city is the first which one of the greatest rivers of the world has seen rise upon its banks," he wrote. "The 800 beautiful houses and the five parishes which Le Mercure [a publication of Law's to induce emigration] gave out two years ago, are yet limited to one hundred huts placed without much order; to a large store built of wood; to two or three houses which would not adorn a French village; to the half of a wretched warehouse which the people willingly lent to the Lord and of which He had hardly taken possession before they wanted to drive Him forth to lodge Him in a tent. What a pleasure it is on the other hand to see insensibly growing the future capital of a beautiful and vast country, and not to be forced to sigh as did Virgil's hero in speaking of his dear country consumed by flames . . . but free to be filled with the highest hope that this wild and desert place, still almost covered by canes and trees, shall one day—and perhaps that day is not far distant—be an opulent city and the metropolis of a rich colony."

New Orleans was the real beginning of the white man's preemption of the river. It was an uncertain venture. The Indians, the plague, and the overflow of the Mississippi harassed the little town, and it choked for breath against the strangle hold of greedy manipulation. Yet gradually the bark- and reed-roofed huts gave way to cypress-shingled, brick, and timber cottages and to the more commodious two-story houses of the prosperous. Along the river, axmen felled the longleaf pine for masts, and sawmills cut the cypress into lumber for export. In the swamps, men trapped the beaver and mink and raccoon; and long before Bienville quit his city, the green shoots of indigo, cotton, and corn were breaking through the black earth. A man of courage and vision could see for himself what lay ahead. Wealth was here, in lumber, in agriculture, in the primitive manufactories of silk, brick, and myrtle wax. It waited, inherent and inhibited, in trade with the Indians, and in commerce with the Old World and the new American colonies. Here in this tenacious, ribald, forgotten outpost a valley's treasures might someday be exchanged for the goods and the gold of Europe. The broad, swift river could be the highway to plenty.

But France could not understand these things. And the vision of Bienville would remain unfulfilled for many years after his death. It would be obscured by the clashing of successive overlordships, by natural disaster and civil strife, by political rapacity which thrived under Frenchman, Spaniard, and American alike. Yet, it would persist. And in that persistence an old man could glory and an old man could grieve. For in his young manhood, Louisiana was uncertainly held but it was held by France. At his life's end, Louisiana was no longer French, but it had survived.

CHAPTER 3

Blood of Martyrs

THE VICTORY of General Wolfe on Quebec's Plains of Abraham was to lead ultimately to the most significant political change in the history of the faraway Mississippi Valley. And, for that matter, in the history of America itself. With the defeat of Montcalm, France lost an empire. But the English triumph would also mean ultimate English loss. Hitherto, the westward-surging English colonials of the Atlantic seaboard had been checked by France's grip on the Mississippi; and the political unrest of the colonies had been tempered by their dependence upon England's strong arm for protection against France and Spain. A defeated, displaced France meant an unneeded England.

Now, in perspective, we can see the shaping of the American destiny. But France's settlers of the lower river read no such portents in 1762; and their unavailing protest against being pawns of empire was to be written in the blood of six men.

These six men were the valley's first martyrs to the yet undefined belief in a New World's self-determination.

The tragedy opened innocuously enough. In 1762, Great Britain and France agreed that the navigation of the Mississippi should be equally free to each country, from its source to the sea, and that neither would levy duties on the other. That was satisfactory enough to the trade-starved French colonials, who looked with favor upon the goods and the gold of the English smuggler-traders.

But on November 3, 1762, there occurred a strangely one-sided land deal. Louis XV, the zany monarch of France, transferred to his Bourbon cousin, Charles III of Spain, "all of the country known as Louisiana." So secret was the transfer that not even the Louisianians would learn of it for a year and eight months, and then they would not believe the act irrevocable. And so unexpected was Louis's royal gift that the Spanish minister at Paris accepted Louisiana only conditionally, subject to the ratification of his Catholic Majesty.

Priceless though the territory was, a monarch even less a fool than Louis might have thought himself wise in bestowing it on another. Upon that troublous river wilderness Crozat the millionaire had wasted most of his wealth. There John Law had flung away the savings and the lives of thousands. France itself had squandered forty to fifty million livres on the colony. And, Louis could well reason, for what? Only an interminable succession of failures, of bickerings among governors and intendants, clergy and populace. So perhaps Louis chuckled over his cousinly gesture. The English march, which had swallowed Canada, might be thwarted by Spain. And supercilious Cousin Charles of Spain might get indigestion from this stew of adventures and savages, nobility under a cloud and indentured peasants, harlots, inept soldiers and resentful bourgeoisie, all boiling in their hell's kettle of fever, smallpox, flood, and famine. That would be amusing.

So the pawns are moved. On February 10, 1763, France cedes to Great Britain all her American continental possession east of the Mississippi except for the Isle of Orleans. This tarnished jewel and all the territory west of the river—"all of the country known as Louisiana"—is now secretly Spain's. Canada, too, goes to the conquering Englishmen. And Spain, ally of France, has to cede to England all the lands she owns east of the river. For the time being, Spanish Charles also loses Havana and the Philippines, twelve ships of the line and immense treasures.

And still the Louisiana colonists do not know that they are no longer subjects of France.

In March, 1763, Louis announces that he will disband the troops serving in Louisiana except for four companies of infantry. Kerlerec, last, unhappy governor of Louisiana, returns to France, where, accused of spending ten million livres in four years under the pretext of preparing for war, he is thrown into the Bastille.

The colony is now ruled only by d'Abbadie, director of the Factory, who has the powers of a military commander. His task is a difficult one; for thinking that New Orleans and Louisiana west of the river is French, he tries to act accordingly without proper support.

The English give him the most trouble. In October, 1763, Robert Farmer, taking over Mobile for the English, seizes the French cannon there. D'Abbadie does not believe these were included in the cession, and protests. He protests again, three months later, that Farmer is making Frenchmen take the oath of allegiance or forfeit their property within three months instead of the eighteen months stipulated by the treaty.

He is also coping with a difficult religious problem. The French government, striking at the Jesuits on both continents, has expelled them from Louisiana. Their property is seized and sold for $180,000.

D'Abbadie is convinced that the colony is approaching anarchy. The Louisianians are freely trading with the English ships which are boldly moored just above New Orleans. In his report to the government he warns that possession of Louisiana is precarious for "how can I keep it without troops, without ammunition, and without ships to protect the navigation of the Gulf and to defend the mouth of the Mississippi?" Not even d'Abbadie knows that the colony is not France's to protect.

He comments despairingly on the "spirit of insurbordination and independence which has manifested itself under several administrations."

"Notwithstanding the present tranquillity, the same spirit of sedition does not the less exist in the colony . . . it reappears in the thoughtless expressions of some madcaps and in the anonymous writings scattered among the public. The uncertainty in which I am, with regard to the ultimate fate of the colony, has prevented me from resorting to extreme measures to repress such license; but it will be necessary to come to it at last, to re-establish the good order which has been destroyed and to regulate the conduct and morals of the inhabitants."

Then, in April, 1764, Louis XV informs him by letter that New Orleans and all Louisiana west of the river have been Spain's since November, 1762. The heartbroken director does not disclose the cession officially until October, but rumors precede his announcement by many months. D'Abbadie does not share the valley's consternation long, for he dies in February, 1765, and is succeeded by Aubry, ranking military officer of the colony.

To add to the gloom there arrive between January and May 650 pitiful refugees from Acadia, uprooted and dispersed by the English. The colony's population is further swelled by fugitives from the Alibaman and Illinois districts. And all add their stories to the woeful tale of disaster.

But the Louisianians refuse to take the cession lying down. Upon official word of the transfer, the parishes send protesting delegates to New Orleans. They are the best men in the colony: Lafreniere, soldier son of Canadian parents; Jean Milhet, the colony's richest merchant, and his brother Joseph; Noyan, who is Bienville's nephew; the Swedish noble, d'Arensbourg; Brand, the king's printer; Doucet, Villeré, Pin, Marquis, de La Chaise, Garic, Masan, Massange, Poupet, Lalande, Kernion, Caresse, Dessales, and others.

Hopefully they petition the king. Jean Milhet is sent to France, where he and Bienville will unsuccessfully appeal.

Soon, Louisianians hear that Spanish Don Antonio de Ulloa will be their governor, that he has already reached Havana. But when no Spaniards have arrived by April, 1765, their despair is tinctured with hope and a rising anger. In the unkempt Place d'Armes, where blanketed Choctaws rub shoulders with blond, smock-garbed Germans and tough Canadian woodsmen, the French colonials talk protestingly among themselves. We have been Louisianians for sixty-five years. . . . We are not chattels to be given away. . . . We are loyal but we are not slaves.

But are these the voices of French colonials or a new people? In this same year, in distant, English-speaking Virginia, a man named Patrick Henry is rising in the Assembly Hall at Williamsburg to move the resolutions denouncing the Stamp Act. The implications behind his words will be heard again in the Stamp Act Congress, in the protests of solid Virginia burgesses and the derisive laughter of New England's smugglers. The mystic might hear above these a single voice that rises from the tumbling rush of unreached rivers, in the soughing of endless forests; a voice neither English nor French, an American voice portentous of a splendid dream.

In July, Ulloa writes the Superior Council that he is on his way to assume the governorship of Louisiana. Ironically, in the same month medals arrive from France for four Louisianians as the final, empty gesture of an empty-minded king. But throughout 1765 Ulloa fails to appear. The only newcomers are 216 more Acadians who settle beside the river.

Finally, on March 5, 1766, the Spaniards arrive. The colonists find a dark omen in the thunder and lightning storms which rage along the river from the time the Spanish galleon enters the Mississippi until it ties up at New Orleans.

Sullenly the people watch Ulloa, his small entourage and his inadequate force of eighty Spanish soldiers disembark. The new governor is a small, fastidious man of science, at home among the men and women of wit and learning in Spain and Spanish America, but sadly misplaced here. He must have seemed an odd fish to the critical Louisianians; and even more strange must have appeared this barbaric colony to the aloof, hesitant scholar.

New Orleans could not have offered other than a dismal prospect to this new ruler from Spain. One good carriage road ran for some fifty miles along a low levee from the English Turn below the city to the German Coast. Otherwise the river and wilderness trails offered the only highways. In all Louisiana there were but 12,000 people, of whom half were Negroes, and only 1,893 men "able to bear arms." The city itself was surrounded on three sides by earthen and timber stockades, and along its narrow, pitted streets stood only some 700 dwellings. Even the best of these were simply constructed of brick and timber, no more than raised cottages of eight rooms, built on high foundations eight feet above ground.

And the furnishings! The discriminating Spaniard must have looked with contempt at the tables of cypress, the leather- and cane-bottomed chairs, the branched pewter lamps that were the handiwork of the colony. The more ornate, imported furniture and bric-a-brac which the well-to-do could afford, must have seemed even more out of place in the modest homes. The colonial leaders could on occasion dress bravely in the velvet suits, the embroidered cherry jackets, the blue sateen trousers and the silver buckles of France; and their ladies likewise could show themselves in rouge and patches, in silk and brocaded gowns. But the populace at large went meanly in skins and homespun.

Not that Ulloa had much time for such unfavorable comparisons. He found himself at odds with the colonists from the moment of his arrival. Stubbornly he refused to show the Superior Council his credentials, and announced that he would deal only with and through Aubry, an ugly unsavory figure, mistrusted by the Louisianians. Nor will he take formal possession of the colony until Spanish reinforcements arrive.

Sporadically, Ulloa tries to win the support of the French. But these attempts fail, even the strengthening of the depreciated currency. Soon Ulloa realizes that he cannot please them. And he is disquieted by his investigation of the government's files, which show that almost every governor of the colony had represented the Louisianians as being filled with "the rebellious spirit of republicanism."

In May, 1766, Ulloa permits direct commerce between French and Spanish colonies if the cargoes are carried in Spanish ships. To prevent smuggling two commissaries are appointed to each port of the province, and as a further mollifying gesture, Ulloa names Frenchmen to these posts. They are empowered to purchase articles to be exported. A five per cent duty is levied on all exports, which are limited to lumber, corn, rice, and other agricultural products.

In September, other trade decrees follow. Goods to be imported must be appraised by "impartial persons," and cannot be sold if excessively costly. Those who trade with the Louisianians must accept the currency of the colony and take away with them one-third of their cargo in lumber and other exportable products of the colony.

Obviously, these decrees benefit the consumer. But they incense the merchants, who include most of the colony's leaders. Through Lafreniere they protest to the Superior Council, and so strong are their objections that Aubry verbally suspends the new decrees. The merchants also start a boycott, several of them writing to their connections advising them not to send shipments to Louisiana. As one result, no flour arrives from the English colonies, and the soldiers have to eat rice.

In the midst of this economic turmoil, background of most revolutionary movements, Ulloa leaves in September, 1766, for the Balize, the entry point of the river. No one knows why. Is it to meet the long-expected Spanish reinforcements? The colonists speculate maliciously.

They get no word of Ulloa for several months. Then, early in 1767, Ulloa issues from the Balize a document in which he proposes to take formal possession and empowers the omnipresent Aubry to administer the government until actual possession by additional Spanish troops is accomplished.

His continued retirement at the remote, uncomfortable Balize is still inexplicable. And not until March do the Orleanians learn why the governor has remained there. He is waiting the arrival of his betrothed, the beautiful and wealthy Peruvian Marchioness of Abrado. Now the colonial dames have their innings. So the governor is reluctant to receive his bride in his capital! He must meet her at the river's mouth to prepare her for the crudities of New Orleans! So. . . !

When Ulloa returns with his bride she receives a chill reception. They hold salons thrice weekly, but these fail to win over the ladies. Yet throughout 1767 the colony's opposition to Spain is conducted only through snubs and criticism. Early in the year Jean Milhet has returned from France to report that his appeal was fruitless. Apparently all is ended. The Spanish flag flies at the Balize, and on the Missouri, the Iberville, and opposite Natchez. But because of Ulloa's temporizing, the banner of France has not been taken down elsewhere on the Mississippi. And this gives hope to schemers.

Outwardly, the first eight months of 1768 pass quietly enough. Who but the conspirators knows that a powerful plot against Spain is in the making? Who suspects that its leaders are the strong Lafreniere, Foucault, the intendant commissary, wealthy Masan, Marquis, a captain in the old Swiss troops of France, Noyan and Bienville, both nephews of the old hero, Hardy de Boisblanc, former member of the Superior Council, Doucet, the distinguished lawyer, Villeré, commander of the German Coast, and the great merchants, Jean and Joseph Milhet, Caresse, Petit, and Poupet?

Initially the conspiracy has elements of opéra bouffe, in disarming prelude to the coming drama of brief independence and the final tragedy of Spanish vengeance. The rebels multiply real political and economic grievances with imagined ones. At the core of their anger is a stubborn purpose. Louisiana must be French or it must be independent.

These Frenchmen enjoy themselves in their plotting. Sometimes they meet at the home of Masan, but more often they gather in the pleasant dwelling of one Madame Pradel, attractive mistress of the Intendant Foucault. Among the roses and myrtles and magnolias of her odorous garden they stroll and whisper, and end their meetings with convivial dinners.

But they keep secret the plans for the uprising. Not until October 25, 1768, do Ulloa and Aubry learn what is in the wind. Then it is too late. The conspirators have enlisted the hardy Germans and Acadians. These, led by Noyan and Villeré, march early on the morning of October 28th, with fowling pieces, muskets and pistols, upon the city. The night before the guns at the Tchoupitoulas gate have been spiked. Spiked too is the chance of Spanish success at a meeting of the Superior Council which Aubry has called for this day.

Marquis assumes command of the rebels. Gaily they parade through the town, shouting damnation to the Spaniards. The Spanish frigate moves from the riverbank to safer mooring in midstream. Aubry distributes cartridges to the 110 French soldiers of his command, and orders them to protect the governor and his retinue. Vainly he pleads with Lafreniere to abandon the revolt. Then realizing that the affair had progressed too far to stop now, Aubry goes to Ulloa's home.

The scene there is both heroic and comic. The few Spanish officials have barricaded themselves. Outside the people jeer at the defenders. But no one is doing any shooting. Informing Ulloa that he cannot answer for his safety within the city, Aubry conducts the governor and his wife to the frigate, where they are left with a guard of an officer and twenty men. The other Spaniards remain defiantly in Ulloa's home. All through the day and evening the Orleanians enjoy themselves without this stronghold. Shouting "La bas Espagnol" and "Vive Louis Quinze" they rush close to the beleaguered house, where they deliver themselves of murderous threats. Then they fall back again in happy carmagnole.

But this is the last amusing note. The rebels appear before the Superior Council with a petition, signed by some 600 citizens, demanding the expulsion of Ulloa and his aides, the restoration of old privileges and the granting of new ones.

The Council cannot act immediately for too many members are absent because of "sickness." So another meeting is called for the following day.

This time there is no doubt about the Council's course. Outside the council chamber a thousand insurgents have assembled. They shout that every Spaniard will be killed if they are not expelled. The Council takes up the petition.

It is an unusual document, as is the speech which Lafreniere makes in behalf of the rebels. Attorney general of the colony, and an ardent advocate, the big Canadian declares that Ulloa has disregarded the colonists' right to continue under their former laws and customs. Moreover, Ulloa has been governing without having taken formal possession.

Then, turning from this legally dubious vindication of

the rebels' course, Lafreniere makes a passionate, momentous statement:

"Without population there can be no commerce, and without commerce no population," he thunders. "In proportion to the extent of both is the solidity of thrones; *both are fed by liberty and competition* which are the nursing mothers of the state, of which the spirit of monopoly is the tyrant and stepmother. Without liberty there are but few virtues. Despotism breeds pusillanimity and deepens the abyss of vices. Man is considered as sinning before God only because he retains his free will.

"Where is the liberty of our planters, our merchants and our other inhabitants? Protection and benevolence have given way to despotism; a single authority would absorb and annihilate everything. All ranks, without distinction, can no longer, without running the risk of being taxed with guilt, do anything else but tremble, bow their necks to the yoke, and lick the dust."

From this amazing statement of rights, Lafreniere turns to a citation of grievances. Prior to the coming of Ulloa, he says, the planters had almost overcome their difficulties. "The most remote corners of the possessions of the savages had been discovered, the fur trade had been carried to its highest perfection, and the new culture of cotton, joined to that of indigo and tobacco, secured cargoes to those who were engaged in fitting our ships."

Doubtless an overbright picture. But Lafreniere's summary of contrasting restrictions and indignities under Ulloa sounds convincing enough.

"He has exhibited to the Superior Council none of his titles, powers and provisions as commissioner of his Catholic Majesty; he has not exhibited his copy of the act of cession, in order to have it registered; he has set up the Spanish flag at the Balize, at the Illinois, and at other places; he has, without legal authority, vexed, punished and oppressed subjects of France; he has even confined some of them in frigates of his Catholic Majesty; he has by his authority alone, usurped the fourth part of the common of the inhabitants of the town, has appropriated it to himself and has caused it to be fenced in, that his horses might graze there."

He concludes with these demands: Ulloa must be declared a usurper of authority. He must be enjoined to leave the colony "in the frigate in which he came, without delay, to avoid accidents or new clamors." The Council must ordain that Spanish possession of the colony cannot be permitted without new orders from the French king. And the Council must empower the colony to elect deputies to carry to France petitions pleading for Louisiana to remain French.

The Council obeys. Rather, the Council simply concurs, for a majority are in full sympathy. Its decree against Ulloa is an almost word for word embodiment of Lafreniere's address with the addition of the petition submitted by the merchants and planters.

This petition has presented specific grievances. The Spaniards, it declares, have prohibited direct trade with France. They have banned the importation of slaves, to the ruination of agriculture. And how mortifying to Frenchmen to suffer trade restrictions when the English are openly taking over the commerce of the colony. Special privileges to monopolies have stifled business. Moreover, Ulloa has committed acts of severity against three ship captains. Complainants are sent to the mines. The Acadians have been threatened with expulsion or slavery. The petition requests that privileges and exemptions be continued as before, that all ships from France and America have free access to the river, and that freedom of trade with all nations be granted.

Aubry inserts in the document his opposition to its contents. Foucault, the intendant, one of the original conspirators, hedges. Later he will be guilty of miserable double-dealing, and Aubry of worse.

But all this is in the future. In the exultation of victory, the colonists demonstrate wildly, shouting their allegiance to France and kissing the flagpole from which waves the fleur-de-lis.

The leaders select delegates to carry their petitions and memorials to France. And Ulloa, his few days of grace waning, is transferred on October 31st to a French vessel, since the Spanish frigate needs repairing. For the time being, his retinue remains in New Orleans.

Early in the morning of November 1st, the governor who could not govern these people took inglorious departure. A crowd of wedding party merrymakers, full of wine and patriotism after a night of celebration, cut the vessel's mooring ropes. It drifted dangerously for a short distance downstream while the pranksters howled. This was a fitting farewell, they agreed, to the man who had caused leprous children to be sent untended to the Balize, who had forbidden slaves to be whipped inside the city because their cries disturbed his wife, and whose wife had refused to let her baby be suckled by a French wet nurse.

That afternoon Ulloa sailed down the Mississippi, never to return. In his place would come a man of blood.

Forty days later Spain learned of the insult to its majesty. The infuriated Council of Ministers recommended that Louisiana be held, and the offenders punished.

Nor did France offer the rebels any consolation. Each of many repeated appeals to Louis failed. With each month of the year 1769 the spirits of the Louisianians sank lower.

During the tense period of waiting, a fantastic-sounding proposal was advanced by the Swiss captain, Marquis. Let the free French establish a republic here on the banks of the Mississippi, he said, where the oppressed people of the world could find refuge. The republic would be governed by a leader to be called "protector," and an elected council of forty men. Its capital, New Orleans, would be a free port, with its own currency. Here on the banks of the great river a new nation would rise.

Such was Marquis's dream of an independent American nation. The dream had its brief glowing. Louisianians argued its merits in meetings and in pamphlets. Then followed the dread awakening. In July, 1769, news came that a great Spanish fleet had reached the Balize. The Spanish frigates were crowded with an army under the command of General Alexander O'Reilly.

Of the leaders of the rebellion, only two tried to organize the resistance that under the circumstances would have been preposterous. Marquis placed in his hat the white cockade of France and moved through the Place d'Armes, urging the people to oppose the landing. Only a hundred men joined him. Petit, a pistol in each hand, violently exhorted resistance with no more success.

Instead, the leaders turned to Aubry, who counseled obedience and predicted that no blood vengeance would be exacted. After all, he said, no lives had been lost in the uprising. Why should any die in its peaceful quelling?

On the evening of the 24th, Francisco Bouligny, envoy of O'Reilly, reached New Orleans. He was met by torchlight by the three remaining Spanish officials, Loyola, Gayarré, Navarro, and their friends, now rapidly increasing in number. To Aubry he conveyed O'Reilly's request that the transfer of Louisiana be facilitated. The next night Aubry entertained the Spaniards at his home. The dinner was followed by a promenade through the town, where demonstrations were made in favor of the Spaniards. New Orleans was trying to make amends.

The following morning, Aubry summoned the populace to the public square. O'Reilly is on the river, he said. Any thought of resistance is useless. Do not meet, nor take up arms.

Deserted by the prudent population, less hardy men than the leaders of the revolution would have fled. Perhaps they were lulled by Aubry's repeated protestations that his Catholic Majesty would show clemency. At any rate, armed only with a letter from Aubry, three of them, Lafreniere, Marquis, and Milhet, descended the river with Bouligny to seek out the Spanish general.

At the Balize they were received in state on the deck of O'Reilly's flagship. Lafreniere acted as spokesman. For once, his eloquence failed him. Briefly, almost falteringly, he protested that the colony did not lack in respect for Spain, that it rose only against Ulloa and the subversions of their rights which he had enforced.

"We beg your Excellency not to consider Louisiana as a conquered country. The orders of which you are the bearer are sufficient to put you in possession of this province, and they make a greater impression on our hearts than the arms which you carry with you. The French are docile, and accustomed to a mild government. On your arrival you will find everyone disposed to yield to the orders of the two Majesties. The colony claims from your benevolence the grant of privileges, and from your equity the allowance of sufficient delays for those who may choose to emigrate."

The Frenchmen were facing no Ulloa, and they knew it. O'Reilly was an Irishman who, since his youth, had served brilliantly in the armies of Spain. He was a ruthless soldier, to whom treason was the greatest of crimes, and swift military punishment the best of all protections.

Yet his answer was fairly disarming. He would withhold any decision until he could become "acquainted with the whole truth, to form right conclusions and to examine the reasons alleged for your justification." The doing of the least injury to anyone would cause him deep regret. He was pleased by their attitude. But, he added ominously, how could the colonists think themselves capable of resisting one of the most powerful sovereigns of Europe, or believe that the king of France, bound so closely by blood and friendship to Charles III, would have sanctioned such seditious activities?

At the conclusion of the interview, the Frenchmen dine aboard as the general's guests. Then they return to New Orleans. The interview has convinced them that they need not flee. On August 15th, Aubry meets the ascending fleet, and O'Reilly fixes the 18th as the date for taking possession of Louisiana. The Spanish fleet, twenty-four vessels in all, reaches New Orleans on the 17th. And on the 18th, O'Reilly lands his ships.

Now the mailed fist begins to emerge from the silken glove. The landing is a vivid show of military force. Parallel to the river, the French troops and the colonial militia are drawn up. From the fleet the Spanish troops disembark in solid columns, 2,600 strong, dazzling in their precision. They include all the elements of an invading army, heavy artillery, light infantry, and mounted riflemen. On the Spanish vessels, brightly dressed out, the cheering Spanish sailors cling to the rigging. The city bells peal. The guns of the twenty-four ships of the Spanish armada boom, and are answered by the guns on the square. From the dark lines of Spanish infantry muskets spurt fire. And O'Reilly walks ashore, to the beating of drums and the shrill of fifes, preceded by gaudily accoutered men bearing silver maces. He is received by Aubry, the members of the Council, and other prominent citizens of the city. His orders and credentials are read aloud to the people. O'Reilly loudly informs them that they are now the subjects of Spain. Aubry hands the conqueror the keys to the city gates. The fleur-de-lis of France flutters earthward, and the red and gold banner of Spain rises above the river. At Aubry's order and example, the colonials shout "Viva el rey" five times. From the square, O'Reilly and his retinue proceed to the cathedral, where he is solemnly received. In the church, the Te Deum is sung. Louisiana is Spain's.

The unsuspected day of doom approaches. On the 19th, O'Reilly entertains in high style the French and Spanish authorities and several citizens of substance. But on the same day he demands in writing from Aubry, "the names of the persons who induced the people to commit the offense of presenting themselves with arms in their hands to enforce the violent expulsion of Don Antonio de Ulloa" and to relate "all you may know in relation to said revolution, without omitting to quote literally all the orders, protests, and public or secret documents to which you may have recourse, in order to reduce to, and keep within the bounds of duty, the chiefs and agents of the conspiracy."

As admits even the Louisiana historian, Charles Gayarré, pro-Spanish descendant of the ablest of Ulloa's retinue, Aubry might have refused to play the role of common informer. But he did not refuse. Instead, he answered by relating in detail all that he knew of the revolution and its leadership. His compliance signed the death warrants of six men.

Aubry's letter of betrayal was received on the 20th. On the 21st, O'Reilly struck. He summoned Aubry to him at eight in the morning, and revealed orders of Charles III to arrest and bring to trial the chiefs of the revolution. While Aubry was still with him, O'Reilly summoned, by specious pretext, nine of the leaders. Unsuspectingly, they believed they were being invited to a conference. At O'Reilly's own home, the nine principals were arrested. Three of lesser consequence were taken at the town hall. The nine whom by subterfuge O'Reilly apprehended in his own quarters were Nicolas Chauvin de Lafreniere, Jean Baptiste de Noyan,

Joseph Villeré, Pierre Caresse, Pierre Marquis, Joseph Milhet, Jean Milhet, Joseph Petit, Balthasar de Masan, Julien Jerome Doucet, Pierre Poupet, and Hardy de Boisblanc. Of them all, only Joseph Villeré had prepared foresightedly to flee, and he was the first to die.

Once they were in his custody, O'Reilly upbraided them for their lack of respect for the Spanish crown. The king, he said, was displeased with the writings and the violence against his representatives. The ringleaders must face trial. He ordered them to deliver their swords and placed them severally, under guard, in three vessels and a private dwelling. Villeré had planned to seek the protection of the English but had been deterred, allegedly by a reassuring letter from Aubry. He was placed aboard a frigate, and on it he died. The Spanish official report stated that he succumbed in a fit of frenzy. Others relate that he was killed while trying to break away from his guards to see his wife, who had approached his prison ship in a small boat.

The trial of the survivors followed swiftly. But it was preceded by the granting of amnesty to all save those under arrest, and by the administering of the oath of allegiance to the colonists, "by corps, company and rank" in order of precedence. Almost the entire colony which so short a time before had risen against Spain took the oath of vassalage and fealty. There was nothing else for them to do, for they were too few against so many. But it is noteworthy that of the white population a greater proportion had rebelled—536 male citizens out of some 1,800 arms-bearing men—than was to be the case in the revolt of the English colonies.

On October 20, 1769, the Licentiate Don Felix del Rey, practitioner before the royal courts of Santo Domingo and Mexico, who had been appointed prosecuting attorney general, presented to the Spanish court headed by General O'Reilly the case against the conspirators. It was not a trial as we understand that procedure today. Previously, the judges had minutely questioned the prisoners in their cells. The accused men never saw the witnesses who were brought against them. They were examined in secret, and in secrecy the evidence was weighed. Yet, in any court procedure, they would have been found guilty of the charges. They had risen. They had failed. Their defense, the defense of independent spirits, was of no avail. Too easily answered were their contentions that the Spaniards had never taken legal possession of Louisiana, that the colonists had never taken the oath of allegiance to Spain, that therefore they should be judged according to French jurisprudence. Del Rey had a field day. General O'Reilly had decided that a lesson must be taught and that six men must die. Two each must be drawn from the military, the legal, and the mercantile elements of the ringleaders.

So, on October 24th, O'Reilly, as president of the court, found the accused guilty. One, Villeré, had already died. As for the others, Lafreniere, Noyan, Caresse, Marquis, and Joseph Milhet were sentenced to die on the gallows. Petit, who had cut Ulloa's moorings, was sentenced to life imprisonment. Masan and Doucet received ten years, and de Boisblanc, Jean Milhet, and Poupet six years each. The common hangman was ordered to gather up and burn all the printed copies of the document entitled "Memorial of the Planters, Merchants and Other Inhabitants of Louisiana on the event of the 29th of October, 1768" and all other documents related to the conspiracy.

Appeals to O'Reilly, the harsh soldier, were unavailing. But one provision of his order was amended. Under the French only Negroes had acted as hangmen; and the Spanish deemed that execution of these leaders at the hands of a Negro would be too great an offense against the community. And since no white man could be found to act, the sentence was commuted to execution by a firing squad.

On October 26th, in the Place d'Armes, five Louisianians, contemptuous of eye bandages, stared into the muskets of a platoon of grenadiers. Drawn up in the square were the mounted dragoons of Spain under the observing eye of a ruddy-faced Irish general. Below them, along the river, poised the three-decked frigates, motionless under the banner of Bourbon Spain. In the hushed, small houses of New Orleans, distraught men and women sought to shut out the sound of the fatal volley. And on the following day, while a Negro slave tossed upon a bonfire in the Place d'Armes the memorials to the freedom they had sponsored, a little man in a black robe chanted a triumphant Spanish apostrophe to their failure.

"This, the memorial of the planters of New Orleans, is by order of his Excellency, Don Alexander O'Reilly, publicly burnt. . . ."

Clemency followed the blood purge. The son of Masan went to Madrid, and offered to take his father's place in prison. The Spanish king, moved by his pleadings, pardoned all the imprisoned Frenchmen, who settled in Santo Domingo. Meanwhile, O'Reilly, "the bloody," entered upon a regime which by the standards of the day could be called temperate.

CHAPTER 4

The Woes of Father Dagobert

Balzac would have liked Father Dagobert, the fat, amiable French Capuchin. The stern Spanish friars who flocked to Louisiana after the cession did not.

In itself the story of Father Dagobert's joys and sorrows is delightful. In relation to the clerical history of the Lower Mississippi it becomes significant as well as amusing, for it reveals so distinctly the nature and extent of the religious spirit which rested lightly in the Gallic souls of the Louisiana colonists. More, it is the perfect medium for telling what happened when Frenchman and Spaniard clashed within the church.

Until the Americans came, the Roman Catholic Church held spiritual control along the Mississippi. But papal bulls and excommunication had less threat to the remote, struggling pioneers of France than did hunger and warfare and the more relaxing aspects of the acute business of living. Jesuit and Dominican, in conflict on most matters, were united in their despair of the morals of the colony; but the embattled orders could not put all their energy into remedying matters, for they were fighting not only Satan but each other. First the Dominicans were ascendant, because of La Salle, who had once studied to be a Jesuit priest, and who detested the order. Bienville, gratefully mindful of Canadian favors at the hands of the blackrobed followers of Loyola, blamed much of his troubles upon the Capuchins, the lesser Dominican order, which in 1717 received exclusive ecclesiastical jurisdiction over a considerable part of Louisiana. The Jesuits got a toe hold in 1727, with his approval: a tract of land in exchange for the education of the colony's children. Assiduous workers, they introduced the orange, the fig, sugar cane, and the indigo plant.

As the Jesuits grew stronger, the bitterness between the orders increased. In 1758 came the "Priests' War," in which Jesuit, Capuchin, and their lay allies engaged in "acrimonious writings, squibs, pasquenades and satirical songs," with the women leading the fight. The Capuchins won. In 1763 the Jesuits were expelled by order of the pope from all the French and Spanish possessions of the New World. But in 1772 a new and as determined a threat confronted the French Capuchins. The struggle, hitherto between rival orders within a colony of France, now became a civil religious war, as it were, between members of different nationalities within the same order. For the Spanish priests, intent on control, followed O'Reilly.

And this brings us to Father Dagobert, one of the most lovable characters in the river's history, who found an unexpected ally in a Spanish governor when the tolerant ecclesiasticism of France was confronted by the asceticism of Spain.

❦   ❦

Father Dagobert had lived in Louisiana for thirty-three years before the lean Spaniard, Father Cirilo of Barcelona, came in 1772 to disturb his contentment. True, there had been lesser unpleasantries, but the rotund old priest, now vicar-general of the diocese, had not let these interfere overmuch. When his order had triumphed over the Jesuits, Father Dagobert's part had been neither aggressive nor vindictive. When the French patriots had risen against Ulloa, the good father had simply shrugged his shoulders and given them his blessing. In this he differed from Father Genoveaux, once vicar-general, who had protested the uprising, and had been exiled by the angry Frenchmen. And in the optimistic interim before the vengeful O'Reilly came, Father Dagobert and his six fellow Capuchins gave spiritual counsel much the same as always.

Which was precisely the kind of shepherding acceptable to the not overly devout Orleanians. For thirty-three years they had loved the unruffled father. They were proud of the fine house in which he and his fellow Capuchins lived, albeit it was not the bare abode which some priests might prefer. They chuckled at the old man's weakness for weddings and wedding wine, drank with him at these convivial events and bragged that here was a cleric who could understand and forgive the frailties of human nature. They smiled appreciatively at his three-cornered hat and comfortable civil raiment which bore no likeness to priestly, brown robes. That Father Dagobert! What a splendid, understanding old fellow! What an easy confessor! What a lover of good food and snuff!

And what if he did ad lib the churchly ritual? Had he ever boasted of being learned? Did he pretend to have mastered the ordered procedures, the consistently proper dates for fasting and holy days? What if his masses and marriages and christenings were not in the exact manner prescribed in faraway Rome? He did know the litanies, and enjoyed them. The congregation also took pleasure in the sight and sound of old Father Dagobert roaring lustily the familiar chants. Their priest suited them and they suited their priest.

Because he was what he was, they even winked when Father Dagobert, who had given his sympathy to the French rebels, readily rendered homage to the conquering Spanish Caesar. Wisely, O'Reilly left the old fellow and his Capuchin brethren alone. But three years after Spanish justice had taken the lives of the six patriots, the Spanish Capuchins arrived to take the souls of their survivors in charge. In the name of the bishop of Cuba, Father Cirilo and four assistants disembarked to conduct an investigation of the religious life of the colony. Father Dagobert didn't know their purpose. Nor did he know that Father Genoveaux, in angry exile in Cuba, had stirred up this hornet's nest. In friendly, festive welcoming, he led his people to the levee to greet his Spanish brethren. And this was the first and last pleasant relationship between the French pastor and the austere men who came as inquisitorial reformers. Father Genoveaux returned with the Spanish priests, and neither he nor they waited long to disturb the serenity of Father Dagobert's life. Less than a month after his arrival, Father Cirilo wrote his first accusing report to the bishop of Havana. On reading it and those which followed, one can conclude only that the best to be said of him is that he took his investigation and the discipline of the church very seriously.

The first letter harped upon the smaller things. These French Capuchins show naught of poverty. Their shirts, breeches, and stockings resemble the garb of the laity rather than that of the clergy. Father Dagobert, that worldly one, carries a watch in his fob, has a clock in his room and a $270 clock in the refectory where the French Capuchins eat with silver knives and forks. Worse, they use small silver spoons for coffee, "as if wooden spoons were not good enough for Capuchins." Their furniture is the most lavish, their table the best spread in the capital. And they dine in private apartments, when they wish, waited upon by bright young mulattresses and unmarried Negresses.

Cirilo asks for power to deal with these and other situations. He wants the right to direct the church, the nuns, and the Capuchin plantations which the French priests are so badly mismanaging. The accusations pile higher. The masses pro populo are not being said. The priests take no notice of the apostolic bulls and letters which have been issued for the last thirty years. None of them confess in the confessional which Father Cirilo piously acknowledges that he has found by use to be uncomfortable and stifling. Instead, these self-indulgent Frenchmen sit in an armchair in the vestry with the penitent kneeling at their side. Father Dagobert has even been known to doze thereon. The Capuchins attend dinner parties and are reported to play cards. The nuns "live as they have always done, without being cloistered and as if they were not nuns at all."

This first letter also deprecates other colonial evils. Slaves live and die in a state of concubinage with the consent of their masters. The home of the priests is also inhabited by Negro girls, children of the mulattress who has domestic direction of the convent, and whose sister is in a delicate condition. So thorough is the inquisitive Spaniard that "I procured to see one day at four o'clock in the morning a white man sallying out of the chamber of this mulattress. Others leave the convent at night to meet their lovers. . . ." Cirilo recommends their expulsion to the plantation, or virtual imprisonment at night under lock and key.

Only one letter has been written, but the quarrel is already public property. Perhaps Father Dagobert himself brings his plight to the attention of the governor, Don Luis de Unzaga, whom he has already found to be a forthright and an understanding man. Don Luis seemingly has scant liking for meddling monks. Or perhaps, in his brief residence in the colony, he too has come under the genial spell of Father Dagobert. Certainly he has discovered already that there is a difference between the people of the Old World and the New which extends even to their religious practices. Whatever the reason, this former colonel of the Regiment of Havana becomes Dagobert's needed friend.

Apprised of Father Cirilo's coming, he has already written before his arrival to the Bishop of Havana.

Louisiana "under the King of France, her former mas-

ter, enjoyed the fullest and most entire liberty," wrote the
governor to the bishop, in anticipation of Father Cirilo's
mission. Father Dagobert is "a pacific man, much liked by
the people and those placed under his jurisdiction. . . . All
these friars are excellent men and give the good example;
but among them are some who are well informed and others
scarcely informed as to the duties of their sacred calling;
all however labor zealously to the best of their abilities and
knowledge, and they are familiar with the great poverty and
destitution of their parishioners." Dagobert, Don Luis writes,
was esteemed by Count O'Reilly and by all Spaniards for
his kindness and prudence. As for the convent's mulattresses,
they were born on the Capuchin plantation and have merely
been afforded shelter. This is contrary to the canons of the
church, of course, "but your Grace will know how to cure
this distemper without cauterizing the patient." He recommends that Father Dagobert be kept at least for another
year, despite such minor shortcomings as the condition of
the ecclesiastical records which are in "ridiculous disorder."

And Don Luis ends his first intercession with a vivid
picture of colonial deviations from ordered religious practice:

"It is not the practice here to force anyone to submit
to the church, and the process of excommunication is held
in abomination. I assure your Grace, however, that those
who live outside the pale of the church are very few. These
people are devout, respectful and edifying in their deport-
ment when in church. But to go to confession and receive
the sacrament is a thing unknown with the male part of
the population. They look upon it as an act of hypocrisy
and as treating with levity the holiest sacrament whose
mystery they worship with the deepest and humblest veneration. Hence it results that they approach for the first
and last time the Communion table on reaching the age of
puberty."

The governor also reminds the bishop that the church

in Louisiana enjoys no immunities or privileges, its jurisdiction being confined entirely to matters spiritual. Marriage is held a civil contract only, and affiancing, nullifying or validating a marriage contract, and the granting of a divorce or temporary separation are given to the secular power alone.

This letter had antedated by eight days the arrival of the Spanish Capuchins. Cirilo was unaware of the tolerance of Don Luis, and in his own first letter to the bishop he had assumed that Don Luis would see things his own way. But by September 14th, the bishop had confirmed Father Dagobert for another year, in keeping with Don Luis's suggestion. This is too much for Cirilo, who on September 15th writes two explosive letters. In the first of these he indicts Dagobert for giving comfort to the French rebels—though neither O'Reilly nor Unzaga thought him deserving of censure—and charges that the old priest instigated the expulsion of Father Genoveaux to gain power. Besides, says Cirilo, Father Dagobert has forgotten to notify his parishioners of Ember Week, and when Cirilo reminded him of this oversight, he happily suggested postponing the fast days to the following week.

Cirilo's second letter of that day is a masterpiece of clerical savagery.

". . . I shall merely say that the very Spanish name is an object of abomination to these friars, because they cannot bear the sight of the things which are of God, and which appertain to our divine religion, and because these friars or monsters think that we have come to repress the abuses which they love, and to reform their evil ways. Therefore they hate us, and such is the reason why we cannot obtain from them even what is necessary to the so very limited wants of a poor Capuchin—such, for instance, as a table to write on, an humble box wherein to put our wearing apparel, paper, ink, quills and other trifles. When they have bags so full of dollars, we are obliged to have recourse to our friends to relieve our necessities.

"What is most deplorable is to see in the convent the concubine of the friars, for such is the reputation she bears. She has three sons, although who her husband is God only knows. They eat at our table and off the plates of Father Dagobert, who, without shame, or fear of the world at least, if not of God, permits them to call him papa. She is one of the mulattresses who are kept in the house. She is the absolute mistress of the whole establishment, and the friars have for her so much attachment that they strive who shall send to the cherished paramour the best dish on the table before any one of us is allowed to taste it. . . .

"As to the Eucharist, that mystery which makes the angels tremble with awe, we found that the sacramental elements were so full of insects which fed on them, and presented so disgusting an appearance that it was necessary to fling them to the jakes as if they had been the veriest filth. So great is the detestable negligence of these men that I think they are the disciples either of Luther or Calvin. . . .

"This Father Dagobert is a great hand at giving with the sacrament the benediction to the people, whenever it is desired by them. Thus, in a little more than a month, he gave it eight times. He is no less fond of making processions, for which he has no authority, and for which there is no necessity; and what is still more singular, when thus going out in procession, he abandons the Host without leaving any priest to watch over it. . . . Nor is less the indecency with which in sight of the exposed Host, these priests demean themselves in the choir, where they are seen stuffing their noses with tobacco, crossing one leg on the top of the other, staring round in every direction, scandalizing the people, and moving the very angels to wrath.

". . . and with regard to Father Dagobert, here is in a few words how he lives: he rises at six in the morning, says or does not say mass (such mass as he says!), preparing himself in this way for the duties of the day. He then goes to church, hardly makes the proper genuflection, claps on his bonnet, says his mass which does not last a quarter of an hour, without any of the prescribed ceremonies, uncovers his head, makes another genuflection as for grace and taking his three-cornered hat, which is a very superfluous and unworthy appendage for a Capuchin, he goes (without saying any Ave Maria, except it be for goodly dollars, and in abundance) to a somewhat suspicious house, where he plays until the dinner hour."

Midway in the attack, Cirilo recommends that Father Dagobert not only be relieved of his position, but should also be expelled from the colony, and sentenced to proper penance. Then he turns upon Don Luis, Dagobert's ally:

"Your Grace, knowing so well the good nature and the pacific dispositions of the governor, will easily conceive how it is that he is desirous of giving satisfaction to these friars, not because he is not fully aware of their misdeeds, not because he does not see that there is no punishment which they have not deserved, and that it would be proper to drive them out of the land, as himself has expressed it to me, but because, when these Capuchins knew the Spaniards were coming up the river, they stirred up the town and persuaded the governor that, if they were sent away, all the people would also depart. . . . But your Grace must not believe in the general emigration with which we are threatened. It would be confined to a few of Father Dagobert's relations, who would starve if they were not supported by him. . . .

"I have not failed to throw out a good many insinuations to these priests, but their uniform answer is that they are not Spaniards, and that, besides our mere assertion, they have no other proof that your Grace is the bishop of this diocese . . . the perversity of these men is such that they are not satisfied with being wicked themselves, but that they also wish us to follow their example, and to abstain from fasting and observing the holydays. As an excuse for their doings they say they are not Spaniards. I can assure your Grace that they spare no efforts to make me like one of them, and to induce me to wear a shirt and stockings and to become as lax in my morals and habits as they are. . . .

"It is said that these priests have secreted all the silver plate and money which they possess. This is very bad, but of very little importance to us who know that with the help of the king and of God, we shall never be wanting in anything and shall have bread enough to live. . . ."

Cirilo ends on a fawning note, with the prayer that God will help the bishop in directing the Spanish Capuchins to weed the vineyard.

During this period, the bewildered Father Dagobert has written but one letter, an humble missive on September 14th to the bishop, thanking him for having appointed him vicar-general—the post which he had already held by appointment of the bishop of Quebec when Louisiana was a part of that diocese. In this letter, Father Dagobert simply gives an account of his ecclesiastical administration, lists the reforms which it requires, and asks the guidance of the superior wisdom of his apostolic chief. But he has been more active in another quarter. He has gone piteously to his friend, Don Luis, begging relief from the abuse of the Spanish Capuchins and Father Genoveaux; and he has even suggested that he and his French brothers return to France.

Don Luis fights for the old Frenchman. On September 26th he denounces the conspiracy of "some unquiet spirits against the poor French Capuchins whom they wish to be censured justly or unjustly." Don Luis stoutly defends Father Dagobert in this letter, criticizes Cirilo for being lacking in prudence, and ends with the sage comment that "many of the synodical regulations cannot be applied to this province without injury to the interests of the king, the number of whose vassals might be diminished considerably if those regulations were attempted to be carried into execution."

Cirilo continues with undiminished venom. On November 14th he writes two more letters which are so vehement as to be omitted from the account of the Louisiana historian, Charles Gayarré, who has preserved the story for us. Refusing to quote them, Gayarré comments that "those letters in some of their parts are very much in the style of certain passage in Juvenal and Suetonius which are hardly compatible with the chastity of modern languages."

Nor has the quarrel been settled even by July, 1773. Don Luis again intervenes, and from this point on the story concerns principally this stoutly tolerant defender of the French Capuchins. In a new letter to the bishop, the governor admits that Father Dagobert has not yet executed all the orders of the bishop, particularly regarding the expulsion of the black women from the convent. But "I felt no hesitation in giving him time for summoning to his aid the necessary fortitude to throw out of doors a set of people whom he has raised and kept about him from the cradle."

Don Luis also gives Father Genoveaux a clean bill, his letter revealing that that erstwhile troublemaker now "keeps aloof from both parties" and does not merit the denunciation which he also has received. Then the governor strikes hard.

"In your last communication you said that you were informed that each of the French Capuchins had received one thousand dollars for his share of the perquisites collected during the year for the funeral rites and ceremonies only, and that Father Dagobert made light of the bull of the Santa Cruzada. Both assertions are false. The first will provoke a smile, and the second a sorrowful indignation. How is it possible not to laugh at the impudence of the first assertion, when it is known that there is not in New Orleans and its environs a population of two thousand souls of all professions

and conditions; and the greater portion of those people are
so poor that, when they die, they are buried with no other
charges or expenses than four reales paid to the man who
goes to the graveyard to give them sepulture. . . ."

Don Luis is even more contemptuous of the charge
that Father Dagobert made light of the bull of Santa Cruzada, the original object of which had been to grant indul-
gences to all Spaniards who engaged personally in waging
war against the infidels or contributed to such war.

"All that I could learn concerning the alleged contempt of Father Dagobert for the bull of the Santa Cruzada
is that, in conversation, he said that it was unknown in
France and that in the Indies it was valuable only on account
of the graces and privileges attached to it. I have conveyed
to the knowledge of the king that it is obnoxious to his subjects in this province; that all means of persuasion are vain
to reconcile them to it; that they consider it as a tribute
paid to the clergy; that they look upon it with horror, and
that they would prefer to it any other tax or exaction. . . ."

Now the bishop's wrath is diverted to this governor,
who is beginning to sound as heretical as the French Capuchins. Angrily demanding an explanation, he receives a flowery answer in which Don Luis protests his admiration for
the bishop but retracts nothing. Unsatisfied with such eva-
sions, the bishop demands of the Marquis de la Torre, governor and captain general of Cuba, that the indolence of
Don Luis be stimulated. The marquis also writes Don Luis.
In reply, the embattled governor informs him that the interests of the king are not being harmed in this priestly battle;
that the Capuchins are being wronged, and that the bishop
should visit the colony himself to discover the true state
of things.

"The people here will remain quiet as long as they are
gently treated," he discerningly comments. "But the use of
the rod would produce confusion and ruin. Their dispositions

are the result of the happy state of liberty to which they have been accustomed from the cradle, and in which they ought to be maintained, so far as is consistent with the laws of the kingdom."

Governor Unzaga also carries the fight to a higher authority, the Bailiff de Arriaga, one of the king's ministers. And this last letter which we read is brilliant in its understanding of nationalistic distinctions. The governor savagely criticizes the bishop for indiscreet severities in threatening the French with excommunication and the "application of the discipline of the Inquisition, under the jurisdiction of which they were not born, and to which they are not accustomed." He decries the bishop's action in reserving for himself the revenues from the granting of dispensations, hitherto the chief source of income for the Louisiana clergy.

"There is no such moral deformity as has been depicted to his Grace," he writes. ". . . What is it to the king, for instance, whether the French Capuchins consider the teal as amphibious and eat it on fast days, and follow other practices quite as insignificant, and which through immemorial custom have been thought to be legitimate among these people? . . . The people here are neither vicious nor addicted to debauchery, nor opposed to our habits, although in many respects those habits disagree with their tastes. They have some of their own, as other people have, to which they are much attached—and this is very natural. These habits are not in conflict with the primordial obligations of society; they are not to be eradicated at once, but must be removed gradually and almost imperceptibly. . . .

"The prelate exalts the virtues of Father Cirilo. I do not know whether the ambition which lurks beneath the coarse woolen gown of the monk can be held up as a pattern of virtue, but I am sure that for a monk to have sown dissension between his brethren and the prelate who is their superior is an act sufficiently mean to make him fall from

that pedestal of probity to which his Grace wishes to raise
him on account of his opposition to imaginary licentious-
ness. . . .

"An enlightened prudence and a good deal of toleration
are necessary here, for although this is a Spanish province,
and although Count O'Reilly endeavored to make its inhabitants forget the former domination under which they
lived so long, still I cannot flatter his Majesty so much as
to say that the people have ceased to be French at heart,
and that in them is not to be found that spirit of independence which causes resistance to oppressive laws. But I will
affirm that they are susceptible of being submissive and
loyal subjects, that they entertain great veneration for their
ancient laws, and that the state of felicity they now enjoy
is a guaranty to me that they are not to be suspected of
being disposed to fail in their duties toward the crown.
Therefore do I endeavor to keep them in the colony, and
to secure their love and services for the king without caring
in the least for what I deem to be fooleries."

This letter virtually ended the strange little clerical
war. The government of Spain temporized, wisely; the bishop
of Cuba was upheld in most of his actions in regard to
Louisiana, but Don Luis was not censured. The clergy were
ordered to make their peace, and apparently they did. Father
Cirilo, in 1781, was made bishop of the town of Tricali,
Greece, and was also appointed coadjutor to his former
patron, the bishop of Cuba, and directed to exercise his
episcopal functions in Louisiana. Father Dagobert, serving
out his year, remained in Louisiana, died there, and was
heartily mourned by his flock. And Don Luis's evaluation
of the French spirit was not contradicted by time. The
Spaniards brought their laws, and a better architecture, and
order to Louisiana. But the Spanish religious spirit never
replaced the adaptative interpretation which the French colonists and their priests gave to the edicts of the church. If

this observation should be debated, New Orleans itself can be offered in proof, as much today as two hundred years ago. Among the Catholics of the lower river, and among the Protestants who came later, the feast day is still preferred to the sackcloth. And this truth, established so long ago, is an important key to understanding.

CHAPTER 5

Black Code

THERE were other colonists.

Along the slave coast they lay where they fell, and when the black flesh had dropped away the bones whitened in the black jungle and on the white shore. Over them stumbled black feet, chains clanking, to the hell ships that sailed to another jungle across the world. The black, rotting corpses slithered over the ships' sides, and the white bones drifted deep beneath the green, shocked surface of the sea. And some black feet felt earth again, earth of the English colonies, and Spain's, earth of French Louisiana's uncleared lands.

White empire had need of black bodies for the forest's felling, the river's conquest, for fields which were to undulate with tobacco and rice and indigo. So the black men and women sweated along the Mississippi, less than fifty of them in the first year of New Orleans, then seven thousand in the brief blowing of John Law's bubble. Seven thousand survived the death-touched ships' holds to die in the fever swamps of the lower coast and in the forests of the upriver plantations. And more came, to live and die, and to beget for their masters. Tenaciously the Negro endured along the river when the white man could not, breaking the soil, sowing the harrowed land, hammering upon the forges, mixing the mortar for Bienville's town.

But not always willingly. These first, fierce Banbara laborers from Africa could endure more than the white man, and were easier to hold than the Indians who knew this wilderness; but they were not a tractable folk. This puzzled the French. Were not their stomachs fairly filled with rice and beans, and with meat when the hogs abounded? And were they not permitted their own strange stews of rabbit, musty alligator, lynx, opossum? They were housed too, and surely the palmetto-roofed hovels withstood rain and winter chill as well as did their African dens. As for clothing, there were the rough, woolen capes to hide the nakedness of which they were not ashamed, and the oxhide sandals which could be stuffed with straw against the cold. They were free to breed like animals in the fields and huts. Those with talent could in time win their freedom through skilled fingers, and others because of the generosity of their masters or the unwillingness of white fathers to keep their mulatto offspring in servitude. But the Banbaras were a sullen and thankless lot, two hundred and twenty-five years ago, and thus became a problem. The problem of the Banbaras, and of the other black men who followed, has not been solved on this or any other river.

Bienville tried. For forty years of French domination of the valley, the Negro lived under Bienville's Black Code. Then the Spaniard came, and there were difficult economic and social readjustments for the Frenchman. But the Black Code remained virtually unchanged. And finally the Americans owned the valley. Yet not until seventy-five years ago did changing domination mean change in the status of the Negro. Sometimes the fields along the river produced wealth, and sometimes only a living or less; but except for the quantity of the rations and the temperaments of the masters, the first one hundred and fifty years of the slave Negro along the river were pretty much the same. The Black Code endured.

It is simple to understand why. The Negro was property and profit. He was also a specter of fear, and not without reason. The code simply placed safeguards upon the property and against the specter. And reading it, and knowing that it survived in all its essentials for one hundred and fifty years, it becomes easier to understand the roustabout and the field hand and the house servant of the Mississippi today ... and easier to understand the black rebel.

Let us turn the pages of the Black Code, and try to imagine the misgivings of Bienville, the colonial leader. We know that in his day he was just, and shrewd, devout and a soldier. He is trying to protect white lives and black property. But first, if only in deference to the Faith, Bienville is concerned with black souls. Not quite first, for Article One, unexplainable today, simply decrees the never-enforced expulsion of Jews from the colony. The next four articles make it imperative for masters to impart religious instruction to their slaves, permit the exercise of the Roman Catholic creed only, decree confiscation for Negroes placed under the supervision of any other persons than a Catholic, and also for Negroes found working on Sundays or holydays.

Of the fifty-four articles in the Black Code it is not necessary to do more than summarize most of them. One, however, is worth reading in full, for it is the embodiment of an unending problem. Remember, the code was drawn up in 1724, when the blood of black slaves and white masters had not yet been so intermixed as to produce the beautiful, sensuous women who were to delight the Creole blades a half century later. Yet miscegenation was already a moral concern. This is the unenforceable edict:

We forbid our white subjects, of both sexes, to marry with the blacks under the penalty of being fined and subjected to some other arbitrary punishment. We forbid all curates, priests or missionaries of our secular or regular clergy, and even our chaplains in the navy, to sanction such marriages. We also forbid all our white subjects, and even the

manumitted or free-born blacks, to live in a state of concubinage with slaves. Should there be any issue from this kind
of intercourse, it is our will that the person so offending,
and the master of the slave, should pay each a fine of three
hundred livres. Should said issue be the result of the concubinage of the master with his slave, said master shall not
only pay the fine but be deprived of the slave and of the
children, who shall be adjudged to the hospital of the locality,
and said slaves shall be forever incapable of being set free.
But should this illicit intercourse have existed between a
free black and his slave, when said free black had no legitimate wife, and should said black marry said slave according
to the forms prescribed by the church, said slave shall be
thereby set free, and the children shall also become free
and legitimate; and in such a case, there shall be no application of the penalties mentioned in the present article.

The regulations for the protection of the Frenchmen
against slave violence were more effective because of the
savage force of the reprisal. The slave in New Orleans and on
the plantations had many proscriptions to remember. If he
carried an offensive weapon or a heavy stick, he was whipped,
unless he was on a hunting mission for his master. He could
not gather with other slaves under any pretext, whether on
the plantations or the highways, or in the forests. The whip
punished the first offense, the brand of the fleur-de-lis the
repetition, and death the aggravated incident. Masters who
permitted such gatherings faced heavy fines. Should a rebellious slave strike his master, his mistress, or the husband
of his mistress, or their children, forcibly enough to produce
a bruise or draw blood, he died. And the death penalty
could be given for the stealing of horses, mules and cows,
and articles of like value, though lesser thefts merited only
the whip and the branding iron.

The Black Code also sought to discourage any thought

of freedom through flight. A runaway absent for a month had his ears cut off and his shoulder branded. For a second like offense he was hamstrung, and branded on the other shoulder. And should the persistent cripple flee again, he suffered death when caught.

But not all of the code was brutal or discriminatory. Definitely, Bienville wanted to protect the slave against the cruelty of sadistic masters, and, within limits, against hardship greater than the recognized norm. A slave not properly fed, clad, and housed according to the minimum requirements of the code could complain to the attorney general of the Superior Council, who was empowered to prosecute. And, Bienville ordained, "it is our will that this regulation be observed in all accusations for crimes or barbarous and inhuman treatment brought by slaves against their masters." Masters were ordered to feed and provide for slaves disabled from working because of old age, disease or other cause; if this law was disregarded, the master was obliged to pay eight cents a day to the government for the maintenance of the slave in the nearest hospital.

The colony's officers of justice had the power to institute criminal process against masters and overseers who killed or mutilated a slave, and to punish such murder according to the atrocity of the circumstances. Neither voluntarily by the master nor through judicial seizure could husbands and wives be sold separately when belonging to the same owner; nor could children under fourteen be separated from their parents.

And finally there is Article Fifty-four, perhaps as ironic today as then. "We grant to manumitted slaves the same rights, privileges, and immunities enjoyed by free-born persons," it reads. "It is our pleasure that their merit in having acquired their freedom shall produce in their favor, not only with regard to persons, but also to their property, the same effects which our other subjects derive from the happy circumstance of their having been born free."

Laws are dry, but not the stories which they provide. The Black Code could not confine courage or cruelty or kindness or lust. When the Americans came, the spiritual domination of the Catholic Church gave way along the river to the ecstatic, physical appeal of Protestant extroversion. The slave was then allowed to worship in any faith. And though the forbidding framework of the code underwent no other essential change until emancipation, desperate hate—or desperate love for freedom—brought the black men together repeatedly for unsuccessful uprisings. Samba, the Banbara, led the first of these, under the persuasion of the Chickasaws in 1730 when the Indians plotted destruction of the French through a red and black alliance. As in most slave rebellions, a slave talked. A Negro woman was hanged, and Samba and seven others died on the wheel. But it wasn't simply freedom that Samba desired. Perhaps he had been a king in his own land. Whatever his reasoning, his dream was the establishment of a government of the rebel Banbaras, who would kill every white, and continue to hold all other black men and women in slavery.

As elsewhere in the New World, every rebellion failed. Black heads grinned from pointed stakes along the river and at the city gates. Gashed, twisted black bodies shuddered upon the wheel, or cringed beneath the lash and the iron. Cropped ears and branded faces reminded other recalcitrants that the Frenchman and the Spaniard and the American were alike in their color and their mastery.

But black courage was not evidenced in rebellion alone. Under France slave and free man fought the Indians. The free men of color fought for the Spaniard and the American against the English, and for the English against the Spaniard. And when the Yankee gunboats held the river, the Negro fought again for himself.

Least of all did the code prevail against the urgings of white bodies and black. The dark, savage women of Africa, the yellow girls of Santo Domingo, the bright courtesans of the young colonial aristocrats won their own kind of freedom. The flaming tignon headdress of the easy quadroons became magnets instead of prescribed badges of their race and station; and though their sons learned the trades and the submissiveness required of dark skins, their tawny daughters needed to remember only the oldest skill of all.

This is but the first glimpse of the race which we shall meet again and again in this story; and the purpose here is simply to place the Negro against the legal and social background to which he has been limited for two-thirds of his residence along the river. In its development his part has been impressive and scantily recorded. He burned the canebrakes and drained the swamps and sawed the cypress for the plantation homes. His strength built the first levees, and adds to their earthy magnitude today. The Negro opened up the true cotton kingdom which lies along the river, plowing and picking, toting the bales aboard the steamboats and firing the overtaxed boilers. In the war which was to bring him freedom, his overwhelming presence along the manless river struck deep at the South's sense of security; and the manipulation to which he was subjected in his first years of liberty endured longest along the river, and with the most unhappy consequences.

In his own folklore, the Lower Mississippi has a preponderant part. From the softer life of the Atlantic seaboard he was sold down the river to the newer, life-sapping domain of cotton. Around the river the roustabout and cotton picker and levee-building convict have fashioned their songs and legends. Today the Negro clings to the river in greater numbers than to any other area in the South. His good-time towns are the river towns, New Orleans, Vicksburg, Natchez, and Memphis. And to the river and its towns and its green acres he is still almost as indispensable as in the days of Bienville's code. When that code was devised, the Negro was a soul to be guarded against heresy, a savage threat to masters already beset, a piece of property valuable enough for physical preservation, and a human being deserving of some protection against inhumanity. His women were to be untouchables in mocking contradiction to clandestine fact.

Now the code is dead, but along the river its assumptions persist.

CHAPTER 6

Rule of the Dons

I F THIS could be a detailed history of the successive overlordships of the Mississippi Valley, closer attention would be given to the Spanish occupation than the brief years of their actual occupation would appear to warrant. The Spaniard pronouncedly affected the governing processes, the architecture, the economics, the civil law, and even the social and racial peculiarities of the river people of France's Louisiana. Only the language of the colony remained unchanged.

That part of New Orleans, the Vieux Carré, described as a little French city within a city prideful of its ties with France, is more Spanish than French in its architecture. Most of the old town was destroyed by fire in 1788, and the homes and buildings which rose from the ashes had the Spanish patio, the Spanish wrought-iron railings, the multi-colored plaster-over-brick walls of Spain. The civil law which even today makes Louisiana unique among the states, is principally of Spanish imposition. The mating of Spanish and French produced the New Orleans Creole, a distinct people whose dark-eyed women were then and are now so frequently of unusual beauty. To that paradoxical land of plenty and hunger, of violence and gentleness, of crudity and a certain culture, Spain brought its own paradoxes of religious rigidity and the temporal ease of mañana; military surveillance and temporizing amiability, enterprise and indolence.

The Spaniard found New Orleans a little city of some three thousand oddly assorted people, whose dissolution and

poverty and chaotic conception of individual liberties had
not been improved by the parental neglect of France. Yet,
here along the Mississippi were all the ingredients for a
productive empire, capable of giving ample sustenance to
its inhabitants. Fish and game abounded in the water and
on the water's edge. To the settlements and the port of
New Orleans, intrepid huntsmen and trappers returned from
four hundred and five hundred leagues upriver, from the
wilder Illinois country with the skins and dried meat of
bear and deer and buffalo, the pelts of smaller fur-bearing
animals, and firkins of bear's grease. The West Indies alone
provided a hungry market for the cedar and cypress and
sycamore timber of the Mississippi's forests, and the inland
towns and the Indian villages were as ready to trade for the
goods which the huge bateaux and pirogues brought upstream.

France had not taken advantage of its wealth; or perhaps in trying to take undue advantage, France had stultified
the producers. Spain did not intend to make the same mistake. Spain had an especial reason for strengthening Louisiana. Even with all land east of the Mississippi forfeit to
England, the sprawling colony could be the great buffer between the British and Mexico and Central America, the
possessions dearest and most valuable to the dons. The treaty
had put the busy English in Mobile and Biloxi on the gulf,
on the Tombigbee, in the Illinois country, and along the
river at Baton Rouge and Natchez. Only a thriving, popu-
lous, disciplined colony could stand firm against further English expansion.

O'Reilly was no indecisive, sulking Ulloa. Undoubtedly
his execution of the insurgent leaders was a savage mistake,
but he was to make no other grave errors in government.
Swiftly he acted to gain a secure hold on the river, and
to win over the colonists. Outside of the recently rebellious
New Orleans area the settlers swarmed to the posts to scrawl

their names, or more frequently their X marks, beneath the oath of allegiance. On the upper river the colony remained French except for the handful of Spanish officers whom he dispatched there. In all the years under Spain less than a dozen Spaniards settled in upper Louisiana, which was divided from the lower half of the province at the southeastern corner of Missouri.

Wisely, O'Reilly gave minor official posts to Frenchmen. He enrolled the French in the city militia, and paid them well. For lieutenant governor he selected an honored Frenchman, Athanese de Mézières, who had emigrated to Louisiana in 1733 and had served as captain under Bienville, de Vaudreuil and Kerlerec, and was a mathematician and language scholar of note. O'Reilly also ended the custom of owning Indian slaves, and at de Mézières's suggestion revived the old French tradition of giving gifts to the Indians.

The first such renewal of these gifts shows that little change in the natives' wishes—or at least in what they got —had occurred since De Soto's day. The Spaniard's presents included a hat trimmed with galloons, an ornamental shirt, fusils, blankets, cloth, a copper kettle, powder and ball, vermilion, glass beads, needles and thread, axes and adzes, knives, awls, wormscrews, flints and steels, hawkballs, mirrors, tape, wire, tobacco and brandy, hatchets, salt, a medal ribbon, and a Spanish flag. To hold down the stealing of livestock from Spanish Mexico, O'Reilly forbade the purchasing of mules and horses from the Indians.

Other of O'Reilly's laws seem strangely harsh today. But they were not harshly enforced.

But the Spaniards proceeded to bog themselves down with a bureaucracy which enriched some of them and tainted a great many with graft. O'Reilly made Louisiana a province. He abolished the Superior Council, and as captain general he was the ruler of Louisiana, answerable only to Havana and Spain. Under him acted a profusion of officials, divided unnecessarily into provincial and municipal categories. The provincial affairs were administered by an intendant; by a governor, who reported to the captain general; a comptroller, auditors, commissaries, surveyors, interpreters, port captains, notaries, comandantes, whose multiplicity—and frequent duplicity—were to find a Louisiana parallel more than a hundred and fifty years later. To govern New Orleans he set up an aldermanic body, the Cabildo, composed of a governor and six regidores, with judicial and administrative functions. The posts were sold openly, for the benefit of the Spanish crown. And with them went such juicy plums as the alférez real, or standard-bearer; the alcalde mayor provincial, who was a chief of police—and judge and jury—in minor cases; the alguacil mayor, a criminal and civil sheriff; and the depository general, who acted as treasurer on a three per cent commission. Jobs outside the domain of the regidores were also sold, particularly the position of mayordomo or mayor, and the profitable post of syndic procurator general, a sort of attorney-generalship in which the holder "assisted" the public in court matters, for fat fees, whether the citizen wanted his services or not.

With the colony in order, and docile, O'Reilly left for Havana and Spain. But before his going, he had strengthened a friendship which would help to alter the course of the continent. Shortly after O'Reilly had assumed control, the colony ran short of provisions. At this juncture there arrived in New Orleans Oliver Pollock, a venturesome Irish merchant from Baltimore with a cargo of good flour. Because of the colony's pressing need, Pollock could have realized an enormous profit. Instead he offered the cargo at actual cost.

Not to be outdone, O'Reilly insisted on giving him a fair profit. A firm friendship developed between the two Irishmen, so closely linked to Spain. Pollock had quitted the English colonies for Havana, where he mastered Spanish, and from Havana he had come to New Orleans. And in New

Orleans, thanks to his friendship with O'Reilly and his successors, Pollock amassed considerable wealth because of business favors.

When the American Revolution began, Pollock's achievements and his sympathy with the cause of the colonists caused Philadelphia to appoint him its New Orleans commercial agent. His ensuing and scantly noted service to the American cause deserves to rank with that of Robert Morris. In New Orleans, Pollock purchased munitions and supplies, shipped them to Philadelphia by way of the Mississippi and Ohio and then overland from Pittsburgh to Philadelphia. Patrick Henry also appointed him special agent for the colony of Virginia during the revolt; and as such he was responsible largely for the financing of George Rogers Clark's expedition against what Virginia considered its Northwest Territory. From his own resources, Pollock raised $300,000 for the revolutionists. After the war, the United States was slow to repay. As a result, Pollock was imprisoned for debt in Havana. He was liberated by Galvez, third Spanish governor of Louisiana, upon Galvez's elevation to the captain-generalcy of Cuba. And Oliver Pollock paid off his debts, amassed another fortune, and died an old man at Pinckneyville, Mississippi, in 1823.

The friendship of two Irishmen brought wealth to one of them. His wealth served the American rebels. From the Mississippi came gold and supplies and the backing that was to wrest more land from England than was bounded by the thirteen colonies. Perhaps, had it not been for Oliver Pollock, English Canada might today have extended southwestward to the Ohio and the Mississippi.

But that lay ahead. Meantime O'Reilly was succeeded by Don Luis de Unzaga y Amazaga, an able man who had been commander of the Havana regiment. Aware of the desperate need for trade and supplies, Unzaga winked at the illegal traffic along the river between the English and the

French. From the English schooners and merchantmen, hundreds of slaves were clandestinely landed. Their employment made possible the development of the great plantations, and the great plantations in turn contributed largely to the growing wealth and stability of the colony.

And now, to their respective banks of the river, and into New Orleans, England and Spain were bringing colonists by the hundreds. Natchez, Baton Rouge, and the Felicianas, in England's new territory, were being swelled by increasing numbers of former officers and soldiers of the regular and colonial forces who were awarded large land grants in reward for participation in the Seven Years' War. Field officers received five thousand rich acres, captains three thousand, with corresponding reductions down to privates, who were given one hundred acres. Spain tried to catch up with like liberality. In the interior of Spanish Louisiana grants of a square league were allotted, and along the river large tracts, eight to ten arpents long and forty arpents deep, were parceled to such heterogeneous new settlers as Malagans and ill-suited Canary Islanders, and even refugee French from the land now British. Under Unzaga the king of Spain tried an unsuccessful experiment, the establishment of a public school. It failed primarily because Spanish was to be the language taught there, and the French would not permit their children to learn the alien tongue. In connection with the school the first public library was established. It held eleven Spanish books, five French, and fifty-two Latin. The texts for the public school were imposing enough to frighten away pupils with or without a patriotic devotion to their own tongue; for in addition to three hundred Castilian grammars and one hundred Castilian spellers, the textbooks included two hundred Sallusts, fifty Cicero's *Orations,* twenty Ovids, twenty Virgils, ten Terences, ten Julius Caesars.

In 1776, after six years, O'Reilly was shifted to Havana.

His successor, Don Bernardo de Galvez, was the youngest governor and the most brilliant military strategist to represent Spain in the New World. Fortune had served the handsome, 31-year-old soldier lavishly. He had been commander of the Louisiana regiment under Unzaga, and was the son of the viceroy of Mexico and nephew of the president of the Council of the Indies, the most powerful official, next to the king, in Spain. It was to be the Englishmen's misfortune that Galvez did not like them. Moreover, he was in opportunist sympathy with the American revolutionists, the commencement of whose struggle coincided with his taking of office.

Almost his first official act was to smash the English smugglers. Eleven richly laden English ships were seized and the captains warned against further attempts. Galvez could afford to be independent of smuggling, for Louisiana was now enjoying good times for the first extended period in its history. Trade, at first restricted to six Spanish cities, had been extended to the French West Indies, Cuba, and Vera Cruz. Money flowed freely in the colony. Slave labor was clearing more and more acres, and the incoming ships of Spain unloaded new citizens for the settlements and forest clearings of Spanish Louisiana.

The prosperous colony was at first only mildly interested in the conflict on the Atlantic seaboard, and then only because it meant trouble for England. The French could not forget that the English had been the first to wreck their colonial empire. To the Spaniard, the expanding English possessions, already at the Mississippi, were a threat to the west and to Central and South America. The success of Clark and his Kentucky Long Knives, financed by Oliver Pollock, against General Hamilton, the "hair buyer" of the Northwest, elated them. The French Louisianians were pleased with Clark's treatment of the French still in the Northwest Territory, and the Spaniards were likewise proud that Don Francisco Vigo, a wealthy St. Louisianian, had also contributed heavily to Clark's finances.

They were less pleased with the exploits of a certain Captain James Willing whom the Americans sent downriver to sound out the former Tory officers on the question of whether the West Floridians would join the American rebellion. Willing, who had unsuccessfully engaged in business in Natchez, was a thorough scoundrel. Learning that the Mississippi River Englishmen were loyal to the king, he exaggerated their opposition, and returning to Pennsylvania persuaded the government to let him bring force against them. The settlers, particularly the large plantation owners, had welcomed their former townsman as a guest, despite political differences. He repaid their courtesies by leading a gang of freebooters down the river, pillaging and destroying the very homes to which he had been welcomed. The aroused English strengthened their forces at Fort Panmure, Fort Bute, and Baton Rouge, while France and Spain waited, hungrily, for the propitious moment to strike the old foe. The moment came with the American victory at Saratoga. France entered the conflict on the side of the Americans, and Spain declared its own separate war against Britain.

The Spaniards' vital part in the humbling of Britain, to Spain's own eventual disadvantage, will be told in more detail in the story of England's brief tenure on the river. Galvez smashed the English along the Mississippi, and at Mobile and Pensacola, making the lost Floridas Spanish again. The treaty of 1783 confirmed Spain in her possessions, and the specter of American questioning of her claims had not yet arisen. So Galvez, warrior idol of Spanish America, was elevated to lieutenant general, given the title of count, and appointed captain general of Louisiana and the Floridas, and governor general of Cuba.

An interesting sidelight on the swift commingling of the French and Spanish appears in the rolls of the Louisiana regiment which Galvez led against the English. The old French names had been partly Iberianized in the spelling, but there is no mistaking the Don Jacobo Dubreuils and Don Elias Toutant Beauregards who appear in profusion among the sonorous Don Francisco de Cartavonas and Don Buena Ventura Oruetas. For all practical purposes French and Spanish were one. It was not to be as easy for these Latins of the Mississippi to go through the long and yet undreamed-of final transition.

A regulative lawmaker followed a soldier as governor of Louisiana. Don Estevan Miro, likewise colonel of the Louisiana regiment, became governor in 1785. Under Spain, the province's population had increased from less than 14,000 to 31,000 and upon it Spain had lavished great sums. In 1785, Spain spent an average of $16.55 per capita on the government and rehabilitation of Louisiana. In the same year, North Carolina's per capita cost was 15 cents. But apparently Louisiana's morals had not risen with its population or governmental expenditures.

So one would suspect after reading between the lines of Miro's proclamations. Everyone must attend mass, and no one can work on Sunday. Stores must close on Sunday and the Sunday dances of the slaves in the public squares to the tomtom rhythms of the jungles cannot begin until after the Sunday night services. The Negro, quadroon, and octoroon women must be disciplined. Concubinage is to be strenuously dealt with. Women of color cannot accentuate their charms with beguiling French caps or Spanish mantillas. Instead they must wear the tignon. The women of color easily circumvented the purpose of the order; for the tignon, a Madras headdress striped in yellow and red, white and blue, and brown and white, became a jauntily provocative creation.

Equally fruitless were other edicts, as they were fruitless in New Orleans before Spain and have been ever since. Gambling with cards and dice was banned, as was the carry-

ing of dirks and other concealed weapons. No liquor could
be sold to soldiers, Indians, or slaves in taverns or otherwise,
and no citizens could assemble without a permit. To hold
down traffic in stolen goods, the purchase of goods from soldiers, Indians, and slaves was prohibited. And the still
slovenly Orleanians, who had to be forced to join in fire
fighting under penalty of fines or imprisonment, were warned
to drain their streets, to keep hogs at home, and remove all
dead animals from the street.

Miro, albeit something of a bluenose, was kind to the
waifs of war and territorial transfer. Hundreds of Acadians,
still impermanently settled, who were sent to the colony at
the expense of the king of France, were given lands. From
bloody Santo Domingo, hideous with massacre, came white
survivors, and many a light-skinned Negro concubine, to find
homes and a new life in Louisiana. And the Protestant English Tories of Natchez and Baton Rouge were won over to
the Catholic Church in great numbers, not by threat, but by
the persuasiveness of young Irish priests, brought to Louisiana for that purpose.

But the stubbornness of Spain, her contempt for the
power of the new republic of the United States, was to lead
to her own eviction. From the middle eighties to American
acquisition, the story of Spain in Louisiana is one of wran-
gling and intrigue over the limits of her holdings and the
rights of American navigation of the river. The succeeding
governors of the final Spanish years and the life of Louisiana
itself can be merged in the broader picture of greed and mis-
understanding and world-juggling of the restless Napoleonic
period. Before we look upon that shady canvas, we must
glance at the English of the river, who came as conquerors
of two European empires, and who vanished from the Mississippi before the young vigor of rebellious colonial Englishmen and the genius of Galvez, the American republic's
monarchistic ally on the river.

CHAPTER 7

The English Come and Go

THE ENGLISH reached the Lower Mississippi too late.
Had they gained territorial possession earlier, their genius
for colonization and trade might have enabled them to hold
their winnings against all comers. They might even have succeeded in their strange plan for an upriver city through
which they hoped to throttle New Orleans.

But they did not arrive in force until 1764, after the
partitioning of France's Louisiana. That date preceded by
just twelve years the lightly viewed beginnings of an Atlantic
seaboard incident involving their own dogged kind. Instead
of having to subdue only this handful of colonials, England
was to face three enemies—France and Spain and the seaboard
recalcitrants.

So, in just fifteen years the English were to lose their
hold upon the Mississippi; but in that short period theirs was
the first successful effort to make the Mississippi pay its
colonizers handsomely.

The river wasn't new to the English in 1764. Sixty-five
years earlier, Bienville had noted that the natives of a Lake
Pontchartrain village had been attacked by a party of
Chickasaws led by "two men calling themselves Englichi."
The story would be repeated many times throughout the period of French domination of Louisiana, and in many other
lands; the old tale of English subalterns in desert and wilderness, leading natives on obscure forays for reasons even more
obscure to themselves.

For more than half a century English agents tempted the Chickasaws, the Cherokees and the Creeks. Smuggled English goods supplanted French merchandise, and England grew bolder as France grew weaker. Before 1764 the English ranged the river as intruders. Now, in 1764, they came as owners of all of French Louisiana east of the Mississippi save the Isle of Orleans.

There were many along the river who hated these English: the Acadians whom they had deported, the French whose New World empire they had destroyed, the Spaniards whom they had humbled in Europe and largely dispossessed in America. But the Englishmen came bearing gifts of ready commerce and trade in slaves. They brought the promise of a happier political abode for the freethinking Swiss and German settlers of Louisiana, and for those independent French who hated tolerant England less than they hated absolute Spain.

The Spaniards, precariously lodged on the Isle of Orleans, greatly feared these English newcomers, and with good reason. Spain had not stirred herself from 1764 until O'Reilly arrived to exact vengeance in 1769. In the intervening five years, the English trading sloops had filled the river. English merchandise stocked the shelves of the French subjects of Spain; and the Louisianians, with the slaves England had sold them, were crossing the boundary to settle in English territory.

And at Manchac, 115 miles above New Orleans, the dread English were building a rival town.

By the time O'Reilly arrived, the English had practically a monopoly on the river trade. In an early report, Francisco Bouligny, O'Reilly's observant aide, notes dismally that in the year O'Reilly came, the commerce of the colony amounted to some $600,000 annually, of which only $15,000 was carried by ships of Spain. Ten to twelve English ships, and one or two floating stores, stocked with merchandise, were always on the river.

"The English traders furnish the planters and take their produce in payment," he writes; "and so universal is the forbidden practice of trading with the Englishmen that to stop it would require a guard in every home.

"An Englishman in Jamaica freights a bark of 150 tons for $1,500 at most to come to the Mississippi. He loads with articles he takes on credit, and with 20 or 30 Negroes. With the product of the goods he reimburses the capital and pays the freight, and a profit remains. He sells three-fourths of the Negroes, and with the remainder who are always the best, he settles at Manchac, and in a few years he is wealthy. . . . If no means are taken to prevent the development of that establishment, it will absorb ours and will be a menace for the vast kingdom of Mexico."

This was no idle fear. New Orleans was the terminal point of the great river highway. Down the Mississippi from the northern interior swept the rich cargoes of peltries and tobacco, salted buffalo meat and tongues, venison and cured hams, tallow and bear's oil and lead. Between St. Louis and New Orleans the posts and settlements which dominated the river were those of the east bank. The east bank was England's, all except the Isle of Orleans. And the English were planning to choke New Orleans by intercepting the upriver trade at Manchac, only 115 miles above the city.

The word "isle," in connection with New Orleans, has no meaning now. Its meaning to the Spaniard in 1769 was foreboding. The New Orleans area was then completely surrounded by lake, river and gulf. Its western boundary was the Mississippi, extending southward to the Gulf of Mexico. The gulf rimmed the Orleans "isle" at the south and to the east. And from the east ran the historic gulf-to-river water passage. This short cut which Iberville discovered and Bienville preferred began at the conjunction of Lake Pontchartrain with the gulf itself. Pontchartrain in turn was linked to Lake Maurepas. And Lake Maurepas was joined to the Mississippi by a little river now called the Amite, and by Bayou Manchac which swerved southeastward from the Mississippi to merge with the Amite.

The Manchac, which is the Choctaw word for rear entrance, no longer exists. It was filled in by Andrew Jackson's troops to guard their rear from a possible gulf-to-lakes-to-river flanking movement by the British before the Battle of New Orleans. But in 1764 and later this bayou and river passage from the Mississippi to the lakes to the gulf was potentially the most powerful natural weapon which the British could use against Spain. The Bayou Manchac and the Amite were together called the Iberville River. The bayou was navigable, though with difficulty, during the four months of the annual spring overflow. The Amite could accommodate craft of six feet draft. And the British planned to dredge narrow, debris-clogged Bayou Manchac so that it could be used by ships as large and for most of the year.

The importance of this plan is readily understood. In the struggle for supremacy in the Mississippi Valley, the decision would go to the nation which controlled, near the river's mouth, the commerce of the valley and of interior Canada. Establish a thriving town and a strong fort at Bayou Manchac, link it to the lakes and gulf with a year-round channel, and New Orleans could be cut off from this vital trade. Close to New Orleans as it was, Manchac could be headquarters for the contraband traffic with the eager Orleanians. Here slaves could be sold and powwows held with the tribal chiefs for whose support and business the Europeans vied. Here a strong military force could dominate New Orleans. And no matter what steps Spain might take to bar the river from New Orleans to its mouth to ships from England, the English could laugh. For they could still reach the Mississippi by way of the lakes and the Iberville passage.

The English went into action immediately after the cession of the east bank in 1763. In January, 1764, Major Robert Farmer left Mobile with two small transports loaded with troops of the 22nd Regiment for New Orleans.

There boats were awaiting them. Farmer reported that "a captain of the 34th Regiment has gone with them as far as where the River Iberville communicates with the Mississippi, in order to examine whether it is not practicable with fifty or sixty men to clear that river so that Boats drawing three foot water may pass into the Mississippi and not be exposed to the dangerous Navigation of entering the mouth of that River and to being at the mercy of the French in passing New Orleans."

At that time the English weren't sure that France would turn over New Orleans and the west bank to Spain. So Farmer comments that if west bank Louisiana remains French, all the Frenchmen in the Mobile colony—now England's— will emigrate to Louisiana; but if it becomes Spanish, the Mobilians will remain where they are. This retention of the settlers "will be a means of making this Country of more importance to England." And Lord Halifax, writing later to Governor George Johnstone of West Florida, comments that "there is no room to doubt that Cession [of Louisiana to Spain] will speedily take place . . . if you find, upon inquiry, that a number of Swiss or Germans, likely to become good subjects and useful settlers, are desirous to remove into Your Government, You will offer them every proper Encouragement in Your power in order to acquire to that colony so desirable an advantage."

Truly the English were dreaming grand dreams. Lieutenant Philip Pittman surveyed the Manchac site and reported:

"The inhabitants and traders who reside at Pointe Coupée, at Natchitoches, Attakapas, Arkansas, the Illinois and the Post of St. Vincent's on the Wabash, would rather trade at this place than at New Orleans if they could have as good returns for their peltries and the produce of their country; for it makes a difference of ten days in their voyage, which is no inconsiderable saving of labor, money and time. The goods which these people take, in return for their peltry, furs, tobacco, tallow and bear's oil are spirituous liquors, grocery, dry goods of all kinds and all the articles necessary for their commerce with the savages."

Pittman notes that in high water vessels going up the Iberville must lower their masts as the tree branches hang low and intertwine, arborlike, over the river. He recommends, in addition to dredging Manchac, that "the trees should be cut down forty feet back from the riverside, so that a road might be made for carriages when the waters are low, at which time the bed of the river [Manchac] is dry from the Mississippi; when the waters are high it will still be necessary for the navigation as vessels may be tracked up by horses or men to the Mississippi, in the same manner as lighters in England."

The execution never matched the dream. In 1764, a Captain-Lieutenant Campbell put fifty Negroes to work clearing the Manchac. But, unfortunately, they cleared the upper end, at its confluence with the Mississippi, first. The laborers tossed the felled logs, the cane and other rubbish into the channel before the lower end had been cleaned. And the Mississippi swept down in the spring of 1765, before the job was finished, piling logs and debris downstream upon the still uncleared drifts and jams below. The congestion was worse than ever before, and the Manchac was never opened to deep-draft navigation, though the plan was not abandoned.

Governor Johnstone rejoiced prematurely in Campbell's work. In December, 1764, he wrote from Mobile to Sir John Lindsay in England:

"I am sure it will give you an equal pleasure with every Man in this province to hear that the passage by the Iberville to the Mississippi is now so opened and cleared by Captain Campbell that it may be depended on as a fact; that vessels of six feet water may pass from Lake Pontchartrain through this channel as soon as the Mississippi rises . . . the opening of the Iberville is regarded by all as one of the luckiest events which could have happened to this colony; but to render the effect entirely certain, it is judged necessary to take Post at Point Iberville, with six cannon, two officers and forty men. The advantages which will attend the occupying of this Post, besides keeping so material a passage open and protecting the navigation in this passage, will be the securing our possessions on the north of that Channel and *rendering New Orleans dependent on us for all things instead of our being dependent on New Orleans."*

Though the raging Mississippi made a mockery of Campbell's engineering, the English went ahead with the fort, which was completed in 1765. A little backwoods fortification of log houses and stockade, it was garrisoned by some 25 officers and men of the 34th, and named Fort Bute in honor of the prime minister. These troops were later replaced by redheaded Scots Fusiliers who intermarried freely with the settlers, and today along that river one finds red-haired men and women of Creole and Spanish and German descent, and dark Latins with burry Highland names.

The channel clearance problem was unsolved, but the Manchac settlement thrived. From Maryland came sober German farmers. The first English colonials arrived early, from Roanoke. They were to be followed by loyalists fleeing the repugnant radicalism of the seaboard, or availing themselves of the land grants to veterans of the Seven Years' War. Attracted by the higher lands, England's generous trade policies and the examples of success, Frenchmen, Swiss and Germans from Spanish Louisiana brought their families and belongings to this English Promised Land. Up and down the river the English thrived. Their ships controlled the river's commerce. Their plantations prospered. And Bouligny noted that the British "keep a delegate at Manchac who does nothing but attract the Indians who are on our lands, especially the Arkansas."

Below the Iberville, the Spanish watch with envy and fear. Though heavily subsidized, their pitiful Canary Island settlers prove failures. Bouligny, first among the Spaniards to evaluate and warn of the English menace, writes that all the Louisianians are purchasing illegally from the English.

"They all say to themselves 'If there was an investigation I would be ruined with my wife and my children,' " he observes. "Full of this fear those who have gained the most . . . are the first to leave the colony with all their relatives. They sell their plantations and settle among the English at Manchac."

By exaggerating the liberty that is theirs under England, says Bouligny, these settlers set a bad example. Then he gives an inadvertently revealing comment on the evils of colonial restrictions: "The harm would have been much greater were it not that they cannot sell their plantations and leave the province. The decline has been such that houses and lands formerly worth from $8,000 to $10,000 are selling today for $1,000 to $1,500."

Across the Iberville River, England's uncleared lands bring more than the cultivated earth of Spanish Louisiana.

❦ ❦

By 1777 the English had wrought a miracle of colonization and trade. Manchac's commerce in furs and peltries alone was amounting to some 700,000 skins a year, with a value of 100,000 pounds sterling. Natchez was still a village of twenty houses, and Manchac not much larger. Yet along the river scores of comfortable, solid homes gave proof of the prosperity of the colonists under England.

Situated only about forty feet from the riverbank, these brick and mortar and cypress houses nestled whitely cool among their gardens and beneath the water oak and magnolia. In the shadow of the great forest a straight and level road ran the nine miles from Manchac and the Mississippi to the bayou's conjunction with the Amite. Along it moved the laden oxcarts and wagons in a two-way traffic.

The people who lived in these gently rolling highlands were at peace with their Spanish neighbors of the lower lands. From the small Spanish fort below the Iberville it was only a bowshot to Manchac, where the warehouses of Messrs. Swanson and Company, Indian traders, emphasized England's mercantile dominance. The two little settlements, one prosperous and the other a failure, were joined by a narrow wooden bridge.

Fort Bute itself was lightly held. Its garrison was composed of a Captain von Haacke, and twenty men of the German-speaking, Waldeckian regiment from New York. Farther upriver, at Baton Rouge, were stationed other German and Swiss troops, of the 60th Regiment, all stanchly Protestant seaboard settlers who spoke little or no English and who were officered by Hessians brought from Germany.

This fort at Baton Rouge, manned by five hundred men, surrounded by ramparts of rammed earth and high palisades, and mounting 13 cannon, was England's strategic fortification on the lower river. The fort was strong, so strong that even the reports of the mounting rebellion in the American colonies didn't worry these blond, earth-loving soldiery, or their Scots comrades, many of whom remained here as settlers. With their civilian neighbors of Dutch Highlands above Manchac they enjoyed the fruits of husbandry. Under their protection were harvested the indigo and cotton. From the gardens of the farmers came the fresh vegetables and the maize on which they fared; and the fields along the river

were thick with the sheep and cows and goats of the self-
sustaining folk.

Beneath the protecting guns of Baton Rouge everyone
felt secure. The American colonies are far away, they said,
and Howe and Burgoyne will cook their goose soon enough.
Here at Manchac and Baton Rouge we will hold the river
for England and make a paradise for ourselves. This fellow
Galvez is making a little trouble for us in New Orleans, but
we are not at war with Spain. And Spain does not dare con-
front England again.

❧   ❧

This fellow Galvez, who became acting governor in
1777, is young, ambitious and warlike. He has endeared himself to the French of New Orleans by his marriage to one of
them and by his loosening of trade regulations. So successful
is this latter action that he reports that within a year he has
cleared the lower river of English traders. Near New Orleans
he seizes contraband trading ships of the English, and he is
collaborating with Oliver Pollock in helping the American
colonists. Under the Spanish flag, laden sloops strain past
Manchac and Baton Rouge and Natchez, bound for Pittsburgh and Philadelphia with supplies for the revolutionists.

It is soon no secret that New Orleans is aiding the
rebels. The English engage in desultory retaliation. Occasionally their forts fire upon this Spanish shipping. Englishmen board Spanish vessels, and break open letters even
though they bear the king's seal. The war moves closer to the
Mississippi.

Meanwhile, unsuccessful in his attempts to win over the
English to the Revolution, the blackguard Willing, whom we
have briefly encountered, returns to New Orleans in 1778.
He receives from Galvez $10,000 worth of arms, ammuni-
tion, and supplies for the tenuously held American posts on
the upper river. Willing also recruits freebooters in New Or-

leans, and sets out with them to raid the Natchez planters. While Galvez winks, the booty from this raid is sold in New Orleans for $37,500 to enrich the American cause.

Also with Galvez's consent, Pollock causes to be spread among the English a rumor that two thousand Americans are coming down the river. With the memory of Willing's drunken raids fresh in their minds, this is enough to keep the English passive in their support of the king. By the summer of 1779 they are desperately worried, though unaware that the expected blow will come from the hand of Spain. In far-off Paris, the rebel Americans win a diplomatic victory that means disaster for the English of the Mississippi and eventual defeat for England in the colonies. France recognizes the independence of the colonies and concludes a treaty of alliance and commerce. Instantly she and Great Britain are at war. Wily Spain offers to mediate. The English refuse, and Spain declares a separate war of her own.

Galvez learns before the British do at Bute and Baton Rouge that their two nations are at war. Immediately he plans to take Manchac and all of West Florida before the British are prepared. From a slipshod British lieutenant at Bute the Spanish commandant at Galveztown worms information on British troops movements. Through this unwary youngster and from other sources Galvez discovers that the British intend to reinforce the Manchac district. In complete secrecy he makes ready to strike first.

On August 17, 1779, nature intervenes almost successfully in behalf of the English. The most violent hurricane in the history of New Orleans ravages town and river front, buffeting the exposed port from three in the morning until ten. The flimsier homes and mercantile buildings and many plantation homes are destroyed, and every boat on the river front is sunk. Even the crops are razed. The French and Spaniards are distraught over their loss.

"Now imagine how I feel finding myself all at once

without any of the help on which I depended to put my ideas into execution," Galvez reports. "As although I should not like to give them up hastily, it would even be impossible for me to take the first step, not only due to the absolute lack of boats and canoes, which are all lost, but because the militiamen . . . who are desolated and who in the majority have taken refuge with their families among the ruins of their homes and even underneath the earth, I believe had rather be sacrificed than be separated from their unfortunate parents, wives, sons and brothers, left to grief and to the roughness of the weather in the fields."

The Spaniards salvage two canoes. These are sent in search of expected vessels bearing reinforcements and to look for ships which may have been driven downstream and not sunk.

"Not knowing really the whereabouts of the *Volante*, which in addition to being a suitable vessel for the execution of my ideas, was carrying 66,000 pesos and 1,200 barrels of flour, very appropriate for the subsistence of this city, especially since the small quantity that they had had got wet to a large degree on account of the wind having removed the roof of the king's storage where it was stored, I have been obliged to send instructions to all the commanders to the effect that they stop execution of what I had ordered to do, and that they try not to make any movement that could indicate to the Englishmen any fear on our part; but that nevertheless they keep the greatest vigilance, and advise me of all changes that they may notice. This misfortune is so perceptible because of the fact that we are the only ones whom it has left without any means and from whom it has taken all assistance; inasmuch as the Englishmen had no vessels to lose, they still have their people, their fort, their artillery, and ammunition in the same standing as before."

But Galvez refuses to let the disaster interfere with his plans. The day after the storm he summons the people of

New Orleans together. By his personal appeal and histrionic talents he stirs the hurricane-cowed colonists to action. Again that night he reports by letter to Intendant Navarro:

". . . after having made the most lively speech on the present state of their losses and of the critical constitution of the houses, I made them understand that more than ever, I needed on this occasion to see verified their promises they had made me so many times, especially because I was in possession of a document from my Captain General in which he advised me that Spain had declared the independence of the Americans and that it was necessary to protect our establishment from the assaults and hostilities that the Englishmen could commit against them, as a result of this happening; I made use of said means without involving the name of the King, to place before them the facts, without which neither the Englishmen . . . if as it is supposed, they have not advice of the declaration of war, will dare to attempt an offense, even if they see me with all my people before them."

Then, employing the "means which the Almighty favored me to explain myself," Galvez passionately appealed to the Orleanians to support the king and himself. The emotional populace responded enthusiastically. Galvez had won the first round against hurricane, time, and the English.

By August 23rd the *Volante* had been found dismantled but fit for repair. The other two principal missing vessels, the *Kaulican* and the *Baliza*, were discovered downstream undamaged. Moveover, the hurricane's force had spent itself twenty leagues upriver. Galvez ordered all larger canoes from this unscathed area to be sent to New Orleans for use in the transportation of baggage and artillery.

❦   ❦

On August 27th, there marched from the gates of New Orleans a bobtailed expedition whose importance and exploits have been badly neglected. Behind Galvez trudged 170 Spanish veterans, 330 poor recruits from the Canary Islands, 20 musketeers, 60 militiamen and 80 free Negroes and mulattoes. By his side rode the American, Oliver Pollock. As the army moved up the German Coast it was swelled by motley volunteers, six hundred farmers and trappers joining from the German Coast, Opelousas, and the Attakapas country of the Acadians, and Pointe Coupée. One hundred and sixty friendly Indians also attached themselves to the expedition. The army lacked baggage and an engineer. Between it and Manchac were 115 miles of poor roads and trackless forest.

Before Manchac was reached on September 6th, a third of the force had been lost because of sickness and straggling. Not until his men were in sight of Fort Bute did Galvez tell them that war had been declared and that his instructions were to attack. The little English fort was poorly defended, for the English, apprised of the approach of the Spanish force though unsure of its intent, had left but three officers and twenty-four men to fight a delaying action while Baton Rouge was put in a state of defense.

The Spanish militia attacked at dawn, while the regulars were posted east of the fort in expectancy of an attack by four hundred English troops who were rumored to be approaching. A Frenchman, Sieur Gilbert Antoine de Saint-Maxent, led the militiamen through an embrasure. The little garrison surrended with the loss of one enlisted man killed. The Spanish suffered no casualties.

On September 13th, after a six-day rest because of increasing illness, the army marched upon Baton Rouge. At the head of his Pointe Coupée volunteers Carlos de Grand-Pré circled the fort and took positions between Baton Rouge and Natchez to cut communications. The Pointe Coupée men captured two minor posts, at Thompson's Creek and Fort Graham on the Amite, without loss to either side.

But Baton Rouge was not to be taken so easily as Manchac. The fort was surrounded by a nine-foot ditch, eighteen feet wide, and behind its thick earthen walls were 400 regulars, and about 100 militiamen with 13 pieces of heavy artillery. Galvez decided to lay siege instead of making a direct assault.

To his first element of surprise he now added deception. The militia, the Negro troops, and the Indians were stationed in a forest near the fort with orders to blaze away. Uselessly, throughout the night, the English soldiery answered with musketry and grapeshot. Meanwhile, under the concealment of darkness and the din of fire, the Spanish regulars erected artillery batteries behind a garden wall.

When the English discovered the guns of the Spaniards it was too late, for they were well protected. At dawn of September 21st an artillery battle began. By 3:30, the fort was in ruins.

From behind its battered walls emerged two English officers, under a flag of truce, from whom Galvez demanded surrender not only of Baton Rouge but of Fort Panmure at Natchez, garrisoned by 80 grenadiers. The English could do nothing but comply. Out of the fort marched 375 regulars and 100 militiamen. And with them came a rare prize, Lieutenent Colonel Alexander Dickson, commander of all the British settlements on the river.

Galvez permitted the white militiamen and the free Negroes who fought with the English to return to their homes. To the soldiery, he gave terms and treatment so magnanimous that Colonel Dickson later wrote from New Orleans: "I must in justice to His Excellency Don Bernardo de Galvez, say that the officers and soldiers who are prisoners of war at this place are treated with the greatest generosity and attention, not only by the officers but even the Spanish soldiers seem to take pleasure in being very civil and kind to the prisoners in general."

Under those terms, the prisoners were obliged not to

bear arms again against Spain. They were permitted to march from the fort "with all the military honors, baggage, horses, drums beating, matches lighted at both end, colors flying, two pieces of field artillery with their ammunition for fifty rounds, and thirty-six rounds for the infantry."

Before being conveyed to Pensacola, they were paroled in New Orleans under a guard so small that had they gone back on their paroles they could doubtless have taken the city. Galvez with most of his troops had left to attack East Florida.

Meanwhile Spain was triumphant on water as well as land. On Lake Pontchartrain, an American-manned sloop which had been fitted in New Orleans by William Pickle, an American and friend of Pollock, captured the large British privateer, *West Florida*. And Vincent Rieux, native New Orleanian, commanding a sloop cruising the lakes, had ventured up the Amite River as far as Bayou Manchac. There he placed his fourteen Louisianians in ambush on the riverbank and surprised a British barque, heavily armed and laden, with its crew of twelve sailors and fifty Waldeckian officers and grenadiers.

There was glory for all. Galvez praised the Acadians, who had particular grievance against the English, for their especial zeal. He reported that the free blacks and mulattoes had on all occasions acted with as much valor and generosity as the whites.

During the siege Galvez lost only one man killed and two wounded. Natchez capitulated without resistance, in accordance with the terms accepted at Baton Rouge. The campaign of a month and a day had netted three forts, 556 British regulars, many sailors, militiamen and free Negroes, and eight vessels. And, as Galvez reported, Spain now held on the Lower Mississippi "430 leagues of the best lands, of the most fertile and richest of the Mississippi, with better establishments and with more inhabitants devoted to the furriery business than on the other side of the river." Which in itself was a tribute to the English colonizers.

❦   ❦

Galvez then swiftly moved against Mobile and Pensacola in a brilliant sea campaign that lies outside the province of this story. Soon the English had lost the Floridas and the river forever.

But before their hold was so suddenly broken, they wrote one heroic chapter of their own. After the capitulation of Fort Panmure at Natchez, Galvez had garrisoned it with but fifty men. The English planters of the Natchez area, many of them veterans who remembered their victories in the French and Indian War, recaptured the fort through siege and stratagem, persuading the defenders that they had laid mines beneath its walls. The English held the fort, expecting relief from Pensacola. But Pensacola itself fell to Galvez, and the Natchez English fled. They were all but friendless. The Americans would treat them as enemies. The Spaniards might punish them harshly if they were caught. So many of them decided to make their way across country to Savannah, Georgia, which was still in British hands. They split into two parties and struck out. One group was captured by the Americans. The other, after a terrible 131-day journey, reached Savannah.

The Spanish were kind to the English who remained. None of them paid with their lives, and few with their property or by confinement, for the retaking of Natchez. Most of them accepted the domination of Spain, which they preferred to that of the American colonials. The brief war along the river had been costly neither in lives nor in property. In the remaining years of Spanish rule, the English readily adjusted themselves to their conquerors.

With the going of the English, Manchac dwindled. By

1785 it was a dying settlement of less than fifty people. The Spanish had no interest in Manchac except to destroy its threat to New Orleans and their suzerainty on the river. Today there is no Manchac at all.

But the jubilation of the Spaniards was to be brief; for if England had been a thornbush in the river garden of Spain, this new nation which Spain had helped to create was to prove an irresistible blight to the garden's flowering in Spanish hands. The long day of the Americans was approaching.

PART TWO

American Dawn

CHAPTER 8

Mr. Ellicott Takes a Trip

ON SEPTEMBER 16, 1796, a plump, thin-lipped Pennsylvania Quaker named Andrew Ellicott, and a small party of companions, left Philadelphia by horseback for Pittsburgh. Mr. Ellicott was a man of parts, surveyor, astronomer and mathematician, and, on occasion, soldier and diplomat. His specialty, however, was the solution of vexatious boundary problems for the federal and state governments of the restless little United States.

Now Andrew Ellicott was about to undertake the settlement of the most vexatious boundary line he was ever to run. On this trip to Pittsburgh, and thence down the Ohio and the Mississippi to the Natchez area, he was traveling under appointment of President Washington as commissioner to determine once and for all the boundary between the territories of Spain and those of the American Republic.

It was to be a ticklish job, and not one to which a Quaker would ordinarily be assigned. But Ellicott was unorthodox in his Quakerism. He had served through the Revolution as a major, and had no aversion to fighting in a good cause. Now forty-two, placid-looking Andrew was venturing down the Mississippi in the dual role of a surveyor and—in case the Spaniards remained balky—an agent provocateur.

Less than a year before, on October 27, 1795, Spain and the United States agreed under the treaty of San Lorenzo that the Spanish would withdraw from the east bank river territory above the 31st degree parallel. It was also agreed

121

that the Americans would be given navigation rights on the Lower Mississippi, and would be permitted to use New Orleans as a port of deposit. The debated boundary line was to have been run immediately after the signing of the treaty.

Ever since the Americans had won independence, Spain had fought a diplomatic delaying action to keep them from gaining this valley territory and to bar them from the river. Her reasons were sound enough. She hoped to separate the western colonies, particularly Kentucky and Tennessee, from the United States, so as to form a buffer between the expanding Republic and her own rich colonies of Mexico and the Southwest.

The United States claimed the disputed territory on the grounds that before the Revolution the Mississippi River had been set as the western limits of North Carolina. What was once an English boundary should now be an American one, the United States told her Spanish ally, even though Spanish garrisons held the Natchez country.

The territory remained in dispute from 1783 on, for during the Revolution Spain had claimed all the east bank as far north as the site of Memphis. The controversial strip ran from the 31st degree—the present north and south border of Louisiana and Mississippi—for about 100 miles; or, roughly, to just above present-day Vicksburg. Spain hung on to her little forts at Natchez, Walnut Hills—now Vicksburg, and even at the Chickasaw Bluffs at Memphis, which was far above the area under debate; possession, she reasoned, was nine-tenths of the law, or even more against a struggling new nation.

The Natchez territory had attracted many British immigrants from 1763 to the Revolution. Overwhelmingly they sided with the Spaniards. After the war, American Whigs, most of them men of substance also welcomed by the Spaniards, flocked to Natchez. So did other Americans, less desirable to Spain. Thomas Jefferson sagely welcomed the

migration of his fellow citizens. He wrote to Washington
in 1791:

"This invitation of the Spanish is meant for our people.
Debtors will take advantage of it and go off with their property. Our citizens have a right to go where they please. It
is the business of the states to stop them till their debts are
paid. This done, I wish 100,000 of our inhabitants would
accept the invitation. *It may be the means of delivering to us
peaceably what may otherwise cost us a war.* In the meantime, we may complain of this seduction of our inhabitants
just enough to make them [the Spanish] believe we see it a
very wise policy and confirm them in it."

Hysterically afraid of any threat to gold-producing
Mexico, the one thought of Spain since American independence was established was to keep the United States away.
One stratagem was to play upon the disaffection existing between the Kentuckians and Tennesseans and the eastern seaboard states. Another was to build a buffer colony in Louisiana, composed of American settlers who would embrace
Spanish rule in exchange for lands and free trade.

So, pursuing both policies, Spain violated her promise
given in the treaty which ended the American Revolution.
The Natchez section was held, despite American protests, for
twelve years. Spain denied navigation of the lower river to
all save a handful of Americans, and boldly proclaimed that
under no circumstances would she permit vessels of the
United States to sail the river.

This denial, she hoped, would further alienate the Westerners from the thirteen states. The Kentuckians and Tennesseans wanted statehood. They felt, and rightly, that they
were being excluded from the national government too long.
They needed vitally a passageway down the Mississippi for
their produce, shipped by way of the Holston, the Cumber-

land, the Tennessee and the Licking, into the Ohio and the Mississippi. So, refusing this right to the Westerners, Spain negotiated the notorious, short-lived Jay Treaty in 1787, with the connivance of the European-trade-minded politicians of the American seaboard. The treaty was to open the ports of European Spain to the oceangoing ships of the United States but secured for Spain a 25-year exclusive domination of the Mississippi.

The explosive results were just what Spain wanted. The Westerners threatened direct action. One group, in which General James Wilkinson and George Rogers Clark were believed to be active, dreamed of an independent republic economically linked to Spain. Others urged that the Westerners become part of Spanish Louisiana. A third group, preferring to remain American, threatened war with Spain and the seizure of New Orleans. The mysterious Citizen Genêt of France conspired with still others to regain Louisiana for France and then extend the tricolor's benefactions to Kentucky.

Plots and counterplots abounded. Wilkinson and his Kentucky followers turned toward the Spanish. So did Clark, who had been unjustly treated by Virginia and was ready to enter Spanish service. A Dr. James O'Fallon tried to induce Spain to let him found an American colony at Walnut Hills, pretending that the settlers would be disaffected Westerners who would oppose American expansion.

The Jay Treaty fell through. So did the devious plans of General Wilkinson for some sort of alliance between the Westerners and Spain. George Rogers Clark settled in Spanish territory and forgot his angry scheming. Under the leadership of Washington, the United States moved toward unity instead of loose confederation, and the resentment of the Westerners diminished. Spain's dream of acquiring the Kentucky and Tennessee territories ended. But she clung to the river. Not until 1795 did Spain sign the new treaty re-establishing the 31st degree boundary and giving navigation rights to the Americans. Even then she had her tongue in cheek, hopefully expecting the collapse of the Republic.

And not until September 16, 1796, did Andrew Ellicott set out to run the line.

❦   ❦

At Pittsburgh, Andrew Ellicott and his retinue, which now included a small military escort, forsook their horses for a Kentucky flatboat and two keelboats. The water was so low that the boats stopped frequently because of damage from rocks on the river bottom. The air was thick for miles around with the smoke of forest fires. But in the journal which he was to publish later Ellicott noted that the Ohio valley produced all the immediate necessities of life in abundance, and in addition such commercial articles as hemp, cordage, hardware, glass, whisky, apples and cider, and salted provisions, which were taken to New Orleans for marketing.

At the junction of the Ohio and the Mississippi the concussion of ice produced a constant reverberation, and the boats were frozen in the falling river which left them embedded in the icy mud. Ellicott wasn't impressed with the confluence:

"Those who are descending the Ohio and Mississippi and have been pleased with the prospect of large rivers, rushing together among hills and mountains will anticipate the pleasure of viewing the conflux of these stupendous waters. But their expectations will not be realized; the prospect is neither grand nor romantic; here are no hills to variegate the scene, no mountains from whose summits the meanderings of the waters may be traced, no chasms through which they have forced their way. The prospect is no more than the meeting of waters of the same width along the sounds on our low southern coast. . . . When the water is low, you have high, muddy banks, quicksand and sand bars; and when full you might almost as well be at sea: for days together you will float without meeting anything like soil in the river, and at the same time be environed by an inhospitable and almost impenetrable wilderness . . ."

Shortly Ellicott might have soliloquized that the impenetrability of the wilderness couldn't hold a candle to the Spaniards' suave efforts to delay his party. Obviously, the order was out to discourage or slow down the Americans, for Spain still believed that the scrap of paper could be voided.

At New Madrid, the Spanish commandant tells Ellicott that Governor Carondelet has ordered the Americans to be stopped until the downriver forts could be evacuated. The evacuation, he says, can't be accomplished until the spring rise.

The party pushes downstream. No Spanish post shows signs of impending evacuation. By the time the surveying expedition reaches Walnut Hills, Ellicott is almost convinced of the bad faith of Spain.

"My suspicions relative to delays being in contemplation by the officers of his Catholic Majesty, to prevent the treaty going immediately into effect, were nearly confirmed," he wrote. "The Commandant, though he treated us very civilly when on shore, had us brought to by the discharge of a piece of artillery, which was wholly unnecessary, as we were near the landing and making for it as fast as we could."

The party had reached dangerous ground. The Spanish government resented Ellicott's presence. So did scores of pro-Tory settlers. Below Walnut Hills, Ellicott received a letter from Governor Don Manuel Gayoso de Lemos, suggesting that the American military escort remain at Bayou Pierre, above Natchez, until the Spanish soldiers could be evacuated. Increasingly suspicious, Ellicott talked matters over with Colonel Peter Bryan Bruin, a loyal American who lived at Bayou

Pierre. On Bruin's advice, he decided to leave his troops here.

Forgotten Bruinsburg, their halting place on Bayou Pierre, has an interesting little place in American history. Andrew Jackson had owned a trading station at Bruinsburg, and there sold Negroes to the planters. When Rachel Robards went to Natchez to get her divorce from Lewis Robards in 1790, she stayed at the home of Thomas M. Green, Jackson's close friend and business associate, at Bruinsburg. Jackson came down in 1791 after the Spanish divorce was granted, and married Rachel in the home of his friend. The settlement was a hotbed of pro-American settlers; and when Ellicott raised the American flag there on Washington's birthday, he completely won them.

On February 24, 1797, the American mission, which, minus its military escort, numbered but thirty men, arrived at Natchez. Sensing trouble, Ellicott sent his commissary to procure all possible ammunition from friendly American settlers. He pitched camp a few miles above Natchez, and at the end of the month, hoisted the American flag. Within two hours came a demand from Gayoso that it be hauled down. Ellicott refused.

But instead of a backwoods showdown, the party encountered only Spanish subterfuge. Ellicott learned that in New Orleans Governor Carondelet was postponing evacuation of the river ports on the assumption that Spain would cede the disputed territory to France. An invitation to visit Carondelet in New Orleans was received, but Ellicott politely regretted.

Meanwhile, a band of drunken Indians surrounded the American camp, shouting threats and making nuisances of themselves, obviously at the instigation of the Spaniards. Ellicott, his patience enforced because his troops were still at Bayou Pierre, asked Gayoso to approve the consolidation of his tiny forces. The Spaniard replied that the Indians were merely restless because the American flag had been raised, and suggested that the party proceed downriver to the 31st degree, together with the military escort.

Ellicott counters with the observation that under the treaty the commissioners were to meet in Natchez; to which Gayoso protests that Spain would consider the arrival of American troops in Natchez a grave insult. In the same breath, he invites the harassed Quaker to be his house guest. Ellicott, however, prefers his tent, and at the conclusion of the interview decides to order his troops to join him.

The soldiers have almost reached the Natchez river front when Gayoso gives reluctant consent to the accomplished fact. The troops bivouac across the river. The Spanish garrison begin to evacuate their artillery from the fort, then ostentatiously wheel them back into position. Ellicott learns also that the Walnut Hills fort is being strengthened instead of deserted.

Now the preponderantly American population of Natchez is angrily preparing for action. Andy Jackson's friend, Mr. Green, had already offered to raise a hundred volunteers to seize the fort. Alas for Mr. Green, he talked too much, and Gayoso had him arrested. He escaped, in Gayoso's words, "conscious of his criminality."

Ellicott writes in his journal that the alarm is now so great that the people can be prevented from acting offensively only with difficulty and that "a general commotion in favor of the United States would take place in the course of a few weeks. The difficulty was how to direct its effects to the advantage of our country without committing our country."

As the weeks of suspicious neutrality pass, the little American escort is strengthened by recruits. To Gayoso's protests, Ellicott answers that they are Americans. Actually, most of them, while Americans by birth, were drawn from the territory's citizenry, and were therefore subjects of Spain.

They are strengthened by the arrival at Walnut Hills of another American detachment under Lieutenant Percy Pope. Ellicott notifies him by secret message to come down, cryptically adding "provided it could be done without bloodshed, and to ascertain this fact he must make the attempt."

Shortly these reinforcements arrive—with "permission" from the Spaniards. They are joined at Ellicott's camp by the force across the river. Consolidated at last, the Americans can act more boldly. Ellicott even borrows from the temporizing Gayoso enough tents for Pope's ill-provided soldiers.

Yet, through cajolery and veiled threats, Gayoso continues to hold up the evacuation and the survey. He says that the forts must be refortified because the English are about to descend from Canada into Spanish territory.

Meanwhile, in New Orleans, Governor Carondelet tells Philip Nolan, a supposedly friendly American who had been allowed to capture and sell wild horses from the Spanish west, that he is determined to quiet the trouble in Natchez by giving "the Americans lead and the inhabitants hemp." He asks Nolan if he will take part in a punitive expedition. To which Nolan—who was to be executed by Spain in 1801 for conspiracy—replies ambiguously, "a very active part."

Despite rumors of attack and the accelerated reinforcement of the forts, Ellicott stoutly holds his ground. On May 2nd he tells Gayoso:

"You were apprized of my determination to remain at this place until we proceed to the tracing of the boundary or recalled by the executive of the United States."

The bumbling Gayoso had made a serious mistake in proclaiming that the British were about to make a foray. In the Natchez area lived many Britishers and Tories, who hated the Americans and who had been well treated and honored under Spain. But they still cherished the dream that the British flag would wave again over the river. Foremost among them was wiry old Anthony Hutchins, a colorful 80-year-old British officer who had come years before to the Natchez country to claim a French and Indian War grant. Hutchins had remained indomitably English. He fought Spain on the river when she became the ally of the Americans, and was the principal victim of Willing's raid. Fleeing after the failure of the British coup in Natchez, he ultimately returned and became the leading citizen of the conservative, wealthy planters. Throughout his life he worked in behalf of England, never despairing of the return of the Cross of St. George. Gayoso's warning of British forays served only to set the hopeful Britishers apart from Spain and to make the Americans more determined than ever.

❦   ❦

Then, on June 4th, there occurred in Natchez one of those ridiculously insignificant incidents which have so frequently resolved historical crises.

An itinerant Baptist preacher named Hannah had attached himself to Ellicott's camp. The good brother was treading on posted ground, for only Catholics were permitted to worship in Spanish territory. Ellicott, however, gained permission from Gayoso for Hannah to hold a meeting in the camp itself.

The revival attracted a "tolerably respectable audience" from the American party and the Protestant settlers of the neighborhood. The hell-fire sermon was not particularly good, Ellicott noted, but since it was given in nominally Spanish territory it was a well-received novelty.

Elated at his success, and fortified by too many swigs from a demijohn, Hannah set a weaving course for the Irish Catholic section of Natchez, bent on proselyting. There he discovered what many others have found out before and since, namely, that the Irishman does not take kindly to the doctrine of Luther and Calvin. The angry parishioners joy-

ously administered a severe thrashing to the interloper. Badly
battered, the preacher betook himself to Gayoso and peremp-
torily demanded justice, threatening reprisals if his assailants
went unpunished.

Gayoso asked him to reflect a few minutes and then repeat his request. Even more intemperately the backwoods
divine inveighed against Spain and Catholicism. So Gayoso
ordered him to prison, where he was placed in the stocks to
sober off.

When Ellicott heard of the toper-preacher's misfortune
he requested his release. Gayoso refused. The next morning
the Scotch-Irish Covenanters and their Protestant brethren of
the outlying district were raging so violently—probably
through Ellicott's good offices in spreading the news—that
Gayoso and his officials took to the fort for safety. The Americans milled through the streets, demanding Brother Hannah's release. This, they shouted, is a deliberate attack on a
citizen of the United States. Spain is determined to enforce
her civil and religious laws in territory that belongs to us.
The rioters were further outraged by news of Carondelet's
latest proclamation, which declared falsely that the United
States was sending troops against Spain.

Then Ellicott got in his most telling argument.

"You must be prepared to defend yourselves," he told
the irate Americans. "After all, no one can with propriety
expect the United States to help you until you show by an
election that you want to belong to the United States."

Promptly, a document calling for such an election was
drawn up, circulated and signed. Completely cowed, Gayoso
asked for an interview with Ellicott and Pope. The astute
Quaker acceded as "a private gentleman." Gayoso told them
he had heard of the "seditious circular," and Ellicott answered that ever since the treaty of 1795 these people had
been American citizens.

After his interview Gayoso published a proclamation

asking for peace. Its copies were contemptuously torn down and destroyed, for the Americans were in no mood for further temporizing. They had formed militia companies, and were now ready to strike. Poor Gayoso retired again to the fort, and ordered its fortifications strengthened.

On June 17th a Spanish patrol fired on a patrol from the American camp. Ellicott doused his lights, for a piece of Spanish artillery was trained on his tent. But no one was hurt in this first and last resort to gunfire.

Gayoso requested another interview. At its conclusion Ellicott described in his journal this requiem to the majesty of Spain:

"The next morning the governor left the fort, and by a circuitous route, through thickets and cane brakes, made his way to the north side of his aide's plantation, and thence through a cornfield to the back of the house, and entered the parlor undiscovered, where I joined him . . . My feelings were scarcely ever more affected than in this interview with Governor Gayoso. The humiliating state to which he was reduced, by a people whose affections he courted, and whose gratitude he expected, had made a strong and visible impression upon his mind and countenance. His having been born and educated with high ideas of command and prerogative, served but to render his present situation the more poignant and distressing."

❦   ❦

Gayoso asked for a compromise.

"No terms would now be expected that were not safe and honorable to the people," Ellicott answered. "They have felt and know their strength, and would only agree to disband and return home by being admitted to enjoy a qualified state of neutrality until the treaty between the United States and his Catholic Majesty should be carried into effect."

The triumphant Americans met at the home of a Mr. Belts, eight miles from Natchez, on June 20th to elect a "committee to keep the peace." Selected as members were Anthony Hutchins, Bernard Lintot, Isaac Gaillard, William Ratliff, Cato West, Joseph Bernard, and Gabriel Benoist. By unanimous if not spontaneous vote Ellicott and Lieutenant Pope were added to the committee.

Gayoso remained courtly to the last. He offered the committee the government house. Instead, the members chose a new building of Sir William Dunbar, which Ellicott had secured free of charge.

Two days later the committee dispatched to the governor a letter setting forth this temporary bill of rights:

1. Believing they were citizens of the United States under the late treaty, the citizens had assembled and . . . are not to be prosecuted for that account.

2. The people above 31 degrees are not to be embodied as a militia or called upon to aid in any military operation except in case of Indian invasion.

3. The laws of Spain shall be continued and on all occasions shall be executed with mildness; but nevertheless the inhabitants shall be considered to be in an actual state of neutrality.

4. To the utmost of the committee's powers it will endeavor to preserve the peace.

On the same day Gayoso and José Vidal, secretary to the Spanish government, signed and agreed to the manifesto. The next day the governor and his officers quit the fort for their cool, shuttered homes.

"Thus ended this formidable tumult without a single act of violence having been committed by the inhabitants of the country," wrote Quaker Andrew.

Immediately he began impressing Gayoso with the need of a permanent committee to keep order, for the adroit agent wanted men on whom the United States could completely rely. So the thoroughly cowed Gayoso called for the election of a permanent Committee of Safety. To this new body, elected in July, only Bernard, Benoist, Gaillard and Ratliff were re-elected. Anthony Hutchins, enraged at the way things were going in favor of the Americans, refused to run "on account of his age and infirmities." The new members were Ellicott's early confidant, Peter Bruin, and Daniel Clark, Philander Smith, Roger Dixon, and Frederick Kimball. The last was the only member whose "sentiments were doubtful." With the situation completely under control, Ellicott reported:

"The committee was no sooner organized than it was evident its measures would be directed to the attainment of two objects: first, the securing of the country to the United States, and secondly, the preservation of peace and good order in the settlement. The first was contrary to the wishes of the officers of his Catholic Majesty, and the second to those attached to the British interests, to which may be added another class, who had nothing to lose but hoped to gain by the tumult and disorder."

In this, he was pointing at old Anthony Hutchins, whom he suspected of trying to divide the Americans so that the territory might again fall to the British.

The irate old Britisher stalked out of the first meeting of the committee. Soon Gayoso was intriguing with him to form another committee more favorable to Spain. Then, on July 26th, Gayoso was made governor general of Louisiana; and on his departure for New Orleans he advised his successor, Colonel Stephen Minor, not to oppose Hutchins if he should seek the election of a new group.

Hutchins appeared at the next Committee meeting. Courageously he damned the members with "abusive language," telling them, in Ellicott's words, that they were "no committee, that they were dissolved, and that he would direct the election of another; that it was a hard pill and rough for them to swallow, but he would force it down their throats."

Bruin, the American, turned upon him.

"Colonel Hutchins," he shouted, "you appear to be acting the dictator and at the same time affect to be waving the American flag of Liberty, but they are incompatible. The cap of Liberty ill becomes you who opposed by arms the independence of the United States."

The committeemen rumbled their approval, and the colonel rushed from the room, shouting incoherently that the committee was dissolved. Shortly, following the failure of an election for which he obtained Minor's permission, he was circulating a petition which among other matters roundly denounced Ellicott and Lieutenant Pope. Later, many of the signers, including Preacher Hannah, swore that they never saw the page attacking the two Americans. At any rate, Ellicott saw to it that the petition, which was addressed to Congress, was intercepted and returned.

Old Hutchins made one last gesture against the hated Americans. When the rumor spread that a Spanish expedition was setting out from New Orleans under Colonel Carlos de Grand-Pré, Anthony offered to raise two hundred men to re-establish Spanish rule. But Grand-pré did not turn up, for American reinforcements arrived. Anthony sulked out the rest of his life in the Natchez which he had hoped to regain for England.

Andrew Ellicott had no easy time with his counterstrokes. For one thing, he lost a fourth of his party to yellow fever in the summer of 1797. He went down with the fever himself, but not before the pills of a Dr. Rush of Philadelphia had given out. These pills, by which Andrew swore, were composed of two grains of calomel and a half grain of gamboge held together with soft soap. Recovering in seven days, Andrew concluded that the yellow fever strikes when "a portion of the system, for some cause or other, [is] rendered unfit for animal life and therefore obnoxious to the healthy part, which from a natural impulse is constantly endeavoring to expel the morbid matter which is probably thrown off by both the external and the internal juices." He recommended the use of clean clothes next to the skin, cathartics, and frequent bathing.

Meanwhile, many citizens of Natchez and some members of his own party gave him more trouble than did the fever. Their ill reports have clouded the reputation of the stubborn agent; and even before he left Natchez, a new Committee of Safety complained of Pope's military interference and asked that Ellicott be recalled or confined strictly to the business he had been sent to do.

It is apparent now that Ellicott had more business to undertake than simply to run the line. As a condition precedent, he had to enlist the support of the Americans of the district and he had to meet plot with plot. There is small doubt that in his troublemaking activities he had the approval of the United States government. He made enemies in plenty. But he won the Natchez area, and he ran his line.

In March, 1798, the Spanish garrison troops finally filed from the fort. On the same day the American troops marched in. As the rear guard of the Spaniards took to their boats at dawn, Quaker Andrew Ellicott walked into the fort and looked about with satisfaction. That much of the job was done.

Late in 1798, Ellicott's axmen began felling the dense cane at the 31st parallel into sixty-foot pathways. They set the hollow, four-foot stubble afire, laughing as it exploded like musketry. Governor General Gayoso met the surveyors near Bayou Sara, a short distance from the line. "We met and saluted in the Spanish manner by kissing!"

Ellicott wrote. "I had not been shaved for two days. Men's kissing, I think a most abominable custom."

But with that embrace from the defeated, effusive Spaniard, Spanish interference all but ended on the river.

❧   ❧

Five years later, Napoleon Bonaparte, his expeditionary force destroyed by the fevers of Haiti and the resistance of its free black men, gave up his plan to occupy the Louisiana Territory which Spain had secretly retroceded to France in 1800. Instead, in disgust, he sold the vast valley to the United States.

The young American giant had swallowed the Mississippi.

CHAPTER 9

Those Kemper Devils

I MAGINE the present state of Florida as the butt of a long Spanish pistol, which in 1803 was forged to a barrel extending narrowly westward along the Gulf of Mexico until its muzzle rested against the Mississippi.

This territory of symbolic shape, divided by the Appalachicola river into Spanish East and West Florida, was the last domain of the dons east of the Mississippi. Its northern limit in 1803 was Quaker Ellicott's 31st degree parallel, a line which, forming now the north-south boundary between Louisiana and Mississippi, continues across a gulf-bordering strip of Alabama, and merges with the present northern boundary of Florida. On the south it jutted from the Gulf Coast to the Mississippi, meeting the river a few miles below Baton Rouge.

Lay a ruler on that northern border on your map, and you will see how uncannily the blocked-off section does resemble a pistol. The likeness was even more real to the Americans who swept into the valley in turbulent waves just before and following the Louisiana Purchase. Spanish West Florida separated the segment that was New Orleans from the rest of the east bank. In the pistol's muzzle, from Baton Rouge to the confluence of the Red and the Mississippi, lay the most luxuriant rolling lands on the lower river.

Actually, Spain's rule was light and lax here, as it had been above the 31st degree, and there was no proscription against settlers. What angered the American newcomers was that the area had been omitted from the purchase. Even Spain's expedient custom of appointing minor officials from the old Tory group and the friendlier American grant-takers did not mollify the majority of the late arrivals. They were Americans. They wanted West Florida to be American.

To understand the omission of West Florida from the purchase, we must study the chessboard of treaties from 1763 to the purchase. In 1763 the defeated French had ceded all the territory west of the river, and New Orleans on the east bank, to Spain. The remaining French territory on the east bank, as far north as some 125 miles above Natchez, went to England. England administered it as part of her West Florida division, with the seat of government at Pensacola. Then during the American Revolution Spain's Governor Galvez attacked the British, capturing Baton Rouge, Natchez, and Pensacola.

Finally, Ellicott secured the Natchez district for the Americans. But south of the 31st degree, Spain clung to West Florida, East Florida, and the remnants of French Louisiana, which included New Orleans.

When Spain returned to France the Louisiana Territory as it had been described in the original cession, she held that only the old Louisiana was being turned over. She still considered the long pistol barrel of West Florida hers. Historically, Spain was correct. Even the representatives of the United States did not believe at the time of the purchase that Spanish West Florida was included in the Louisiana Territory which Spain had returned to France and which Napoleon in 1803 sold to the United States.

But the incoming Americans in the narrow Spanish strip along the river felt that they had been discriminated against by being left out of the purchase. Which brings us to the gigantic Kemper brothers, who first decided to do something about it.

❦ ❦

Reuben Kemper stood six feet six. His two brothers, Nathan and Sam, were only slightly shorter. They were blond, rangy giants who could break in a hogshead barrel with their fists. And they didn't like Spaniards.

The brothers were descended from John Kemper, a German who had settled in Spotsylvania County, Virginia, in 1714. This forebear's son, John Peter Kemper, reared ten children. In 1799 or thereabouts three of his grandsons, Reuben, Nathan and Sam, sought the green promise of the Mississippi Valley.

They picked the district of Feliciana just above Baton Rouge, a land of heavily timbered, rolling hills and grassy prairies. No more beautiful or fertile country could be found then or now along the Mississippi. Here hundreds of Americans, some still resentful Tories and others of rebel stock, had established themselves in the magnolia and hickory and oak forests, felling the trees and clearing the undergrowth to build their farms and set up their trading posts.

As at Natchez before Ellicott, the brash, new Americans were not so favored as were the descendants of the Tories or the French who had come here years before. The nation they represented was a challenge to Old World monarchy. The agents of their upstart government had driven Spain to cede most of her river lands. On the Mississippi, the tough flatboatmen jeered at the Spanish militia as they floated downstream to sell their goods, to carouse, and to terrorize New Orleans. Almost a common front of Tories, Frenchmen, and Spaniards existed in West Florida against the Americans.

Nathan Kemper had become the agent of the Reverend John Smith of Cincinnati, a minister who was also a state senator in Ohio and a land speculator. Smith proved to be an unscrupulous politician, who later was forced to resign from the Senate for complicity in the schemes of Aaron Burr. Sam Kemper had settled in the Mississippi Territory, just over the line from West Florida. Reuben had entered business in New Orleans. It wasn't long before the Kempers were in trouble.

Smith and Nathan Kemper fell out over the rendering of some accounts. So, in the spring of 1804, Smith ordered Nathan off his lands. Nathan appealed to Don Carlos de Grand-Pré, governor of the district. Don Carlos submitted the matter to a "committee of disinterested neighbors." The neighbors ruled that Nathan must leave.

"I'll be damned if I'll do it," answered Nathan. He sent for Sam, and wrote brother Reuben.

"Their palms have been greased," he told Sam. The two brothers agreed that no Spaniard could run the Kempers even the length of a flatboat.

Enlisting the support of four friends, they barricaded themselves on Smith's property. Governor Grand-Pré ordered Alexander Stirling, an elderly Tory who was alcalde of the district, to evict them. In New Orleans, Reuben Kemper asked the American Governor Claiborne to take possession of all of West Florida, pointing out that the injustice done his brother proved an American couldn't get a square deal. Reuben also wrote threatening letters to Stirling, promising vengeance if his brothers were harmed or ousted.

Stirling contented himself with having the neighborhood patrolled. The Kempers sat tight, while the Spaniards and Tories fumed and their fellow Americans laughed. Finally Don Carlos was stirred to action. He dispatched an improvised gunboat to Bayou Sara, the little river settlement where the Kempers were defying Spain. Six men couldn't fight a gunboat, so the Kemper band retreated across the line to the Mississippi Territory, vowing that they would return.

In Pinckneyville Sam and Nathan held a council of war. They considered now that the issue had become something greater than a private quarrel. Their own treatment, they said, symbolized the attitude of the Spanish toward all Americans. Nothing short of rebellion could end the intolerable situation.

The brothers were not scholarly men, but they had a friend who was both a patriot and a scholar. So they went to Edward Randolph of Pinckneyville, told him of their plan to start an uprising, and asked him to write a Declaration of Independence. Randolph obliged with this remarkable little document:

For a people to be free it is sufficient that they will it. Whereas the despotism under which we have long groaned has grown into an unsupportable burthen, and as it is long since admitted men are born with equal rights, we the undersigned inhabitants of that part of the [Spanish] dominion called West Florida, have resolved to throw off the galling yoke of tyranny and become free men, by declaring ourselves a free and independent people, and by supporting with our lives and property this declaration.

Next a flag. The Kempers designed one of two white stars and seven alternating blue and white stripes.

An initial "army" of thirty-odd volunteers responded to their call. On August 7, 1804, this little band invaded Spanish territory.

Their first act of war was to seize a Spaniard, Captain Vincente Pintado, and burn his house and gin. They also captured Stirling and other unfriendly planters and called upon the Americans of West Florida to rise.

But an Englishman, John Means, warned the Spaniards before the rebels had gained any real strength. Moreover, except for a few hardy spirits, the inhabitants of the Florida parishes showed no inclination to join the Kemper army. The Spanish militia confronted the invaders on the road to Baton Rouge. After a flurry of shots, the militia brought up some artillery, and the Kempers retreated to Bayou Sara.

This time they had poked up a hornet's nest. The Spaniards organized a force of 150 volunteers. Michael Jones, a noted Tory partisan of the Revolution, was placed in charge of guards which patrolled the forest roads leading from Bayou Sara to the Mississippi Territory. Seemingly, the rebels were trapped.

But no one wanted to attack the Kempers in Bayou Sara. While the Spaniards waited for them to come out, Reuben Kemper, in New Orleans, dispatched Daniel Clark, an American trader who was esteemed by the French and Spaniards, to Baton Rouge to ask pardon for his brothers. Grand-Pré refused.

So the Kempers and most of their followers simply stole out of Bayou Sara at night and melted through the woods to safety. The war had ended with little harm done to either side.

But seven West Florida Americans, suspected of complicity, were arrested and brought before Isaac Johnson, alcalde of the Second Division of Feliciana. The proceedings, written in English by this Anglo-Saxon official of Spain, consist of twelve interrogations of the accused men. And typical of Spain's easygoing attitude toward the settlers —an attitude animated by fear of American invasion— is the alcalde's notation that before their examination all have been "graciously exonerated from all charges by the clemency of his Excellency, Governor Don Carlos de Grand-Pré." Later the alcalde would himself rebel against Spain, and with more success.

❦   ❦

How do a handful of rebels answer to the question: "Did you ever take up arms against the government?"

Here is George Kavanaugh, replying to the alcalde on September 26, 1804:

"I did, but when I joined the band, I knew nothing

of any declaration of independence, or design to suppress
the king's authority and government, but had been informed
that some inoffending persons were made prisoners by the
austere conduct of the officers at Bayou Sara and that it
was intended to effect their liberation from confinement
for which purpose I went with several others without re-
flecting on the impropriety of such conduct."

George Garnhart answers:

"Basil Abrams acquainted me that [the] government
had determined on having upwards of eighty persons murdered in the night, that it was not known who were to
fall; but he assured me that the whole country would rise
and suppress the government to prevent these great evils."

The alcalde has other questions. On September 27th
he asks the accused men:

Have you on any pretense whatever at any time seized
or taken away from any person within this province any
kind of provisions, or live stock, or horses, mares, or geldings,
one or more; or saddles, bridles or other furniture: or arms
or ammunition, gun locks or other parts of arms: or committed any other depredation or offense against the property
of any one or more of the inhabitants: or do you know
who has been guilty of the above offenses: If you do; name
the offenders and each of them: and the offenses, and each
offender particularly.

The defendants must have smiled inwardly at some
of the responses. Here is Jonathan Clark's:

"The company took Mathew Ofalon's gun from him
and Nathan Kemper put it into my hands. I intend to
return it to the owners as soon as I have any opportunity."

For four days the alcalde conducts his interrogatories.
Have the accused countenanced or assisted in putting inhabitants on their parole not to aid the government against

the insurrection? Yes, that was done. Have they participated in stopping couriers carrying letters and papers? No,
it was done, but not by the defendants.

"What was the general plan of Abrams, Kemper and
their associates?"

Jesse Kirkland does not know, nor do Henry Garnhart,
George Kavanaugh and Levi Sholar. But the rest do.

"To throw off the Spanish authority and establish liberty and independence," says Isaac Sharp.

"To change the government and establish independence," says Jonathan Clark.

"Abrams and the two Kempers said that their intention
was to take Baton Rouge and give it up to the Americans,"
says George Garnhart.

The interrogator wants to know the names of the Kempers' associates. Most of them are in Mississippi Territory
now.

"The original volunteers who assembled to go and did
go to take Baton Rouge fort," says Jesse Kirkland, "were
Basil Abrams, Nathan Kemper, Samuel Kemper, Nathan
Bradford, Henry Bradford, Jr., Leonard Bradford, William
Cobb, Arthur Cobb, William Westbury, Jonathan Clark,
George Garnhart, George Kavanaugh, Edwin Falks, John
Moore, John O'Neal, Hughes, Morgan, Kelly, Isaac Sharp,
Levi Sholar, James Bell, Samuel Perry, Mathew Douchet,
David Beek and myself. David Moore and William Morrison
were made prisoners on our return from Baton Rouge and
afterwards joined themselves to the party."

Kavanaugh remembers that Moses Young and two others
whose names he has forgot joined also, and Jonathan Clark
recalls that Michael Morgan was a member. Thirty-one men
in all, to wrest West Florida from Spain.

Who in the territory has connived at, encouraged or
countenanced the insurrection?

Only a certain Champ Terry, says Levi Sholar:

"It was generally talked among us and depended upon by most of the company that Champ Terry would join us with forty men and that he had said if five hundred dollars were given to him that he would head the party and conduct their affairs. I declared my opinion to them all that I thought Terry was a character on whom no dependence was to be placed, but the rest seemed greatly to depend on him." Champ never showed up.

The defendants insist that no punishments were to be inflicted on the officials if the insurrection had succeeded. Nor were any rewards or appointments spoken of. So, the interrogatories ended and the seven culprits went free. After all, they were small fry.

❧ ❧

But the memory of the Kempers rankled. Across the line in Pinckneyville big Sam Kemper had opened a tavern. Near-by, Nathan was operating a plantation. As the months passed, word of their gibes and repeated threats continued to reach the loyal citizens of Feliciana.

So, these loyalists decided to act outside the law themselves. At about midnight of September 3, 1805, a year after the abortive rebellion, a band of armed planters and picked slaves from West Florida surrounded the Kemper tavern. They had chosen this night for their raid because Reuben had come up from New Orleans to visit his brothers. Perhaps those Kemper devils were plotting fresh mischief.

The raiders did capture the Kempers, but not without a terrific struggle. Kemper family legend has it that the brothers killed seven men with chairs, but this is not substantiated. The Kempers themselves were severely mauled with clubs, bound hand and foot, and carried across the line.

The next day the prisoners were turned over to the Spanish militia, under Captain Solomon Alston, at Tunica

Bayou. The men figuring in the kidnapping indicate clearly the bitter cleavage between the Tory and American settlers. The leaders of the raid, Ira Kneeland, William Barker, and James Horton, were members of old Tory families. Captain Alston, a brother-in-law of old Alexander Stirling, had especial reason to like the Spaniards. His father, John Alston, had participated in the uprising of the Natchez English

against Galvez. He was captured, and imprisoned in Morro Castle in Havana until 1783 when he was released upon the intercession of Prince William Henry, afterward William IV. After gaining his freedom the elder Alston learned that following the uprising a reward of $5,000 had been rashly offered for his head. He returned to Louisiana, delivered himself to Galvez and claimed the reward for his destitute children. The generous Galvez aided Alston, who took the oath of loyalty to Spain and became a prominent citizen of the territory. His son, Solomon, in turn became an officer of the militia.

Captain Alston placed the Kempers aboard a boat and started down the river to Baton Rouge. At Pointe Coupée, in American territory across the river from Baton Rouge and a few miles north, the Americans had established a military post. As the Spanish craft reached Pointe Coupée, Reuben Kemper spied a friend, Dr. Thomas Towles, on the levee.

"Help!" he bellowed before he could be gagged. "It's Reuben Kemper. The Spaniards are taking us down the river."

Dr. Towles ran to the post. Pursuit was speedily organized under Lieutenant William Wilson. Soon the American soldiers overtook and boarded the Spanish vessel, and despite Alston's furious protest that the river was neutral territory, they took Alston, his militiamen, and the battered but jubilant Kempers back upriver to Mississippi Territory.

There, Judge Thomas Rodney freed the Spaniards and told them to get back to their own side of the line immediately. He also released the Kempers under bond to keep the peace, following Alston's testimony of their foray against West Florida the year before.

The admonition to the Spaniards to leave quickly was as wise as the peace bond against the Kempers was fruitless. William Barker, a member of the kidnaping militia group, loitered outside the courthouse for a few disdainful minutes. He was still there when the Kempers emerged. The brothers fell upon the foolhardy Barker and belabored him until they were exhausted and he senseless.

Reuben Kemper wasn't satisfied with this restricted vengeance. He later waylaid James Horton, who had flailed him with especial vigor on the night of the tavern raid, and for days afterward Horton's life was despaired of. And finally Reuben and Sam caught Ira Kneeland, against whom they must have held their strongest grudge. They trussed up Ira, gave him a hundred lashes, and cut slices from his ears with "a dull knife." These slices Sam kept pickled in a jar of spirits in the tavern as a satisfactory memento of the occasion.

The Kempers' reprisals put their abductors in a panic. Captain Alston took to sleeping in a boat anchored somewhere in the Mississippi. Probably because of continued exposure, he died of what the doctors described as dropsy.

Thenceforth no one molested the Kempers. They in turn settled down, Nathan and Sam in the Mississippi Territory and Reuben in New Orleans. But the discontent which they had been the first to express in revolt grew. The Americans of West Florida wanted independence. Even under easygoing Grand-Pré, favoritism and arbitrary fiat were the hallmarks of Spanish rule, and neither was intended to benefit the Americans.

In 1809, Grand-Pré, a Frenchman by birth, was removed from office and sent to Havana on charges of conspiring with the French to seize West Florida for Napoleon. He died there while awaiting trial. His successor, Don Carlos Duhault de Lassus, had a fine military record but was a weak administrator; and he was saddled with a singularly crooked secretary, Raphael Croker. Petty officialdom grew more venal, crimes escaped punishment, and discrimination increased. The West Florida Americans smoldered, biding their time.

Then in 1810 came rumors that Napoleon was about to seize Spanish Florida. Much as the West Floridians disliked Spanish weakness and corruption, they hated Napoleon more. Moreover, this hatred had a tendency to unite Tory and American against the threat of Bonaparte, the inadequacy of Spain which made the threat possible, and the river French who wanted to re-establish themselves.

The rival Tory and American groups drew closer. They began to meet, and to plan ways to combat poor government and foreign menace. Still unsure of each other's ultimate objectives, the leaders found in Freemasonry a common bond and a pledge of secrecy. So, meeting "on the square" in the "five points of fellowship," they conspired against Spain.

Revolt was not their first thought. Instead, following a mass meeting on June 23rd, attended by more than 500 Felicianians, a West Florida convention was held at Buhler's Plains. Here the settlers declared their allegiance to Spain and their unswerving opposition to any pretensions of France. Determined, however, to make local self-government less a travesty, they subsequently nominated officers for a provisional government, with de Lassus being retained as Spanish military governor and first judge. From their own number they selected three associate superior judges, a high sheriff, and civil commandants for Bayou Sara, Baton Rouge, and St. Helena. Only one of the delegates, Manuel Lopez, did not have an English, Scots or Irish name; and he acted as spy for the governor.

Nothing indicates the social diversity of the settlers so well as does the difference between the two men who were to lead the revolting West Floridians. One of the associate judges selected was Fulwar Skipwith, who later was to become governor of the independent West Florida republic. Skipwith was a scholarly, wealthy Virginian, a cosmopolite who had served as American consul general to France, and who had married a Flemish countess. The aristocratic judge and his wife traveled in this frontier country in a coach-and-four, complete with outriders and lackeys.

As "brigadier general" of the militia which they proposed to reorganize, the settlers chose Philemon Thomas, a 46-year-old veteran of the Revolution, a redheaded, raw-boned, uneducated man who ran a small grocery which advertised in his own lettering "Coughpy fur Sail" and "Akomidation fur Man & Beest." He and Skipwith were unlike in everything but their courage and common purpose.

De Lassus pretended to concur in this reorganization and in the ordinances and military structure which the dissenters proposed. He did, however, oppose the selection of Skipwith and the rank of brigadier general sought for Thomas. The governor himself was only a colonel. And behind his seeming complacency, and undeniable weakness for temporizing—even to the extent of dining the convention's leaders—was a determination to suppress the movement.

On September 20th, the settlers peaceably evicted the tiny Spanish garrison from Bayou Sara. That morning, two of Philemon Thomas's men also intercepted a letter from the wily de Lassus to Governor Folch at Pensacola, beseeching soldiers to quell an "insurrection." And the same night, de Lassus again held a "peace dinner" for representatives of the convention, including Thomas. He was unaware that his letter had been taken and that Philemon and the rest of the Americans were now cognizant of his double-dealing.

The next night the settlers determined to strike before Spanish aid might arrive. In the Feliciana country, Isaac Johnson, now a militia major, and Captain Lewellyn Griffith mustered the Bayou Sara Horse, twenty-one strong. The dragoons unfurled a blue flag with a single star, made for them by Johnson's wife, Melissa. Philemon Thomas spurred his horse through the back country, summoning the American "grenadiers." Forty-five in all, they began marching to Baton Rouge and a rendezvous with the horsemen. A handful of others, some of them planters and the rest crude backwoodsmen who called the Spaniards "yallerbellies" and "pukes," brought the combined strength of the two columns to about seventy-five men.

They met after midnight outside of little Baton Rouge, whose dominating fort they intended to capture. The Spaniards had been warned to expect trouble and had alerted the garrison, but did not know when the Americans intended to strike.

Outnumbered, and lacking artillery, the rebels could not hope to make a successful frontal attack, or to lay siege. The fort stood on high ground, and was surrounded by long cypress pickets slanting outward and banked with clay redoubts. At the four corners of the square stockade stood stout bastions, and a nine-foot ditch surrounded the stockade. Twenty pieces of artillery faced the river, with older guns scattered elsewhere. The main gates were protected by four cannon loaded with grapeshot. Seventy-five men, however brave, couldn't storm this stronghold. In command of the Spaniards was popular young Louis Antonio de Grand-Pré, sublieutenant in the army of Spain, and the eldest son of the late Don Carlos. Lieutenant Grand-Pré was determined to prove by his own defense of the fort that his father had been unjustly charged with disloyalty.

Assault was out of the question. But the Americans had another way to skin this Spanish cat. Among the grenadiers was a Kentucky backwoodsman, Larry Moore, even more illiterate than his good friend Philemon Thomas and just as resourceful. Moore pointed out that the cows, which the garrison kept, browsed outside the fort and entered and left it through a riverside opening in the cypress palisades. If the cows could get in, he said, so could his pony, and just as unnoticed. The cows came home at dawn for milking. That was the time to surprise the yallerbellies.

Isaac Johnson secured permission to lead his horsemen through the gap in the palisades. In a thick fog, through which the dawn was streaking, the Felicianians rode quietly up the cowpath to the fort. Mingling with the cows, they were inside and lined up on the parade ground before the sentry noted the scuffle of their horses' hoofs.

"Ole! Que es eso?" he shouted. And again, "Quién vive?" Now he could distinguish the shadowy horsemen.

"Alerta! alerta! alerta!" he screamed. His warning was taken up by his fellow sentries.

Out of the guardhouse rushed Lieutenant de Grand-Pré, followed by panicky, half-asleep soldiers. Straight at the dragoons he ran.

"Amigos," he called in Spanish. "We are more numerous. We do not want to hurt you."

He slashed with his sword, not at the Americans, but at their horses' flanks. The dragoons urged their mounts forward. As yet not a shot had been fired.

Young Grand-Pré ran back toward his command.

"Fuego, fuego!" he ordered.

A ragged crackle of Spanish musketry answered him. But the fight was already out of his troops. Not an American was hit by the volley as they spurred forward.

"Shoot 'em down!" Isaac Johnson roared.

The dragoons fired at the wavering line of Spanish soldiers. Young Louis de Grand-Pré fell mortally wounded with four balls in his body, and with him a soldier, instantly slain. Another lieutenant and two soldiers were wounded. The fort had fallen.

As the Americans were disarming their dazed prisoners, Governor de Lassus entered the fort. A dragoon ordered him to hand over his sword. He refused. Whereupon the settler, unaware of the niceties of war, knocked him down with a musket butt, and was about to bayonet him when Philemon Thomas pushed him aside.

In the early morning's uncertain light, Isaac Johnson hauled down the red and yellow flag of Spain and raised the blue flag which his wife Melissa had stitched. Spain's

last stronghold on the river was lost, exactly thirty-one
years after the day when Don Bernardo de Galvez had forced
the English to surrender this same fort.

Isaac Johnson tied the flag of Spain to his horse's tail.
Then, followed by most of his troop, he galloped wildly
through the streets of the awakening village of Baton Rouge
with Spain's humbled banner dragging in the dust. For the
first time in American history, cavalrymen had taken a
fort. With many a swear word and jubilant, backwoods
yell, the dragoons told the villages that a new republic had
been born on the Mississippi.

Certain formalities remained. Assembling again on September 26, 1810, the West Floridians declared their independence of Spain, drew up a formal declaration, and selected Fulwar Skipwith as governor of the new nation.
Philemon Thomas was appointed commander in chief. John
Rhea, president of the convention, a prosperous merchant,
planter, and former alcalde of Feliciana, was instructed to
seek annexation by the United States and also a loan of
$100,000 to help defend West Florida from Spain. The
young nation's boundaries were more modest than those
of West Florida under Spain, for the rebels extended them
westward only as far as Pearl River, now the eastern boundary between Louisiana and Mississippi.

There also were certain informalities left to attend to.
Opposed to the rebels, in addition to the Spanish themselves, were a number of English-speaking settlers. Principal
among them were Shepherd Brown, William Cooper, and
Michael Jones, the Tory who had hunted the Kempers. The
three began raising men to oppose the victors. They were
hunted down, and Cooper was killed while "trying to
escape."

De Lassus was set free by a Captain David Cook of
the 3rd Regiment of Feliciana, and made his way to New

Orleans. Spain tried him in absentia, and sentenced him to death, but de Lassus lived in New Orleans until he was seventy-eight, and died a prominent and well-liked citizen. Cook was cashiered and run out of the country for helping him escape. De Lassus's venal secretary, Croker, escaped, as did many of the Spanish-Mexican soldiery.

The Republic of West Florida settled down to the business of defending itself against all comers. Believing that the Spanish governor at Mobile might attack them, the Americans decided to carry the fight to Mobile itself. Mississippians flocked into West Florida to help them. And for the first time in the revolt, a Kemper took part. The brothers had not been near enough to join when the brief war began.

❦   ❦

Early in the fall, the West Floridians dispatched Reuben Kemper, now a colonel in the West Florida army, and a handful of men to Mobile. It was planned that he should enlist volunteers in the Mobile area, and then capture the city. Virtually without arms, the Kemper expedition camped in November on Mobile Bay, waiting for guns, ammunition, and supplies. Finally a keelboat loaded with weapons and provisions arrived. In Mobile, frightened Governor Folch wrote on December 3, 1810, to President Madison, imploring him to order American troops to "drive Reuben Kemper back to Baton Rouge," and asking also that commissioners be sent to Mobile to negotiate for the transfer of the city and the rest of the province of West Florida to the United States.

Meanwhile, on October 27th, President Madison had proclaimed that West Florida had really belonged to the United States all along, as part of the Louisiana Purchase. He then ordered Louisiana Territory's Governor Claiborne in New Orleans to enter the territory and take possession as far eastward as the Perdido River.

Claiborne lost little time. By December 1st he had distributed copies of Madison's proclamation throughout West Florida. The successful rebels were indignant and threatened to defend their independence against the United States itself. Skipwith and Thomas planned to resist. Claiborne proceeded to the Feliciana town of St. Francisville, the republic's capital on the river, raised the American flag, and urged the assembled citizens to accept the government of the United States.

Angrily, and with truth, General Thomas answered that "the United States had refused either assistance or protection when it was needed; and now when it was unnecessary, sought to force it on us." The claim of the United States, he thundered, was bad in law and morals and Madison's proclamation a virtual declaration of war. He then promised to defend West Florida with his life.

Claiborne ordered gunboats from New Orleans, and reinforcements. Without waiting for them, he marched the few miles from St. Francisville south to Baton Rouge, encountering no opposition. But when he raised the American flag over the fort, it was torn down. Trouble might have followed, but the reinforcements arrived. The brief life of the West Florida republic ended without bloodshed after seventy-four days.

The intervention of the United States brought disaster to Reuben Kemper's expedition. He and two aides were arrested on the American side of the Florida line and brought home. His men were ambushed by the vengeful Spaniards, who killed four, wounded five and captured seven with a loss of two killed and four wounded. Two of the captives, Major William H. Hargrave and Cyrus Sibley, were imprisoned in Havana for six years. They were finally freed upon payment of $6,000.

The West Floridians protested no more against American domination. After all, that was what they had really wanted all along. They had resented only that the United States had not stepped in before they themselves had secured and proclaimed their independence. Less than five years later the Feliciana Dragoons would be part of Jackson's motley army at the Battle of New Orleans, with Reuben and Nathan Kemper fighting beside the Tennessee riflemen, the free Negroes, the Creole dandies, and the New Orleans American volunteers against the luckless redcoats.

The Kempers of West Florida have a greater significance than is accorded them. They, and most of their fellows, typified the swashbuckling brashness of the American on the Mississippi, cherishing a sense of individual freedom that verged on anarchy. On the lower river, this spirit clashed with the vestiges of monarchical rule east of the Mississippi; and before its impact the tottering authority of Spain went down. Most of the American settlers were tough, quarrelsome invaders. It is no wonder that the resentment of the less violent Spaniards and Frenchmen should have lingered for generations. Trigger-quick to establish their own rights, they were frequently careless of the rights and customs of their predecessors. In this they were simply in tune with the cock-crowing new Republic of the United States. And they made the lower river irrevocably American, first wresting the long muzzle of West Florida from the weak clutch of Spain, then defending the river against England's final thrust.

The planters of the Felicianas still follow today the independent tradition of these ancestors. Bayou Sara, where the Kempers held out against the Spaniards, lies beneath the shifted bed of the river; but little St. Francisville hides almost unchanged in its remote quiet beneath its ancient oaks bearded with Spanish moss. The Felicianas are a beautiful, ripe land today, scarcely ravaged by progress. Their high plantation homes are tucked behind avenues of venerable trees, their low rolling hills are thick with forests and carpeted with meadow grass and clover for browsing cattle.

And perhaps the spirits of the Kemper brothers whispered only a few years ago to these earthy Felicianians. During the dynasty of Huey Long, the two present parishes of East and West Feliciana successfully opposed his tyranny with ballot and guns until the last of Long. Back in 1934 they organized the Feliciana Home Guards to repel any attempt by the Long machine to interfere with their elections. They were not bothered. And when an evangelistic, coarse-mouthed organizer of Long's Share Our Wealth society attempted to make a speech in St. Francisville, a group of Felicianians escorted him and his satellites across the parish line and told him never to return. Nor did he.

As far as the Felicianians are concerned, theirs is still the Free State of West Florida, and Reuben, Sam, and Nathan Kemper are their tribal deities.

CHAPTER 10

Dominique You Squares Accounts

THE MISSISSIPPI RIVER might have been English to-day—

If Creole Major Gabriel Villeré had not escaped from his British captors on the afternoon of December 23, 1814, by jumping through a window of his plantation home, reaching New Orleans the same day to warn Andrew Jackson of their approach;

If the British had immediately advanced upriver to New Orleans that afternoon;

If on the morning of January 8, 1815, a certain absent-minded Major Mullins of the British Army had not forgotten the fascines and ladders so necessary for crossing ditches and scaling breastworks;

If pirate Jean Lafitte's esteem for $30,000 in British gold and the offer of his Majesty's commission had outweighed his Gallic hatred for the British and perhaps an odd liking for the Johnny-come-lately Americans;

And if one Dominique You, late artilleryman of Napoleon and Lafitte's lieutenant and ablest gunner, had not been able to square a few old accounts by outshooting Wellington's gunners.

Such speculation is amiable pastime now. But had any or all of these contingencies gone the other way, the British might have won the lower river. Had they done so, they might have held to it despite later news of the peace treaty

159

at Ghent which had been consummated before the battle. Had they stayed on—well, even conjecture has its limits.

In each instance, the scales tilted in favor of the Americans. The United States won its most one-sided victory. Possession of the Mississippi was clinched. A triumphant army had been portentously molded from Creole, Indian, free Negro, pirate, Yankee trader, and frontiersman. And for succeeding generations the battle produced a succession of narratives and eventual scenarios which have just about exhausted the literary possibilities of the event.

But in the telling and retelling of this final thrusting of the English from American soil, Dominique You has received little glory. He has been overlooked principally because he played a secondary role to Lafitte, and perhaps because his reformation and subsequent impoverishment do not provide inspiration for moral guidance. At any rate, the old artilleryman and navigator whose tomb in New Orleans bears the Masonic square and compass, deserves more than the military honors accorded him after his poverty-ridden death.

There were three piratical Yous—Dominique, Jean, and Pierre—who quit their parental village near Nantes to become seamen. Dominique mastered navigation, and later, as a soldier in the Grande Armée, gunnery. He participated in Le Clerc's ill-fated expedition to Haiti, and later turned privateer. In 1810 the three brothers joined the pirates of Barataria Bay on the Louisiana coast.

Now for a few notes about these pirates of whom so much has been written, factually and otherwise. They held letters of marque and reprisal from the Republic of Cartagena, first of the Latin-American colonies to revolt against Spain. They had harassed Gulf of Mexico shipping long before Jean Lafitte organized them into a compact, merchandising gang of cutthroats. From their headquarters at Barataria Bay, they would descend upon the gulf, theoretically preying only upon Spanish merchantmen but actually not being too selective. For protection and for commerce with New Orleans their Barataria lair was ideally located, connected as it was by an intricate progression of bayous and canals. In New Orleans they sold their smuggled goods to the receptive merchants. But until Jean Lafitte came along, they had operated on a quarrelsome, unregulated basis that lost them many customers and more profits.

The Lafittes, Pierre and Jean, had emigrated to New Orleans from Saint-Malo, France, about 1806, setting up a blacksmith shop. Soon they were acting as smugglers' agents for the pirates. Slim, six-foot Jean was a darkly handsome, sophisticated Frenchman, a linguist who spoke Spanish, Italian, French, and English with almost equal fluency. The brothers prospered as smiths and smugglers. More, they were accepted socially by most of the easygoing Orleanians despite their Baratarian connections. In 1808, Jean Lafitte became disgusted with the disorderly way in which the pirates conducted business, and decided to teach them how to keep their books and their manners in balance. In assuming leadership of the pirates, he had to kill but one objector. Thenceforth, their brawling, weekly auctions of slaves and merchandise at Barataria became well-regulated public sales which the merchants were not afraid to attend.

The pirate nest flourished, the settlement increasing from some 400 buccaneers and 200 jades to a sizable town with a male population of more than a thousand freebooters who manned fifty ships. Lafitte directed the building of thatched cottages, gambling and assignation houses, a huge slave barracoon, and a handsome brick and stone house for himself. As lieutenants he selected Dominique You, who was his favorite, René Beluche, Cut-Nose Chighizola, and Vincent Gambi. In New Orleans his brother Pierre continued to act as agent, boldly displaying goods and as many as 450 slaves at a single auction. Barges maintained regular schedules between Barataria, New Orleans and upriver points, with iron-clad guarantee of deliveries. By 1813 Lafitte was supplying nearly every merchant in New Orleans, and counted them as his friends.

Prospering with his leader, Dominique You must have likewise made friends in the city. Perhaps the veteran artilleryman would have preferred to embrace earlier the honest existence to which he returned shortly after the Battle of New Orleans. If so, he could have had reasons other than a simple liking for orthodoxy. For the Americans, gradually entrenching themselves and making their form of government felt, were not so lackadaisical or complacent as their French and Spanish predecessors. On several occasions the Baratarians had to repel sorties by United States deputies. Incidentally, more than a hundred years later their descendants, no longer pirates but liquor runners, would still be battling deputy marshals.

In 1813, Governor Claiborne set a price of $750 on Jean Lafitte's head. In mocking answer, Lafitte offered a $1,500 reward for Claiborne, and continued to walk the streets of New Orleans, though his brother and others of his following were briefly brought to justice. Neither reward was ever claimed.

The United States, however, was persistent. And in September, 1814, two unrelated events upset the even tenor of piracy. From Jamaica, where an English army of veterans of the Napoleonic Wars was being assembled for an assault on Louisiana, an English naval commander arrived at Barataria. He offered Lafitte $30,000 in gold and a commission in the Royal Navy if the pirate would join forces and reveal the bayou approaches to the city. Lafitte stalled for time, then sent a report of the meeting to Governor Claiborne and the army and navy officers who were frenziedly trying to assemble a force against the threat of invasion. The pirate chief offered himself and his men to the Americans, asking as his reward "an act of oblivion for all that has been done hitherto." Claiborne recommended acceptance, but the military refused.

They had a certain impelling motive in their refusal. A fleet of American gunboats was even then preparing to sail downriver to the gulf to attack the pirates, for the government at Washington had been goaded into drastic action by Claiborne's frequent reports. A few days after Lafitte's message, Commodore Patterson attacked the Baratarians, destroyed their Grand Terre headquarters in the bay, and captured 100 prisoners—including Dominique You and Beluche—and nine ships.

Fleeing through the maze of bayous to New Orleans, Lafitte boldly appeared before Claiborne to renew his offer of service. Claiborne took his proposal up with General Jackson, now at Mobile en route to the defense of New Orleans. Jackson refused to accept the services of the "hellish banditti." But when the Tennessean arrived in New Orleans, he discovered that what he needed most of all was man power. Reluctantly, he accepted the motley addition to his army, and You and his companions were released from the jail.

Jackson's change of heart was made lasting by direful news. An English squadron had sailed from Jamaica on November 24, 1814, bearing a formidable army under the command of Sir Edward M. Pakenham, brother-in-law of the Duke of Wellington. Most of the troops were veterans of the Continental campaigns and the victories over the Americans on the Atlantic coast. On December 12th they arrived off Louisiana, and sailing up Lake Borgne, arrived on December 23rd within nine miles of New Orleans.

Meanwhile Andy Jackson had completed the mustering of the most heterogeneous army ever to fight on American soil. He had brought 884 United States regulars with him. This nucleus had been supplemented by 563 fringe-shirted

Tennesseans under Generals Coffee and Carroll. In New Orleans some 60 American merchants, professional men, and others had enrolled in Beale's Rifles. The Orleans Battalion of Creoles who had earlier refused to fight for the United States added another 365. The city's battalion of free men of color, first in the city to volunteer their services, numbered 210. Hind's Mississippi Dragoons, Pierre Jugeat's Choctaw scouts, and the unsavory Baratarians completed the little army of 2,325 men.

On December 23rd the British surprised the American pickets at Bayou Bienvenue below the city, captured their commander, Major Gabriel Villeré, and occupied his plantation. The doughty major leaped through a window, made his way to the river which he crossed to the west bank, and proceeded in haste to a point across from the city. There he recrossed and warned Jackson. While the British were making the fatal mistake of resting a few hours instead of pushing their advantage of surprise, Jackson gathered his scattered commands, met the British in the dark with rifles, tomahawks and knives, and forced them to withdraw.

A lull of a few days followed. Then Pakenham called up his artillery to blast out the Americans. The British wheeled twenty-four cannon into position. Opposing them were fourteen American guns, manned by the Baratarian jailbirds and directed by You and Beluche. And here the emperor's artilleryman avenged himself. Under his expert laying, every British gun was silenced with a loss of only three American pieces. This triumph was to be of incalculable value on January 8th when the final engagement, known as the Battle of New Orleans, took place. For on that grim day the British were unable to lay down an artillery barrage for their advancing infantrymen whose smoothbore muskets of only 100-yard range were useless before the long rifles of the Tennesseans which mowed them down at 250 to 300 yards.

After the unsuccessful artillery duel, Pakenham rested another week. Then, stung by the taunts of Admiral Cochrane of the British fleet, he decided to attack. On the evening of January 7th a British force on the west bank drove back the Americans, mostly newly arrived Kentuckians. The decisive, east bank engagement did not begin until the morning of January 8th.

That day Dominique You almost missed getting in a second blow. The powder which had been allotted to his battery was of poor quality. So a couple of days before the battle he had sent his brothers Jean and Pierre to the powder manufactory of Optime Bourguignon, near Bonnet Carré in St. John's Parish above New Orleans, to get a supply of good powder. When the battle of January 8th began, Jean and Pierre had not returned. One can almost hear the enraged freebooter cursing his brothers, the British, and fate while his guns pointed uselessly at the enemy. But the brothers arrived with the powder in time for its employment against the doomed redcoats and skirted Highlanders. Perhaps there was a romantic reason for the delay, for later Jean You married Fortune Parent, a step-daughter of Optime Bourguignon, and became a director of the powder plant himself. It is of passing interest that Fortune's father, Adolph Parent, the founder of the manufactory, was originally connected with the du Pont powder company.

Before the rifle and artillery fire of Jackson's army, more than 700 Britishers, including Generals Pakenham and Gibbs were killed, and 1,400 wounded. The Americans took 500 prisoners. Their own loss was but 8 killed and 13 wounded. Soon after the British sailed away.

Among the Baratarians, swearing in many tongues that Andy Jackson was the greatest fighter in the universe, Dominique You's voice was as loud as any. The pirates were delighted. They had proved themselves in behalf of the United States. They had received the approbation of the general, with this especial reference to Beluche and to You with whom Jackson had said that he would willingly storm the gates of hell:

Captains Dominique and Beluche, lately commanding privateers at Barataria, with part of their former crews and many brave citizens of New Orleans, were stationed at Batteries Three and Four. The general cannot avoid giving his warm approbation of the manner in which these gentlemen have uniformly conducted themselves while under his command, and of the gallantry with which they redeemed the pledge they gave at the opening of the campaign to defend the country. The brothers Lafitte have exhibited the same courage and fidelity, and the general promises that the government shall be duly apprised of their conduct.

The government answered handsomely. Upon notification by Claiborne and Jackson of their fidelity in battle, President Madison signed a pardon on February 6, 1815, for every pirate who could prove through the governor that he had fought the British.

But at the scene of their regeneration, things did not go so well for the pirates. First, at the Victory Ball on January 23rd, Jean Lafitte was snubbed, probably unintentionally, by General Coffee and General de Flaugeac. Then on March 31st, Jackson, now the pirate's idol, became the victim of a shabby aftermath of his victory. On his arrival in New Orleans he had been forced to declare martial law because of existing confusion and a seeming desire in some quarters to make terms with the British. Martial law was enforced even after the battle. When some of the Creole troops petitioned for discharge, Jackson placed them in a camp near Baton Rouge, prisoners to all practical purposes.

A general assemblyman petitioned for a writ of habeas corpus, which was granted by a Judge Hall, whereupon Jackson put them both under arrest and deported them beyond his military boundaries on charges of incitement to mutiny. When tidings of the Ghent treaty arrived, civil law was restored, and Judge Hall, rankling over his treatment, summoned Jackson to appear before him on contempt of court charges. On the day of the hearing, Jackson simply appeared, refused to defend himself, and paid a fine of $1,000. A year before his death, Congress made restitution, paying him $2,700 in principal and interest.

The court's action enraged much of the populace, and especially the Baratarians. You, Beluche, and many other former pirates crowded the courthouse and its environs, and when the general emerged, carried him on their shoulders to a coffeehouse where celebration helped to mollify Jackson and themselves.

By this time the pirates must have been at least temporarily disgusted. So, when the dejected Lafitte sailed away on a new piratical venture, You, Beluche, Chighizola and Gambi accompanied him. Soon thereafter, You and Beluche returned to the city, to live out their years as law-abiding citizens.

The story should end here, with a homily on the rewards of virtue. But for old Dominique You there were to be no material rewards. He was popular enough. He entered zestfully into coffeehouse gatherings and Masonic meetings, he helped organize an artillery company. He entered politics as a "Jackson man," but unsuccessfully. He is credited with organizing a plot to free Napoleon from St. Helena. But in 1830, at the age of fifty-five, Dominique You died in poverty. Nor could the closure of business establishments, the flags half-masted in his memory, and the military ceremonies at his grave make up for the forlorn sequel to his coin-rattling, swashbuckling days. Dominique You is forgotten, and Lafitte, who died a pirate, is remembered. There is no monument to Dominique You, no tangible reminder except the weather-worn, brownish tomb with the cryptic symbols in St. Louis Cemetery inscribed to "l'intrépide guerrier sur la terre et sur l'onde." On the battle site of Chalmette there is no bronze marker proclaiming that here an artilleryman of Napoleon made handsome amends to the country whose laws he had broken.

CHAPTER 11

Sudden Death

In 1847, the Cincinnati publishing house of E. E.
Barclay disgorged a paper-back thriller entitled *The Female
Land Pirate—or the Awful, Mysterious and Horrible Disclosures of Amanda Bamoris.*

The preface disclosed that the late Mrs. Bamoris, widow
of Richard Bamoris of Murrell's Men, had poisoned herself
in a prison cell in 1846 while awaiting trial for his murder.
In her last hours, according to the publishers, she had written the story of her life of crime. It opened with this foreword:

Tremble reader! Prepare yourself to listen to a revelation
of crimes of a most horrible nature, related by one of the
guilty accomplices—by one who asks not your sympathies
—by one who, ere this reaches other eyes, will be sleeping
cold in death—by one who will have paid the last great
debt of nature, as a partial atonement for her many sins.
Reader, I am standing on the brink of eternity!

To old-time devotees of the yellow-back shocker,
Amanda's brink-standing autobiography has a familiar ring.
Shortly after her father's death, her mother took in washing
and in 1830 died of consumption when Amanda was a
ripe thirteen. Soon thereafter she was accosted on the streets
by a wealthy gentleman, one holding high office, who took
her to the home of a "relative," named Aunt Patterson.

Auntie was a "coarse featured, masculine woman . . . rather corpulent, and her face, bloated with liquor, gave her a repulsive cast." This is Amanda's, or her publisher's story, not mine.

For three years Amanda dressed in silks, practiced her piano lessons, struggled with the "higher branches of English education." But not a hand was laid upon her. Aunt Patterson explained that the benefactor would marry her when her education was completed.

"At the age of sixteen, I was what the world calls a beautiful female," Amanda relates. "Thus far, not a word had been said in my presence offensive to the most refined taste. But villainy was at hand. The flower had bloomed and was now ripe for the destroyer's surprise."

Alas for Amanda! One night her benefactor entered her room and locked the door. "Suffice that I left that room a guilty woman, but under the strong impression that a few days hence would witness my nuptuals with my seducer. . . . Daily, or nightly I should say, he visited me. He worked upon my passions."

But the villain was married. So by way of avenging her honor, his deflowered protégée stabbed him, though not fatally, and fled Aunt Patterson's evil ménage. To further satisfy her honor, she poisoned a loaf of bread destined for Auntie's table, and sought refuge in Louisville. There she read in the newspapers that Aunt Patterson had died of poison. There also she met Richard Bamoris, a gambling man, and moved with him to Vicksburg in 1833. In Vicksburg, double-dealing Dick tired of Amanda who "got used to it and consoled myself with the society of other gentlemen." In fact, Amanda admits, she gave herself up to a life of voluptuousness. But she remained with Richard, possibly because he had now turned counterfeiter. And finally Amanda discovered that her man was a member of Murrell's gang. To save her own life, Amanda had to join also. In two years she was an accomplice in five murders. Then one day, her original sin appeared in Vicksburg. Amanda, who never forgot an insult, had him abducted and taken to the cave hide-out of Murrell's cutthroats. There her seducer was tortured, cast in a pit, and left to die of starvation.

After Murrell's capture, Richard and Amanda decided to reform. Apparently the decision wasn't a lasting one. In New Orleans, Richard killed one of Amanda's lovers. In turn she shot him to death in a courtroom. Sic transit Amanda.

It is most improbable that the unfortunate Amanda ever existed. But it was easy in 1847 to accept the lurid confession as gospel, for its background was the Lower Mississippi. In no other period and on no other frontier in American history was human life held so callously in disregard.

A lone traveler on the lower river would not have been a good insurance risk in the first fifty years of the American influx, roughly from 1795 to the 1840's. On the Mississippi itself murderous river pirates preyed upon voyagers and commerce. The overland adventurer, at the turn of the century and for years after, had to run the gantlet of the brigands of the Natchez Trace and of the lesser highways through the valley wilderness. In the bucko dives of Memphis, Vicksburg, Natchez, and New Orleans, death or crippling injury were the nightly climax of rotgut whisky carousals. Up and down the river the red-shirted flatboatmen brawled. In New Orleans, Creole blades itched for human scabbards. Everywhere, organized crime and the individualistic spirit of violence vied as the twin handmaidens of sudden death.

The annals of the Lower Mississippi are crowded with the fact and legend of indiscriminate blood spilling and

discriminating pillaging. We can select only a random handful of tales.

A ruffian named Fluger, better known as Colonel Plug,
was the villain of one of the earliest of these stories of
terrorism. A river pirate, the colonel's favorite ruse was to
hide himself aboard a flatboat at night. Once the laden
craft swung downstream, the colonel would scuttle her by
boring holes in her bottom. When the flatboat began to
founder, his associates ashore would row out in skiffs, pretending a rescue. They would save only the cargo and Colonel
Plug. Eventually Fluger was drowned because he miscal-
culated the time element between scuttling and rescue.

On land, the law-abiding shuddered at the deeds of
Big and Little Harpe, who killed and mutilated along the
Natchez Trace. They had achieved bloody notoriety before
the end of the eighteenth century. Accompanied by three
abandoned women companions, Susan and Betsy Roberts and
Sally Rice, the Harpes murdered scores of luckless travelers
along the trace, merely for the maniacal love of killing.
And there was Joseph Hare, who progressed from pick-
pocket to highwayman, terrorizing the countryside above
Natchez. Hare was finally hanged in Baltimore for robbing
the mails. Another was Samuel Mason, respected veteran
of the Revolution, who with his three sons turned wholesale human butcher and robber, placarding his victims with
his trade-mark "Mason of the Woods."

The worst and the last of the land pirates was John
Murrell of Tennessee, whose outlaw organization extended
throughout the deep South. Son of a woman whose tavern
business near Columbia, Tennessee, was a front for a brothel
and thieves' market, young Murrell was a thief at ten and
a highwayman and murderer before he attained his majority.
His mother's paramour, Harry Cranshaw, was his tutor and
first accomplice. For several years, Murrell and Cranshaw

killed and plundered along the Trace, with Mom Murrell selling their loot.

Murrell was able to deceive the wariest citizens, for association with lecturers, evangelists, book peddlers, and other sojourners at the tavern and fellow travelers gave him an unctuous, educated veneer. He even participated in camp meetings, where he was famed as a thunderous preacher. A dapper, friendly little man, he was welcomed in many an unsuspecting home and hostel along the Trace from Nashville to Natchez.

Eventually Murrell gathered a large following, popularly known as the Mystic Brotherhood, which graduated from murder and horse stealing into a real or pretended organization for a slave insurrection. Historians differ on that score; but the brotherhood had members not only along the Trace but throughout the Lower Mississippi Valley. Headquarters were moved from Denmark, Tennessee, to a larger swamp hide-out in Arkansas, some fifty miles up the river from Memphis.

In 1834 the gang was tripped up. A young man named Virgil Stewart was taken into membership. Stewart's own vivid account is that he purposely joined to track down the outlaws. Other reports have it that he was a renegade member of the gang. At any rate, Stewart informed on Murrell, and declared that the brotherhood planned a gigantic insurrection of slaves for Christmas Day, with synchronized assaults in New Orleans, Memphis, and Natchez. Murrell was captured. On the Fourth of July, insurrections were attempted at several Mississippi points, but these were quickly quelled, and white and black ringleaders, including some ostensibly respectable planters, were hanged. Murrell served only ten years in the state penitentiary in Tennessee. He was released in 1844, turned blacksmith, and died a few years later of tuberculosis contracted in prison.

Whenever the citizens of the river caught an outlaw

their retaliation was thorough. Mason and Little Harpe were caught and executed in 1804, and their heads placed on pointed stakes. No mercy was ever shown river pirates on those longed-for occasions when they were outmatched by flatboatmen and travelers. Once, in the early 1800's, the crews of several flatboats secreted themselves on one vessel and floated downriver opposite Crow's Nest, a notorious bandit lair. The unsuspecting pirates swooped out to secure the prize. The rivermen thereupon killed most of them, and then forced twelve captive pirates to walk a plank. While they bobbed in the river, their captors picked them off with rifle shots.

Even had there been no land and river pirates, the incautious traveler would have had many obstacles to the safe conclusion of a journey downriver. If he went ashore at Memphis for a drink, he ran the danger of falling afoul of the denizens of the Pinch, or Pinchgut, a squalid collection of gamblers, prostitutes and fighting flatboatmen who were in their heyday in the twenties and thirties. At Natchez Under the Hill, situated at the base of the bluff on which the city stood, two sordid, brothel-lined streets were infested with low women, gamblers, and gunmen. Sometimes they shot at passing boats just for the fun of it. Usually they enticed the unwary, plied them with drink, then robbed and frequently killed them. New Orleans was even worse because its area of vice was larger. The harassed Louisiana legislature enacted in 1818 stringent measures to curb lawlessness, including the death penalty for armed robbery; and by 1819 Governor Villeré was bragging that "the city is now in the enjoyment of the most perfect security."

But the governor's assurance was premature. Not for many years would New Orleans be safe from the excesses of even the flatboatmen. Masters of rough-and-tumble, the hardy rivermen produced many a legendary hero and heroine. Upriver, their deity was Mike Fink, who could out-shoot, outfight, outdrink, and outwork any other man alive. On the lower river they boasted of Bill Sedley, a giant Kentucky killer whose favorite haunt was New Orleans, and Annie Christmas, who was reputed to stand six feet eight inches high, and who was the leading character in the bawdiest, most prodigious of their yarns. Annie alter-

nated between doing a man's work and catering to man's physical demands. She clawed and gouged with the best, or, when the spirit moved her, outstrumpeted the lustiest of the women whom she recruited for her floating house of prostitution.

As long as the flatboatmen confined their mayhem to themselves, they were let alone in the live-and-let-live tradition of the river towns. But an odd, envious sort of anarchism seemed to animate the rivermen, causing frequent clashes with the more or less sedate society of merchants and professional men who were gradually entrenching themselves in the growing communities. Memphis itself was threatened with destruction in 1842 when the crews of 500 flatboats banded together in an attempt to burn and loot the city because of the slaying of one of their number who resisted arrest.

In New Orleans the flatboatmen were particularly obstreperous. Not content with keeping to the brothel and tavern areas, they frequently wrecked respectable restaurants, theaters and cabarets, engaging the police in free-for-all fighting while the professional criminals roamed unchecked. The New Orleans underworld was hand in glove with the "mauvais Kaintock." Away out on Girod Street, there thrived the most vicious area in the country. It was known as the Swamp. In his colorful history of New Orleans, *The French Quarter*, Herbert Asbury thus describes it:

There the flatboat men and the ruffians of the underworld reigned supreme and the art and practice of mayhem reached their fullest development. Scores of fights occurred in the Swamp every night, and over a period of many years the district is said to have averaged half a dozen murders a week, none of which were ever investigated by the municipal authorities or, for that matter, even reported. The police never ventured into the section; it was a tradition of the Swamp that for twenty years no officer of the law had set foot within its boundaries. . . .

The Swamp comprised an area of half a dozen blocks, crowded with saloons, dance-halls, gambling dens, bordellos, and so-called hotels, all housed in shacks with low gable roofs, built of rough cypress planks or lumber from old flatboats. Most of the bars in the drinking-places were simply boards laid across two or more kegs, and the other furniture was of the same rude sort. . . . Frequently all of the various enterprises of the Swamp were under one roof, and in many the standard rates were so low that for a picayune (six cents) a boatman could get a drink, a woman and a bed for the night—and the practical certainty of being robbed, and perhaps murdered as soon as he fell asleep. . . .

From this teeming cesspool of iniquity issued the prowling bands of thieves, footpads and firebugs which made life and the possession of property more precarious in early New Orleans than in any other city in America. Robberies and holdups were so frequent as to be common-place events, and many of them were preceded by incendi-ary fires, for gangs of arsonists set fire to houses in order that looting might be more easily carried on during the excitement of extinguishing the flames. The boldest of these gangs operated in 1827 and 1828, and early in the latter year concocted a scheme to burn and pillage the entire respectable portion of the city. Plans for the holocaust were evidently prepared in great detail, but before they could be carried out a woman who had been arrested in Mobile confessed the details of the plot to the Mayor of that city, who immediately notified the Mayor of New Orleans, Count Louis Philippe de Roffignac. The garde de ville succeeded in arresting four of the conspirators—two Negroes and two white men—but the others sought refuge in the Swamp and were never apprehended.

No wonder the Creoles hated the invading Americans. But not every menace was imported from the barbaric States. Throughout this period, occasional slave uprisings and fre-quent rumors of such kept the scattered plantations and even the larger towns uneasily on guard. In 1811 a deter-mined revolt occurred in the parish of St. John the Baptist, some 35 miles above New Orleans. Five hundred Negro slaves, organized into companies, officered and strutting to drumbeats beneath outlandish flags, marched toward New Orleans, gaining recruits on the way. On their march they set fire to several plantations. Before they reached the city, militia and regulars from Baton Rouge and New Orleans hemmed them in. Sixty-six were slain, and scores were taken prisoner and hanged on the spot. Sixteen leaders were sent to New Orleans for trial. Found guilty, they were executed and their heads mounted on high poles above and below New Orleans, as far north as the plantation on which the revolt began.

Even in the 1830's, a Negro named Squier and his gang of runaway blacks and renegade whites kept Orleanians in terror. Squier had been a favorite slave of an indulgent owner, General William de Buys, who permitted him to hunt game alone near the city. Soon Squier began taking French leave, and in 1834 he was shot by a planter searching for runaway slaves. His wound necessitated the amputation of his right arm. When the stump healed, one-armed Squier, who was thenceforth to be known as Bras Coupé, fled. Organizing a band of fellow fugitives, he haunted New Orleans, robbing and murdering even in the heart of the city. The Negroes and many whites swore that he couldn't be killed. But one night he slept in the hut of a Spanish fisherman, Francisco Garcia. Garcia killed him as he lay on a pallet and brought his body to the city. For two days it was exposed in the Place d'Armes in warning to thousands of slaves who were forced to march past the gruesome exhibit. Garcia went home grumbling because his reward was only $250 instead of an expected $2,000.

There was yet another racial group which reminded the river settlers of sudden death. After the Revolution, the Indians were the least of the valley's worries. But as late as 1813, drunken, marauding Choctaws raided plantations in the vicinity of Baton Rouge; elsewhere in lower Louisiana farms were abandoned in fear of Indian attacks. Terror of an expected alliance of Choctaws and runaway slaves was so great after a massacre by the Creeks near Mobile in 1813, that Governor Claiborne personally organized the Louisiana militia to protect the white populace against Indian uprisings.

And the Creoles themselves had a well-mannered way of cutting life short. Wearing their brittle honor on their sleeves, these Orleans duelists welcomed the insult that would mean a passage at arms. Unlike the crude Americans, they would not resort to fisticuffs. Instead, they relied on the rapier, the colichemarde, the broadsword, and sometimes the pistol—to which lethal selection the American participants added the shotgun, the rifle, and the bowie knife. The Creoles boasted of their stellar swordsmen, Bernard Marigny, Pepe Lulla the Spaniard, Marcel Dauphin, and Bastile Croquere, a handsome mulatto who could fight no duel in Louisiana because of his color, but who was a sought-after instructor. Dueling, both American and Creole style, was an accepted custom, almost a pastime, which claimed hundreds of lives from the turn of the century to the Civil War and, clandestinely, even later.

One wonders how men survived in this turbulent period. One does not wonder that the spirit of turbulence itself has survived its more primitive manifestations along the river.

CHAPTER 12

The Americans Build A Town

MAJOR MARCUS B. WINCHESTER was the last person you would have expected to meet in 1819 in that tough new wisp of a village on the Chickasaw Bluffs to which its proprietors had given the grandiose name of Memphis.

Handsome young Marcus must have seemed completely out of place among the handful of squatters and the forlorn, whisky-tippling Indians on the bluffs. Not yet out of his twenties, he already had experienced more of glamour than Memphis would ever offer him. He had been a boy major in the War of 1812, serving on the staff of his fighting father, Tennessee's General James Winchester. Taken prisoner by the British at Raisin Creek, Marcus had so captivated his captors that after his incarceration in Canada he had been feted as a hero. So persuasive was his quiet charm that even that castigating Englishwoman, Mrs. Trollope, would come to praise him; and in Washington, tart Ann Royall reserved for young Winchester the best of her few adulatory words.

Major Winchester knew better than did the jealous settlers and Indian traders why he had taken up residence in Memphis; why he strolled of an afternoon dreaming of the future city for which his presence here indicated hope. He had come to these high bluffs on the Mississippi as agent for three canny land speculators. One of them was his father. Another, who was to be the driving force in the creation of this American-built town on the river, was John B.

Overton, retired chief justice of Tennessee. The third was Andrew Jackson, who in addition to his familiar talents for soldiering and politics had an astute if not always ethical sense of land values.

Here on the Chickasaw Bluffs these three had planned to establish a metropolis of the middle valley, midway between New Orleans and St. Louis. Their vision and their manipulations were alike typical of the pioneer speculators in western lands, who, working on the political inside, frequently instigated and nearly always profited greatly from the land rushes which followed the acquisition of the river territory.

The Chickasaw Bluffs had a curiously important relationship to this period of expansion. The warrior tribesmen from whom they had their name were never friendly with the French and the Spanish, though they were amicable enough to the English and later to the Americans. Not until 1795 did Spain secure a foothold on those dominating, strategically important hills. When she did so, she acted desperately and too late, trying to forestall American occupation of the valley territory which England had ceded after the Revolution in complete indifference to its physical occupation by Spain's soldiers. In May, 1795, the Spanish flag still floated on the bluffs, while President Washington denounced Spain's act of possession as "an unwarranted aggression." Spain clung to precarious Fort San Fernando de los Barrancas until 1797, a year and a half after she had technically forfeited all east bank territory north of the controversial 31st degree.

In 1797, however, the Spanish garrison sulkily moved across the river. Close on their heels, in July, came Captain Isaac Guion, ostensibly to bestow presents on the Chickasaws. From the Chickasaw chief, Piomingo, Guion obtained a tract of land, upon which he erected Fort Adams in answer to the Spanish fort across the river. By 1798, Fort

Adams had been replaced by dismal little Fort Pickering, several miles to the south.

Meanwhile, in the 1790's, Jackson and Overton had obscurely acquired large holdings on the lower bluffs. Their acquisition of these lands was illegal in that the territory actually still belonged to the Chickasaws and not to the state of North Carolina which acted as vendor. At the time of their purchase, the only residents of the bluffs, aside from the small garrison, were the dwindling Chickasaws and a few white settlers. Even by 1812, no more than 50 white people tended their squalid pigpens and corn patches in the vicinity. But meanwhile, Jackson, Overton, and Winchester hadn't forgotten their property. In 1818 the Chickasaws ceded their Kentucky and Tennessee homeland to the United States, with Jackson and Isaac Shelby negotiating the treaty. Their removal opened the way for the white man's expansion; and in that same year the new proprietors sent young Marcus to the bluffs as explorer and agent.

By May, 1819, Overton and General Winchester were conducting a survey of the area. After a tortuous and dubious series of transactions, Overton had enormous holdings, with General James Winchester, Andrew Jackson, and the heirs of William Winchester in possession of lesser but sizable parcels.

From the beginning, Memphis would be John Overton's town. Disturbed at the possible political effect, Jackson sold half of his land after Isaac Shelby denounced him for suspicious land activities during the Chickasaw treaty making. On a net investment of $25 he realized $5,000 on this sale, and as much or more on the remainder which he turned loose to clear his skirts for his presidential campaign. It was Overton and Winchester who supervised the laying out of the town into lots. It was Overton who opened a flowery sales campaign in the newspapers of Nashville, New Orleans, St. Louis, Natchez, Cincinnati, Pittsburgh, and Louisville.

And it was chiefly as Overton's agent that Marcus Winchester remained in Memphis. Political and personal double-dealing too long and complicated for description here was to give birth to a brawling, American town.

Marcus Winchester was as alien to his Memphis neighbors as the town's own frontier spirit was alien to Natchez, Baton Rouge, and New Orleans, the French, Spanish, and Tory-stamped older towns of the river. The upstart village got off slowly. In 1819 the wilderness was scarcely dented. Even the Fort Pickering soldiers had been removed several years earlier. Only a half dozen white men lived in or near the new settlement proper: Ike Rawlings, one-time sutler for Jackson and now an Indian trader; and his fellow traders, Paddy Meager, Job Bean, and the Carr brothers. Only rarely did the infrequent steamers pause at the village. By 1823 its population was but 53, and ten years later only 663.

One reason for the uncertain, slow growth was the enmity between proprietor and early settler. As agent for the landowners, Marcus Winchester was resented from the first by the individualistic traders and flatboatmen who wanted no interference with their squatter rights. Grizzled Ike Rawlings hated the young agent with especial venom after Winchester opened a better trading post, stocked with newer trinkets and more palatable whisky to swap for the deer, bear, and beaver skins of the Indians. This animosity between proprietors and people endured for Memphis's first twenty years, with detrimental results. And the struggling town was plagued with rivals: Mound City, Pedraza, and Hopefield, across the river in Arkansas; Raleigh and Randolph near by on the bluffs; and Commerce in Mississippi. Even the river, continually shifting its depths and shallows, seemed to conspire against the Memphians. Flatboats needed shallow eddies in which to land, and Memphis needed the laden, trade-making flatboats. Perversely, the shallows shifted southward, leaving deep water on the village river front. Only steamboats required deep water, and in the early years there were not enough steamboats on the river to make the depths as commercially advantageous as the shallows downstream. And in the late twenties, when the steamboats began to assume importance, the deep water and the shallows swapped places again. The flatboatmen themselves bedeviled the town, running roughshod over its inhabitants, refusing to pay wharfage fees, and for twenty years defying the feeble official efforts to restrain them.

Visitors to Memphis found its pretensions to civilization ludicrous. Bears occasionally roamed streets so muddily precarious in the rainy season that an ox team once drowned on the main thoroughfare. New Orleans might indulge in French wines, but the Memphians drank their whisky straight at the doggery, or tavern, the favorite distillation bringing but twenty-five cents a gallon. They liked their merriment as well as any others, and the rough log cabins frequently shook to the dancing which the occasional evangelists and circuit riders denounced as wicked. Those set-tos would have been scorned in stately Natchez for another reason than sinfulness; here the musicians scraped and thrummed only the lowly fiddle and banjo, and their repertoires for the square dances and mountain reels consisted mostly of such frontier favorites as the "Arkansas Traveler" and "Old Zip Coon."

After the weekly musters of the volunteers, marching to the tune of "Jay Bird Died of the Whooping Cough," quarrelsome Memphians liked to settle grudges on the militia grounds. They were unfamiliar with the Creole rapier. Instead, they got satisfaction with clenched fist, gouging thumb and stamping boots, or with rifle, pistol or bowie knife.

Throughout their frontier symphony throbbed the overtones of backwoods Protestantism. The circuit riders came early to Memphis with their camp meetings and personal exhortations to the backsliding majority. In the surrounding forests, the settlers shouted and jerked as the spirit moved them, courted ardently in the underbrush between sermons, and fortified themselves against the devil from demijohns cached conveniently near by. Memphis produced its own evangelists as well: Uncle Henry Lawrence, a Negro, and the white sermonizers, Elijah Coffee and Silas Toncray. Elijah had left his wife and an evil reputation behind him in Illinois. In Memphis he devoted himself haphazardly to saving souls. Silas, who was in business as a silversmith, watchmaker, engraver, sign painter, druggist and doctor, sought his converts among the Negroes.

In spite of its crude provincialism Memphis had its supporters. At Paddy Meager's old Bell Tavern, Davy Crockett, the Bentons, and Andrew Jackson himself—who looked kindly upon Paddy's daughter Sally—lodged frequently on their business trips and during campaigns. Crockett was an especial favorite and drinking companion of the denizens of the Pinch, a settlement of poor houseboaters on Gayoso Bayou at the foot of the village; and the adroit politician made the Pinchgutters feel that he was one of them. To Marcus Winchester, the visits of these Tennessee giants were like manna, though ultimately his link with Thomas Hart Benton was to lead directly to the great love and great tragedy of his life.

Meanwhile what has the young agent been doing to further Overton's interests? In 1824 Marcus is distributing two hundred gallons of whisky along the bluffs, in furtherance of John Overton's efforts to maintain Memphis as the seat of Shelby, newest of the western countries. In 1826 he becomes the first mayor of the incorporated town. Old Ike Rawlings, who has sufficient following to defeat him, has refused to run. The next year Marcus has resigned the mayorship to become postmaster. He is replaced by old Ike, the enemy of the proprietors. In 1828 Marcus again is mayor, but on the next seesaw for control, Ike returns and serves for five two-year terms, with a Winchester victory only in 1831-1833.

It was during his first years in Memphis that Marcus Winchester defied the deepest rooted taboo of the South, and in so doing he wrecked his own life. His good friend, Tom Benton, had as a mistress a lovely French quadroon of New Orleans. This arrangement in itself was not unusual. Many Orleanians kept dusky mistresses, and in Memphis, Ike Rawlings lived openly with his mulatto housekeeper. There were few of the early Memphis settlers, deprived of women of their own color, who did not have a Negro or Indian woman as concubine. But Tom Benton, who was about to seek a United States senatorship from Missouri, decided that his beautiful, educated mistress would be a dangerous political encumbrance during his campaign and a social liability later in Washington. She must be replaced by a wife. So he endowed her with ample funds and asked Marcus Winchester to act as her trustee.

Instead, Marcus married his accomplished quadroon ward. Thenceforth, throughout their lives, the Winchesters were ostracized socially, though not politically, by the outraged Memphians who tolerated concubinage between the races but would not sanction matrimony. The alliance was seized upon by the enemies of the proprietors, and by the straiter-laced Memphians as a bludgeon for unsuccessful efforts to drive Marcus from the town. But he stuck it out; and strangely he never lost the respect of most of the men of Memphis nor their political support. Years later they were to send this husband of a "yaller gal" to the state legislature. And after his death a Memphis newspaper would recall in the seventies that "there never was a member of any community more esteemed while he lived than Major Marcus B. Winchester, the most graceful, courtly, elegant gentleman that ever appeared on Main Street." Marcus Winchester, embittered by personal tragedy, was to take heavily to drink in later years. His son, an even more tragic figure than his parents, would eventually return to marry one of that race of whose blood only one-eighth flowed in his veins.

In the out-of-the-way settlement, Marcus Winchester found one ally whose presence there seemed even stranger than his own. She was tall Frances Wright, a masculine-looking, handsome Scotswoman, who had been a protégée of Lafayette and was to found near Memphis one of the strangest Utopias ever launched in the United States. Long before Harriet Beecher Stowe had learned to write her name, agnostic Frances Wright was dreaming of freedom for the Negro slaves. First visiting the States in Lafayette's entourage, she returned in 1818 in pursuit of her dream. Through Lafayette's influence she was aided by Andrew Jackson in the acquisition of two thousand acres of land on Wolf River near Memphis. There she established Nashoba, a co-operative colony whose principal purpose was the freeing of slaves.

Her method was to buy slaves and remove them to Nashoba. As soon as the profits from their co-operative labor reached their purchase price they were to become free.

Even aside from his personal life, Winchester was similarly advanced in his attitude toward slavery. A supporter of emancipation, he contributed funds and personal efforts to Frances Wright's doomed experiment. One wishes that an unobserved recorder could have noted the frequent consultations of this custom-defying pair, each so anathematized by conformists, each burning with the same raceless spark.

In 1826 Fannie Wright became ill, and in 1827 she left Nashoba. Her heterogeneous associates, some depraved, some completely impractical, made a travesty of Nashoba, which degenerated into a vicious rendezvous of free love and racial amalgamation. In 1828 she revisited the colony in company with Mrs. Trollope. But finally, in 1829, Frances Wright gave up. The last thirty slaves at Nashoba were emancipated and sent to Haiti.

Although Marcus Winchester wrote despairingly in 1834 that "it matters little whether the railroad terminates at Fort Pickering or Fuller—in either event the young Memphis must be merged with its greater rivals," John Overton's town was destined for importance. Surviving competition, the inroads of the flatboatmen, bitter factionalism, and the head start of the older towns, Memphis with its 27,623 inhabitants was by 1860 the sixth largest city in the South.

The city has never lost its distinguishing quality. Even today it is the most American town on the lower river, closer in social and economic kinship to the Midwest than to the lower valley. Memphis is still frontier Protestant, for most of its Irish Catholic immigrant population was to be killed off by the yellow fever epidemic of 1878; and it still radiates the spirit of the boom-town promoter which animated Jackson and Overton and Winchester. In its conviviality, Memphis takes its whisky neat, and not in the outlandish concoctions of New Orleans. In its politics it differs too; for Memphis is still directed by its proprietary class. Few examples of democratic government in the tradition of the New England town meeting or the multiparty independence of the Midwest exist in the lower valley, and Memphis is no exception to this lack. But the distinction between directed government in Memphis and in New Orleans is basic. Succeeding political machines in New Orleans have not dissociated themselves from the earthy demands of the mass appetite. In Memphis the machine is operated by and for those who are embracingly described as "solid citizens." And in its attitude toward less substantial and non-conformist souls, Memphis is still akin to those earlier residents who condoned accepted vices while making social martyrs of Marcus Winchester and his French quadroon wife.

PART THREE

Valley Flowering

CHAPTER 13

The Sweet Crystals of Monsieur de Boré

An INSECT plague and the most horrible massacres
in New World history combined to give sugar to the lower
river as its first successful money crop.

Sugar was not a new venture when indigo failed and
when the first survivors of Santo Domingo's brutal racial
wars sought refuge in Louisiana, but as an agricultural experiment it had been suspect and unremunerative.

The colonials had always had difficulty in making profits
from their plantations. Indigo had been the first crop to pay
them well. But after the Spanish acquisition in 1765, the
new masters gave preference in indigo purchases to the older
Spanish colonies, where a better quality was grown. Though
fairer regulations later aided the Louisianians, bad seasons
piled upon worse ones. Then in 1793-1794 a strange new
insect, which ate the leaves of the ill-smelling plant, ruined
indigo planting in Louisiana.

Other crops had been tried previously by the farmers of
the river, so neglected by their succession of rulers. The cultivation of myrtle wax, for candles, and silk had been undertaken and abandoned. Tobacco was grown for home consumption only; owing to weather and soil conditions it was
not commercially practicable on the river. Cotton had been
planted since the earliest days, and even by 1768 had become
an article of export. At the time of the collapse of indigo, the
Creoles were beginning to turn more frequently to cotton for

revenue, spurred by Monsieur Dubreuil's invention of a fairly successful gin.

But the manufacture of sugar from the delectable juice of the cane had not been successfully introduced. Yet, it had flourished elsewhere in the New World, particularly in Santo Domingo where one Pierre d'Étienne had brought the cane to the island. In 1751 the Jesuits imported cane to Louisiana. A fleet of French troopships en route to Louisiana touched that year at Santo Domingo. The Jesuits of the island were permitted to ship a quantity of cane to their brethren of Louisiana, together with a number of Negro slaves acquainted with its culture.

So the Louisiana Jesuits planted this cane on a tract of land above New Orleans. The crop matured in the fall of 1751, somewhat to the amazement of the brothers.

The following year, one of the most ingenious of Louisiana settlers tried out the new crop himself. He was the Sieur Claude Joseph Dubreuil, who had emigrated from Dijon in 1719 with his wife and two children, at the age of twenty-four. Settling on Bayou St. John above the city, he readily established himself as probably the most advanced man in the colony. A hard worker, Dubreuil had mechanical as well as agricultural aptitude. In 1727 it was said of him that "his lot is the largest, the finest, the best cleared in the colony. He has been the first to make levees and deep ditches for the drainage of the waters in the swamps to keep his land dry. He gave the idea and made himself from 7 to 8 thousand toises of canals" (a toise being 6 to 9 feet).

By 1744, Dubreuil owned five hundred Negroes, several plantations, brick kilns, and silk manufactories. It was no wonder that this progressive settler erected a sugar-cane grinding mill in 1752. For a while the crop had some success, although cane was used principally for chewing and for making taffia, a heady cheap drink to which the population became immoderately addicted. D'Estrehan, the king's treasurer, and a number of other planters followed Dubreuil. But they couldn't master the granulating process. Bad luck also followed their first exports, for the sugar leaked from the hogsheads, and the cargo ship was so lightened that she almost capsized. By 1769 sugar had been abandoned by all but a handful of planters, who continued to grow it for the local market only, partly because of Spanish restrictions but principally because their sugar was a failure. Only half granulated and wet, it looked like marmalade or guava jelly. The planters had not learned the judicious use of lime nor the proper point of concentration for striking.

Sugar-cane culture continued to decline until the 1780's. In that decade a Spaniard named Solis bought a wooden sugar mill in Havana. He turned out only molasses and rum; and finally unsuccessful, he sold his mill and holdings to Don Antonio Mendez, the king's procurator under Spain. Mendez secured, in addition, the services of a Cuban sugar maker, and in 1791 produced the first real sugar in Louisiana. This, however, was in such small quantity that it was simply a curiosity and not a commercial product.

Then, in the same year, sugar making received unexpected impetus. The first great insurrection of the Santo Domingo blacks brought conflict without quarter. Fleeing the bloody island, a number of Santo Domingans came to New Orleans, the forerunners of a stream of refugees from the intermittent slaughter. Immediately they began to persuade the Louisianians to turn to sugar cane, the only crop with which they were really familiar.

And this brings us to Étienne de Boré, the first successful sugar planter of the river.

❧   ❧

De Boré was a son of the upper valley. He was born in Kaskaskia, in the Illinois district of Louisiana, of a distinguished family of Old World France. His parents returned to

France when Étienne was a small boy, and there he was raised.

In his young manhood he became a Mousquetaire Noir, a royal guardsman, his mousquetaire rank of captain giving him the army grade of lieutenant general. In 1771 he married the lovely daughter of d'Estrehan, and in 1774 he returned to Louisiana to settle on his wife's indigo plantation above New Orleans.

The subsequent decline of indigo threatened de Boré and his wife with ruin. The aging guardsman—he was fifty-four when he abandoned the traditional indigo crop in 1794—met the Santo Domingo newcomers, and listened eagerly to their tale of twenty-five years of sugar prosperity.

Though most of his friends warned him against foolish experimentation, de Boré bought quantities of cane from Mendez and Solis. Then, with thirty Negro slaves, he set out a plantation at considerable expense, built a mill, a drying room, and a shed. He was shorthanded, for able slaves cost from $1,200 to $1,500, and he could not afford them now. He hired the Cuban sugar maker who had worked for Mendez and Solis. And when the cane had ripened in the fall, de Boré watched as the slaves carted it to the mill.

One can almost see the old mousquetaire in the dark, steaming sugarhouse, the battery of caldrons seeming to swell with the heavy yellow juice, awaiting the conclusion of his experiment. Dripping black slaves lift their huge ladles from kettle to kettle, while de Boré, dipping into the ever-thickening fluids, from the succession of containers, continues the testing. Finally, a group of fellow planters, watching incredulously, hear a shouting slave: "It granulates!"

De Boré the foolish one becomes de Boré the savior. That first crop brought $12,000.

The next year two hundred planters were emulating de Boré. And by 1800 the colonial government was so impressed with the new crop that it issued a proclamation suspending the existing prohibition of the importation of Negro slaves. The culture of sugar cane required too many additional hands.

Seven years after de Boré's initial success, New Orleans had become the market for 200,000 gallons of rum, 250,000 gallons of molasses, and 5,000,000 pounds of sugar. The little sugar-cane capital counted a half dozen distillers and a refinery which alone produced about 200,000 pounds of loaf sugar.

Meanwhile, the visionary Étienne de Boré had become quite a personage. From the Old World as well as the colony, important men visited his plantation to inspect this agricultural gold mine. One of the earliest of them was General Victor Collet, an officer of the rising Napoleon, who in 1796 made a voyage of observation down the Mississippi, under the mistrustful eyes of Spain. General Collet noted in detail the method of operation; and he commented that although the only sugar refiner in the colony is in de Boré's service, he is permitted to refine for others when his employer's work is done.

The general's visit had an abrupt ending. Fearing that Collet was plotting with the Louisiana Frenchmen to regain the colony, the Spanish government sent fifty dragoons by land and an armed small boat upriver to seize the general at de Boré's home. He was escorted to the Balize, the entry point at the mouth of the river, and from there dispatched unceremoniously to Philadelphia. The indignant de Boré escaped arrest only because plump, choleric Governor Carondelet knew of his immense popularity with the people.

Two years later there arrived three especially notable guests. They were the Duc d'Orléans and his two brothers, the Duc de Montpensier and the Count de Beaujolais, the sons of Philippe Égalité. The three royal visitors were entranced with Monsieur de Boré's sugarhouse, though they were probably even more delighted by the succession of banquets and balls in their honor. On this occasion de Boré was overshadowed by the colony's most resplendent citizen, the great landowner Pierre Philippe de Marigny, who was reputed to have been worth $7,000,000 at his death. His plantation home, facing the river between Esplanade and the Champs-Élysées, was twice the size of an ordinary mansion, a massive, timber structure with brick pillars, approached by an avenue of oaks which ran from the river to the front portals.

The émigré princes remained in New Orleans for three months, and legend has it that at one banquet the cigars were lighted with $100 bills. They had the run of the city. In Marigny's finest carriage they drove around New Orleans to call on fluttering young ladies, visited de Boré's plantation six miles away, and dined and wined with scores of the loyal young gentlemen of France. When they left, Marigny "loaned" them a handsome sum. And when the Duc d'Orléans became king, he was visited by his New Orleans host.

Nor did de Boré's eminence fit him only for entertaining visitors of note. De Laussat, France's last representative before the cession, had him appointed mayor of New Orleans, a position which he continued to hold during the early years of American domination. His popularity with the French and his sagacity in handling the intrusive Americans justified the comment that de Laussat made at the time of his appointment: "a gentleman renowned for his patriotism and for a character of undeviating independence. I made a powerful appeal to him in the name of his country whose interests required his services and I had the satisfaction to win him over. After M. de Boré and through his influence I secured the services of some of the most distinguished among the colonists."

But Monsieur de Boré was more interested in his beloved plantation than in helping the Americans administer this sullen territory. Surely he had reason to prefer it, for that plantation would have graced any land in any age.

His great house was surrounded by gardens. Shady avenues of orange trees and dense retreats of myrtle and laurel defied the sun. His grapevines were protected by wire netting to keep away the birds, but the pigeons were free to peck at the black cherries on whose overripeness they would become drunk and fall from the trees.

All about was plenty. The plantation produced its own sheep for wool, its geese, ducks, turkeys, chickens, and guinea fowl. Eggs were "gathered by the bushel." Herds of cattle, tended under the direction of especially chosen slaves, provided fresh butter and cheese, cream, milk, and clabber. Bees vied with the tall, purple cane to provide sweetstuffs for the table. De Boré's vast barns were stocked with corn, rice, and hay, and in the outhouses stood a wide selection of carriages. As if the earth did not provide enough, shrimp and fish came from the river; the swamp produced raccoons and possums so esteemed by the slaves; crawfish abounded in the ditches. And considerably behind the house stood a large, stagnant pool, a rendezvous of snipe, water hens, and rails.

From the plantation, cartloads of produce left daily for the New Orleans market before dawn, to be delivered to and sold by two old crones, Agatha and Marie, guardians of the sumptuous town house of de Boré. Josephine, a handsome mulattress, and a duskier aide took the milk and butter to town, returning by ten in the morning with the mail and papers. Altogether the farm produce supplied all the needs of the plantation and brought an extra $6,000 profit, leaving the sugar crop as completely free income.

From the public road, which wound upriver, an avenue of pecan trees led to the enclosure of the de Boré plantation. For more than three hundred feet on each side of the entrance gate ran a brick revetment five feet high, and an earthen, clover-covered rampart, which sloped to a large moat stocked with edible fish, frogs, and eels. Along this road came the visitors from New Orleans, twenty each Sunday; and once a year there arrived the leather-gaitered horse traders from Texas, clanking six-inch spurs as they drove their horses from plantation to plantation.

Within this feudal paradise the blue-eyed, benevolent old sugar king held court. It was almost as formal as Versailles. At dinner he occupied the center of the table, and every guest stood until he beckoned them to be seated. No latecomer could even enter the dining room. But on occasion the old Frenchman would make exceptions. Too old to fight in the Battle of New Orleans, he entertained Andrew Jackson, Generals Coffee and Carroll of the Tennessee troops, and members of their military suites for weeks afterward. Some of the backwoods American officers persisted in putting their feet on the table; but instead of remonstrating, de Boré merely remarked later that their actions were excusable since they followed the customs of their country.

The Negroes of his estate were more generously treated than most. De Boré forbade whipping, though recalcitrants were put in the stocks for a night or all day. The slaves lived in a double row of cabins near the sugarhouse and behind every cabin were a hogpen and hen house, and a garden plot. They were permitted to gather driftwood on Sundays, which they sold for $1 a cord, retaining the money; and they were paid for overtime labor. Clothing was distributed twice a year, the principal garment being a blanketlike frock with attached hood, and a pair of quantiers of cured oxhide, cut in the shape of the foot and laced and stuffed with hay or rags.

The old man prided himself on his ancestry, his civic standing, and the beautiful wife of whom it was said it was worthwhile to travel fifty leagues to see Madame de Boré take a pinch of snuff. But most of all he took pride in the shining sweet crystals which he had proved could bring for-tune to Louisiana's planters. Even the police jurors held their meetings in the sugarhouse before adjourning to the mansion for dinner, and no visitor was permitted to leave before view-ing its wonders.

It was a sight to see. From the cane fields came the tall, dark stalks, tied in bunches and hauled on little mule-drawn wagons to the mill. There, upon a huge table stood three large cast-iron cylinders, arranged vertically in a straight line. The center cylinder, propelled by mules, gave impulse to the other two. On one side of them stood Negroes feeding the purple stalks into these grinders; on the other, slaves caught the crushed cane and returned it for a second feeding. The dark juice thus squeezed out fell into a gutter and from thence ran into a reservoir.

The crushed stalks, the bagasse, were tied in bundles and dried for future burning in the mill furnaces. Today, this refuse of the cane is manufactured into wallboard.

From the reservoir, the brownish fluid went into the first of a series of copper kettles atop the furnaces. And here the skilled refiner supervised the granulating process from the first to the last kettle, directing the skimming of impurities, watching for the motey lightness that indicates the amount of lime needed to bring on the granulation. Finally, the crys-tals form in the boiling sweetness. M'sieu de Boré's sugar is ready.

Sugar made Étienne de Boré and many another Lower Mississippi planter wealthy. Sugar built many of the show-place plantations between New Orleans and Baton Rouge, and sugar's misfortunes turned so many into empty ruins. And sugar today is not the least of the river's will-o'-the-wisps, pursued by planters whose acres are factories of tall waving cane; whose dream is of a long succession of seasons blessed with protected bountifulness, whose political hopes center on the exclusion of the competition of faraway isles.

CHAPTER 14

When Cotton Ruled

IT WAS inevitable that after his ascendancy to the agricultural throne King Cotton should establish his richest baronies on the Lower Mississippi.

The valley's alluvial soil was the most fertile in the nation. It was sparsely settled and cheaply obtained. The river itself provided assured means of transportation of cotton to New Orleans, a principal port of the United States. So as intensive cultivation wore out the older lands to the east, the cotton growers moved from the Atlantic coastal plain, the Piedmont and Cumberland plateaus, and the Blue Ridge and Allegheny valleys to the seemingly inexhaustible lowlands of the Mississippi. With their coming, the river and cotton became inseparable in legend and in fact.

We can arbitrarily set 1830 to 1860 as the dates of cotton's halcyon days on the river. There is nothing arbitrary in the implications of this planter civilization, far reaching then and far reaching now. Nowhere has this ancient and most important of vegetable fibers exercised a stronger directive force upon the people producing it.

Thomas Jefferson believed that agriculture was the basis of the good life as opposed to Alexander Hamilton's reliance upon finance and industry. In this basic distinction, the South followed Jefferson; but cotton twisted the Monticello pattern and made meaningless the Jeffersonian dream of independent husbandry. For even while Jefferson propounded his idealistic conception of the happy state, cotton was rising to haunt him. The Jeffersonian concept, which was the old English and the New England concept of agriculture, envisaged the yeoman supplying himself with food and with home-grown material for clothing. Today, along the Mississippi, this is called subsistence farming and is more preached than practiced. Even now white men and black men suffer from that redirection of agricultural effort in the 1790's, occasioned by economic forces unparalleled in history. A century and a half ago the world was seeking a new textile; and in England the eighteenth-century era of invention had produced machinery for cotton textile manufacture. Only a machine that would swiftly separate seed from lint was lacking.

The American colonies had been familiar with the cotton plant since 1621, when Jamestown's colonists first planted it. But the handmade, finished cloth was poor, and the market remained local. Only the indigent wore cotton homespun, for wool, linen, and silk were available and more desirable to those who could purchase them. When English machinery began production of suitable cotton textiles, the American Revolution cut off the colonies from the English products. This blockade encouraged domestic spinning, and with its rise came the idea of cotton as a money crop. Mark that "money crop" well, for under the spell of cotton profits the South was to break with the Jeffersonian tradition, would produce for sale and not for self, and turn itself into a vast agricultural factory. By the end of the eighteenth century additional impetus to cotton culture came with the decline in profits in tobacco and rice along the lower Atlantic seaboard. Developments dovetailed with fateful precision. England was perfecting the factory system, and machinery for cotton spinning, carding, and weaving. The resultant cotton textiles became good enough to compete with linen and wool, and therefore rose in price. The demand for cotton goods and raw cotton increased enormously. The Levantine countries and the West Indies were incapable of crop expansion, so the southern United States became the great region of cotton production.

The first commercially important result was the cultivation of Sea Island cotton, introduced from the Barbados, which commanded the highest prices in the British market and established an enduring reputation for southern cotton. It was comparatively easy to extract the seed from this long-staple cotton with a crude roller gin, the only separating mechanism in existence prior to 1793. The trouble with Sea Island cotton was that it couldn't be grown elsewhere in the South; and ginning the shorter fibered cotton which could be produced everywhere else was a slow, laborious, and comparatively costly process.

Then in 1793 Eli Whitney fashioned his gin. Such an invention was inevitable, and Whitney was more lucky than brilliant; for the groundwork had been laid and many other persons were also tinkering with gins. Actually, the Piedmont was so confident in 1793 of an immediate invention that it had already planted a three million pound yield of short-staple cotton.

Whitney's box gin was easy to reproduce. So as the device spread under his and rival patents, the last obstacle to the spread of cotton culture vanished. Commercial farming and the slave system united the hill and lowland regions of the South. Land values tripled. Cotton began to push into the tobacco lands of Virginia and the Carolinas. For the first thirty years of the nineteenth century, the cotton boom roared through the southeastern belt. Export demand continued greater than supply. Despite setbacks during the embargo period of 1807-1809 and the War of 1812, cotton expansion continued almost uninterruptedly from the turn of the century until the Civil War. Practically displacing all other textile materials, cotton held from 1825 a near-monopoly in the European market.

What did this mean to the South and especially to the

development of the Mississippi? Most significant was the shaping of a disastrous policy of emphasis upon the slave and of exhaustion of the land. The slavery system fitted perfectly with cotton culture, for the unskilled Negro was most easily adapted to the simple, cyclical routine of the plantation. The black man, the southern immigrant who settled without choice, became the principal investment of the South. In 1790 there were 750,000 of him in the United States. In 1830 he numbered 2,328,000 and in 1860, 4,441,000, of whom four million were southern slaves, investments which quadrupled by the basic, plantation-encouraged process of reproduction.

Thus did cotton embrace the South. But the spread of the cotton kingdom, was impossible without continuous land expansion. Soil wore out. Planters burned with the fever of swelling profits. And as they sought fertile, larger holdings, the gulf and river states, Alabama, Mississippi, Louisiana and Arkansas, inevitably became the second and greater province of King Cotton.

And this brings us to the river. The precise historian must deplore the kaleidoscopic oversimplification of a story, of fantastically complex speculation, land frauds, and colonization. The romanticist must also protest a condensation which neglects the drama of the inexorable southwestward advance. The poet would want to put into words the synchronization of the life cycle of the river and cotton: the thrusting seeds bursting into sunlight in the lush, green spring when the river itself throbs and swells with the maternal burden of a thousand tributaries; the white, autumnal birth of the fibered bolls, when a tired river flows in unthreatening majesty between the fields it has created, fertilized, and at intervals of infanticidal frenzy destroyed.

But to be inclusive the narrative must be unadorned. On the heels of the Louisiana Purchase, cotton conquered the Lower Mississippi Valley in the first quarter of the nineteenth century. In 1800 only 88,000 people, of whom half were slaves, lived in the entire Louisiana Territory, with Natchez as the center of population. Iniquitous Indian treaties cleared new acres, and wholesale land sales began in 1807. The great migration followed the War of 1812, whose loudest mongers had settled in this deep, rich, new South. Land skyrocketed from $2 to $10 and even $16 an acre. In five years, from 1815 to 1820, almost a half million Americans moved south-westward, bringing statehood to Louisiana in 1812, Mississippi in 1817, Alabama in 1819. Across the river, Arkansas counted 14,000 population by 1820; Missouri, 66,000. The older planters of the river—the French, the Tory English, and the earlier American adventurers—who had experimented with sugar, tobacco, and corn as well as cotton, succumbed to the wild urging of the one-crop system. The institution of land killing had reached the Mississippi.

And with the spread of the kingdom, something else reached the river. These newcomers were the sons and grandsons of English and Scotch-Irish colonials who had developed their own kind of culture in the southeastern states. To the uncleared river acres they brought their chattels and their seaboard memories. They blessed their wilderness holdings with proud, poetic, gentle names, steeped in the new romantic tradition of England. They came to exploit the land but not to migrate again from the lands they exploited; for near by lay seemingly endless and purchasable acres to be added to initial boundaries. If their encroachment meant displacement for squatter and poor white and their wastefulness poverty for generations a hundred years unborn, they could not be concerned. Always, westward, for their descendants, the land would be bright; politically, socially, economically, their inseparables of inexhaustible lands and the institution of slavery would endure. Or so they thought, when they thought about it at all. Slave labor was suited, they observed, only to cotton's simple sequence of cultivation. The slave was easily fed, for corn made hogs and both made for cheap provisioning. He was amenable to working in gangs under overseers. He was a cash commodity in case of a pinch. And there would always be new lands for him to cultivate.

From the hedonistic enterprise of the river planters of the thirties grew a pleasant culture which in turn created a pleasant legend. Of the culture, there remains principally a scattering of wide-porched, stately homes. The planter legend has outbuilt the grandest of these; and the latter-day destruction of this myth would have been a pity had not the reality itself been a prideful thing. The men who built these homes were not cavaliers and but rarely of cavalier stock. But they developed their own kindly, sturdy aristocracy. Most of them were not cultured in the erudite definition of contemporaneous Boston or even Virginia; for colic and yellow fever remedies, a sure eye and a green thumb were more important than philosophy, literature, and art on this new frontier. Primarily, they were simply farmers on a large scale. As a class they were autocratic by virtue of their sovereignty over men and broad acres, headstrong, mostly provincial in outlook, extravagant, violent, careless. But not even the most painstaking demolisher of the river planter myth can successfully dispute that as a class they were also amazingly hospitable and tenacious and clannishly loyal and generous; good livers who admired and sought to own beautiful homes, fast horses, and not infrequently a comely slave woman or two. Earthy longings, but not without merit.

❦   ❦

I intended to make this chapter just the story of a representative cotton planter in the river's agricultural heyday. Yet to the understanding of any such person this preface has been necessary; and the brief delineation of the agricultural background has been no more difficult than the selection of an archetype of the prosperous river planter. I am convinced that almost every plantation owner on the Lower Mississippi kept a diary and that every one of those diaries survived high water, low cotton, and the war. Those I have scanned—and they are many—are fascinatingly human documents. Some record inordinate successes, which are not typical, and some mirror bleak failures, which also are not typical. From them all I have chosen the record which was kept by one Bennet H. Barrow, as presenting an example between the extremes of great wealth and abysmal collapse.

Bennet H. Barrow beat the southwestern land push by being there when it started. He was the youngest son of William Barrow II who migrated to the Felicianas in Louisiana near the end of the eighteenth century and who was a leader in the West Florida rebellion. The elder Barrow's plantation, Locust Grove, was situated some twelve miles north of St. Francisville, which lies on the river above Baton Rouge. He grew and marketed his cane and cotton so successfully that at his death his estate was inventoried at $214,930.80. His holdings included 348 slaves and 7,160 arpents of land—an arpent being a French measurement varying from .84 to 1.28 acres—divided into six plantations.

Young Bennet inherited the Locust Grove plantation of 1,400 arpents. At nineteen he married Emily Joor, renamed the plantation Highland, and in 1830 began an independent farming career. He kept his diary from 1833 to 1846, and the story which follows is taken from his jottings.

The yearly cotton planting at Highland averaged from 600 to 750 acres, with yields ranging from 375 to nearly 700 bales. Barrow liked to note favorable comments on his crops: "they have seen no crop at all to compare with it, from half leg to waist high bolled & formed as well as can be for the season several grown Boles on a stalk." But when worms, grasshoppers, lice, and plant diseases struck his fields he would become depressed: "never saw worse look cotton, twisted trash beat in it & stained cotton blown so as not able to trace the rows, worms Eating all the Leaves off."

While cotton was Highland's money crop, the rolling Feliciana land produced many others in happy contrast to the insufficient diversion that later was to plague the river. For the livestock, the plantation grew oats, hay and fodder, corn and peas. A slave crew tilled a communal truck garden. Behind the Negro quarters stood an orchard of peach, plum, apple, and other fruit trees. Tobacco was grown, but only for home consumption. The Highland barns sheltered seventy to eighty head of horses and mules; and in the meadows grazed oxen, kept to drag timber from the swamps, and some two hundred beef cattle. Large herds of hogs and sheep and flocks of chickens were raised to help feed the plantation's nearly two hundred slaves. Most of the work was performed manually, but Barrow's gins and presses were steam driven, and in the late thirties he converted his sawmill and grinding mills from horse to steam power. In not too orderly fashion he practiced the latest farming methods of the time, grafting fruit trees, rotating crops, manuring fields, and scattering leafy molds from the timber tracts upon the cultivated lands.

Bennet Barrow earned from his plantation a more than comfortable income, though he turned much of his cotton and sugar-cane profits into additional acreage. Returns from his yearly cotton sales fluctuated from $7,000 to $25,000. At his death he owned six plantations, as did his father before him, with a total acreage of 5,000 arpents. He was a shrewd land dealer, purchasing more than he sold. Infected with the universal desire to keep acquiring land, he was continually borrowing from banks and individuals to finance his acquisitions, usually on purchase terms of one-third cash down with the balance in three years. A good financial risk himself, his carelessness and readiness to endorse the notes of friends cost him about $22,000 between 1836 and 1846.

An English physician, Dr. Desmond, a man "of uncommonly gentlemanly manners—modesty and chastity," nicked him for something more than $10,000. The doctor skipped the country, leaving Barrow to make good the notes he had endorsed. Sadly young Barrow recorded in 1840: "This crop would have paid every Dollar I owed—but owing to my Endorsing—will take two more crops to clear me of Debt— never Endorse . . . for a man Extravagant and careless in business . . ." At the same time he wrote: "my course will be a Lesson to my children—that is never to loan what is not your own—if you owe anything pay it first—I borrowed money for other persons 'friends' & now have to pay it over. Mind Who proffesses to be your friend—you see a man working hard & economizing help him, but see a fellow dressing fine, using fine language & they are What is called clever fellows—let them pass." Yet in 1844 he was still being victimized: "sincerely wish every rascal and persons causing me to be in Debt in Hell riding a red hot iron."

An altogether human man, Bennet Barrow. And none knew this better than his slaves. Only once did he record the sale of slaves. This was in 1836 when he realized $1,760 in New Orleans for Big Sam and Amy who were "not worth $5." Nor did he believe in the overseer system. He employed overseers only until 1837, at which time he decided to get rid of them and with the help of his "Drivers"—slave foremen—supervise the hands himself. In 1837 he noted: "more Whiping to do this fall than all together in three years owing to my D mean overseer—never will have another unless I should be compelled to leave—they are a perfect nuisance." And in 1839 he commented: "I hope the time will come when every Overseer in the country will be compelled to addopt some other mode of making a living—they are a perfect nuisance cause dissatisfaction among the negroes—being more possessed of more brutal feelings—I make Better crops than those Who employ them."

He supervised his slaves' labor closely, studying their working habits and telling them how to do better jobs. In 1840 he observed: "I am well paid for my trouble in teaching my small gang to Hoe, never saw such hoe hands as they are, two years ago took two on a row—now Eaquel to a woman, in dricting [directing] them to make a slow and sure lick in one place & to cut the full width with the hoe every time—unless reminded of it they would stand & make 4 or 5."

The Negroes at Highland were well fed and adequately clothed. At Christmastime they received money and apparel as presents. "I prefer giving them money at Xmas to their making anything, thereby creating an interest with you & yours—if a negro is suffered to sell anything he chooses without any inquiry being made, a spirit of trafficing at once is created to carry this on, both means and time are necessary, neither of which is he of right possessed. A negro would not be content to sell only what he raises or makes or either corn . . . or poultry or the like, but he would sell a part of his allowance allso, & would be tempted to commit roberries to obtain things to sell."

There were other opportunities for the Barrow slaves to win gifts. He liked to divide his field hands into rival crews to pick crops and to perform other plantation tasks. The losers gave the winners a dinner, and the winners in addition were awarded prizes.

Barrow seemed to be especially concerned with the material welfare of his slaves. New wells were dug frequently and old ones cleaned. Cabins were repaired each year. Barrow constructed a dance hall for his slaves in 1838. The Highland jail, infrequently occupied, was always kept cleaned. In his clothing allowance, the Highland Negro received two suits or dresses a year, two extra pairs of shoes for the winter, new blankets every third year. All slaves over four years old received five pounds of "good clear meat" a week, and hogs, sheep, and cattle were slaughtered in large numbers, especially during holidays. In unusual contrast to other planters, Barrow bought much sugar and molasses and sometimes flour to vary the meat, corn meal, and garden vegetable diet.

Not a churchgoer himself, he tolerated rather than encouraged religion. Trouble among slaves on a neighboring plantation in 1844 arose, he believed, from their being "preached to for 4 or 5 years years past—greatest piece of foolishness any one ever guilty of . . . no true Christianity among church going whites—& how expect to Preach morrality among a set of ignorant beings—proper discipline may improve them & make them better." Yet he was himself concerned in his own way with the morals of his slaves. Marriage was encouraged on Highland, miscegenation opposed. In 1837 he wrote: "had a general Whipping frollick. White man sending for some of my women by one of my boys, one eyed Sam —A load of buckshot will be the dose if I can see them or find them."

The health of the slaves was carefully watched. The plantation routine was nevertheless frequently upset by cases of lockjaw, pleurisy, rupture, colds, and other injuries; and the doctor bill ran more than $500 in some years, for medical attention was quickly sought when an illness or mishap occurred. To vary the monotony of labor, celebrations were frequently permitted: "finding no cotton to trash, sent for the Fiddler & made them dance from 12 till dark."

Barrow could be stern when events warranted. Highland was run by a rigid set of slave rules, for "a plantation might be considered as a piece of machinery, to operate successully all its parts must be uniform and exact." The slaves could not marry away from the plantation nor wander from it during holidays. Their working hours were precisely prescribed and enforced. Runaways were severely punished.

"I had rather a negro would do anything Else than runaway," Barrow wrote. He usually rounded up such fugitives himself. Of a habitual leave-taker he wrote: "ran and trailed about a mile, treed him, made the dogs pull him out of the tree, Bit him very badly, think he will stay home a while." Of another: "dogs soon tore him naked, took him Home Before the other negro[es] at dark & made the dogs give him another over hauling." Occasional entries read: "my hands worked badly—general Whiping," and "whipped every field hand this evening."

But Barrow deplored wanton cruelty. Of one neighboring family he commented: "a meaner set than the Howells do not live—cruel and unjust to the extreme." And again: "went to Town man tried for Whipping a negro to Death. trial will continue till tomorrow—deserves death—Cleared!"

He recorded the death of favorite slaves with feeling. Of Old Orange, "a more perfect negro never lived, faithful, honest & purely religious, never knew him guilty of a wrong." And of George, who drowned, "a very great loss. one of the best negroes I ever saw, or knew. to his family as a white person." He was quick to defend his slaves against unjust accusation. Hearing that a neighbor had blamed a Barrow slave for a fire in his gin, Barrow wrote that he planned to visit him and "if he says it was Dennis, I will curse him & if I ever catch one of his negroes on this side of the creek will make them see sights."

The abolitionist movement was one of three national issues that caused him to express concern, the others being the annexation of Texas and corruption in office. Contemptuous of northern advocates of freedom, he wrote during a visit of two "D. Yankees" of the "impudence of their section of the country"; and goaded past enduring finally gave them "a hint to leave that no Southernor would mistake—ordered their horses back."

Never an aspirant for high office he served his own locality continuously from 1833 to 1846 as overseer of his

road district, overseer of the poor, member of the grand jury
and of the police jury, a parish governing body.

Despite the demands on his time incident to directing
the continuous operations of a large plantation—sowing and
harvesting the money staples and the food and feed crops,
clearing land, sawing timber, repairing buildings and implements, supervising two hundred slaves—Bennet Barrow
found plenty of time to enjoy himself. The family owned
a small steamer, the *Nimrod*, for hunting and fishing. Barrow and his neighbors rode to hounds, and hunted deer, bear,
opossum, alligator, and wildfowl at night by torchlight. They
fished in Radcliff's Lake and Big and Little Bayou Sara.
But best of all, the Barrows loved horse racing. Barrow was
the second largest stockholder in the St. Francisville Race
Track, and for a while was official timer and a consistent
wagerer at the famed Louisiana Jockey Club in New Orleans. He and his brother William owned two horses of especial note, Fanny Bell and Josh Bell, the latter lauded by the
Spirit of the Times in 1842 as "one of the best horses of the
year." These thoroughbreds won several purses of more than
$1,000 each.

The Barrows and their neighbors didn't have to travel
far for entertainment. Visiting with resultant "frollicks"
was their most frequent diversion. In 1842 Bennet and Mrs.
Barrow "kidnaped" several young ladies and invited other
guests to Highland. "Would not let any leave," he chronicles.
"Got a violin player from Town . . . Let them rest & knap
during the day some times . . . playing smut—at dark began
to dance . . . never have seen A collection so sudden & so
perfectly free easy and happy for two days & nights, all
restraint thrown aside   never enjoyed myself so much." His
high, cool home must have been a frequent rendezvous.
Above the fireplace hung his portrait, painted by Tom
Thorpe, of Bee Hunter fame. In the large rooms of Highland his children studied under private tutors and tried to

master dancing and music lessons. On his library tables lay newspapers and magazines, the Charleston *Mercury*, the Woodville *Republican*, the *Spirit of the Times*, and others; and occasionally he added such new volumes as Johnson's *Life of Henry Clay* to his inherited small library.

"Here am I sitting with the Baby in my lap," he wrote in 1836. "Emily [his wife] criticizing the History of Georgia —Caroline & John at all kinds of mischeif." And the next year: "attempting to learn James and John their book— had rather drive a team of mules."

We will leave Bennet Barrow here with his wife and children around him. It is nearly a hundred years since he made the last entry in his diary, and almost that long since cotton has been undisputed and untroubled in its rule of the lower Mississippi. I am satisfied that Bennet Barrow's intimate, unsophisticated self-portrait and the record of his plantation fairly present the moderately successful planter of his period on the river: a man not enormously wealthy but prosperous; an out-of-doors, forthright sort of fellow, neither brilliant nor dull; solid in his virtues and likable in his weaknesses; trying his decent best to be kind and fair within the limits of a system of human bondage that in itself could be neither kind nor fair.

CHAPTER 15

Ol' Miss Meets Her Master

IN 1796 A GROUP of inventive and perhaps lazy Pennsylvania Dutchmen built a queer craft near Pittsburgh. It was a crude side-wheeler whose cumbersome paddles were turned by eight horses on a treadmill below deck. The Pennsylvanians expected great things of their paddle-wheeler which took them down the Ohio and the Mississippi with "prodigious swiftness." Their horse-powered freight boat would conquer the current and thereby secure a profitable return cargo from shippers delighted with its promised speed.

There was nothing wrong with their idea except that their poor nags broke down completely when they were pitted against the Mississippi's current on the upstream trip. The disillusioned voyagers abandoned boat and horses at Natchez and set out across country for home. And up and down the river folks said to each other that no newfangled contraption could ever best the river. Those fool Dutchmen ought to have known that sails and strong arms and occasionally a horse tow on the banks were all the force which man could sensibly employ against the Mississippi.

In all the years of Mississippi commerce men had found no better means of propulsion than these. The explorers and traders had adopted first the light bark canoe of Canada. Then, because there was no birchbark on the lower river, the French and the English turned to and developed the pirogue, hewn from the trunk of the cedar or walnut, until it was so large that bulkheads divided its freight compartments. To it they occasionally added a mast. Later river craft differed basically from the pirogue only in construction, for all were propelled by paddle, oar or sweep, with occasional sails and shore tows. The flat-bottomed mackinaw, the bullboat made of taut bison hide, the wide, military galley, and finally the legendary flatboat and keelboat became familiar to the trade-hungry valley.

Of them all, the flatboat and the keelboat dominated in the opening of the Mississippi to commerce and settlement. By 1810, approximately a million people had settled in the western territories, all of them dependent almost entirely upon the river highways. The flatboats carried them and their wares and their later necessities downriver on a one-way voyage which ended at New Orleans with the dismantling and sale of the flatboats for lumber. Built solely to take travelers and merchandise downstream, they were cheap, strictly utilitarian in design, and more often jerry-built than not. Their eight-foot holds were stacked with cargoes of staple foodstuffs, liquor and durable goods, the passengers living on the roofed deck or in unfilled corners below. They were steered from the stern by a 40- to 50-foot oar, with a smaller oar at the bow, and sweeps on each side.

At the turn of the eighteenth century they dominated the river trade. In the first six months of 1801 the exports from the United States to Spanish New Orleans were carried in 450 flatboats, 26 keelboats, a brig, two schooners, and seven pirogues. In 1817, 529 flatboats and 300 barges tied up in New Orleans; and even from 1820 to 1830, when the steamboat was beginning to monopolize the Mississippi commerce, 3,000 flatboats descended the river annually.

But the keelboats, the first queens of the river trade, couldn't survive the steamboat's competition as did the one-way ugly ducklings. The keelboat was a two-way traveler which couldn't compete on the upstream trips. Long, narrow, and trimly built, with a functional beauty of their own, these Pittsburgh boats did an amazing round-trip business until they were crowded out. They could carry up to 80 tons of freight, and though they made all possible use of sail the upriver trip was primarily a fight of men against the river. And a tough breed were the keelboat crews who rowed or poled the 7-footers and strained from the banks against the long cordelle. Our story here is about the steamboats, but it is worth while to quote a stanza from "The Hunters of Kentucky," which immortalized the overused phrase "alligator horses." The song was written by Samuel Woodworth—who also wrote "The Old Oaken Bucket"—in praise of the Kentucky riflemen who fought under Jackson at New Orleans. But an audience of keelboaters, hearing it sung at the French theater in New Orleans, whooped their adoption of this verse as their own:

> We are a hardy, freeborn race,
> Each man to fear a stranger;
> What e'er the game, we join the chase,
> Despising toil and danger;
> And if a daring foe annoys,
> No matter what his force is,
> We'll show him that Kentucky boys
> Are alligator horses.

Yet an Englishman named Isaac Watts had already harnessed a force before which the hardy, freeborn keelboatmen would vanish from the river.

Watt's steam engine coughed the prelude of the machine age. Rumsey and Fitch experimentally applied this new source of power to propelling boats; and then Robert Fulton, surviving disappointment and bitter attack, produced the *Clermont*. At last man had a vessel which was not tied to the winds or to his own animal strength.

Even so, the adaptation of the steamboat to such an untamed river as the Mississippi was despaired of by most shipping men. No such boat could survive the falls of the Ohio, nor the malignantly shifting channel of the Mississippi, nor the monstrous current. The man who experimented with steam on the Mississippi would be remembered only for his folly.

But another Dutchman challenged the river. He was Nicholas J. Roosevelt, a shrewd, adventurous New Yorker who, soon after Fulton had proved his steamboat, had taken out a patent on side-wheelers. Fulton himself, and his partner, Chancellor Livingston, meanwhile had been trying to protect their debt-burdened company by acquiring state steamboat monopolies. Shortly after, Roosevelt, who was making a nice thing from paddle-wheel royalties from independent operators, became a member of the company. The enterprising trio then began to plan the extension of their operations to the rivers of the western country.

First, however, they must learn the requirements of the turbulent western streams so different from the mild Hudson. So Roosevelt decided to take a flatboat trip down the Ohio and the Mississippi to study and report on river conditions, the possibility of profitable trade and the type of boat best adapted to the big rivers. This was to be no ordinary journey, for to the despair of his conservative friends, the adventurer and his bride decided to make it a honeymoon trip. The flatboat was accordingly fitted out with a bedroom, dining room and pantry, and a gay awning was hung over the deck. In this rarely luxurious craft the honeymooners, a pilot, cook, and crew of three set out down the broad Ohio in 1809.

Everywhere Nicholas was warned that the Ohio and the Mississippi were too swift and too treacherous and frequently too shallow for steamboats. Nevertheless, he went ahead, compiling his statistics on potential business; and in the fall the couple returned to New York by Atlantic coastal steamer and stagecoach, enthusiastic over the possibilities.

Back home, Nicholas persuaded Fulton and Livingston that the western country was ready for steamboating. So in March, 1811, the partners of the new Ohio Steamboat Navigation Company arrived in Pittsburgh for the launching of the *New Orleans*, a slate-blue, two-masted side-wheeler, which imported New York craftsmen had built for them at a cost of $38,000. A trial run on the Monongahela followed a month later. And then the two Roosevelts set out again for the Lower Mississippi, despite protests that a woman should not take such a dangerously experimental voyage.

At Cincinnati, at Cleveland, at dozens of obscure river ports, disbelieving citizens crowded the river front. A favored few came aboard at each stop. But there was no convincing them. They were unanimous in warning that the *New Orleans* might go some distance downstream but it could never buck the current. They were unconvinced even though Nicholas treated unsuspecting dinner guests at Louisville to a short upstream spin, and later, celebrating the birth of his first baby in Louisville, jubilantly steamed the *New Orleans* back to Cincinnati. Soon thereafter, with the mother and baby aboard, the *New Orleans* shot the razor-rock falls of the Ohio. The first obstacle had been overcome.

Now the epochal trip of the *New Orleans* was to be dwarfed by a cataclysmic performance of nature. Anchored below the fall, the steamboat was suddenly rocked by enormous waves. Around her the clay bluffs crumbled. She tugged crazily at her anchor, quivered until it seemed her timber would come apart. On her maiden voyage the *New Orleans* had been caught in the terrible series of tremors known as the New Madrid earthquake, probably the worst nonvolcanic earth shock in American history.

Much of the remainder of the trip was nightmarish. Through almost continuous disturbances the *New Orleans* churned slowly downriver, groping for old channels now vanished, looking vainly for familiar island landmarks, sight-ing strange new lakes. From the shore fear-mad Indians and settlers called to the adventurers to turn back. The Mississippi's swells were oceanic. Its red, earth-stained flow was clogged with uprooted trees, and great, twisted snags spewed up from the river bottom. At New Madrid, the ground had been split into wide, seemingly bottomless fissures running southeast to northwest. The *New Orleans* plowed stubbornly on. Better to keep going than to tie up. Finally the desolate region of the shocks lay behind them.

At untouched Natchez a shouting populace welcomed the pioneers. And here a chance-taking planter loaded a shipment of cotton, consigned to New Orleans. It was the first steamboat cargo on the Mississippi. On January 12, 1812, the *New Orleans* arrived in the city for which it was named. Nicholas Roosevelt, his bride, and the crew of the *New Orleans* had shown that it could be done.

❦ ❦

For two years the Ohio Steamboat Navigation Company enjoyed monopolistic privileges on the river. It demanded and received fees for every steamboat built in the West. The embryonic traffic, which still went no farther upriver than Natchez, was theirs. Then Captain Henry M. Shreve, no eastern financier but a western riverman, tackled them.

Henry Shreve was the son of a fighting New Jersey Quaker who moved west after the Revolution. The boy grew up on the rivers, making trading journeys by barge, keelboat, and pirogue down the Ohio and into the western country before he was out of his teens. He opened the fur trade between St. Louis, Pittsburgh, and Philadelphia in 1807, and in 1810 broke the British lead trade monopoly on the Mississippi.

The success of the *New Orleans* was a challenge to this successful bargeman, who soon became a stockholder and commander of the stern-wheeler *Enterprise,* built at Brownsville under the patents of Daniel French and Daniel Smith, and launched in 1814 at Bridgeport on the Monongahela.

The *Enterprise's* first trip was almost as eventful as that of the *New Orleans*. In December, 1814, Shreve brought a cargo of supplies for Andy Jackson's army from Pittsburgh to New Orleans. He capped the trip by running the British batteries below the city to deliver military stores to Fort St. Philip, then turned landsman long enough to help serve a 24-pounder in the Battle of New Orleans.

Not yet had a steamboat traveled far upriver. So, in the spring, Captain Shreve headed north for Louisville. Aided by the flood, which lessened the river's current as it spread out, he made it. For all but the most adamant disbelievers the test was conclusive. Steamboats could go both ways on the Mississippi.

Meanwhile, Shreve had run afoul of the Livingston company. The *Enterprise* had been seized in New Orleans on the charge that Shreve was violating the Easterners' monopolistic rights. While the case was argued lengthily in the courts, the *Enterprise* continued to ply the river.

Shreve was paying little attention to legal interferences, for a revolutionary idea had come to him. The trouble with the river steamers, he reasoned, was that they sat too deep in the water and therefore grounded easily. A river steamer should sail on the water, not in it. So, in 1816, he had his own kind of steamboat built at Wheeling. It was a grotesquely notable departure. The *Washington* had a flat, shallow hull and a high-pressure engine. Instead of setting the engine and boilers in the hold, he placed them on the main deck. And above the main deck he built a second deck, in a design which was never improved upon. The *Washington* was a side-wheeler with the engine in the waist between. Her cabins were curtained bunks divided by narrow aisles leading to the dining rooms. Her engines were driven by steam pressure high enough to do away with the pull of condensing exhaust steam. And all the later steamboats of the river differed from the *Washington* only as they improved in size and power and gimcracks.

Naturally the river people were delighted. But not the Easterners. When the *Washington* reached New Orleans in the fall of 1816, she was inspected by Edward Livingston, the old chancellor's business agent.

"You deserve well of your country, young man," he told Shreve. "But we shall be compelled to beat you if we can."

Shreve could neither be bought nor scared off. On March 12, 1817, the *Washington* left Louisville for New Orleans on her second voyage, accomplishing the round trip in the then incredible time of forty-one days. Doggedly, Shreve fought the Livingstonians in court for three years, spending his entire fortune in the battle. The litigation ended with complete victory for the antimonopolists. The court held that the Livingston monopoly was unconstitutional and void. Captain Shreve became a river hero and a river legend. He had licked the New Yorkers. He had revolutionized steamboat design. The great era of the Mississippi paddle-wheeler had begun.

❦　❦

With restrictions removed, steamboat building and steamboat trade opened the Mississippi. To the two million people who lived in the valley in the 1820's it meant economic and social contact with the rest of the nation. The valley developed with breathless swiftness. In 1814, New Orleans had wonderingly witnessed 21 steamboat arrivals. In 1819, there were 191; in 1833, more than 1,200 steamboat cargoes were unloaded. By 1840, New Orleans was the fourth port of the world, with its exports far greater than its imports. The lordly paddle-wheelers swept downstream at 10 to 12 miles an hour and upstream at 6, and nothing could compete with them. In the two decades after the launching of the *Washington* the river boats built on Henry Shreve's design outweighed in tonnage the combined shipping of the Great Lakes and the Atlantic seaboard.

Mississippi, Tennessee, Kentucky, Ohio, Illinois, Indiana, Michigan, Missouri, Iowa, Wisconsin—all these were finding their markets in New Orleans. And the paddle-wheelers' contribution to the building of the valley was indirect as well as direct. They carried emigrants and traders and travelers so cheaply that no other transportation by water or land was worth while. Their holds were tight with cargoes both ways; Europe-destined cotton, imports consigned to the western country, seaboard commodities transshipped at New Orleans for the teeming valley. Even the clearing of the river bottoms was in part the doing of the steamboats, for settlers, making a living by selling cordwood for the hungry boilers, opened more land than a less profitable reason would have caused. In 1846 the produce exported from New Orleans was valued at $72,000,000, and imports $35,000,000. The valley's steamboat tonnage was 15,000 tons more than that of the Atlantic ports, even exclusive of New Orleans; Bienville's starving town had twice the shipping business of New York.

❧   ❧

Yet steamboat traffic never became as safe as it was profitable. The old Arkansan in a coonskin cap wasn't exaggerating a great deal in 1843 when he took indignant leave of a steamboat tied up for repairs. Other passengers urged him to continue the upriver trip.

"No, this is the last time I ever mean to put my foot in one of those eternal contrivances," he called back. "I have been five times run high and dry on a sand bank, four times snagged, three times sawyered, and twice blown up sky-high. I calculate I have given these creatures a pretty fair trial, and darn my breeches if I ever trust my carcass in one again. Take care of my plunder. I will call for it at St. Louis."

From 1810 to 1850 more than four thousand people were killed or injured in steamboat disasters on the Mississippi. Insurance rates on cargoes ran from one and three-quarters per cent of the value on the first two hundred miles above New Orleans to four per cent and more on the upper river. From 1831 to 1833 one in eight of the river steamers was lost through boiler explosions, burning, or foundering on snags or sand bars. Because the paddle-wheeler's average life was calculated at only four or five years, it became the unfortunate practice to build them cheaply, install inferior engines, and employ poorly paid, incompetent engineers. And that piled Pelion on Ossa. The principal source of trouble was the boilers, especially when sporting captains raced their boats. Month after month the newspapers of the river chronicled ghastly disasters. In one such, Henry Clemens, brother of Mark Twain, lost his life with more than a hundred others, when four of the *Pennsylvania's* eight boilers blew up while she was loading wood sixty miles below Memphis. Fires were an even more frequent cause than explosions, for the wooden superstructures and hulls and the cotton cargoes were quick to ignite.

None knew better than Mark Twain of the other danger of the river, inherent in its swift rage, treacherous shallows, changing channels, and lurking snags.

"There's only one way to be a pilot," Bixby told the young cub, Sam Clemens, "and that is to get the entire river by heart. You have to know it just like ABC."

Which was literally true. Worse, the ABCs changed so often. No one has described the demands which navigation made upon that monarchical, sure-eyed being, the river pilot, as has Sam Clemens, who faithfully set down and followed the advice of Mr. Bixby.

"My boy, you've got to know the *shape* of the river perfectly. It is all there is left to steer by on a very dark night. Everything else is blotted out and gone. But mind you, it hasn't the same shape in the night that it has in the daytime."

"How on earth am I ever going to learn it, then?"

"How do you follow a hall at home in the dark? Because you know the shape of it. You can't see it."

"Do you mean to say that I've got to know all the million trifling variations of shape in the banks of this interminable river as well as I know the shape of the front hall at home?"

"On my honor, you've got to know them *better* than any man ever did know the shapes of the halls in his own house."

"I wish I was dead!"

"Now I don't want to discourage you, but—"

"Well, pile it on me; I might as well have it now as another time."

"You see, this has got to be learned; there isn't any getting around it. A clear starlight night throws such heavy shadows that, if you didn't know the shape of a shore perfectly, you would claw away from every bunch of timber, because you would take the black shadow of it for a solid cape; and you see you would be getting scared to death every fifteen minutes by the watch. You would be fifty yards from shore all the time when you ought to be within fifty feet of it. You can't see a snag in one of those shadows, but you know exactly where it is, and the shape of the river tells you when you are coming to it. Then there's your pitch-dark night; the river is a very different shape on a pitch-dark night from what it is on a star-light night. All shores seem to be straight lines, then, and mighty dim ones, too; and you'd *run* them for straight lines, only you know better. You boldly drive your boat right into what seems to be a solid, straight wall (you knowing very well that in reality there is a curve there), and that wall falls back and makes way for you. Then there's your gray mist. You take a night when there's one of these grisly, drizzly, gray mists, and then there isn't *any* particular shape to a shore. A gray mist would tangle the head of the oldest man that ever lived. Well, then, different kinds of *moonlight* change the shape of the river in different ways. You see—"

"Oh, don't say any more, please! Have I got to learn the shape of the river according to all these five hundred thousand different ways? If I tried to carry all that cargo in my head it would make me stoop-shouldered."

"*No!* you only learn *the* shape of the river; and you learn it with such absolute certainty that you can always steer by the shape that's *in your head,* and never mind the one that's before your eyes."

"Very well, I'll try it; but, after I have learned it, can I depend on it? Will it keep the same form and not go fooling around?"

Before Mr. Bixby could answer, Mr. W. came in to take the watch, and he said:

"Bixby, you'll have to look out for President's Island, and all that country clear away up above the Old Hen and Chickens. The banks are caving and the shape of the shores changing like every thing. Why, you wouldn't know the point above 40. You can go inside the old sycamore snag, now."

So that question was answered. Here were leagues of shore changing shape. My spirits were down in the mud again. Two things seemed pretty apparent to me. One was, that in order to be a pilot a man had got to learn more than any one man ought to be allowed to know; and the other was, that he must learn it all over again in a different way every twenty-four hours.

What the river people like to remember about the steamboats is not the danger and the economic importance of their traffic, but the splendor of their reign. We see the golden days of the packets as a series of bright, sharply defined prints by Currier and Ives. Here speeds the race between the *Natchez* and the *Robert E. Lee*. Here the *J. M. White*, unbeatable greyhound of the river, gets up steam. Here sit the suave gamblers, ready to separate the celebrating planter from his cotton crop proceeds or his plantation itself. Here friendly, deft Negro waiters balance heaping trays of the crispest fried chicken and the hottest, most luscious biscuits in the world before Carnival-bound guests at the captain's table. Here smile romance and profligate ease and adventure on the great brown river rushing headlong down a continent.

And these nostalgic, mental etchings, so cherished by the river folk, are in the main true to one side of life in the days of the steamboats' glory. There can be no exaggeration of the exploits of the *J. M. White*, pride of Captain Billy King, who moved the paddle wheel aft to take advantage of the second swell and thereby built the fastest boat on the Mississippi. The river captains raced for side money, for the business advantage of arriving first with their passengers and cargoes, and for pride in their throbbing craft. In the boiler room sweating engineers and firemen, careless of the hiss of the safety valve, exacted the last dangerous ounce of pressure for the honor of their packet and the pleasure of trailing a plume of smoke in the face of a defeated rival. The record breakers cut Shreve's New Orleans to Louisville run of twenty-five days to impossibly swift trips. Four days, nine hours, and thirty-one minutes by the *Eclipse* in 1853. Twelve minutes less for the *A. L. Shotwell*. On the New Orleans to Natchez run, the *Comet's* five-day and ten-hour record of 1814 was lowered by 1870 to seventeen hours and eleven minutes, a record achieved by both the *Natchez* and the *Robert E. Lee.*

Nor did destruction deter the masters. The *Brandywine* went up in flames in 1832 while racing the *Hudson* above Memphis. More than a hundred of her crew and passengers were lost. In 1837, the *Ben Sherrod* caught fire and exploded, with death to some two hundred. So with a score of others. Yet steamboat racing continued to its storied climax when the *Robert E. Lee* bested the *Natchez* in a race from New Orleans to Cairo.

It must have been great fun for passengers so swept away by the spirit of competition as to forget the risk. Frequently they would assemble on one side of a packet, straining to glimpse the competitor ahead or behind until the boat would list so badly that her outside boilers would begin to get dry. Then the captain would have to order: Trim boat—too many on this side! The author of *The Western Pilot,* Samuel Cummings, even gave advice to passengers in a chapter entitled "Hints to Steamboat Travellers":

If another boat is gaining on your boat; and about to pass you, let her go along, don't run out on the side of the boat next to her, for it is every passenger's duty, in such a case, to watch the boat he is on, and assist in keeping her on an even keel—while in company with another boat, your steam is generally as high as your engineer thinks it prudent to carry it—with a hot fire under your boilers, which sends a blaze through the flues in the boilers, from one end to the other—and boat put of trim, so that the water is running from the boilers on one side of the boat to the boilers on the other, until the top of the flue in the boiler, in which water is running from, becomes dry—the top of the flue soon becomes red hot, from the fire passing through it, and of course, softens with the heat—at the same time, the pressure of steam between the shell of the boiler and flues becomes greater, until the flue is collapsed —the iron is torn asunder at one end or other of the flue, and there is an explosion.

Racing was not the only delight of river travel. A passenger could content himself merely with eating; or if he was a gambling man himself he could sit in on the interminable poker games. Usually he was fleeced, for the river gamblers were adroit and frequently dishonest. The curious foreigner or Easterner, making his first trip down the river, could find endless interest in the wild lowlands through which he sped, in the colorful hubbub at the landings, and in the poignant songs of the black roustabouts.

> Farewell, brothers, if you's gwine fo' to go,
> We'll weep fo' to see you' face once mo'.
>
> On de levee by de river side.
> I've left my girl in New Orleans
> Fo' she is young, jes' in her teens.
> On de levee by de river side.

In the opulent heyday of the packets, the builders vied to outdo each other in ostentation. The great main cabins, or lounges, resembled the ornate lobbies of metropolitan hotels, heavily carpeted, glowing with brilliant cut-glass chandeliers, hung with oil paintings on the outer door of each stateroom. Their dining rooms boasted of 24 stewards and 13 desserts. At each end of the main cabin of the *Eclipse,* the most decorative packet of the fifties, stood gilt statuettes, one of Henry Clay and the other of General Jackson. It provided sleeping rooms for servants and a piano for the use of passengers, and advertised 48 bridal chambers. Surely these river monarchs gave a glimpse of *The Arabian Nights* to the multitude of planters, army officers, business-

men, and plain, ordinary travelers who crowded the state-
rooms on every trip.

The river restrictions of the Civil War trumpeted the
coming doom of the packets, though they prospered for
a decade and more afterward. During the war shippers,
denied the use of the river, became accustomed to the freight
lines of the intrusive railroads which had first begun to
slice through the west in the 1840's. At first these grubby
interlopers had served simply as connecting lines between
the interior and the waterways. Then the growth of the levee
system gave the railroads a greater measure of security and
their beds began to parallel the river. During the war years,
the growing efficiency of the railroads and the relief which
they offered from the high marine insurance rates converted
the shippers. Even after the western waterways were again
safely available, this new shipping method held its customers.
Never again did the packets approach their former commercial importance. By 1887 there was not a town on the
Lower Mississippi of more than 1,000 population—except
for Bayou Sara in Louisiana, for which the hungry river
was already reaching—that did not have a railroad connection. By the same year, there remained only one regular
steamboat line from Cincinnati to New Orleans. The regular Louisville boats had vanished as had the established
lines to the Cumberland and Tennessee rivers. And when
the Interstate Commerce Commission decreed in 1887 that
the Louisville and Nashville Railroad did not have to conform to the long and short haul clause where water competition was present, the steamboaters gave up the ghost.

Old-timers on our river brood when they recall the
death of the great packets. It is all but impossible now
to travel on the Mississippi as a steamboat passenger; and
on our stretch of the Mississippi only the brave, shabby little

Tennessee Belle reminds the watcher of the gimcrack giants of the past.

It is useless to remind the old men that the barges of the Inland Waterways Commission are carrying more water-borne freight today than ever the packets did. They will answer that it is not the same. The tows of black steel barges nose through the water ahead of their tugs like pre-historic sea monsters, and there is neither beauty nor glamour in them. The river veterans remembering, if only dimly, the death rattle of the paddle-wheelers are not satisfied.

And some of the younger people of the river are uneasy because of something else which they think is new to the river. A few years ago a maritime union strike tied up an inland waterways tow at our town which had been inno-cent of strikes and unions alike. The crew tried to picket the barges on our river front, for it was planned to send strikebreakers aboard. The police interfered with the pickets. My newspaper's photographer got a good picture of a police-man drawing a gun on an unarmed picket, and that picture was circulated in distant places to the disapproval of some of our citizens. They used the strike and the picketing and the long-postponed advent of union action on the lower river to point up their criticism of the present-day assertive-ness of the common man. Nothing like this could have happened or would have happened, they said, in the old days of the river.

I thought that disproof existed, but I did not find it until later in the files of the New Orleans *Daily Delta* of May 14, 1854, wherein a nameless correspondent looked askance at an earlier turbulence as prevalent on the Missis-sippi as on the Ohio. This is what he reported:

Happening a short time ago on the Ohio River in a steamboat, we noticed a curious occurrence on the boat landing at a town near the place of her departure. The freight had been taken in, and the boat was about to shove off, when there was a rush of the deck hands toward the gangway. They were however quickly repelled, and several of them knocked down by stout men with billets of wood, who stood guard on the wharf. On inquiry, we found that the system of thus forcibly compelling the hands to execute their contract, had become the necessary though unwritten law of the Western rivers. But for these violent proceedings, the hands would have gone ashore in a body, and compelled the boat, either to advance her rates or to lay up for several days, thereby inflicting a severe loss upon the proprietors,—and this, too, after the hands had shipped at certain stipulated rates for the whole voyage. When the boat had once got out of port, the hands resumed their work, seemingly content, despite their chagrin in being thus compelled to observe their agreement. Now, this very force and violence, so necessary and just, have been legalized in reference to our sea vessels; and it ought to be in regard to the navigation of our larger rivers. There is a lamentable defect in our whole legal system, so far as it concerns the very large and valuable interests of internal steam navigation. The Federal law wisely throws around our sea service many guards and securities, which are unknown on the Western waters. The power and discipline of the ship are maintained at the same time that the interests and welfare of the sailor are guarded with parental care. The captain has full power to maintain order, to administer punishment, to suppress mutiny by violence, to handcuff, chain and imprison his refractory men. The engagement of the sailor is rigidly enforced according to his shipping papers, and whilst in port, he may be imprisoned for desertion or abandonment of his contract. But how different on our Western steamboats! The captain has no law but that of force, and his force is frequently inadequate to suppress mutiny, to protect the property of the boat, much less to enforce the contracts of his hands. It has happened several times quite lately that large boats have been taken possession of by deck passengers, who have devastated the property of the boat, have grossly maltreated the captain, officers, crew and other passengers, and committed violences which would scarcely be credited in a community of law and order.

A recent occurrence of this nature will illustrate the extent of this violence, and the means by which alone it can be suppressed. The elegant steamer S. F. J. Trabue, on one of her recent trips up the river, had nearly three hundred deck passengers, of whom one hundred were very unruly and violent characters of the class of Pittsburgh coalmen. There were also a good many inoffensive countrymen from the Wabash, who were returning home, after selling their produce in the city. Shortly after leaving port, the coalmen commenced a series of the most brutal violences on the Wabashers,—knocking them down and kicking them,—and when the Captain interfered they snapped pistols at him, threatened to throw him over-board, and take possession of the steamer. Now, it happened that they had mistaken their man. Captain Tucker was the very last person to submit to such violence. Quietly arming some of his most trusty men with billets of wood and knives, he went in among the mutineers, and after warning them to desist from their violence, and receiving in return threats and resistance, he gave the signal, when his men fell upon the villains, knocked them down, beat several of them into quietude, and tied the others. For the remainder of the voyage there was peace on board. During the *mêlée* five of the mutineers jumped overboard. It was obvious to all on board, that but for this prompt and decisive action of the Captain, his splendid boat would have fallen into the hands of the very worst description of characters that can be found in the West. And yet, the Captain who thus saved his steamer and cargo and the women and children entrusted to his charge, had no sooner stepped ashore in Louisville, than he was served with writs to the amount of $10,000, for damages done to the deck passengers, who had mutinied and threatened to take possession of the steamer. Probably, on the trial, it will be shown by some ingenious attorney, that there could be no mutiny on a steamboat navigating our interior streams; that that is an offence which can be committed only on the high seas, and that Captain Tucker, instead of making the law and executing it himself, should have landed and appealed to some judicial tribunal to suppress the violence. No doubt, law will be found to sustain this view of the case. We shall regard the Captain fortunate, if he escapes without loss from the proceedings already instituted against him.

So perhaps we have not changed altogether for the worse. The witchery of river travel and commerce has vanished, but other and less desirable aspects also have gone. No lives are being lost on the Mississippi today because of malconstruction, commercial foolhardiness, or the inefficiency of operators. No shipmasters stand at the wharves to beat back the recalcitrant deck hands. And on no boat or barge that moves upon the Mississippi do the roustabouts or crew-men scramble like animals for scraps from the first-class table, set out for them in pannikins and sportively made available at the shout "Grub pile!" It may be that in the sacrifice of enchantment for the few we have gained on the Lower Mississippi, as elsewhere, something of dignity and security for the many.

CHAPTER 16

This Was Natchez

Rebecca Mandeville, who might have been scissored from a *Godey's Lady Book*, kept for six months in 1848 a diary of her life in Natchez.

William T. Johnson, a free quadroon barber, began recording his own gossipy notations in 1835, and continued them for sixteen years until he was killed in a property line dispute.

If you were to take their respective journals with you on a springtime pilgrimage to Natchez, you would have difficulty in reconciling them either to each other or to the Natchez tradition now on display. And this is just a way of saying that the river people of a century ago couldn't have lived up to the architectural majesty they created.

In a Natchez April today you wouldn't trouble to think of Rebecca Mandeville or William Johnson. It is pleasanter and easier to fit old Natchez to a pattern of brave gentility shrouded in candlelight, and of quiet breeding that is the presently dismissed handmaiden of wealth, and of community integrity as unassailable as the classic proportions of a Corinthian pillar.

Yet, the Natchez of the garden club guidebooks does its forebears an injustice in forgetting the lustiness that the Negro barber chronicled or the humdrum insipidity of a woman's life so long ago. For, if you place these realities in proper perspective, you will come nearer to understanding the culture of Natchez a hundred years past; a culture which triumphed over pistol-barreled crudities and imported artificialities alike.

Natchez has reason to be proud of that culture of which her mansions are the remaining outward symbol. Its development was English-American, little affected by the French and Spanish foundations upon which it was imposed. Even prior to the nineteenth century the first Scotsman and English Tory, the Irish adventurer and American republican had come from New England and the southern Atlantic coast and the interior to take up the lavish land grants of Spain. And when Spain's reluctant fingers were finally pried loose, they were followed by others like themselves.

Long before the 1820's brought cotton's historic, vanished dominance, there were great homes in Natchez, and not those of planters alone. They were built by soldiers, by lawyers, doctors and politicians, by river captains and merchants. The singular fact is that regardless of occupation this Natchez aristocracy was homogeneous at the start, and it became more homogeneous and caste-conscious through a quite thorough system of intermarriage. The Natchez gentry seemed to be animated by a common desire to build stately homes, to furnish them lavishly, and to ensure their retention by their own kinsmen. Only in this latter hope they fell short. And that is sad, for they differed from later exploiters of the river in that they had come to stay.

To the question, what were they like, there is no inclusive reply. They would have given one answer. Their less fortunate contemporaries would have had another. Looking back at them and their time, we would find yet a third. Perhaps, in the written words of two dissimilar residents of Natchez we can find something of all three.

❧   ❧

This is the insipidly placid Natchez of Rebecca Mandeville, member of the gentility:

February 29, 1848: [She goes for a walk and] didn't get home until near teatime . . . found Joe quite nervous watching for me for a Gentleman was in the parlor with father, and from the name [she thought] he must be some relation of ours from Goshen, and if so must of course stay at our house. Well, I took off my bonnet and we were considering the propriety of sending for father to inform us upon the subject when in comes the worthy gentleman to confirm our suspicions, and tells me that I must go in the parlor and see Capt. Wilkins, a cousin, but a perfect stranger to us. . . . Oh! horrors!

March 2: After dinner, trained my Brazilla vine up to the gallery and read newspapers until dark . . . been reading papers ever since tea and will now read a chapter in the Bible and then repose.

March 10: I was carrying some lunch to Joe this morning when I heard a man's step on the stairs, peeped and seeing that it was a stranger flew back into the dining room, set down the plates and went to meet him. . . . I was directing him [to find the overseer] to the best of my ability . . . when all of a sudden I became aware that his eyes were fastened upon my face, and thought how carelessly I had twisted up my hair and put my clothes on this morning. I can only congratulate myself, though, on my good luck, for one minute later and I should have met him with my hands full of toast and sweetmeats—rather an embarrassing predicament for a young lady and gentleman, strangers to each other too.

[On the Bluff, Rebecca] saw there an unusual number of ladies, also a ringleted man who looked as if he thought himself very handsome.

March 13: Went to church twice yesterday—wore my new blue dress for the first time. "Tom Thumb's" carriage and horses have been going about the streets today. The whole concern is quite a curiosity. We went this afternoon to see the minute General and I forgot when looking at him that he was not a child, he is so well formed and so tiny. I could not kiss him, though, so when the crowd of females were making the room resound with their busses, Jose and I sat close in a corner, so were passed by unseen, and escaped the disagreeable necessity of refusing the little fellow a kiss. Strange fancy some women have of lavishing their kisses in public! My face burnt at the very idea. . . . After bringing Jose home, I took Sissy and went on the bluff—put 2 or 3 ginger nuts in my bag first and eat them up there—dreadfully plebian! but they tasted very nice for I had not eaten any dinner and was unromantic enough to feel hungry. I would never do for a heroine of romance after such an act. I am sleepy now too.

March 28: [She reads] some very interesting letters written at the time of the late Duke of Orleans' marriage and giving a full account of it, describing him and his lovely bride.

April 11: Quite a commotion in town by the presentation of the Sword to Gen. Quitman, wanted to go out and pay some visits, but did not like to walk the streets when so thronged.

April 12: [Rebecca and Joe go to a tea party] I don't think I ever passed a pleasanter evening—the party was composed of eight of us young girls and about as many gentlemen all in good spirits and ready for enjoyment—had two tableaux, scenes from Ivanhoe, in that where Rebecca presents the casket of jewels to Rowena. Joe represented the Jewess to perfection.

April 21: [It rained on the night of Oakley Fair, for which Rebecca had made three penwipers and dressed a doll, and she was too ill to go.] Should like to be there very much, now—at least I feel so when my imagination calls up the brilliantly lighted room, gay articles displayed for sale, happy faces and merry laughter—but I never let my mind dwell upon disappointments for I think with Campbell "to bear is to conquer our fate."

May 1: Sewed this morning and began to read Hyperion with Jose—about six o'clock, Joe, Sissy and myself regaled ourselves with vanilla ice at Stanwood's, then proceeded to the Bluff where we met and talked with a number of our acquaintances.

May 11: [Rebecca records going to the] concert given by the Oyshean family [and the next evening to] a little opera by Mr. Nash's pupils [and to see] a copy of the Last Supper by da Vinci, copied by Craighoff.

June 1: Feel most wretchedly—attribute it to being up until nearly 3 o'clock last night—Jose and I were at a little party at Dahlgren's—enjoyed myself very much—escorted home by Mr. Cochran—yesterday morning got a New York paper sent by Capt. Wilkins. Jose quite sick today owing partly to last night's dissipation. Dr. Davis came to see her this morning—we engaged him in conversation and an hour slipped away very pleasantly before he took his "congé.". . . Mr. Shipp sent me an exquisite bouquet of choice cut flowers this afternoon. Mosquitoes devouring me.

June 24: Met with a disagreeable adventure this afternoon. Jose and I tired and worn from bottling straining some sirup made in the morning, dressed ourselves, took Sissy and sauntered upon the Bluff to breathe the fresh air —it being rather late we did not sit there long—on our way home when in front of Mr. Henderson's store, I was startled by hearing our name and something said about pleasure of our acquaintance, turned my head just in time to see an impudent looking man stop in front of Jose and hold out his hand, when Jose with a most Siddons like air drew herself up and said "I have not the honor of your acquaintance"; "not acquainted, hey," said the man with an impudent leer, and marched off fast enough to be soon out of sight—he had come up along side of Jose who heard him distinctly say "good evening Misses Mandeville shall I have the pleasure of your acquaintance." I do not know the man's name though he frequently attends our Church —it seems he knew ours, which only makes his impudence the more gross—to dare to insult a Mandeville! how my blood boils at the thought.

June 27: Walked on the Bluff, accompanied by Father, the only person we have told of the man's impudence and who says the man ought to have his head broke. He carried a walking stick which I begged him not to use if he should see the object of his indignation, whom we fortunately did not meet.

July 17: Poor Emmeline [a slave] died on the ninth, all of us around her doing our best to keep her from going —it being Sunday a great many of her colored friends came here and followed her remains to their last resting place—many bitter tears did we all shed over the poor creature—it is strange how we become attached to our servants and they to us.

That was the stilted, circumscribed Natchez of a genteel young lady of fashion.

William Johnson's father was a white man, his mother a mulatto woman. Freed by his father when he was twelve, he moved in 1830, when he was 21, from Port Gibson to Natchez where he set up as a barber. Five years later, Johnson married another former slave who also had been set free with her mother by a Natchez banker.

Barber Johnson, who loaned money on the side to the spendthrift white men, prospered between 1831 and 1850, became a planter and slaveowner himself, and proprietor of three barber shops and a well-patronized bathhouse with the gentility as his clients. He and Ann Battles, his wife, had ten children. Three of his daughters taught in the Natchez Negro schools. A son served in the federal colored militia after the Civil War, and later became an extensive renter of plantations.

In 1940, the Louisiana State University Archives secured Johnson's diary and other papers from the widow of a prominent Negro doctor who was Johnson's grandson. They are now being edited for publication. The Johnson papers were found in the attic of the large, two-story house which William Johnson had filled with four-poster beds, solid furniture and an adequate collection of books and sheet music. The diary, illustrated with rough, graphic sketches, is the principal exhibit of the collection.

From it emerges the earthy Natchez of remarkable William Johnson, barber, money-lender, chronicler and occasional confidant of the aristocracy. Here is the little city that modern Natchez has forgotten and Rebecca Mandeville never knew:

————*1836:* "Mc [Robert McCarey, a fellow free barber] and myself had a tolerable good Dinner. We had as follows —Mc had 2 bottles of Claret, 1 bottle of champagne, Egg Bread, pork, broiled chicken and beef steak. I had a piece of good bacon, wheat bread, oysters in fritters, one large bottle of Anneset, one dozen oranges, one small bottle of Muscatele wine. He had a bottle of brandy and honey."

March 17, 1837: "Tonight there was a passel of Irishmen collected together near the market house and every person that passed they struck with sticks or something else. Dr. Denny was returning from Mr. Rain's dinner when the Irishmen knocked him down and beat him like the mischief. They cut his head and nose pretty severe. They struck the sheriff also. The fencibles turned out and put two or three of the Irish in jail."

——*1837:* [A citizen is chasing slave wenches] "Oh, the Rascal I would give $100 if some gentleman would only catch the low minded dog and cow hyde him well. It would do me so much good."

September, 1837: "An Election came on to day for Major General of 2d Division of Malatia of this state. General Quitman & Mr. Besancon [editor of the *Free Trader*] had a fight—Mr. Besancon made a thrust at him that would have killed him had not a piece of silver in the pocket of the general arrested the progress of the sword. They were separated by the sheriff or some other gentleman. . . ."

December 4, 1837: Johnson rents his slave, Lucinda, to a man who is "just a going to House Keeping" for $12 a month. He later refuses to sell Lucinda for $750.

December 6: Two men crossed the river to fight a duel, but the parties interfered and the matter was settled amicably. "I'm truly glad it ended that way."

Some white men have signed a paper to have permission given Robert Smith to remain in Natchez. Smith, the white men say, is "an honest and as correct a colored man as there was in Natchez." But Johnson knows better, as Smith was arrested in New Orleans for buying goods from a slave. A relative of Johnson's in New Orleans went his bail, and when Smith ran off to Natchez he left $500 with Johnson's relative to cover the bail. But Johnson thinks it better that no point be made of letting Smith remain, for the white men say that if Smith can't stay, none of the people of color should.

December 12: "Col. Bingaman spit in Col. Morgan's face and cursed him and then threw a chew of tobacco in his face—on account of his suing the Col. in N.O." Colonel Bingaman is also listed by Johnson as one of a group which he designates as the "most wealthy and intelligent part of this community." Johnson gives two candlesticks with glass covers to the colonel.

A man wakes him at 11:30 to borrow his bathtub "for his brother who was very ill with a cramp in his stomach."

January 9, 1838: "A Frenchman opened a lot of goods direct from France. He had as much as could do and more to wait on the people." Johnson bought a pair of boots at $7, two stocks, one plain and one satin, and a pair of pantaloons, the entire bill amounting to $19.50.

March 10: "We had rain nearly all day tho they were not very Heavy Showers. Today there was a Race out at the track and I went out to See it. The Nags belonged to Colonel Bingaman, Col. Smith and Mr. Minor. Capt. Mc-Keath [Bingaman's horse] won the first heat very Easy. And in coming up to the stand His rider Dismounted and the Blankets was thrown on him and when Mr. Minor saw that he Spoke of it to Mr. Prior, and Mr. P. returned him a very impertinent answer and told him that he was too Damd Smart and to mind his own Business. This made Mr. Minor Mad and he left the matter for the judges to Decide on and they decided that Col. Bingaman should not Start his horse again, that he was Ruled off or out of the Race. The Col. then stated that it was a Damed Rascally Decision and there followed a great deal of abuse to the judges . . . they proclaimed it out that Col. Bingaman could not start according to Rule. He Swore that he would Start His Horse. With that Mr. Minor sent his nag home. Mr. Smith ran his mare Slowly around—but the Horse ran pretty fast Double Distanced her—for she did not Run. Mr. Prior abused Mr. Minor a good deal. It was laughable to see the following men abusing the Judges [he lists them], first one and then the other was at it."

March 1: Johnson whips his slave who got drunk the night before and ran off three times during the day. "Gave him a pretty severe thrashing with the cowhide, then he was perfectly calm and quiet and could then do his work.

'Tis singular how much good it does some people to get whipped."

March 21: He advertises a runaway as "an unsound slave," offering a $200 reward or a sale price of $300. Later another of his slaves runs away, and sends him word that he'll never do it again if Johnson won't punish him.

April 5: "Today is quite cloudy and business quite dull. I got the barrels to give baths today for the first time and Mr. Ayres called and took a bath. The first this season and paid the cash for it."

He notes also that some men have crossed the river to fight but that the sheriff of Louisiana arrives and puts each under $1,000 peace bond.

——, *1839:* "Mr. Jenkins was caught in bed with Mr. Parker's old big black woman. Buster and another man was caught in bed with old Lucy Bristle. Hard times indeed when such things occur."

April 23, 1841: He writes that the children of a white father have been sent to him to learn trades.

July 1: "A Mr. Turner and Mr. Miderhoff has a Scuffle. It Commenced in this way. Turner Commenced on Miderhoff with a cowhide, fell by accident at that time. Mr. M. Jumped on him but other was too strong for him. Miderhoff Jumped off and ran away. Left his hat in the fight. He fought pretty well for a very Short time . . . and at the blow of the fight he made a Splendid run it was indeed very good time that he made the Run. . . ."

July 3: "Mr. Miderhoff's card in the morning papers also in hand Bill form reads thus

To the Public

I hereby denounce N. E. Turner a base poltroon and an arrant Coward this Scoundrel made an assassin like attack upon me night before Last at Dusk when I was unarmed and did not Expect an attack . . .

when yesterday a friend of mine Called on Him to Cross the river he basely Sculped from responsibility by saying that he was not a fighting man."

August, 1841: He writes that Judge Tenney has been killed in a duel in Arkansas, with Seargent S. Prentiss as his second. The news has been brought down by Steamboat. All parties left Natchez to go there to fight it out, with rifles at 30 yards.

Many free persons of color are having to leave Natchez by order of the Court of Inquisitions, and the others are having peititions signed for individual permission to remain in Mississippi. (The Inquisition was a vigilante organization which ran out of the state free negroes suspected of abolitionist activity.)

August 24: "Lotts of F—P—C— are running around Town with Petitions to have the Priviledge of remaining in the state, tis laughable almost, Wellington was out into the Country this evening to have his Petition Signed and he got the following Gentlemen on his Paper: Dr. Steven Duncan and Col. A. D. Bingaman—Dr. Calhoun—Col. Wilkins —Mr. R. C. Evans, Mr. I. Routh—Mr. S. S. Elliotte—those Names are enough to make any Common man Proud—those Names are an ornament to any Paper—Those are Gentlemen of the 1st order of Talents and Standing.

May 7, 1842: A man who had advertised that he was going to send up a balloon, announced to the crowd that he would not do so until the next day. A mob quickly destroyed the balloon and were about to thrash the owner when the "lady that they had in company begged them not to."

June 6: Louisianians across the river catch a runaway slave "that helped kill a man by the name of Todd—living near Red River—they burned him up Soon after he was taken. They caught one more of them and they Brought him to the Concordia jail . . . they shot the other One but Did[n't] kill Him. . . ."

September 4, 1842: "A party of persons Sheverderied [charivaried] Mr. John Williamson Last night they were finally stopped by the Sheriff—and Police officers—for they have never had a chance at him Since he married before—and this they gave him because he made use of Some Language that Some men did not Like—when Mr. Patterson was Married—they were dressed in all manner of Shapes. One was Dressed Like his wife with a behind as Large as they could well make it to Look. The thing went off well I am told. . . ."

August 9, 1844: Excitement over elections is rising. "Natchez Guards at there Armory had a meeting and a marching and wound up thare meeting with a fight. In the first place Shanks and the Capt. Page had a quarrel, after a little Capt. Page and W. W. Woods has a fight. Page caught him around the necke and choked him wonderfully, untill he was Separated. Great times we have there."

August 16: A slave who had been beaten to death with a fence picket with a nail in the end is dug up and an inquest held. But no one wants to pay the $50 coroner's fee to open the skull, so the verdict is left at death from congestion of the brain. . . . "Thus it was and thus it is."

August 27: "Today there was a trial before Esqr. Potter and the Parties were a Mr. Gibson vs. the Daughter of Poor Old Sam Gibson, who the world Knows to be free, but during the Inquisition She and her mother went out to stay with this Gibson and now he puts up a Claim to her by saying that Sam G. her father belonged to his father and that he had went out of the state and was set free and returned to it again. Thus he became the property of said Gibson under some old Law passed so says Potter in 1807—Greate God, what a Country, the suit went in favor of Gibson. . . ."

Such was William Johnson's Natchez, turbulent, callous, and frontier-spirited, whose men were not yet as civilized as the homes they built.

❦　❦

In the river's springtime, the two garden clubs of Natchez bespeak their rival pilgrimages. If you are near the river then, you should attend them. Perhaps only the outward spectacle will please you: the Confederate balls and tableaux, the broad mimicry of the showboat, the women in hoopskirts and men in stocks and pale trousers who greet you in the homes of Natchez, show you their treasures, and talk with intimate glibness of their noted dead. Perhaps you may feel also a passing tightness in your throat at the beauty of these estates, at the pleasantness of these friendly mimes, at the conscious contrast between the serene old mansions and the newer bustle of awakening Natchez. And unless the perfection of wood and marble and fading oil, intricate Chippendale and uninterpreted personal relics assume disproportionate importance, you will think too of the flesh and blood of a hundred years ago, whose descendants are these costumed guides. Once the owners gave identity to the houses in which they lived. Today the houses identify their historic shadows. Nor are they shadows only of the sheltered, pitapat Rebeccas, or of the blister-tongued, tobacco-spitting Colonel Bingamans. There was also majesty here.

This was the stuff of which that majesty was made. . . .

Here is austerely beautiful Monmouth, shrouded in mossy oaks, its brick walls and square-pillared porticos as sturdy as they were a hundred and twenty years ago; its wrought-iron banisters as delicate as on the day of their fashioning. A New Yorker, kinsman of the great Schuyler family, built Monmouth out of his vast wealth.

But John Hankinson and his wife walked through this green, sloping parkway only a short time. In 1824 they found a yellow fever victim dying near Monmouth, and despite his dread illness they sheltered him. In a week, all three were dead.

In 1826, another New Yorker acquired Monmouth. He was John A. Quitman, and he was to become Mississippi's greatest hero. Soldierly, handsome John Quitman was the organizer and first captain of the Natchez Fencibles, dashing in their uniforms of French blue, with silver buttons, silver lace, and a profusion of braid. Newcomer to Natchez, he won an heiress for his wife, but fearful that he would be termed a fortune hunter he drew up in advance a marriage contract in which he relinquished all rights to his wife's estate. Then he proceeded to win his own fortune at the bar, and his longer-lasting fame in battle. When the Mexican War broke out, John Quitman was made a major general. At the head of his Mississippians he led the storming of Belan gate and the assault on Chapultepec castle. And it was one of his young Fencibles, Frederick Macready of Natchez, who raised the American flag over the citadel of Mexico City.

Congress awarded John Quitman a sword in honor of Monterrey, though he never liked it as much as the keen blade forged for him by Reese McDonald of Natchez who made the first bowie knife. His fellow Mississippians elected him governor, and women in white gowns sang "Hail to the Chief" and tossed flowers before his white horse at his inauguration. He might have become president, but in 1851 he was arrested while governor for breach of neutrality in espousing the cause of Cuba. He resigned the governorship. Later he was elected to Congress, and died in 1859 of poisoning, far from white Monmouth, after a banquet for President Buchanan.

Here is Montaigne, the Swiss-French château where another Mississippi soldier lived. General William Martin didn't help win a war; and he would have liked to remain with his lawbooks in 1861, for he had opposed secession. Yet he fought for his state, first as captain of the Adams County troops which he reorganized just prior to the war's outbreak. William Martin bought $15,000 worth of arms for his horsemen from the Ames Company of Massachusetts, which knew well the reason for the purchase. The New England arms merchants, appreciative of the order, gave him a handsome sword. As a general under Joe Wheeler, he escaped a Yankee trap at Shelbyville, Tennessee, but lost his Yankee sword. Ten years later it was returned to him, and it is still held by his descendants.

The invaders of the river were not kind to the Martins of Montaigne. When Natchez was occupied, Union troops stabled their horses in the drawing room, mutilated the woodwork, smashed chandeliers, and looted the furnishings. Then they turned the house over to a gang of freed slaves and poor whites.

Here is The Briars, simple in its dignity, the plantation house where saturnine Jeff Davis courted and married raven-haired Varina Howell in 1845. She was nineteen, and he an uncommunicative, mature man, still embittered by the tragic death ten years before of his first bride of three months. Dark, gently born Varina Howell, whose naval officer father was a cousin of Aaron Burr, left the Briars for a broken-hearted destiny. Her tall husband, who had acquitted himself well in Mexico, became congressman, secretary of war, and then the strange, aloof president of the Confederacy, and prisoner in chains in Fort Monroe. Through it all, unsophisticated Varina Howell stood at his side; and perhaps the drama of Jeff Davis would have been less compelling had not a brooding man found beauty and companionship in Natchez.

Here is spacious, wide-galleried Ravenna, behind its high iron fence, radiant with giant wisteria, crimson tulips, and masses of azaleas and roses. It was the Natchez home of the fighting Metcalfes of China Grove plantation. Here and at Spanish-built Cherokee you might learn of orphaned George Metcalfe, the young filibuster who miraculously came home to Uncle Oren's.

George Metcalfe was a trouble-hunter. After the Mexican War, in which he was believed to have been the youngest soldier, the boy joined his elder fellows of Natchez in 1848 in espousing the freedom of Cuba. The Cuban patriot, General Narcisco Lopez, came to Natchez to raise money and volunteers for the struggle against Spain. Enthusiastic Natchez contributed her dollars and men, and feted Lopez as her own hero. The Natchez *Courier* reported that "the flag of free Cuba was displayed across Wall Street on Sunday evening and again on yesterday and attracted much notice. It was a flag of blue and white stripes on a triangular field. We shall certainly be glad to see a meeting held in this city for the purpose of sympathizing with the heroic demonstration now being made in Cuba by her patriotic sons and we will cheerfully co-operate."

Young George enlisted. So did his younger brother, Henry. To disguise their identity, the lads gave their nationality as Irish, a quirk which was to save their lives. When the steamer *Pampero* sailed from New Orleans with its 450 Cuba-bound filibusters, the Metcalfes were aboard. With them were other Natchez adventurers, Sam Reed, Victor Ker, M. H. Ball, G. M. Green, William H. Holmes, John Hopkins, William Little, James Stanton, James M. Mandeville, K. A. Fourniquet, Charles A. Robinson, and many another young Mississippian.

The first news of the adventurers was good. The patriots had captured a general and set up a provisional government. Then came the hideous sequel. General Lopez was defeated and captured at Bahia Hondo. Fifty-one Americans were butchered, the rest held for trial. Lopez died publicly in Havana beneath the grip of the garroter.

The Natchez volunteers who survived the battle were thrown into dungeons to await the Spanish firing squads. And of them all, only George and Henry Metcalfe came home. The brothers were believed by the Spaniards to be Irishmen, and thanks to the intervention of the British consul were not executed. Instead, they were sent to Spain in irons, and finally released. Shortly after they returned home, Henry, broken in health, died. But George Metcalfe, the 22-year-old veteran of two wars and an Indian expedition, never lost his love for a fight. A decade later he went off again, this time to battle for his state and the South. Afterward, with no more wars in sight, he settled down to teaching school.

Here is the second Cherry Grove, and linked with it the memory of Clifton, both of them the homes of the proud French Surgets. Pierre Surget built the first Cherry Grove on his Spanish grant in 1788, out of the profits of a cargo of pig iron. Destroyed by fire, Cherry Grove was restored in the 1860's. But there was no restoration of Clifton, the fabulously magnificent mansion of Captain Frank Surget, grandson of Pierre, and the first millionaire of Natchez. When the Union soldiers came, cosmopolitan Frank Surget gave a dinner for a number of northern officers. But he overlooked inviting Captain Peter B. Hays, who was in charge of fortifications. The next day Captain Surget was curtly informed that a fortification must be erected on the precise location of his home.

The family was able to save only their silver and a few

personal belongings before the wrecking crew blasted and pulled down Clifton, destroying even the gardens and grottoes. The crushed Surgets decided to go to France forever; and though Captain Surget died before embarkation, his widow sailed later alone, and lived out her life abroad.

There is many another home at which you will want to pause on your pilgrimage to Natchez, and many another name to give glory to each: Windy Hill Manor, where Aaron Burr was welcomed by his old friend, Colonel Benjamin Osmun, after his arrest for conspiracy; and Connally's Tavern on Ellicott's Hill, where the Irishman Blennerhassett awaited Burr and later planned their defense against the charges; and Elgin, the stately home of Dr. John Carmichael Jenkins, notable botanist and horticulturist, whose fruit-grafting experiments ended with his death of yellow fever in 1855; and Longwood, where died Seargent S. Prentiss, the lame, silver-voiced tippler, perhaps the most notable man ever to represent Mississippi in Congress; and Myrtle Grove, the home of Captain Thomas P. Leathers, who skippered the *Natchez* in her losing race with the *Robert E. Lee*; and Arlington, with its great Tuscan columns, whose earliest mistress died on her first night within its walls; and Stanton Hall, four years abuilding in 1815, replica of the ancestral home of the Irish Stantons of Belfast; and Longwood, the unfinished, five-story Moorish dream of the dark-eyed scientist and Union sympathizer, Dr. Haller Nutt, who deserted his unfinished home at the outbreak of the Civil War; and red-brick Gloucester, the estate of fanatical, suspicious Winthrop Sargent, who came from New England to be the first governor of Mississippi Territory.

And there are others whose names fall softly: Rosalie and Belmont, D'Evereaux, Linden, Auburn, Cherokee, Elmscourt, Landsdowne, The Forest, and Saragossa. Each has its unending story of hope and change and lost greatness and despair. Some, still remembered, have fallen in peace and in war before fire, the common enemy. You stand before the iron-railed double stairway which is all that remains of Concord, home of Gayoso, last of the Spanish governors, and remember that it is nearly a hundred and fifty years since the reluctant dons retreated. Now a century and a half of Americans have built their homes upon these shaded bluffs.

Listening while the descendants and successors of these old builders tell of them, you become aware of two disturbing truths. So few created these ancestral legacies, and even fewer held to them. Over and over in Natchez history, even to the present, the same names are repeated time and again—the Minors, the Surgets, the Merrills, the Dunbars, the Swifts, the Shields, the Davises, Ogdens, Jenkins, Bryants, Stantons, the Huntingtons, Dunlops, Metcalfes, Brandons, and Duncans, the Williamses, Kers, and Gillespies. Stout English and Scots and Irish names they are for the most part, and persistent in survival here, where fewer surnames than homes have vanished. They were only a handful to begin with, and for the most part they kept to themselves, hoping to perpetuate their holdings and their blood pride by intermarriage. Not always were the results as happy as those lords of the Natchez bluffs would have wished.

As late as the spring of 1942 you would not have ended your Natchez pilgrimage without visiting Glenwood, which the newspapers call Goat Castle; a forlorn relic of beauty, where a pathetic old man and woman had discovered that the public's enjoyment of their eccentricities could help them keep body and soul together. For your entrance fee they would let you snicker at the chickens and goats which seemed more at home in the desecrated drawing room of fey, mocking Glenwood than they.

You would have left Goat Castle, uneasily seeking a more understandable present, wanting to remember only a past undeserving of this tortured link with tomorrow's spring.

CHAPTER 17

Good-Time Town

Had you been even a moderately prosperous planter or businessman of the 1850's you would have found many an excuse to board a New Orleans-bound packet as often as you could.

Behind any excuse would have lain a motive as compelling now as then. New Orleans was—and is—the good-time town of the Mississippi; a city of beguiling sin, a strangely foreign playground for the Americans of the upriver plantations, a racing mecca of the nation. True, one did not so describe it to a pious wife or head-shaking elders. It was better to explain that New Orleans was the business heart of the valley and the cultural metropolis where the opera thrived and the drama was honored. Which was also true.

So we are disembarking from the fast New Orleans-Natchez packet with cotton money in our pockets and a longing to spend it. Being country folk, we are impressed by the sprawling city of almost a hundred thousand people, along whose river front the masts and funnels of sleek ocean-going ships and river boats stand as thick as trees for five miles. After the open, clean-smelling air of our plantation, we are somewhat annoyed at first by the unpleasant smells rising from rotting refuse and horse stables, mule yards and Negro slave pens, and from the gas-bubbling green slime of the gutters. Probably we do not connect this odor of decay with the terrible death rate of this gay town, three times as high as that of any other city its size in the country. But we do understand why more flowers are sold here than anywhere else in the United States and we hasten to buy a boutonniere from a levee-front vendor who is darker than we thought a Spaniard or a Frenchman would be.

We forget the offending odors as our public carriage approaches the high-domed St. Charles Hotel which we have chosen because its cool magnificence surpasses its hospitable, flower-bordered competitors. This St. Charles, principal rendezvous of the river planter, is the most ostentatious hostel in the South, girt with classic Corinthian columns and a magnificent granite-slabbed promenade. Yet we will spend little time inside, for besides the races there are so many diversions that we cannot find time for them all.

First a stroll, after the steamboat trip, into the near-by French Quarter. We have been warned to be wary here, for although New Orleans is a far safer place than it was twenty-five years ago the careless pedestrian still runs some risks. We have heard of the gangs of purse-snatching children, harbored by two notorious harpies who provide white and Negro waifs with clothing, meager supper, and crowded sleeping quarters in return for their hauls. Though these gamins specialize in cotton and sugar from the wharves, they are not above a try at pickpocketing.

Before the great whitewashed cathedral facing the Place d'Armes is lined a crazy string of old hacks, barouches, and cabs whose Negro drivers chatter in atrocious French and drink root beer. An Italian organ grinder cranks Old World melodies in the park while rapt children munch figs as they listen; and a disharmony of stringed instruments comes from the hodgepodge of cafés, saloons, and restaurants about the square, where the Creole Orleanians, still persistently aloof from the American interlopers, sip orange-flower water, eau sucré, cognac, and strong coffee. It reminds us that we must eat at least one epicurean meal in this neighborhood, at Victor's or at the Café de Quatre Saisons; and, since the thought makes us hungry, we buy an apple and a banana from a dirty fruit peddler in a striped jersey shirt and fur cap. As we eat, our attention is distracted by the beat of a drum. The drummer is an ill-dressed man who is calling: "Lost child! Lost child!" together with a description of the missing youngster. We cannot help him, so we stare idly at the windows of a well-stocked hardware store, filled with iron pots, copper utensils, casks and spikes, and long-legged iron spiders and griddles. We place a handsome order there for the plantation. Then our curiosity draws us to the helter-skelter French market place where the raw display of 'possums, 'coons, crawfish, eels, and frogs makes us smile at the tastes of Frenchmen.

Shortly, we drop in at The Gem on Royal Street, most elegant of the drinking houses of the city, which is open only to "gentlemen in white kid gloves and burnished boots." Our feet sink into the thick Saxony carpet as we relax in a cushion-lined iron settee; and we order a tall rum punch and talk over the sights we intend to take in before the opening of the races. Certainly we want to see the crack pistol shot of the Common Street gallery who can snuff a candle at twelve paces twenty times in succession. We hope, too, that Paul Morphy, the greatest chess genius in history, will give another exhibition before he leaves on his European trip. Down in the huge amphitheater in Washington Square there are the bullfights where the finest and largest bulls of the Attakapas, country of the Acadians, are taunted and slain by Mexican matadors, here on invitation of the mayor and council. And we must not forget the cockfights, the dog-fights, and sundry unusual matches such as one we have heard of between a dog and a hundred rats.

And before we return home, we must assuredly look in on one of the two German gardens, the Tivoli and the

National. We have heard an odd story of the dancing of those otherwise sedate Germans of the lower river who, eyes shut, hold each other so closely that their cheeks touch, while they spin vigorously, bouncing like India rubber. Cool, rustic places, these German gardens, tree shaded and thick with sturdy tables and benches. Fat waiters shuffle on the shell walks, carrying baskets filled with beer jugs. And in the center of the garden stands the dance house where a dozen German brass players trumpet their waltzes. Only five cents a dance.

Our third punch is giving us unruly ideas. The German gardens are respectable, middle-class, for all their color, and one's dancing companions there are really quite proper. But there is another place, we remind each other, where the partners are neither proper nor escorted. At the Pontchartrain Ballroom, dress and masked balls are still being conducted with white demimondes in attendance—or in waiting—four nights a week, and quadroons for three nights. The women are masked and it is impossible to recognize them until later. We have heard that there are nearly twice as many men at the quadroon bal masqués as at those where the white adventuresses are queens.

Yes, it is the city of sin. They tell us that every steamboat captain has a second family in New Orleans; that in the glittering houses of assignation, unwise women of some prominence make pin money; that the Orleanians even rent handsome slave women for from $12 to $20 a month. Of course, we will tour as spectators only. And not a word when we get back home. Another punch, waiter!

A cannon shot interrupts our scheming. Eight o'clock. It is the curfew for less fortunate people of color, the slaves of New Orleans. Recalcitrants caught out after the curfew get twenty-five lashes and a night in the calaboose, and their masters must pay a $3 fine. If the master wishes, his troublesome slave may be whipped at the calaboose for one cent a stroke. Here in New Orleans the waiter boasts, in answer to our questions, that they know how to keep the slaves in line. At 25 cents a day, troublesome black women are linked together in the workhouse chain gang, to clean the market and shovel the dirt and rubbish of the streets. Black men are simply beaten. And worse than beatings, they can be frightened by being told that they will be sold to an Irishman. Those sales bêtes, the Irish draymen, m'sieu! The worst masters of all.

This reminds us that we must attend a slave auction at The Arcade, as a house servant on our plantation is probably dying. We will need another well-trained man. Here at The Arcade only healthy, stout men and women are herded from the traders' pens to the blocks. The Arcade has a good reputation. Its guarantee that the chattels are free of vices and maladies, as prescribed by law, and its description of age, capabilities and blemishes, can be accepted as gospel. Yes, we'd better drop in on the next sale, even though prices are higher this year than last. Next year might be even worse.

It's too late now for the theater; besides, we're sleepy after our card-playing trip downriver and those potent drinks at The Gem. But before we leave New Orleans we must attend every presentation in town. The season this winter has been brilliant. The Star Theatre has been packed for Barney Williams, king of Irish characters, and his wife, Julia Dean, who have earned in California the stupendous sum of $500 a week; Anderson, the masterly Hamlet, and those incredible Ravels. There has been almost none of the hissing which, in moderation, is as proper as applause.

The Ravels are the talk of the year, except among those who prefer Shakespeare to dexterity. Fresh from Havana, where the troupe earned $52,000 in some thirty exhibitions, the tightrope walkers, the gymnasts and pantomimists are drawing $1,400 houses nightly. We must see their favorite pantomime, the Green Monster, who disappears by means of a rope fastened to his back. And Dan Rice, who, playing the White Knight, gets into a cupboard and vanishes out the back, though you believe he is still there. You gasp when a tin sword is thrust inside, and a child in stuffed clothes emerges and proclaims that he is the White Knight, mashed into a dumpling. They say that many of the audience believe his story.

The headliners at the Star, the Varieties, and the Amphitheatre are endless: the Batemans, Mrs. Stuart, Mrs. Logan, Anderson, Jansen, Silsbee, Van Amburgh, Gottschalk, Jullien, Sontag, Borghese of the Orleans Opera, Soto. The Odd Fellows Hall is society's mecca, with Sontag making the greatest hit since Jenny Lind. And Dan Rice's burlesque of *Uncle Tom's Cabin* is just what the damned Yankees deserve. We must even see W. H. Lynne as Henry IV, if only to say we went.

Only one thing tweaks our consciences. Sunday is the gala day in this French Catholic city. So unless we are to miss much of the excitement, we will have to forget the warnings of our upriver pastor against Sabbath violations. Well, when in Rome. . . . And Sunday is not really Sunday here, but a day of extraordinary pleasures. The martial review of the soldiers is held on Sunday. The bullfights are reserved for this day alone, as are the death-defying ascensions of a daring Frenchwoman balloonist. As soon as the Masses are over, the people are promenading, crowding the cafés, the oyster bars, and coffeehouses, betting on cockfights, idling happily in the Cathedral Square.

And on Sunday, the best horse races. . . .

As river planters we would have felt pleasurably alien to this city so different in population, in architecture, in attitudes from the overwhelmingly English-Scotch-Irish American settlements of the Mississippi. Yet here in New Orleans the upriver Anglo-Saxon sportsmen and pleasure seekers carried on their principal sports activity. In every year of the quarter century before the Civil War, horse racing was the great, crowd-drawing pastime of New Orleans; yet, it was participated in almost entirely by the Americans. The Creole of New Orleans loved gambling, but from inclination and from necessity he was not a horseman. He did not have the money to indulge in horseflesh as did the cotton-rich planters above New Orleans. Moreover, since the Americans had first espoused racing, even the wealthy Creoles eschewed it as participants, if for no other reason than that the still-resented Americans dominated the sport.

We look at a program for this spring meeting of the New Orleans Jockey Club. Who are the owner-entrants? Such men as William J. Minor of Natchez, Alexander and William Barrow of Feliciana, William J. Green, William Wynn, Thomas Wells, Mountfort Wells, George Long, Henry A. Taylor, James Jackson, Colonel A. L. Bingaman. Not a Frenchman, not an Orleanian; only the river planters, racing for uncommonly high stakes and providing a gay two weeks' season for the South. First a week at the Metairie Course, then another at the Louisiana Course, in crisp, bright March. The horsemen brag of the tracks, far springier than the eastern turfs. The envious Northerners answer that it is not the difference in turf that enables the river's horse to make better time. The Orleans racers are allowed free time between heats, and they carry a year's less weight. But these are academic matters, lacking interest to most of the thousands who throng to Metairie in March.

We take an omnibus to the Metairie track, speeding along the white, 20-foot Shell Road where stock grazes behind continuous fences, until we halt at the Toll Gate to pay the admission fee. On the grounds, we note that the animation of many spectators is being prolonged at the liquor booths on the race track grounds. The bars, the refreshment rooms, and the great, barnlike building of the gamblers are crowded. It is not enough simply to bet on the horses. Here the gentlemen of chance preside over the green tables, thumbing the marble balls and elusive dice. Always time for a few plays before the races.

There are no scrubs in the Metairie paddock. For years the river planters have been building up a great racing breed by the best sires out of the best dams in two continents, so that the South "has not only been holding her own, but surpassing the North and herself again, in the point of time, astounding the world and now challenging 'Mother England's' derby." No horsemen in the world give more attention to the care and training of their horses than do such owners as Colonel Bingaman, General Wells, and Duncan Kenner. In the biggest races, as in Lecompte and Lexington's three meetings, as much as a hundred thousand dollars would change hands in New Orleans alone. The spectators, as many as twenty thousand for an outstanding event, would come to Metairie from throughout the South and even from distant New York.

Among those twenty thousand we would have mingled, nearly a century ago, without wondering whether this kind of life in New Orleans would end. Nor has it, save superficially.

PART FOUR

Years of the Locust

CHAPTER 18

Gunboats on the River

THE CONFEDERACY's back and much of its spirit was broken on the Mississippi.

Jefferson Davis, the unapproachable, stubborn aristocrat of Natchez, failed strangely to understand that his river was more important than Richmond; that the Confederacy could have lost its capital, a dozen Virginia battles, and the state itself with less disaster than it suffered from weakly defending the Mississippi. Never during the war was the lower river, from New Madrid to New Orleans, defended in force except at Vicksburg. Then it was too late.

The North knew the river's worth. Its conquest would mean cotton for northern mills. It would reopen river traffic for the strangling Midwest and separate the eastern part of the Confederacy from the men and supplies in Texas, Arkansas, Missouri, and western Louisiana. It would hasten the spiritual degeneration of the river's soldiers, tempting them to desert to protect the lonely plantation or to indulge in the demoralizing traffic in contraband cotton that made unholy partners of enemies. Most terrifying of all, it would make possible the enlistment of nearly two hundred thousand former slaves and the recruiting of an equal number for manual labor in the Union's behalf.

Perhaps, at the onset, the northern leaders didn't comprehend all these possibilities. But they had vision enough to make the conquest of the Mississippi their most persistent offensive objective.

This is how the Union captured the Mississippi.

In the first year of the war, the Confederacy held the middle river, with forts at Columbus, New Madrid, Island Number 10, and Fort Randolph. New Orleans was protected by two old forts 75 miles below the city. Relying on these fortifications and on the armies east and west of the river, the South did not fortify a single river town.

The North struck swiftly at the Mississippi. Grant moved into Tennessee, and Forts Henry and Donelson fell on the Tennessee and Cumberland rivers in February, 1862, forcing the evacuation of Columbus. In March and April, General Pope captured New Madrid and Island Number 10. The men in gray couldn't halt the Union armies at Shiloh on April 6th and 7th, and the blue lines moved southward to the Memphis and Charleston Railroad. In conjunction with the overland drive, a Union river fleet had pushed down the Mississippi, defeating a Confederate flotilla at Fort Pillow in May. In early June, Fort Pillow, threatened from the rear by the Union forces and menaced by the victorious Yankee gunboats, was abandoned. On June 7th the Union fleet virtually destroyed the Confederate gunboats before Memphis. Practically undefended by troops, Memphis had no other course but surrender.

Meanwhile, in April, 1862, Farragut had damned the torpedoes and brilliantly run the Confederate batteries below New Orleans. On April 25th, his warships were anchored before New Orleans. And that great prize of the river, just as scantly defended as Memphis, capitulated. In May, Farragut took Baton Rouge and Natchez; then he attempted, with the assistance of a small land force, to capture Vicksburg. The attack failed, but except for that still unfortified town on the bluffs, the Union was in practical control of the Mississippi.

Such is the bare outline of an incredibly quick success which would be completed a year later with the siege and surrender of Vicksburg. Behind it is a story of equally incredible shortsightedness on the part of the Confederacy. Not that the South could have halted Grant in Tennessee; but the key cities of the river were left unprotected and unfortified in the belief that the scattered forts could stop the gunboats. The troops which might have defended the towns were concentrated elsewhere.

As it was, the Union navy was the deciding factor. Thanks principally to Captain James B. Eads of St. Louis, the Yankee gunboats on the middle river were far superior to the Confederacy's. Eads had built seven gunboats, nick-named "the turtles," in sixty-five days. They were flat-bottomed vessels 175 feet long, their sides projecting only a foot above water, and surmounted by plated casemates 150 by 50 by 8. These odd monsters mounted thirteen 6-inch rifles, and were capable of a speed of nine miles an hour. In addition this fleet had two other ironclads, and three former passenger steamboats, eight rams, and 38 mortar boats, which were scows mounted with 13-inch mortars and towed by tugboats. All in all the fleet on the upper and middle river included 45 assorted gunboats and 38 mortar boats.

In the fight off Memphis, the Confederate gunboats had a total of only 28 guns as against 68 on the Union flotilla. Seven of the eight Confederate warships were sunk or dis-abled. Below New Orleans, Farragut's strongly armored iron-clads steamed past futile Forts Jackson and St. Philip, after the barricading chains strung across the river had been cut away.

After the capitulation of New Orleans, only the later heroism of the Vicksburg defense tempered the humiliation and the despair of the river people. Especially did volatile New Orleans suffer in spirit. The Creoles had boasted that debonair, fire-eating Pierre Gustave Toutant Beauregard was the greatest soldier in the world; that Lee himself must be good because "I 'ave heard Beauregard speak well of heem."

Their brilliant Jew in Davis's Cabinet, Judah P. Benjamin, could outsmart any Yankee alive, they knew. As for fighters, their Zouaves, their Washington Artillery, their crack volunteer infantry companies had more élan than any troops in the Confederacy.

Now none of the river's fighting men could loosen the avaricious grasp of General Benjamin Butler, commander of the occupying forces.

It had not taken Butler long to earn the lasting hatred of the Orleanians. Before the city's formal surrender, a landing party from Farragut's fleet had raised the American flag over the United States mint. A young Orleanian, W. B. Mumford, hauled it down and hoisted the Stars and Bars. Mumford was hanged at Butler's order, shortly after his troops occupied the city on May 1st. He suspended two newspapers which had praised the destruction of cotton stores just before the city's capture. He suspended another because its editor was in the Confederate army. He organized three regiments of colored troops, "the darkest of whom," according to his ironic report, "is about the color of the late Daniel Webster." He connived in the illegal speculations of his brother, who made a fortune in New Orleans. Popularly he was believed to be confiscating silver, art pieces, and furniture belonging to Confederates for his own profit.

But what damned him forever was the notorious "woman order," promulgated after he became enraged at the contemptuous attitude accorded his soldiers by women of all classes in New Orleans. The order read:

Headquarters, Dept. of the Gulf.
New Orleans, May 15, 1862

General Order No. 28

As the officers and soldiers of the U. S. have been subject to repeated insults from the women (calling themselves ladies) of New Orleans in return for the most scrupulous non-interference on our part, it is ordered that hereafter when any female shall, by word, gesture or movement, insult or show contempt for any officer or soldier of the United States, she shall be regarded and held liable to be treated as a woman of the town, plying her vocation.

The mayor of New Orleans was removed from office for protesting against the order. Jefferson Davis, branding Butler an "outlaw," put a price on his ugly head. Northern newspapers condemned the order, and Secretary of State Seward apologized to the British chargé for its phraseology.

New Orleans replied in its own way. Legend has it that a pottery maker sold chamber pots with Butler's picture on their bottoms, and that they were especially favored by the city's prostitutes. Ladies carried cambric handkerchiefs with the Confederate flag embroidered in a corner. A tempestuous Creole wrote in *Le Carillon,* a New Orleans French newspaper: "What belly has vomited you forth, in what den were you conceived, how could so scaly a reptile not rend your mother's entrails when you were born?" Friends shipped him secretly to Paris to save him.

Yet despite harsh treatment, including heavy levies on the wealthier Confederates, New Orleans was luckier than some of her sister towns along the river. Baton Rouge was thoroughly pillaged after its capture. As the North's grip on the river became more secure, what seemed like systematic vandalism increased. The villages of Donaldsonville, Louisiana, Columbia, Arkansas, and Greenville, Mississippi were put to the torch because guerrillas in their vicinities persisted in firing upon the gunboats from the banks.

Until the war's end, irregulars and home guards did their best to protect outlying plantations from marauders, running off wandering white and Negro troops and raiding plantations "leased" to loyalists. That they had sympathy from some of the Union officers is evident in a report of

Lieutenant Roe of the gunboat *Katahdin*, which was patrolling the river below Baton Rouge in the Donaldsonville area. The report was written a few days before Federal troops burned Donaldsonville:

I respectfully request instruction if the *Katahdin's* guns are to be used for the protection of soldiers upon a marauding expedition. And if I am to use them in protection of drunken, undisciplined and licentious troops in the wanton pillage of a private mansion of wines, plate, silk dresses, chemises, female wearing apparel. I cannot further prostitute the dignity of my prefession as I conceive I have done today. I blush to report that while the troops were thus engaged, I pointed my fire upon guerrillas hovering in the rear,— apparently occupied in preventing such acts of U. S. troops.

In the Natchez area, several mansions and farmhouses were burned, and libraries, pictures, even clothing piled up and set afire. Many homes were robbed by looting soldiers. Episcopalian ministers were ordered to bless the President of the United States in the customary prayer in which they had substituted the phrase "President of the Confederate States." One, the Reverend William Henry Elder, refused. He was banished. Another complied at a Christmas service. Four young women left the church in protest. They also were ordered out of town. Throughout Mississippi, Sherman, rehearsing his devastating, later march through Georgia, destroyed corn, cattle, hogs, sheep, and poultry.

Pillage and petty tyranny were bad enough. But the most demoralizing blow was to come. Earlier in the war, and prior to the Emancipation Proclamation, President Lincoln had refused to permit the enlistment of slaves in the Union army. In January, 1863, the bitterly contested decision was made. Two months later, Lincoln wrote Governor Andrew

Johnson of Tennessee, who had advocated the use of Negro troops:

> The colored population is the great available and yet unavailed of force for restoring the Union. The bare sight of 50,000 armed and drilled black soldiers upon the banks of the Mississippi would end the rebellion at once.

The results were not so decisive as that, but they were successful enough, especially on the river where there was the greatest concentration of Negroes in the South. It is difficult to overemphasize the effect of this step upon the civilian population of the Lower Mississippi. Most of them lived on isolated farms and plantations or in small towns from which the majority of the able-bodied men had departed. They expected nothing less than massacre at the hands of the Negro troops.

Yet, in view of the number of Negroes who were enlisted and used along the Mississippi, the acts of violence were comparatively infrequent. Those that occurred, however, were widely reported, and served not only to terrorize the civilians but to enrage the Confederate soldiery into bloody retaliation, as at the recapture of Fort Pillow when Forrest's men indiscriminately slaughtered the Negro garrison.

Altogether, some 180,000 Negro troops were raised in the South, of whom, according to Captain J. S. McNeily, the Mississippi historian, 24,000 were recruited in Louisiana, 17,800 in Mississippi and 20,000 in Tennessee. Some of them served as faraway substitutes for Northerners who paid them to take their places in the conscripted forces. After the fall of Vicksburg, the Vicksburg *Herald* carried frequent advertisements from shirkers in New York, Massachusetts, Ohio, Michigan, Wisconsin, and elsewhere offering handsome bounties to any Negroes who would join the Union army in the advertisers' stead.

It was inevitable that incidents of lawlessness on the river would increase with the arming of the undisciplined Negroes and that the filthy Freedmen's camp established along the Mississippi would become a center not only for the debauchery of the black soldiers but for white northern troops as well. The sharp rise in robberies and murders caused Grant to report on August 30, 1863, that he saw "signs of negro insurrection."

A few examples of Grant's "signs" suffice. On Deer Creek, a rich plantation section in the Yazoo-Mississippi Delta, marauding Negroes killed several white planters. In Vicksburg, Negro soldiers shot in the back and killed a citizen who had struck a Negro sergeant. At historic Woodville, below Natchez, aged Judge Edward McGehee, his wife, and three ill daughters were dragged from their home by Negro soldiers searching for guerrillas who had fired upon them from that neighborhood. The judge was beaten over the head, his wife felled with the flat of a saber, while a white officer from Kansas looked on.

As the score of murders and robberies mounted, forty citizens of Oak Ridge, Mississippi, asked Sherman's permission to unite to protect their families. Refusing their request, Sherman answered:

"We are justified in treating the inhabitants as combatants and transporting you all across the sea. . . . I have only reduced these points to writing that you people may have something to think about and divert your minds from cotton, niggers and petty depredation."

Of the river planters who escaped such inroads many suffered complete loss of property through a legalized method. In October, 1863, Secretary of War Stanton ordered a confiscatory policy. The river, he said, had to be lined with a loyal population to ensure uninterrupted navigation. All property of "disloyal persons" was proclaimed as belonging to the United States and "when required may be taken."

Plantations of "loyal men" could be retained or leased to other loyalists, but persons of doubtful loyalty must take a loyalist as partner.

It sounded like Jubilee. Abandoned plantations were leased to political favorites who were permitted to enlist their own guards to protect them from raiding Confederates. After such guerrilla raids, indemnity was exacted from the disloyal and a fine of $10,000 levied if a loyal lessee was killed. Jefferson Davis's plantation was turned over to the Freedmen's Bureau.

"Jeff Davis' plantation is all covered with these negro farmers," exulted the Yankee-edited Vicksburg *Herald* in 1864. "Just where the rebellion was hatched shall rise up the Demonstration that black men need only the opportunity to solve the great problem that has so vexed the politicians."

Black men don't own the property now, and the great problem is still unsolved.

Jubilee on the river! Except for one drawback: Nathan Bedford Forrest, in command of the Confederate Department of West Tennessee, Mississippi, and Eastern Louisiana, was still on the loose. His irregular cavalry repaid terror with terror. Forrest, in peacetime an almost illiterate Memphis slave trader, was a daring cavalryman, a brilliant strategist, and a killer. When his raging horsemen swarmed in upon Fort Pillow and took no Negro prisoners, he wrote on the scene: "My men . . . are a-cillin um." Forrest raided Yankee-held Memphis, captured Holly Springs, cut Union communications and destroyed supplies, hindering Grant's Vicksburg campaign and Grant's pacification of the river even after it was entirely in Union hands.

Forrest also protected the South from its own marauders, the bands of deserters, stragglers, horse thieves, and robbers who plundered the plantations in the last two years of the war. In the river counties, his men ran down the bandits who called themselves Confederate soldiers, the illegal traders in cotton, the mule and horse stealers, and the increasing groups of Confederate deserters, showing little mercy to any of them.

The Reverend Stephenson Archer of Greenville remembered the thoroughness of Forrest's men. In the memoirs which the old clergyman published before his death, he recalled that he was once requested to marry a couple at Winterville, then known as Ireys Plantation:

I met Captain Evans within a mile of the place. He said, "Where are you going, sir?"

"I am going to marry Miss Copeland to Lt. Johnson."

He replied, "It ain't any use. I have just had him shot and flung into the river."

"Why, you are mistaken!"

"No, it's a fact."

"What did you do that for?"

"He stole Mr. Halsey's mules, and I had orders from General Forrest, who commands the cavalry in this section, to shoot all such marauders, and simply executed my orders."

I repaired to the house, and found that what he told me was literally true.

Not even the redoubtable Forrest could halt the two factors most disturbing to the Confederate war effort along the river. One was the decline of the fighting spirit itself after the fall of Vicksburg, on July 4, 1863. The other was the contraband traffic in cotton.

Thirty-one thousand men surrendered at Vicksburg. The captured troops were paroled. As parolees, they aided the Union's cause vastly more than they could have as captives, for they spread despair wherever they went. And all through the Confederate armies, the men who had come from the river thought bleakly of armed Negroes, of confiscated lands and destitute families. It is not unfair to say that the ruling desire of a great many was simply to get home.

In 1863, General Daniel Ruggles of Mississippi wrote to General Joseph E. Johnston: "The spirit of volunteering ceased to exist . . . this want of patriotic fervor is traceable to a number of causes, coming under the ruling desire to save property." From September to November, 1863, an estimated 26,000 deserters went to their homes in Alabama and Mississippi alone.

And in the terrible, last months of the Confederacy, Robert McHenry, a prominent Arkansas planter, wrote thus to President Davis: "The soldiers, I am sorry to say, are deserting and going home to the enemy in consequence of the cotton speculation. . . . A large part of the cotton returned to Richmond as being burned, has been stolen and sold to the enemy."

The illegal trade in cotton was undoubtedly the most potent factor in the decline of the war spirit and the accompanying moral degeneration so especially evident in the river counties. In ten counties of Louisiana and Mississippi within a hundred miles of Vicksburg, almost one-seventh of the South's 1860-1861 crop of 4,861,000 bales had been produced. The blockade had piled up increasing millions of bales. Then, with the Union occupation of the river came a profitable if unlawful outlet for the great cash crop.

Speculation and smuggling contaminated both sides. In January, 1863, C. H. Dana, assistant to Secretary of War Stanton, bitterly noted that "the mania for sudden fortune out of cotton, raging in a vast population of Jews and Yankees scattered throughout the country, has to a large extent corrupted and demoralized the army. . . . Every colonel, captain or quartermaster is in secret partnership with some operator in cotton, while every soldier dreams of adding a bale of cotton to his monthly pay."

General Grant himself wrote in July, 1863: "I venture

to say that no *honest* man has made money in West Tennessee in the last year, while many fortunes have been made in this time." So aroused did the general become that in the same year he ordered all Jews out of his military district, an order which was later countermanded by Lincoln as discriminatory.

A commanding officer of the Natchez district netted $10,000 in three months. Soldiers conspired with rebels to smuggle and sell the precious lint. It was precious indeed. Cotton which had sold in New York for 31.2 cents in 1861-1862, had risen to 67.21 cents in 1862-1863, and had soared to the unheard-of price of 101.50 in 1863. Dollar cotton! It was enough to make thieves of the most honest, traitors of the most devoted, business associates of the bitterest enemies. And it did.

"I hate the very name of cotton as the source of so much contamination of our people," wrote Louisiana's General Richard Taylor, the son of old Zachary, in his memoirs, *Destruction and Reconstruction*. The general was looking back to the day in 1864 when he ordered that every bale of cotton belonging to private individuals should be destroyed wherever it was likely to fall into the enemy's hand. The command was more honored in the breach than in the observance.

Efforts were made to destroy such cotton, but more escaped than was burned, even though cotton burning was ordered by the government itself. Memphis was an especial center of illegal trade, not only in cotton but in all contraband, throughout the war, for it was close to loyal territory. Through Memphis passed cotton on its way north, and medicines, clothing, minor luxuries, destined for homes and shops further south.

Cotton speculation was even worse immediately after the war. After Appomattox, some five million bales were piled up in the South, of which the Confederate government owned only a fraction. But most of it was seized as "Confederate cotton" by agents of the Treasury Department, who worked under a contract which gave them a portion of all cotton so identified and seized. The planters were helpless. To regain cotton lawfully theirs they paid a "toll" to unscrupulous agents, amounting to not less than twenty bales in a hundred. Frequently, two or three tolls were levied. The Treasury decreed that all cotton seized in the Atlantic and Gulf states must be shipped to Simon Draper, United States cotton agent in New York, and that cotton seized on the waters of the Upper Mississippi should go to William P. Mellen, agent at Cincinnati. After retaining their agreed-upon quarter or half of the seized cotton, the subagents in the field would send the balance to a middleman, known as the supervising agent. This participant took another cut of the cotton, and sent the rest to Mellen or to Draper. These gentry again would manipulate the cotton, a favorite procedure being to show inferior samples so that the cotton would be bought by their friends at low prices. Draper was a penniless man before he became cotton agent. He died a millionaire. Thus was the South dispossessed of its cotton. Thus did many a philanthropist get the wherewithal for philanthropy.

I have gone beyond the war on the river without dwelling upon the most heroic episode of its conduct—the siege of Vicksburg. I have done this purposely, for Vicksburg deserves separate consideration. The intensity of the siege, the heroism of defenders and attackers, the bulldog persistence of Grant illuminate the war's river phase which otherwise is lacking in military stimulus. It was a death-fight. Of the Union's 25,000 dead who are buried in Mississippi, 17,052 fell at Vicksburg. Of the Confederacy's losses, consider the Vicksburg Cadets, which afterward mustered six men of 123, and the Vicksburg Sharpshooters, who counted one alive of 124.

After the fall of Memphis and New Orleans in 1862, it did not seem possible for Vicksburg to offer any defense. General Beauregard was sent in April to fortify the town, but only six batteries were ready in May when Farragut attacked. He failed, and attacked again in June with a fleet which mounted 106 guns and 16 mortars, and with field pieces emplaced on the Louisiana shore. Failing again, the admiral reported that Vicksburg could not be taken without an army of 12,000 to 15,000 men. More men than that would die before the city fell.

While the gunboats hovered upstream and below, the Confederates, at last realizing the city's military value, desperately strengthened it with men and guns. Fortunately for the defenders, numerous Union delays prevented the investiture of Vicksburg until the end of December, 1862. First, Sherman struck. Then Grant drove at the bluffs again and again in a series of campaigns as important to the tactician for their failures as for the final success. The bloody frontal assaults were repelled. Then Grant drove General J. C. Pemberton's army into the city proper. After thousands of men had died on each side of the Vicksburg breastworks, Grant decided that the city could be taken only by siege. Thereupon, he invested Vicksburg with 71,141 men and 248 guns. The Union dug twelve miles of trenches, in which men were blown to bits by Confederate mines, and from which they burrowed to blast the defenders sky high in turn. So close were the opposed rifle pits, redans, and redoubts that hand grenades were used, and shells were lobbed from hollow logs reinforced with metal bands. The residents dug caves in the Walnut Hills, and stuck it out.

By June 28th, the rations of the defenders, outnumbered two to one, were only a stale biscuit and a piece of fat bacon a day; and the civilians were faring even worse. Mule meat was fought for. So desperate was the food situation that General Pemberton, in command of the defense, was told by a subordinate that "this army is ripe for mutiny unless it can be fed." By July 1st, scarcely a building in Vicksburg stood undamaged from shellfire. A third of the surviving Confederate force was in hospitals, and most of the others sickly from hunger and sleeplessness.

On June 28th, a week before the city's surrender, the Reverend Thomas Markham wrote this letter to his wife:

Burg June 28th 1862

My Dear Wife

This morning will long be memorable in the history of our Hills City. Last night for about an hour I witnessed a most magnificent exhibition—the firing of shells from the mortar boats. Each shell would sail up slowly into the sky looking like a moving star, & after reaching its altitude would drop swiftly to the earth exploding as it fell, the flash lighting up the horizon as the mortar fired, the ascending shell the boom of the mortar reaching us after the shell came into view, the lighted passage of shell to earth & explosion as it struck & all this repeated every 15 seconds sometimes 5 & 6 together in air & bursting on ground made up the grandest spectacle I ever witnessed. I witnessed from the front of Hazelett's house sitting there with several gentlemen.

I slept at Brown & Johnston's. Wheeler kindly offering me a bed.

This morning at 4 o'clock all Burg was aroused by a bombardment more frightful and terrific than I had conceived bombardment. I heard the rapid heavy firing but was dreaming struggling I suppose to waken. Charles Chilton who slept below stairs called to me to get up & leave the house as danger was most imminent. I rose dressed & hastened out—went over to Hendon and White's & found Ed Brown & John Randolph in front & asking where the boats were—

firing filled the sky in every quarter—John went with me
to the rear, there were two frigates one right opposite &
one below opposite Prentiss house, their big guns flashing &
bombing, others coming up & firing below. One sight was
enough. I at once left but had better have stayed. I made
for Country, going out Grove St. Shell bursting above &
about me, & grape shot sweeping street beside me, my escape
was marvellous. As I went on I overtook men women &
children on foot infants in arms & some few families on
drays. I went out to Mr Cox^s & found fugitives filling the
yard & road. But all was quiet. All were to impressed to
scream or shriek.

6 Gunboats swept by our batteries. We disabled two &
sent them back & injured the others—so says men at the
guns. One Soldier was killed & 9 wounded at our batteries—
one gun dismounted & one burst.

Mrs Gamble was killed at her house. A no. of houses
were struck. Catholic & Presb^n–& Meth. Ch^s, our house (a
shot went thro. front gallery roof) not much damaged.
But I will write from Uncle George Markham where I am
going to-day with Tom Roach who takes me out in a
buggy. . .

On July 4th, Pemberton, badly outgeneraled but not
outfought, surrendered. No matter how heavy the cost,
Grant had dealt the Confederacy a mortal blow. The South's
net loss included 46,000 men of whom 31,000 were prisoners
of war, 260 cannon, and 60,000 small arms. The river was
irretrievably gone. And far away in Gettysburg, the broken
armies of Lee were preparing to quit the hills and fields of
Pennsylvania. The South's death knell was clanging for all
to hear.

Such is the story of the river and the war. I would like
to add one small, human postscript. In a thick portfolio of
family letters and other documents which date from 1797

to this century, I found a lengthy missive written to my great-grandmother by a young Orleanian, a private in the Confederate army. He was in love with my grandmother, who, according to family lore, generously engaged herself to sixteen soldiers simultaneously at the outbreak of war. He writes from Natchez, where he is supervising the building of fortifications by slaves. After fulsome paragraphs on honor, patriotism, and hope of success, he apparently becomes indignant over the courtship competition of those more highly placed. So he comments:

> Wayside
> Near Natchez, Miss.,
> March 1, 1863

True, Lieutenant Olivier is a very worthy and nice young gentleman—very nice, Miss Anna. But so is the youth who marched beside him and wore a ragged jacket while Lieutenant Olivier wore a gold-laced frock and sash and sword. Ne crede colore. The largest honors of this war are due not to the generals who planned for they have been cowardly and incompetent as often as they have been brave and able. Not to officers who laughed and gambled in gay clothing while the men grumbled and fought in rags, for those who carry muskets are as brave and often as intelligent as those who carry swords. The men, the ragged and dirty men, the long-bearded and sometimes shoeless men, have done the work thus far—and will do it to the end. So I beg of you, Miss Anna and Miss Cora to look beyond the lace for evidences of true worth and wave to the weary looking, rough-shod privates, for they have been your real and efficient protectors.

> Jos. B. Lyman

CHAPTER 19

Bottom Rail on Top

CAPTAIN J. S. MCNEILY retired from the editorship
of the Greenville (Miss.) *Times* some fifty years before I fig-
uratively succeeded to his uneasy chair. I never knew him,
for he died in 1924, long before I came to the Delta. Yet I
am continually conscious of this long-ago predecessor. Kindly
older citizens sometimes compliment me by remarking that
an editorial had something of his force. Others, less tactful,
shake their heads when a local crisis arises, and mourn the
lost days when the captain would have straightened out the
situation with almost a single scratch of his brimstone-
tinctured pen.

Even if I did not have such reminders from our vanishing elder statesmen, I would know whereof they speak; for
our ill-kept files of seventy-five years ago are scorched with
the man's scorn and garlanded with his bitter courage. I am
sure that many another newspaper file along our river is
likewise trade-marked. Never in American history has there
been another such conjunction of time and place in which
editorial wrath could feed so unceasingly upon indignity or
outspoken resolution be so dangerously tested as in that
shameful decade of Reconstruction on the Lower Mississippi.

The river people had no monopoly upon distress and
degradation during Reconstruction. Yet the river was peculiarly suited to the corrupt purposes of the carpetbagger and
scalawag, and the radical intent of their vengeful masters in
Washington; and their talons clung longer to plunder and

political control here than elsewhere in the South. There are ample reasons for this extended tenure. Land was cheap, cotton profits seemingly assured; and the knowing adventurer could find shorter cuts to the land's wealth than by its tilling. After the war, the river's towns and acres were still intrinsically the richest in terms of production and taxation alike. Racially, the river region was the most one-sided black belt of the South, where the white men were vastly outnumbered and the emancipated Negroes a politically pliant mass. New Orleans and Memphis, once thriving ports, were ripe again for commercial development and for plunder. And the unyielding planters of the river symbolized most vividly to Thad Stevens and his crew the hated southern slave-owning aristocracy which must be ground in its own pride.

Against this unhappy background, Captain McNeily's resistance epitomizes the defiance of the typesetting editors of the small-town southern press. These men were physically hemmed in by federal bayonets. Their enemies held the guns to intimidate, the political strength to nullify at the polls any protest, the economic power to bribe or destroy. Some of these obscure newspapermen died violent deaths. A few succumbed to temptation. But most of them kept publishing their little hand-set weeklies, contemptuous, savagely critical voices in a hopeless wilderness. Someday a scholar whose patience matches his admiration, will write a fitting history of Reconstruction journalism in the South. I wish I could. I would give old Captain McNeily a volume to himself.

He was Mississippi born, on a plantation near Woodville, of a family of soldiers and planters who came to the present Wilkinson County when Mississippi was held by Spain. The war interrupted his education; the University of Mississippi closed its doors when its young men, J. S. McNeily among them, entered the Confederate army. He served with the 21st Mississippi, ultimately commanded by his brother Preston, throughout the conflict, participating in all the bloody campaigns in Virginia. The war over, he returned to Woodville, to join the staff of the venerable *Republican*, whose name was no indication of its politics. Crushed by the South's defeat and family sorrows, he soon decided to emigrate to Mexico. An older friend, Major Van Eaton, persuaded him to go to Greenville instead, in 1868. From then until 1892 Captain McNeily edited the *Times* in that little river town which the Yankees had burned during the war and which the carpetbaggers continued to gut for ten years afterward. Later he would write several scholarly volumes and monographs on the tragic period, the most noted of which is *War and Reconstruction in Mississippi.*

Captain McNeily need not have remained in this purgatory. There were foreign nations which would have offered him the sword which so many of his fellow officers accepted, and there were protesting newspapers in the North which would have made him their dissenting voice. But he stayed in the muddy, broken town, never making more than a modest living and in frequent danger of jail or assassination, until, incredibly, the battle was won.

We have space here only for glimpses, not all of them discouraging, of those grim days. The captain had stanch allies; the first William Alexander Percy, whom they called the Grey Eagle of the Delta, General Wade Hampton and Colonel Christopher Hampton, Merritt Williams, a triggerquick veteran who became one of the largest landowners in the South, Colonel Matt Johnson, Captain William Hunt, Captain Watt Stone, and many another old soldier who kept fighting the enemies of peace. And he found new, unexpected coworkers. Such a one was Major James E. Negus of the Union army. He was a Pennsylvanian, who had completed his education at Stuttgart in Germany, returning from Europe to enlist with the 15th Pennsylvania Cavalry. Shortly after the war he met General Wade Hampton, the great

champion of South Carolina, who owned thousands of acres
on the river in Mississippi. Gigantic Wade Hampton, who
once killed a bear with a knife, and the cultured Pennsylvanian took a liking to each other. They agreed to enter
business together on the river, and founded Wade Hampton
and Company, dealers in general merchandise, with a wharf-
boat at Skipworth, below Greenville. Major Negus married a
Greenville girl and from his first days on the river he was
actively in sympathy with the Southerners. Major Negus
remained in the Delta after Wade Hampton left to lead
South Carolina's struggle. Today, the president of the First
National Bank of Greenville is Wade Hampton Negus, the
Pennsylvania major's son.

And there was Holt Collier, now a legendary figure
along the river. Holt had been a slave, a black, erect, handsome man, who was the best hunter and surest shot in
Washington County. He fought for the Confederates with
his master, and when he returned he refused to be recon-
structed by "white trash and uppity niggers." Instead, so an
authenticated story goes, Holt Collier even killed from
ambush a Yankee who had threatened his master. Years later,
white-goateed Holt Collier took President Theodore Roosevelt
on a bear-hunting excursion in the Delta. When he died, his
funeral was attended by scores of the white men whose cause
he had espoused against interlopers and his own race.

But alien white men like Major Negus and black men
like Holt Collier were exceptions. The mounting tale which
Captain McNeily reported from his exchanges, and his own
observations, was one of horror, near-anarchy, unparalleled
despoliation, and stubborn resistance. By the time he assumed
the editorship of the *Times*, the Klan, entrenched in middle
Tennessee since its founding at Pulaski in December, 1865,
had spread westward to Memphis, to Arkansas, and to parts
of Mississippi, though it did not function as such in the river
counties of the state. Editorially, Captain McNeily applauded

its early activities. In Memphis, the nearest city, rugged Nathan Bedford Forrest headed the entire Invisible Empire. Memphis had become a difficult place after a bloody race riot in 1866. The city at that time was garrisoned by undisciplined Negro troops, who committed frequent robberies, assaults and even murders. Finally, in May, 1866, a three-day racial conflict resulted in the killing of 46 Negroes and 2 white men, the wounding of 75, and the destruction of 91 Negro homes, 4 Negro churches, and 12 Negro schools.

Forrest directed the Klan with the same punitive thoroughness which had characterized his command of the Confederate irregular cavalry in the closing months of the war. His night riders terrified the Negroes. On the river they were famed especially for a coup in Arkansas, where in 1868 the Negro and scalawag militia were committing wanton depredations. Alarmed at the Klan's extension to Arkansas, carpetbagger Governor Clayton had declared martial law, and purchased four thousand guns and ammunition in Detroit for immediate delivery. By mistake the arms reached Memphis. Governor Clayton arranged to have them reshipped by chartered steamer to Helena, Arkansas' river port town, southern steamboat captains in the regular river trade having refused to handle the consignment. The chartered steamboat, the *Hesper*, set out late in the afternoon of October 15, 1868. A hundred masked men, many of whom had suddenly deserted a fashionable ball on news of the *Hesper's* sailing, commandeered the tug *Nellie Jones* and set out in pursuit. Twenty-five miles downriver the Klansmen overtook the *Hesper*, boarded her and threw the guns into the Mississippi.

Such triumphs were jubilantly reported throughout the valley. But these minor victories of the Klan could not overcome oppression. The South was down and almost out. The abolitionist, and the white and Negro politicians on the scene, intended to keep her down for their own profit. In later years, Captain McNeily would record in scholarly detail the rape of his state. Now he could only protest.

The Reconstruction formula differed little in each southern state. The Confederates returned to their impoverished towns and untended farms. Their own early efforts at reconstruction failed to satisfy the northern extremists who after Lincoln's assassination controlled the government. Into the South swarmed the locust plague of carpetbaggers to league themselves with local opportunists, usually poor whites, and the gullible Negroes, most of them ignorant, many of them vengeful. They secured and maintained power by the bayonet, by control of the election machinery, by disfranchising thousands of former Confederates and enfranchising and bloc-voting the Negro. Violence begot violence. The South was systematically looted. And finally the white South, employing any workable methods from ballot stuffing to intimidation and murder, regained political control.

Concerning Reconstruction, two popular misconceptions exist. One, immaterial except for reasons of historical accuracy, is that Reconstruction was a continuous, unbroken era. The other, persistent in the South, is that the Negro was largely responsible for the misgovernment and the looting, the humiliation and the terror which were Reconstruction's earmarks.

Actually, there were four well-defined periods within the approximate decade of Reconstruction. The first lasted less than a year. During this time the southern states remained under military government. The second period of nearly two years witnessed the South's generally successful efforts to meet President Andrew Johnson's mild terms for regaining self-rule and statehood. This period ended with the vicious Reconstruction Act of 1867, which returned the seceding states to military rule and which brought the evil flowering of carpetbaggery. The fourth period begins with the readmission of the southern states to the Union, completely under the heels of the interlopers, and it ends with the triumph of the native whites over the scalawag-carpetbagger-freedmen coalition.

The Negro in Reconstruction served as dupe for the plunderer and as the political instrument with which the fanatic northern group led by Thaddeus Stevens intended to reshape the South's economic, political, and social structure. In the long run the Negro was to be the principal victim of Reconstruction in the South, for he remained there to suffer in many and in undeserved ways for the crimes and mistakes into which the white adventurer led him. If he followed white radicals along suicidal paths, this allegiance was the result of his simple emotional response to the promise of Jubilee. If the vicious and lawless among his number committed grave misdeeds, it was in great part because they were armed and abetted by the predatory stranger. A people enslaved throughout their residence in a free land, and liberated only by a bitterly destructive war, could not have been expected to look first to their defeated masters for political guidance. Their tragedy was that political equality and political responsibility were too suddenly thrust upon them, and that the men who should have taught them the proper meaning of these privileges were more interested in good pickings than in good citizenship.

Obviously, the white southerner of Reconstruction could not make a philosophic distinction between the leaders and the led, when both threatened his security, his political freedom, and his very life. Thus Reconstruction built higher the barriers to understanding at the expense of those who needed most to understand and to be understood. Nor has the shadow of the barrier lifted, though there are signs of light. No apologies are required for either the white man or the black man of the Reconstruction South. Under the circumstances, neither could have reacted to the virus other than each did.

❦ ❦

We will look at Reconstruction only in Captain McNeily's Mississippi. On June 13, 1865, President Andrew Johnson appointed William L. Sharkey provisional governor of Mississippi, as the first step toward restoration of civil rule. Similar appointments were made in other southern states. The provisional governor was empowered to call a convention "composed of delegates chosen by that portion of the state loyal to the United States," which should alter or amend the constitution and otherwise act to return the state to its constitutional relationship with the federal government. The military commanders of the several districts and the federal military and naval officers in the South were authorized to assist the provisional governors.

Sharkey was in every way acceptable to the Mississippians. As a lad of fifteen he had fought under Jackson at New Orleans. He had been a prominent Whig, an opponent of secession, and a strong Unionist. For eighteen years he had presided as chief justice of the high court of errors and appeals in Mississippi. In his public and private life he was unimpeachable, and even the strongest secessionist had respected his contrary views.

While the radicals fumed and demanded continuance of military rule, Governor Sharkey proceeded with a temperate program to restore civil government. Prominent Mississippians, taking the oath of allegiance, attended the constitutional convention as delegates. The president was Judge J. S. Yerger of the river's Washington County. An opponent of secession himself, Judge Yerger had lost one Confederate son in battle, another from fatal illness while in service, and his own home had been burned by Union soldiers.

The convention duly rendered the ordinance of secession and the institution of slavery null and void, and provided for immediate Congressional and state elections. It memorialized Congress, with more courage than wisdom, in behalf of imprisoned Jefferson Davis and former Governor Clarke and for the removal of Negro troops from the state.

Immediately, the northern radical group seized upon the convention's failure to establish political rights for the Negroes. Thad Stevens was beginning to ride the whirlwind. Crying for "black heels on white necks," Ben Butler demanded "confiscation of Southern lands and their colonization by discharged soldiers and loyal negroes." The Freedmen's Bureau joined the hue and cry.

As the storm gathered, Governor Sharkey further goaded the northern extremists by authorizing white volunteer militia companies to cope with spreading criminal acts, committed by both whites and Negroes. Most of the military in the state at the time were Negro soldiers, many of whom contributed to the misdeeds they were supposed to prevent. In 1866 there were only 39 white commissioned officers and 1,071 white soldiers in Mississippi, and 338 Negro officers and 8,784 Negro soldiers, none of them regulars. Federal army officers vehemently opposed the creation of the white militia. But President Johnson permitted it, thereby providing another item for Stevens's personal bill of particulars. And even though the white and Negro militia did not clash, the radicals termed the "Sharkey plan" a scheme to reorganize the rebel army.

Tempers on both sides swiftly became red-hot. The President further angered the avengers by making it possible for owners of "abandoned lands" taken by Negroes and "loyalists" to recover their property by receiving presidential pardon, which he freely gave. General Slocum, military commander of the state, resigned in September, 1865. Later, campaigning for secretary of state on the Democratic ticket,

he gave in a speech at Syracuse his eyewitness picture of
Mississippi in this first year after the war:

Half the Negroes in that section are at once seized
with a desire to see the Yankee military judge, and to see
how their old masters or mistresses would act on being
brought before him. Complaints are made against the kind-
est and best people in the country. The immediate result
is despondency and anger on the part of the whites—discontent and indolence on the part of the blacks. . . .

You seldom hear of the numerous cases where the freedmen have laid claim to the lands of their former masters,
and have quietly informed them that they held title under
the United States government, and have persistently refused
to do anything but eat, loiter and sleep. They fail to tell
you of the cases where, just as the harvest is to commence,
every hand has suddenly disappeared from the place, leaving
the labors of a year to decay in the field. They fail to tell
you of great bands of colored people who leave their former
homes and congregate in the cities and villages or settle
on a plantation, without permission from the owner, seeking
only food and utterly careless of the future. On the very
day that I left Vicksburg a poor woman came to me with
a complaint that at least fifty Negroes, not one of whom
she had ever before seen, had settled on her farm and were
eating the few stores she had laid aside for winter use.

Our sympathies are due to the white as well as to the
black race, though we have no constitutional right to control either. The difficulties surrounding this question can
only be met and overcome by practical men.

For a while, reconstruction of Mississippi by Mississippians proceeded under Sharkey's concept. It was a backbreaking task of rehabilitation. One-third of Mississippi's
adult white male population, as of 1861, was disabled or

dead. In 1866 one-fifth of the state's revenues was spent for artificial limbs. Currency remained deranged. Floods in 1867 overran much of the Delta, the state's principal revenue yielder then and now.

But the first two years were holidays compared with what would follow. In 1867 three Congressional-approved commissioners, General Grant, Major General Carl Schurz, and B. C. Truman, toured the South. Their report on southern loyalty was generally favorable, but the radicals, refusing to accept their findings, countered with stacked committee hearings in Washington to which no Mississippi Democrat but only white and Negro federal officers, Treasury agents, and similar payrollers were invited. These gave a sinister picture, which was what Seward, Sumner, Stanton, and Stevens wanted. Johnson was unable to block the notorious Reconstruction Act of March 2, 1867, under which the southern states were converted into military districts, Mississippi and Arkansas forming the fourth.

From now on the bottom rail was on top with a vengeance. Union League organizers swarmed through the state —and the South—fraternizing with the Negroes in barrooms, cabins and fields, signing them up as loyal voters, impressing them with oaths, passwords, military drills, and gaudy ceremonies. The great objective was to mold the Negro into a solid Republican block. Meanwhile civil officers were forcibly removed by the military. The editor of the Vicksburg *Times* was jailed for denouncing General Ord as a despot. Another Mississippi editor, E. M. Yerger, shot and killed Lieutenant Colonel Crane, acting mayor of Jackson, as the climax of another abuse of judicial power.

Under federal bayonets army officers and Negro registrars conducted registration of voters for the election of delegates to a new constitutional convention. The count of qualified voters was 46,636 whites and 60,167 Negroes, with Negro majorities in 32 of the 61 counties.

Of the delegates which these voters sent to a weird deliberative assembly in 1868, 17 were Negroes, of whom eight were ministers; 29 were scalawags, 19 were white conservatives, and the remainder, about 30, were out-of-state carpetbaggers. The thirty-two counties with Negro majorities sent 70 delegates; the 29 white-majority counties sent 30 delegates. Members of both factions at the constitutional convention went armed with pistols and dirks. The delegates voted themselves $10-a-day salaries and forty cents a mile travel allowances, exorbitant sums for the time. Reporters were excluded for not placing "Mr." before the names of Negro delegates. Most of the Democratic handful resigned. Of these conventions in Mississippi and elsewhere, Claude Bowers wrote in *The Tragic Era:*

In Mississippi, the convention cost a quarter of a million, and four obscure Republican papers were paid $28,-518.75 for publishing the proceedings. In Arkansas, where each member was voted ten newspapers, the mileage graft was shameless, and the printing was let to a politician without competition at an astounding figure.

There was graft everywhere; for the constitution-makers of the day expected to be office-holders on the morrow, and all were in training.

Most of the constitutions were monstrosities, proscriptive, and frankly designed to serve the purposes of party. Incendiary talk marked the proceedings. While a Mobile delegate, supported by the carpetbaggers, clamored lustily for the legalization of intermarriage, the scalawags opposed; but as a rule the negroes showed more judgment and a keener appreciation of the realities than the white demagogues. . . . Everywhere, except in Georgia, the conventions centered on the disfranchisement of large blocks of whites, and wrote this infamy into the fundamental law—for this was the real purpose of these conventions.

Ending their work to the satisfaction of the Washington radicals, helping themselves to as much public plunder as was within reach, the conventions closed in jubilations, and in North Carolina there was a real thanksgiving, with the notorious General M. S. Littlefield, who was to get more than his share of the loot under the governments of "loyal" men, singing "John Brown's Body."

These documents, framed by ignorance, malevolence, and partisanship, sounded the death-knell of civilization in the South.

Except in Mississippi, the southern carpetbag constitutions were ratified. Mississippi, waging a back-to-the-wall fight with no holds barred, defeated the new constitution 63,860 to 56,230 on the issue of white disfranchisement. In 1869, however, the constitution was accepted with the disfranchising clause omitted. So in 1870 the state was readmitted to the Union. In the same year it ratified the Fourteenth and Fifteenth Amendments to the Constitution.

Until 1870 the state was administered by a succession of military commanders, Ord, Gillem, McDowell, and finally, and most lamentably, General Adelbert Ames, a 34-year-old West Pointer who seemingly forgot an irreproachable military career when he turned politician. Perhaps his selection of Ben Butler as his father-in-law had something to do with it.

Among Ames's earliest acts was the annulment of state laws providing artificial limbs for maimed Confederate veterans and excepting them from the poll tax. On one occasion he used troops to liberate two of his county officials convicted of embezzlement. He ordered his post commanders to disregard writs of habeas corpus from either state or federal courts. He dismissed practically every civil officer in the state in favor of his own appointees.

Under Ames, both as military governor and later as

civil governor, Mississippi reached the lowest depths of Reconstruction. The Republican ticket, backed by Ames and President Grant, swept into office in the first election after the state's readmission. J. L. Alcorn, an ambitious former slaveholding Mississippian, was governor and James Lynch, a mulatto, secretary of state. Three white carpetbaggers and three scalawags completed the state ticket. The rich river counties, Washington, Adams, and Warren, sent entire Negro delegations to the Republican legislature of which 46 members were Negroes. This campaign had been marked with unrelenting terrorism on both sides. Negro mobs and Negro militia rioted in many areas. Nor were the whites slow to retaliate. A Negro convention delegate named Combash gathered a following and ran amuck through Sunflower County in the Delta. Dr. Tully Gibson, a planter and physician, led a group of friends against Combash's raiders, killing several of them. Later, the doctor was slain by soldiers and deputies while resisting arrest for his attack on Combash. The Negro leader himself had his career ended by the Ku-Klux, who hanged him.

The campaign was also highlighted by the activities of the Loyal Leagues. In Captain McNeily's *War and Reconstruction in Mississippi* appears this pathetic glimpse of a League initiation:

The initiation was, to the negro, very solemn and impressive. They usually met on Saturday night at the cabin of some prominent negro, or in some vacant outhouse. Armed sentinels were posted on all the approaches to the house. In the center of the room, which was rarely capable of holding one-fourth of the number assembled, was placed a table, or old goods box, on the center of which rested an open Bible, and a deep dish or saucer filled with alcohol and myrrh, which was lighted; above this altar, so-called, was suspended a United States flag, and also a sword. The candidate was blindfolded outside and was led in by the arm and required to kneel at this "altar" and place his hands upon the open Bible. The president of the League called upon the chaplain to pray. He invoked the divine blessing upon the "poor benighted brother who was about to pass from the night of bondage in slavery into the marvelous life and light of freedom." Short passages from the account of Moses leading the children of Israel from Egyptian bondage were then read, when the candidate was catechised, something after this fashion—(a prompter answered the questions, and the candidate was required to repeat the answers):

"What is your name?"

"Jim Cruise."

"Are you a white or colored man?"

"A colored man."

"Were you born free, or a slave?"

"A slave."

"Are you now a slave or a freedman?"

"A freedman, thank God."

"Who freed you?"

"Abraham Lincoln, bless God!"

"Who helped him to free you?"

"The army and the 'Publican party."

"Who fought to keep you in slavery?"

"The white people of the South and the Democratic party."

"Who then are your best friends?"

"The 'Publican party and Northern soldiers."

"Whom do you want to hold all the offices in this state and govern it, make and execute its laws?"

"The 'Publicans, the friends of the poor colored man."

"Suppose the Democrats carry the elections and get back into power, what would become of you and all the colored people in the state?"

"We would be put back into slavery. God forbid!"

All—Amen! and amen!!

An oath was then administered to the candidate which he was required to repeat after the prompter:

"I, Jim Cruise, do solemnly swear on the holy Bible, in the presence of God and these witnesses, that I will ever remain true and loyal to the Republican party; that I will always vote the Republican ticket; that I will keep secret all the signs, pass words, and grip of the Loyal League; that I will obey all the laws, rules, resolutions, and commands of the League of which I am a member; that I will forever reverence the name and memory of Abraham Lincoln, the author and father of my freedom, and that I will observe and keep in holy remembrance each anniversary of the Emancipation Proclamation, and that I will teach my children to do so. That I will never knowingly vote for any Democrat for any office lest I be put back into bondage and slavery. That I will never disclose the name of any member of this League, or of any League of which I may become a member, nor tell the place of meeting of the same; that I will not testify against any member of this, or any Loyal League, concerning anything done by the League or its order, or the order of any of its officers.

"For a violation of this oath, or any part of it, for the first offense, I agree to receive fifty lashes on my bare back; and one hundred lashes for the second offense; and for the third, to be secretly shot to death by any member of the League appointed for that purpose, so help me God!"

The blindfold is then removed and the candidate receives the following lecture:

"My Brother: You have just been brought from the darkness of bondage and slavery to the glorious light of freedom. You behold above you the flag of freedom, beneath whose folds the soldiers of the Union marched and fought; and the sword, the implement with which they struck from your hands the chains of slavery, and made you a free man. You behold on your left, a pot of sweet incense which constantly rises toward heaven. So let your gratitude, sweetened with humanity, and strengthened with courage, ever ascend to God in acknowledgment of the blessings of freedom."

He was then invested with the grip, sign of recognition, pass word, and sign and cry of distress.

Can we blame the Negro?

🌼   🌼

Following readmission to the Union in 1870, it was necessary to elect to the United States Senate a successor to the unexpired term of Jefferson Davis. The radical legislature selected the Reverend Hiram Revels, an Indiana-bred mulatto who had been educated at a Quaker school. For the following full term Governor Alcorn was honored. Ames received the other senatorship. Thus Mississippi's first three senators after readmission were a renegade southerner, a northern adventurer, and a Negro. Revels's career is not without interest. He had been in the public eye in St. Louis when his head had been split open by a beer bottle in a riot in a church. In Leavenworth he had lost a libel suit arising from an accusation that he had misappropriated $1,160 in church funds. In later years, however, after the white Democrats returned to power in Mississippi, he was appointed president of a state Negro college, and acquitted himself well. Today, in our river town, the Revels Memorial Church is the only tangible reminder of his leadership.

The river counties suffered heavily in this heyday of Reconstruction. The Negro and carpetbag officials vied in robbery of the public till. In Yazoo County, A. T. Morgan, a northern white man with a Negro wife, grew rich as sheriff. In Washington County a carpetbagger named Webber stole an estimated $200,000 in six years as sheriff and as deputy to the Negro who succeeded him. The overwhelmingly black state militia was led by brigadier generals and colonels of their own race who drew comfortable salaries for leading what was dubbed "Alcorn's Sedentary Militia."

All this is a small part of the record, which could fill many unhappy volumes. Elsewhere on the Mississippi the carpetbagger's reign was as bad or worse. In Louisiana, where the stakes were higher, there was more looting than terrorism; in threadbare Arkansas, more terrorism than robbery.

But resistance did not die in men's hearts. In time many in the North also sickened of the spectacle. And as the South gained friends elsewhere, the invaders, falling out among themselves, began to lose courage. A significant example of expression of intersectional sympathy occurred in Vicksburg in 1874. There were only three white officeholders in the county. At election time the Republican candidate for mayor was a white man under seventy-seven indictments, with seven illiterate Negroes running on his ticket as aldermanic candidates. In April, 1874, this group was defeated by opponents running on a reform ticket supported not only by the Democrats but by many moderates among the white and black Republicans. The resignations of the sheriff and chancery clerk were then demanded. They quit office hurriedly but later the sheriff appealed to the Negroes to help him regain his post. On December 6th, a Sunday, a number of Negro ministers urged their congregations to arm themselves and restore the sheriff to office; and Governor Ames ordered out a Negro militia company to suppress the whites. The Negro troops and mob were met by volunteer white militiamen, led by Confederate officers. In that volunteer group were a hundred former Union soldiers, serving under their former enemies. In the battle, 29 Negroes were killed and 30 taken prisoner, with a loss of two white men.

All such incidents were reported, savagely editorialized upon, and, in instances, participated in by my predecessor, Captain McNeily, as the old files of the *Times* vigorously attest.

Finally, in 1875, Mississippi's Democrats overthrew the carpetbaggers, winning a legislative majority, impeaching the Negro lieutenant governor and superintendent of education, and forcing Ames to resign as governor, a position to which he had been elected after resigning as United States senator. The Democrats stuffed ballots, intimidated the Negro masses, and even killed to regain control.

This is all hard to understand today. But a quotation from the disregarded minority report of eight members of a Congressional committee, which investigated the Ku-Klux Klan in 1871, might be helpful to the outsider:

. . . when the negroes were formed into military organizations and the white people of these states were denied the use of arms; when arson, rape, robbery and murder were things of daily occurrence; when the great mass of the most intelligent whites were disfranchised and the ballot was put into the hands of the negro by the government at Washington; when every promise made and every law enacted was broken and disregarded by the Federal authorities whenever it suited their purpose to do so; when even the courts were closed and the Federal officers, who were made by Congress absolute rulers and dispensers of what they called justice, ignored, insulted and trampled upon the rights of ostracized and disfranchised white men while the official pandered to the enfranchised negro on whose vote he relied; in short, when that people saw that they had no rights which were respected, no protection from insult, no security even for their wives and little children, and that what little they had saved from the ravages of war was being confiscated by taxation and rendered valueless by the debts for which men who owned nothing had pledged it, and saw that all their complaints and remonstrances, however honestly and humbly presented to Congress, were either wholly disregarded or regarded as evidence of a rebellious and unsubdued spirit, many of them took the law into their own hands and did deeds of violence which we neither justify nor excuse. But all history shows that bad government will make bad citizens; and when the corruption, extortions and villainy of the governments which Congress has set up and maintained over the Southern states are thoroughly understood and made known, as we trust they will be some day, the world will be amazed at the long suffering and endurance of that people.

Recollection of this grisly period hinders both the white man and the black along the river today. For the memory of ten years of wrong has resulted in continuing mistrust, and a perpetuation of wrongdoing itself.

CHAPTER 20

Bring Out Your Dead

MEN could count 152 names for the noisome
Thing, but no true cure. It struck without warning. First,
the flushed, yellow face, the drunken look, the chills and
fever. The eyes become bloodshot, glistening, or apathetic,
and sharp pain needles through the eyeballs, the head, the
entire body. From the erupted skin pours an odorous per-
spiration. The tongue cracks, thirst is overpowering. Then
the delirium, black vomit, hemorrhage—and miraculous recovery or merciful death.

Some called the Thing the American pestilence. Others
knew it as the fever of Spain, the disease of Siam, the vomito
negro, or the bilious putrid fever. To the stricken Carib
Indian it was the dread cocolitzle. Many bandied its nick-
name, yellowjack. But most frequently it was spoken of,
simply and fearfully, as yellow fever.

Safeguards abounded. A man could drink limewater,
eat garlic and onions, swallow huge doses of quinine or
cathartic pills. Some sprinkled sulphur in their boots. Others
gulped gin and sulphur, and wore liver pads. Stricken towns
sprinkled chlorinated lime, or saturated the air with carbolic
acid, or fired cannon into the offensive atmosphere to halt
its spread.

And there were a score of remedies. The humors could
be drawn by the application of heavy blisters on the head
and kidneys. Opium to quiet the patient, quinine—200
grams in three days—to cure him. Bleeding, preferably at

the back of the neck. And since water was bad for the victim, only four spoonfuls a day.

But when yellowjack stalked, none of these precautions, none of these panaceas really seemed to work. One garlic-reeking citizen would live. Another, redolent with onions, sulphur, and whisky, would die. Those who were willing to face the truth knew that they did not know what to do for the yellow fever, or even what it was. They could only do their best, meanwhile accepting that favorite description of a learned man of medicine: "Yellow fever is a disease produced by invisible germs floating in the atmosphere taken through the blood into the lungs, and afterward propagated by excreta and invisible emanations." And that helped nobody.

Old in the world when New Orleans was emerging from a swamp, yellow fever was accepted as an inescapable hazard, particularly along the Lower Mississippi. New Orleans seemed especially susceptible to its ravages. From 1767, when the disease was first recorded there as such, though it struck much earlier, few years passed without attacks so frequent as to be endemic. The French blamed its arrival upon the Spaniards who came with O'Reilly. And in October, 1796, Spanish Intendant Ventura Morales made this detailed observation of the plague:

An epidemic which broke out in the latter part of August, and which is prevalent to this day, has terrified and still keeps in a state of consternation the whole population of this town. Some of the medical faculty call it a malignant fever; some say that it is the disease so well known in America under the name of "black vomit," and finally, others affirm that it is the yellow fever which proved so fatal in Philadelphia in the autumn of 1794. Although the number of deaths has not been excessive, considering that, according to the Spanish registry, it has not yet reached 200

among the whites since the breaking out of the epidemic . . .
still, it must be admitted that the loss of lives is very great,
because, although those who died out of the precincts of
the town, and the protestants who perished (and they were
numerous) have not been registered, nevertheless the number
of deaths exceeds, by two thirds, those which occurred in
the same lapse of time, in ordinary years.

A peculiarity to be remarked in the disease is that it
attacks foreigners in preference to natives, and what is singular, it seems to select the Flemish, the English, and the
Americans, who rarely recover, and who generally die the
second and third day after the invasion of the disease. Such
is not the case with the Spaniards and the colored people,
with whom the recipe of Dr. Masderall has produced marvelous effects.

The years tolled death. In the last decade of the eighteenth century, New Orleans was free of yellow fever only
in 1792. No precise records of yellow fever deaths were
kept until 1817, when 80 were listed. In 1847, yellow fever
claimed 2,306 victims in New Orleans. In 1854, there were
2,435 deaths; a year later, 2,670. A high mark was reached
in 1858 with 4,845, and in 1867, 3,107 bodies were carried
away in the yellow fever carts.

Nor was New Orleans alone in its misery. Yellowjack
ranged up the river, striking in Baton Rouge, Natchez,
Memphis, in all the smaller towns and on countless plantations. The fever struck elsewhere too in the United States.
Boston, New York, Charleston, Philadelphia, all had their
epidemics, introduced by the trading ships from the Latin-
American countries and from the lower river. But New
Orleans was the most crowded graveyard of all, its death
rate from the fever 100 per cent higher, and even more.
The Orleanians replied to criticism by saying that yellow
fever was the "stranger's disease," pointing out that mortal-

ity among the natives was only a fraction of that among newcomers.

In the gutters of the city, the stagnant, clotted pools lay unnoticed. In the swamps beyond, foliage and animal matter rotted into green scum, and no one cared. Men slapped at the buzzing little pest that no one had yet named the *Aëdes aegypti*. The people of the Lower Mississippi shrugged their shoulders and sought specifics. Certainly, yellow fever sometimes swept upriver. But folks were comparatively safe, except in New Orleans. Even New Orleans was no death trap save in July, August, and September of a big fever year.

Then came 1878.

🌿   🌿

Memphis in 1878 was a filthy, bankrupt city. No one could understand what kept the town together. Its taxable wealth had shrunk from $30,000,000 in 1874, to $20,000,-000. The municipal indebtedness had reached a staggering $5,500,000, and one-third of the taxable property had been confiscated for nonpayment of taxes. Though the population was double that of 1860, trade was little better. Homeless Negroes, searching for jobs or Jubilee, thronged the streets as paupers and petty thieves. Memphis scrip and bonds, totaling $960,000, were worth 23 cents on the dollar. War, Reconstruction, and political debauchery had brought John Overton's town to the precipice.

In no way was the demoralization of Memphis more apparent than in its lack of sanitation. Dirty wells and cisterns supplied the drinking water which before the war had been taken from the Mississippi and the Wolf. The Memphis *Ledger* described the streets as "huge depots of filth, cavernous Augean stables with no Tiber to flow through and cleanse them." Even the pavements were decaying. In

The Biography of a River Town, Gerald M. Capers, Jr., pictures this Memphis of 1878:

Front yards, back yards, avenues, alleys and gutters were full of garbage, refuse, dead animals and stagnant water, all producing a stench which, but for the adaptation peculiar to the olfactory sense, would have driven human life from the town. The whole corporate area, with its thousands of "privy vaults," drained into Gayoso Bayou, a stream which had once been several miles in length, but which in the seventies had for many years been merely a series of stagnant pools, separated by dams of decaying organic matter and human excrement.

This was the Memphis in which a Mr. and Mrs. Bionda operated a snack house on the river front, a haunt of hungry and not too squeamish boatmen when ashore. Mrs. Bionda, like everyone else, found it convenient to empty the slops and garbage into the gutter or the near-by shallows.

Perhaps Mrs. Bionda was throwing out the refuse one August night in 1878 when she swished carelessly and too late at a mosquito. Her mind was probably on other things. Yellow fever, for instance. For three months Memphis had been nervously discussing the great fever epidemics to the south. As far back as May the businessmen of Memphis, apprised that yellow fever was raging in the West Indies, had petitioned for a quarantine. The council had refused. In July the Memphis newspapers had reported an epidemic in New Orleans. Thereupon, a quarantine station was established at railroad points outside the city. In August, it was rumored that in near-by Grenada, Mississippi, yellowjack was raging. Memphis became panicky. They remembered another August, in 1873. A New Orleans steamboat had left two sick men at Irish-populated Happy Hollow under the bluffs. Yellow fever had broken out in the settlement and spread throughout the city. Twenty-five thousand Memphians had fled. Of those who remained, 2,000 had died, and 5,000 others had been stricken and recovered. Memphis wanted no repetition of that terrible onslaught.

Mrs. Bionda died on August 13th. Her death was reported the next day as the first yellow fever casualty, though actually two Negro children and a white man had previously succumbed. The rooms of the snack house were fumigated with carbolic acid and copperas, and the surrounding streets disinfected.

Twenty-two new cases were reported on the day of the announcement of Mrs. Bionda's death. Memphis went berserk with fear. A wild new flight from the city began. By the middle of September, 25,000 of the population had departed; this left only some 20,000, of whom 14,000 were Negroes. Of the 6,000 whites who remained, a majority were poor shanty Irish. Before the epidemic was to run its course, 17,000 of these Memphians were to be stricken. More than 4,000 of the whites would die, but less than 1,000 of the 14,000 Negroes.

The crazed rush had ended by early September, for all who could or would flee had done so. Memphis was a ghostly city, its trade and traffic suspended, its living caring for the sick and burying the dead. The early morning stillness was broken only by the cry, "Bring out your dead," as the burial carts made their rounds, and in the unearthly hush even the buzzing of the green-bottle flies, trailing the wagons to the graveyards, sounded loud. White funeral notices hung limp from houses and fences, and at the end of the last journey, drunken gravediggers waited beside the stacked coffins and shallow pits.

The men and women who remained when they could have fled, particularly the doctors and Catholic priests, acted with unending heroism. The priests had remained behind with their poor parishioners, the Irish. Twenty-four died.

Fifty doctors, including many volunteers from other towns, succumbed. The "besom of destruction" felled all but one member of the staff of the *Ledger,* four of the *Avalanche* and two of the *Appeal,* but these survivors contrived to publish the news, meanwhile nursing their fellow reporters and printers in the printers' infirmary.

The epidemic clothed some with unexpected majesty. "Down the Jericho Road," in the prostitution district, Annie Cook ran the Mansion House, a sumptuous bagnio on Gayoso Street. She discharged her prostitutes, and opened her gaudy rooms to yellow fever patients whom she nursed herself. On September 6th, Annie was stricken. A week later the *Appeal* carried this epitaph:

> Annie Cook, the woman who after a long life of shame, ventured all she had of life and property for the sick, died September 11 of yellow fever which she contracted while nursing her patients. If there was virtue in the faith of the woman who but touched the hem of the garment of the Divine Redeemer, surely the sins of this woman must be forgiven her.

Ironically, another woman, described as "an accomplished Louisiana whore," who had not volunteered to help, recovered.

The conduct of the Negro police and Negro militia was likewise praiseworthy. The McClellan Guards, the Negro soldiery, and the Bluff City Grays, the white military organization, united in patrolling the streets and guarding the tent camp near the city where thousands of Memphians, financially unable to travel farther, had congregated. Negro male nurses courageously remained with their charges, and though rumors of rapes of sick women by some of these nurses persisted, no such crimes were ever proved.

But if heroism abounded, so did examples of cowardice

and worse. Survivors caroused madly. A drunken white man was found on the nude body of a dying woman who had sent for him. Attendants pillaged the dying and the dead. A prominent citizen who was out of town when the epidemic began, refused to enter the city even after being told of the death of his wife, her stillborn baby, and another child.

Courts-martial were established to deal with robberies. The decomposed bodies of a family of four, their bones "in a puddle of green water," attested to the reluctance of many of the living to approach the dead. Two decaying bodies on a principal street remained untouched for days. A naked, delirious woman, terrified of a drunken nurse, fled unclothed beyond the city limits, calling for her husband. Rats ate the body of a Negro woman, lying untended near the *Appeal* office, and died. A mother was found dead with the mouth of her lifeless baby clinging to her breast.

And there were unusual and grimly comic incidents. A woman died, but her healthy child was born posthumously. A 12-year-old girl, deaf, dumb, paralyzed on one side of her face, and suffering from St. Vitus's Dance on the other, recovered from the fever and regained all her faculties. Negroes dressed the bodies of the dead in carnival costumes. In St. Patrick's Cathedral services were being held for an Irishman, when the shrouded figure stirred, sat up, and yelled, "What the Hell are you doing?"

The nation responded generously to the appeals of Memphis. The Howard Association, a charitable society, spent more than half a million dollars, and supplied 2,900 nurses. Thousands of dollars poured in from farmers, bankers, ranchers, and merchants in the North and West and South.

The fever raged throughout the long, unusually warm summer's end and early fall. In mid-October frost covered the middle South. Then a freeze followed, and the epidemic ended. Seventy-five per cent of the whites who remained in the city had died, but less than ten per cent of the Negroes.

It is obvious from records of this and other epidemics that the Negroes of the South had somehow developed a comparative immunity to yellow fever.

Memphis had been hardest hit in this terrible year, but Memphis was not alone. In little Greenville, Mississippi, 150 miles below Memphis, 1,000 of its population of 2,300 had suffered yellow fever and 400 had died. In New Orleans, 4,046 deaths, the second highest number of victims on record, were reported. Fugitive Memphians, fleeing from the scourge that many carried with them, had spread the fever throughout the Mississippi Valley and beyond. Kentucky and middle Tennessee were heavily infected. And fear of yellow fever brought severe economic damage to the entire valley.

In this greatest of epidemics, yellowjack had chosen the most propitious of all times to strike. The lower river was battling to overcome the despair and the wreckage of Reconstruction. The epidemic of 1878 hindered its efforts, reduced its population, by death and desertion to healthier climates, and made its greatest cities, Memphis and New Orleans, almost synonymous for the scourge itself.

It is impossible to exaggerate the retarding effects of yellow fever, and those lesser deadly scourges, smallpox, cholera, malaria and dengue, upon the progress of the valley. Through the nineteenth century disease stalked virtually unchecked along the Lower Mississippi, destroying thousands of its settlers, driving thousands of others to quit the baleful land of fevers, deterring uncounted numbers from seeking their fortunes in the rich, unexploited valley. Most of the Negroes remained, even after emancipation gave them the right to move freely, for they were comparatively unscathed. But they contributed toil, and not vision or capital or leadership, to the river; the strength of their bodies was their lone endowment, and they could not transfer immunity to their masters.

Yet the people of the river clung to their lowland towns

and fields, doggedly suffering the chills and fevers and out-
lasting their curse. Had Reed and Agramonte and Carroll
lived and proved in 1800 instead of 1900 that yellow fever
was transmitted by the *Aëdes aegypti,* the results in lives
saved, in territory developed, and in human contribution
to the nation's aggregate strength would have rewritten the
economic history of those hundred years. The tiny mosquito,
intermediate host to a virus as yet unidentified, cursed the
valley with destruction. For a sorrowful, death-ridden century, a fleet, whining insect had its way against ignorant
courage.

CHAPTER 21

Who Killa da Chief?

IN 1887 THE spasmodically graft-sickened citizenry of New Orleans began an overdue housecleaning of what was politically and morally the most degenerate city in the United States.

Even among the river towns whose rowdiness made the wild West of the eighties seem like a Sunday-school picnic ground. New Orleans was gutter-low. From 1840 to 1860 the city had been plundered by a succession of machine-ridden administrations whose thoroughness was peculiarly a product of the political talents of the intruding Americans. The depths of political anarchy, reached in the bloody Know-Nothing riots of the fifties, had been followed by wartime occupation and military rule which further enervated the populace. Then, Reconstruction had held the people helpless for more than a decade after the war.

The eventual restoration of local Democratic rule was itself a travesty, for the Democratic ring took up where the carpetbaggers had left off. Politician, prostitute and crook were blatant in their confederacy and bizarre in their expressions of mutual esteem. The New Orleans red-light district became the most gaudily magnificent, and the New Orleans barroom bullies and cutthroats the most mayhem-minded and unimpeded in the nation. In the early eighties civic responsibility seemed as dead as a bloated catfish bobbing against the levee.

But in 1887 and 1888 the disgusted citizens enrolled

behind the Young Men's Democratic Association, a virile organization of younger business and professional men. The association's volunteer rifle companies compelled an honest election. The city government was purged, and Joseph Shakespeare was elected mayor. His principal pledges were to reform the police department and to belabor the underworld.

To accomplish this Augean task, Mayor Shakespeare appointed as superintendent of police one David C. Hennessy, a 31-year-old patrolman in the private Harbor Police and a former city detective. Hennessy went about his new job with zest and vigor. The police force received a thorough going-over; the pot-valiant gunmen of the district quieted down. But Hennessy had already been marked for death even before he assumed the superintendency; not by home-grown terrorists or infuriated politicians but by the dread Sicilian society of the Mafia with which he had first tangled eight years earlier.

Since the early seventies, thousands of Sicilians had poured into New Orleans, with the encouragement of agents of rival steamship companies and such benevolent groups as the Prisoners Aid Society. Some were simply impoverished and deserving seekers after a decent chance in life. Many were the scum of Palermo and Naples, either affiliated with or dominated by the mystic Camorra and the equally dangerous Mafia society.

The Camorra, a sort of hierarchical government by blackmail, had existed in the stews of Sicily since 1417. Its members swore fidelity to the band, pledged that they would never denounce a companion or have recourse in law. In the New World, as in the Old, it thrived on robbery, assassination, and taxation of Sicilian vendors of food and clothing, operators of games of chance, or any enterprise in which money changed hands. The Camorra maintained a fund for the corruption of police, for legal defense, and for the widows of deceased members and the families of men under sentence.

Similar to the Camorra, but perhaps even lower in origin, was the Mafia, also known as the *Stoppaghliera,* which was likewise bound in conspiracy against law-abiding society. The gendarmes of Sicily were delighted to speed the departure of these throat-slitters in company with the woebegone paupers and lesser prison birds upon whom they preyed. Under the complacent eyes of corrupt police and indifferent officials, the Mafia and Camorra in New Orleans pursued their ancient and evil ways unhindered. The unwritten law was that they were to leave the Americans alone. That gave them immunity.

Writing in the *American Law Review* of June, 1891, on what had by then become famous as "The Mafia Case," Robert H. Marr, a prominent New Orleans attorney, bitterly described these new citizens of the city:

For a number of years a large and steady stream of Sicilian immigration has been flowing in upon New Orleans; and while among the newcomers there have certainly been some who have become excellent and substantial citizens, yet it must be owned that this immigration has been in the main of a thoroughly undesirable character, being largely composed of the most vicious, ignorant, degraded and filthy paupers, with something more than an admixture of the criminal element. . . .

The localities of New Orleans infested by Dagoes are faithful reproductions in inhabitants and surroundings of the most squalid quarters of Naples, having the same dingy buildings, the same intolerable stench and all pervading filth, the same universal unkemptness of person and the same deafening clatter and chatter. So far the only Americans with whom they have manifested any inclination to assimilate are the mulattoes and octoroons; with these they principally cohabit.

The description is haughty and unsympathetic, yet in its harsh outlines true enough. Certainly the miserable Sicilians were a people apart in this city which had been such a melting pot for others of equally unblessed background. Apparently, little heed was paid to their lawlessness, and little sympathy extended to the tribute-paying masses. By 1890, the number of Sicilian assassinations in New Orleans had reached ninety-five. It was impossible to obtain convictions, for no witnesses among the Sicilians could ever be found. And most of the other citizens didn't care anyway. If the Dagoes wanted to kill themselves off, they said, so much the better.

But Dave Hennessy had interfered with the Sicilian gangsters even before he became chief of police. In 1880 the leader of the Mafia in Sicily was the notorious Leoni. His second in command was dwarfish Guiseppe Esposito, a ferocious, simian-looking murderer. Near Palermo they had captured in 1880 an English clergyman, and had cut off his ears when no ransom was paid. The enraged British government demanded action from Italy. Troops killed Leoni and captured many of his band. But Esposito and several others escaped and were smuggled to New York. From there Esposito came to New Orleans, changed his name to Radzo, and turned oyster fisherman, brazenly christening his lugger *Leoni* and nailing the Mafia chief's flag to its mast.

Soon Esposito deposed Tony Labruzzo, the small-time leader of the New Orleans Mafia. Labruzzo unwisely complained to the Italian consul, who in turn asked the then chief of police, Boylan, to have Esposito shadowed until he heard from the Italian government. Dave Hennessy and his brother Mike were assigned to this detail. Soon thereafter they arrested Esposito in Jackson Square. Private New York detectives acting for the Italian government spirited him downriver in a skiff, and put him aboard a New York-bound steamer. From New York, Esposito was returned to Italy where he spent the rest of his wretched life in irons.

Ten days after Esposito's arrest the Mafia assassinated the informer Labruzzo. Five years later Mike Hennessy was slain in Houston. But Dave Hennessy had longer to live.

The New Orleans Mafia continued to flourish. In the mid-eighties it was led by Charles and Tony Matranga, and numbered at least three hundred active members. The Matrangas introduced a new Mafia wrinkle by turning labor racketeers. Their intended victims were the Provenzano brothers, who had a monopoly on unloading the fruit boats and who employed several hundred fellow Sicilians. The prosperous and politically powerful Provenzanos were not Mafias, but they had always paid their tribute and kept their mouths shut. Now the Matrangas simply ordered the Provenzanos off the docks, attacked their workers, and finally took over the stevedoring monopoly, lowering the hourly wages from the established 40 to 60 cents to a pitiful 10 to 15 cents, and pocketing the difference. The Provenzanos opened a grocery. The Mafia ran them out of business. Finally, in self-defense, the Provenzanos employed their own hatchet men, and some half dozen gangsters died in the ensuing war. Then early one May morning in 1890, Tony Matranga and two of his bodyguards were wounded from ambush. The Provenzanos and three of their gunmen were arrested, indicted, and their trial finally set for October 17, 1890.

Hennessy liked the Provenzanos. Also, he had decided that the Mafia must be destroyed. Assiduously, he had already begun collecting evidence on the society, and had discovered that some hundred Sicilian murderers were at large in the city. Through correspondence with the Italian police, he had assembled thick dossiers on these culprits, many of whom were wanted in Italy.

In July, 1890, the chief received an anonymous death letter. But Hennessy persisted in the investigation against which he was warned. And in October he announced that he would give evidence against the Mafia at the trial of the Provenzanos.

❧   ❧

The night of October 15, 1890, two days before the trial of the Provenzanos was scheduled to open, Hennessy left his office at eleven o'clock. He was afoot, and accompanied only by a friend, Captain W. J. O'Connor of a private detective agency. At Rampart and Girod streets they parted, Hennessy continuing alone on Girod Street where his home stood. A few seconds later O'Connor heard a burst of shotgun fire, then a scattering of pistol shots. Rushing back to the dimly lit, murky street, he found Hennessy crumpled upon the steps of a ramshackle house. He was bleeding from four wounds in the body.

"The Dagoes got me," he gasped.

The next morning he died in Charity Hospital. On his deathbed he said that he had not recognized the individual identities of his assassins, but insisted they were Italians.

Hennessy's statement was borne out by others who had seen the gunmen running away. Moreover, the shack from which they had fired was occupied by Pietro Monasterio, a Sicilian cobbler, and two Negroes. Investigators found near by five "Mafia guns"—shotguns sawed off at the barrels to ten inches, and hinged to shortened, hollowed stocks so that the barrels could fold within them. Hooks were inserted in the stocks so that the weapons could hang on the inside of the coat.

The people of New Orleans were infuriated. A $15,000 reward for Hennessy's murderers was posted, while many

Sicilians, frightened by threats of wholesale lynchings, placed advertisements in the newspapers, denying any connection with the Mafia. Fifty prominent citizens were appointed by Mayor Shakespeare to co-operate with the authorities in the hunt for the criminals.

An incontrovertible mass of eyewitness and circumstantial evidence was shortly accumulated. On November 20th, the grand jury indicted eleven Sicilians for murder and shooting to kill: Peter Natali, Antonio Scaffidi, Antonio Bagnetto, Manuel Politz, Antonio Marchesi, Pietri Monasterio, Bastiano Incardona, Salvador Sunzeri, Loretto Comitez, Charles Trahina, and Charles Portza. Eight others were indicted as accessories before the fact: Joseph P. Macheca, James and John Caruso, Charles Matranga, Rocco Geracci, Charles Patorno, Frank Romero, and a boy, Gasparo Marchesi, who was alleged to have run ahead of Hennessy whistling a signal to the assassins.

The Mafia was no less busy than the city government. In behalf of the accused men, an outstanding array of counsel was employed. More important, the defense had secured the services of Dominick C. O'Malley, a notorious private detective with a genius for jury fixing. O'Malley, a County Mayo Irishman, was to have a spectacular life in New Orleans. During his long career he would be shot fourteen times. Eventually, he would own a newspaper, the New Orleans *Item*. At the time of the trial, however, he had been in New Orleans only a short time, but long enough to serve ten months in the workhouse and to appear in court nine times on charges of jury fixing, intimidation of witnesses, and carrying concealed weapons.

On December 22nd the nineteen Sicilians were arraigned. On February 6th, the trial of nine of the accused began in a tense courtroom before Judge Baker. Eleven days were taken to select a jury. In the process 1,375 citizens were summoned, 46 challenged by the state, 82 by the defense, 560 for cause, 95 excused by consent, and 12 empaneled. The remainder of those summoned were not found.

Witnesses testified to seeing Scaffidi, Bagnetto, Marchesi, Politz, and Monasterio run from the scene of the slaying. Other evidence showed that Macheca, Matranga, the Carusos, Geracci, Palermo, and Sunzeri—all Sicilian leaders and men of means, who were charged with being accessories—had gathered at the Academy of Music until 10:45 on the evening of the murder. From there they had gone to a restaurant where they had wined and dined until one o'clock in the morning, finally ending up at Fanny Decker's house of prostitution. There they had "acted excitedly," drunk heavily of wine, and one of them had shouted that "we are Dave's enemies and want people to know that we are!"

During the trial, Politz became violent, and finally testified against his fellows. But a steady procession of Sicilian witnesses gave alibis for each of the defendants.

Rumors of jury tampering accompanied the progress of the trial. The grand jury later reported that Lionel Adams, chief defense counsel, and O'Malley had the names of five hundred talesmen on February 22nd, although their identities were not supposed to be public for several days. Meanwhile, the temper of the citizens rose. A grimly mocking parody of the Sicilians' shoulder-shrugging question "Who killa da chief?" became a password of anger.

On March 12th, the jury received the case. It was instructed to acquit Matranga. The case against Incardona had been abandoned by the prosecution. Verdicts of guilty as charged were demanded for the rest.

The next afternoon a discomposed jury returned its verdicts: not guilty in the cases of Incardona and Matranga, as arranged; not guilty also in the cases of Bagnetto, the Marchesis and Macheca, and mistrials for Politz, Scaffidi, and Monasterio!

It was as obvious then as it is now that someone had reached the jury. While the Anglo-French population of New Orleans was trying to comprehend the stunning miscarriage of justice, the defendants reveled at a wine supper served in the parish jail. Sicilian market vendors decorated their shops with gay bunting. At the oyster-lugger landing a Sicilian gang tore down and spit and stamped upon an American flag, then hoisted it, union down, beneath the flag of Italy. State's witnesses barricaded themselves in their homes, while rejoicing Mafias and their adherents shouted in the streets that the Mafia would run the town from this night on.

🏵 🏵

The jubilant Sicilians didn't know it but they were enjoying only a brief and final hour of triumph. Their mistake, and the mistake of the jury fixers and defendants, was that they failed to understand these Americans of the river.

At five o'clock, shortly after the end of the trial, 28 New Orleanians met in the law offices of William C. Parkerson, who had been the leader of the Young Men's Democratic Association in their fight for good government. Parkerson, a heavy-set, handsome six-footer, was a talented member of the bar, blue-blooded, the father of three children. In this grim gathering he was selected to lead "a movement to correct the failure of justice."

The next morning, March 14th, the newspapers carried this notice:

Mass Meeting

All good citizens are invited to attend a mass meeting on Saturday, March 14, at 10 o'clock a.m. at Clay statue, to take steps to remedy the failure of justice in the Hennessy case. Come prepared for action.

The notice was signed by these Orleanians, whose names provide almost a Who's Who directory of the day: John C. Wickliffe, B. F. Glover, J. G. Pepper, C. E. Rogers, F. E. Hawes, Raymond Hayes, L. E. Cenas, John M. Parker, Jr.; Harris R. Lewis, Septime Villeré, William M. Railey, Lee McMillan, C. E. Jones, J. F. Queeny, D. R. Calder, Thomas Henry, James Lea McLean, Felix Coutourie, T. D. Wharton, Frank B. Hayne, J. G. Flower, James Clarke, Thomas H. Kelley, H. B. Ogden, Ulric Atkinson, A. Baldwin, Jr., A. E. Blackmar, John V. Moore, William T. Pierson, C. L. Stegel, E. T. Leche, W. S. Parkerson, Henry Dickson Bruns, William H. Reeves, Richard S. Venables, Samuel B. Merwin, Omer Villeré, H. L. Favrot, T. D. Mather, James P. Mulvey, Emile Dupre, W. P. Curtiss, Charles J. Ranlett, T. S. Barton, C. J. Forstall, J. Moore Wilson, Hugh W. Brown, C. Harrison Parker, Edgar H. Farrar, J. C. Aby, Rudolph Hahse, C. A. Walscher, W. Mosby, Charles M. Barnwell, H. R. Labouisse, Walter D. Denegre, George Denegre, R. H. Hornbeck, S. P. Walmsley, E. H. Pierson, James D. Houston.

One of these signers, John M. Parker, Jr., was to become a governor of Louisiana and Theodore Roosevelt's Bull Moose running mate in 1912.

Long before ten o'clock on the morning of the 14th a dense crowd had massed along Canal Street. It did not include Dominick O'Malley. Though courageous enough, the fixer had wisely gone into hiding. So had several jurors and Sicilian leaders.

Parkerson, Walter D. Denegre, and John C. Wickliffe were the speakers.

"Affairs have reached such a crisis," Parkerson said, his deep, soft voice compelling quiet, "that men living in an organized and civilized community, finding their laws fruitless and ineffective, are forced to protect themselves. When the courts fail the people must act. What protection or assurance of protection is there left us when the very head of our police department—our chief of police—is assassinated in our very midst by the Mafia society, and his assassins again turned loose on the community? The time has come for the people of New Orleans to say whether they are going to stand these outrages by organized bands of assassins; for the people to say whether they shall permit it to continue. I ask you to consider this fairly. Are you going to let it continue? Will every man here follow me, and see the murder of D. C. Hennessy vindicated? Are there men enough here to set aside the verdict of that infamous jury, every one of whom is a perjurer and a scoundrel?"

Briefly he also denounced O'Malley. He was followed by Denegre, then by Wickliffe, who announced that Parkerson would be captain, James D. Houston first lieutenant, and himself second lieutenant of the citizen avengers.

Immediately thereafter the signers of the call formed military ranks and the march upon the parish prison began. Behind them hundreds of other Orleanians fell in, many with shotguns protruding from beneath their overcoats. And behind this organized group tagged the mob. Scores who had not brought weapons armed themselves at a Canal Street gun store.

At 10:25 an assault was made upon a side street entrance of the prison. Speedily the gate was battered open. Wickliffe and three others guarded the opening, permitting none except selected men to enter. Inside, the prison was in turmoil, as white and black inmates screamed in animal fear that all prisoners were to be killed.

The prison had scant protection. Sheriff Villeré had left on an unsuccessful search for soldiers or police. Obviously, the state and local governments had connived in the attack. Captain Lemuel Davis, in charge of the prison, locked all prisoners except the Sicilians in their cells. These he turned loose inside the prison, telling them to hide themselves as best they could.

Outside the waiting mob yelled itself hoarse with "Who killa da chief?"; whistled the "Dago whistle," and howled for the Mafias' blood. And soon the blasting roar of shotguns reverberated from inside the high brick walls, the cramped cells, and the flagstone courtyard of the prison.

The leaders had ordered spared the lives of the five Sicilians who hadn't been tried, the boy, Gasperi Marchesi, and Matranga and Incardona against whom no case had been proved. They granted no mercy to the remaining eleven, condemned by Parkerson and his fellow signers as being guilty beyond doubt. Hunting their victims down, the executioners emptied their weapons into the bodies of the Sicilians, then stepped aside to let their associates also fire upon them. Politz and Bagnetto were dragged from the kennel of Captain Davis's terrier and hanged outside, one to a lamppost, the other to a tree. Macheca, Scaffidi, and Marchesi were shot to death in their third-floor cells, from which they had refused to flee. The other six were riddled in the exercise yard of the women's department, where they had sought refuge. One of them, Monasterio, shammed death after the first volley, but was subsequently detected and killed.

The executions were over in an hour. Parkerson climbed to a window sill, breathing heavily, and addressed the crowd outside.

"I have performed the most painful duty of my life today," he said. "Now go home, and may God bless you and the community." A few moments later he was being carried toward his home on the shoulders of cheering men.

For a few hours it was feared that a general slaughter of Italians would follow. Even the Italian consul was threatened. But the mob spirit subsided without further bloodletting.

The repercussions were violent and varied. In New Orleans the newspapers praised the executions and gave practically a blow-by-blow description of the slayings. The New Orleans Grand Jury refused to indict any of the participants. Instead, it defended their actions and denounced O'Malley's "assiduous and corrupting influence" and the loose immigration laws. Every commercial organization in New Orleans, including all the exchanges, also endorsed the killings.

Signor Corte, the Italian consul, reported that the mayor and the governor had winked at the plot and its consummation. In protest, Italy withdrew her minister from Washington, and darkly threatened war. In answer, several thousand Texans joyously offered their services in the defense of New Orleans. And in the city itself, the Orleanians compacted to "run every Dago out" if there was any retaliation.

Actually, all but two of the Sicilian victims had become American citizens, and all but four were machine-registered voters, citizens or not. The two Italian subjects had criminal records in Italy. But the Italian government continued to fume, while American newspapers divided over the issue almost on a sectional basis. The South generally applauded. The Columbus *Dispatch* and the Philadelphia *Times* likewise approved. The Boston *Transcript* and the New York *Tribune* inveighed the loudest and longest against the Orleanians, but few Louisianians saw those papers anyhow so no feelings were hurt.

The disputed merits of the case turned into a bonanza for such national weeklies as *Frank Leslie's Illustrated Newspaper*, the *Illustrated American*, *Public Opinion*, and *Truth*. In *Truth*, Professor Alessandro Oldrini, of the Geographical Society of Italy, denounced lynching, exonerated the Mafias, and demanded the employment of the Italian fleet against New Orleans and the punishment of Parkerson. On behalf of the lynchers, Wickliffe, himself a newspaper editor, wrote illustrated articles for *Leslie's* and also answered Oldrini in *Truth*.

Italy could or would not understand the distinction between federal and state jurisdiction in such matters. So diplomatic exchanges, from which Louisiana itself remained aloof, dragged on until April, 1892, when the United States paid approximately $20,000 out of the contingent fund of the State Department.

With these slayings, the threat of the Mafia in New Orleans ended. Years later the Black Hand society tried to take its place, but unsuccessfully. One Italian child was kidnaped and murdered, in 1907, but his abductors were brought to justice. Later, in 1929, Black Hand extortion letters were received by several Sicilian grocerymen in Tangipahoa Parish, fifty miles above New Orleans, where many Sicilians had removed to become farmers. I remember the incident because it gave me my first scoop as a cub reporter in New Orleans. My home was in Tangipahoa Parish. The grocerymen told the two local police, who enlisted the aid of my father and two other citizens who liked excitement and disliked blackmail. The officers and volunteers disguised themselves on the night the pay-off was to be made, and proceeded in an intended victim's car to the spot where the money was to be deposited. The rendezvous was to be marked by a red lantern. They saw the lantern in a field, and stopped the car. My father, top-heavy with .45's, got out while his companions crouched with 30-30 rifles in the car. But no one approached. Dad told me the story, and it was a "Sunday feature section, page one exclusive." So far as I know that was the last Black Hand effort in the New Orleans area.

❦   ❦

The Mafia case has significance aside from the thoroughness with which the New Orleans citizens exacted vengeance. Beyond reasonable doubt, the lynched Sicilians were guilty of the death of Hennessy and of numbers of their fellows. So, too, in a legal sense, the citizen vigilantes were guilty of murder. But the basic blame can be discovered in Parkerson's challenge to his Canal Street listeners: "When the courts fail the people must act." That basic blame falls upon the jury fixers, the bribe-taking talesmen, the corrupt politicians who had permitted the Mafia to thrive so long as it preyed only upon its own people. It falls upon the cynical abusers of lax immigration laws. It falls upon the body politic, which slumbered for generations until a mocking aftermath of an unendurable crime shocked them into lawless action.

And this tolerance of violence until it strikes near home is still characteristic of the lower river. As long as Sicilians slew only Sicilians—as long as Negroes kill only Negroes—few cared then and few care now. Law is still a matter of personal enforcement or personal neglect. It is not the happiest characteristic of the valley.

CHAPTER 22

Golden Octopus

FOR THOSE who live on the Lower Mississippi there are few ways, honorable and otherwise, to become a multimillionaire.

The surest method is to secure exclusive rights to a foolproof, monopolistic gambling concession. This can be done if you know the right people—or perhaps the wrong ones—particularly in New Orleans where the gambling spirit infuses the population to a degree unmatched anywhere else in the nation. Yet no matter how firm your connections or how one-sided your device, it is doubtful that you would ever be able to operate on as grand a scale, for as long a period, or with such social irreproachability as did the polished owners of that great, golden octopus, the Louisiana Lottery.

The Louisiana Lottery could have earned millions from the ready purses of the Orleanians alone. Even today, millions of dollars are being filched annually by policy racket, slot machine, gambling hall, and racebook-making concessionaires in that amoral Latin city. New Orleans gambled under France, under Spain, under the United States, and under the Confederacy. Gambling has always been in her blood. But the lottery made New Orleans only one of its many green fields. The lower valley, the nation, and even the world became its pasture.

In the years immediately following the Civil War, an eastern gambling syndicate, C. H. Murray and Company of New York, had as its chief assets a number of state lottery charters. Louisiana was not among these states, an omission that was noted musingly by Charles T. Howard, the debonair New Orleans representative of the company.

Howard, a Baltimorean by birth, had gone to New Orleans in 1852, when twenty years old, to work for a steamboat company. Two years later the young fellow, now agent for the Alabama Lottery Company, had married an attractive Creole. For the next seven years he followed an unobtrusively successful career as lottery representative. When the Civil War began, he enlisted first in the Confederate navy, then in the Crescent Regiment of New Orleans in which he served as sergeant until sickness led to his discharge. After his recovery he joined the cavalry, and remained on active duty until the end of the war.

Returning to the shattered city in 1865, he engaged in his old occupation. It was without onus and one in which a living could be made, for the most penniless Orleanian was willing to scrape up a dime or a dollar for a lottery ticket. Howard affiliated himself with the Kentucky Lottery, one of three operated by the Murray syndicate. And finally, he persuaded his fabulously wealthy eastern employees that a Louisiana lottery would prove a bonanza.

First, of course, certain political amenities had to be observed. Louisiana's carpetbag legislature was out for all it could get, a characteristic not peculiar to any one period in the state's history. So Charles Howard helped the lawmakers, almost evenly divided between the two races, to improve their financial statuses. By special arrangement, the General Assembly met in 1868 and presented to Howard and six associates a state lottery monopoly. Later two of the incorporators would swear that at least $300,000 was spent in the first seven years to buy votes; and in 1886 a

Shreveport barber, who had been a legislator in 1868, brought suit to recover two hundred shares of lottery stock which he said had been carried for him in the name of one of the lottery leaders.

The terms of the monopoly were simple enough. The legislature granted a 25-year charter and exemption from taxation in exchange for a $40,000 yearly payment to the New Orleans Charity Hospital. Except for behind-the-scenes manipulations, there was nothing illegal or even culpable in the transaction. As early as 1826, lottery funds had kept two New Orleans elementary schools and one central high school alive. In 1865 the state legislature had as one important source of revenue the licensing of lottery vendors who were selling Havana lottery tickets. In 1810, Christ Church in New Orleans had been authorized to raise $10,000 by lottery for its building; the debts of the First Presbyterian Church had been wiped out by a $20,000 lottery; and throughout the first half of the century the Catholic churches had turned to the lottery constantly to build and to pay debts.

However, public disapproval of the lottery system was developing even in 1868. Many protesting citizens expected Carpetbagger Governor Henry Clay Warmoth to veto Howard's lottery bill; but he did not. So in 1868, the seven incorporators, Howard, Philip N. Luckett, Robert Blower, Jesse R. Irwin, F. F. Wilder, John Considine, and Charles H. Murray received a 25-year charter, which would become effective January 1, 1869. The capital stock was $1,000,000.

Nine days after the incorporation, the seven incorporators signed away their rights to three members of the Murray syndicate: John H. Morris, Zachariah Simmons, and Charles H. Murray himself. Of the three, only Morris is important to this story. The assignees formed a new trust, named Howard, Simmons and Company, with enterprising Charles Howard receiving a quarter partnership and the presidency. Three years later Murray and Simmons withdrew from the company, and Howard became managing partner to Morris.

Morris, the new, dominant prospector in this still unexploited gold mine, is a figure as fabulous as he was unostentatious. Not until 1879, when the lottery had attained social respectability, was it generally known that he was Howard's close associate.

Son of Francis Morris, internationally noted turfman and gambler, John Morris was thirty-six years old when he became Howard's all but silent partner. Born at Throgs Neck, New York, he had graduated brilliantly from Yale at eighteen. In 1857 he met in London and married beautiful Cora Hennen, member of an unimpeachable New Orleans family. Her father had served with Jackson's bodyguard, became a leader of the New Orleans bar and later state Supreme Court justice, and had raised a large family in rigidly devout Presbyterianism. Morris had inherited an interest in the Murray syndicate from his father; and from his father he had inherited also a love of horses and of gambling. He was an early president of the New York Jockey Club, and acquired three great horse-breeding farms in Texas, Westchester County, New York, and England. After his marriage, and later residence in Louisiana, he made a showplace of Mount Hennen, his father-in-law's country estate across Lake Pontchartrain from New Orleans, stocking it with pheasant, deer, and fish and sending blooded stallions to improve the livestock of the farmers near by.

In the first few years of the Howard-Morris venture the profits were not large. For one thing, the Louisiana Lottery had not perfected its sales appeal. For another, the lottery owners were discovering that politicians never stay bought but have to be constantly repurchased. For twenty-five years the lottery maintained what was jocularly called the "bribery fund." Its outstanding contribution came in 1877 following the notorious Hayes-Tilden presidential election. Although, as historians agree, Tilden defeated the Republican candidate, he was euchered out of victory when Louisiana's deciding electoral votes were blandly handed over to Hayes on the promise that the state Democratic ticket would be recognized as victorious. To facilitate the swap, which restored Louisiana's white Democrats to power, the lottery presented the political bosses of New Orleans with $250,000; in return, it was agreed that when the next constitutional convention convened another 25-year charter would be granted.

But this deal did not sit so well with many Louisianians. The lottery became the principal issue in the state election of 1879, and an antilottery legislature was elected. It swiftly repealed the charter.

Hurriedly the lottery interests went to work on the ensuing constitutional convention, which had as its chief purpose the amending of the constitution to ensure "white supremacy" for all time. The lottery's legislative specialists trumpeted the sad condition of the state's finances and the means by which lottery could save Louisiana from debt repudiation. In one way and another they succeeded in having articles placed in the new constitution extending the lottery, without the monopolistic feature, until January 1, 1895. It was ordered that all lotteries would end on that date. The convention also declared in another article that "gambling is . . . a vice and the General Assembly shall enact laws for its suppression."

But the lottery men had won a great victory. The constitution was to be submitted to the people, and had to be approved or rejected by them in full. With the clause restoring the lottery to life incorporated in the document, the Louisianians either had to accept the lottery or reject the constitution that would mark the end of Reconstruction. So the voters swallowed the pill.

Thus, 1879 was the real beginning of the octopus. From

that time until its protesting death, its tentacles covered
Louisiana. After 1879 the lottery had to worry only about
keeping out the competition which the constitution permitted.

The business, meanwhile, had begun to thrive. A few
years after its original charter was granted in 1868, an astute
Alsatian physician, Dr. Maximilian A. Dauphin, was brought
in as manager. His first concern was to convince the public
that the drawings were honest. To do this, he employed two
Confederate heroes, General Pierre G. T. Beauregard and
General Jubal A. Early, to supervise the drawings. For not
more than two days' work a month, the pathetic, impoverished soldiers, whose honesty could not be challenged, received
$30,000 a year each.

The public quickly concluded that these two noble
patriots could not be connected with a crooked business. Nor
was the lottery dishonest in its drawings. There was no need
to be. Dr. Dauphin based his awards on the lottery of Venice,
which had been universally condemned because it paid only
52 per cent of its gross in prizes. But, since Louisiana's legislature had relinquished all policing powers over the lottery,
the octopus cleared almost 50 per cent. Its contemporaries in
other states had to distribute from 70 to 85 per cent of their
intake.

So, under Dauphin, the lottery stock rose from $35 a
share in 1879 to $1,200 in 1890. The prizes the lottery offered
were attractive enough. A whole 25-cent ticket could win
$3,750; a 50-cent ticket drew $7,500; a dollar ticket,
$15,000. A $20 ticket could draw $300,000; the semiannual
$40 ticket, $600,000. This highest sum was never won,
although a New Orleans barber received a $300,000 prize.

From 1890 until its death, the lottery ran hog-wild.
Its agents swarmed everywhere. Two drawings were held
daily, and tickets, fluttering on green and white strings,
could be bought for as little as a dime in almost any shop,

grocery, or drugstore in New Orleans. Branch offices flourished in New York and Boston, each doing a $50,000 a
month business; in Chicago, which did $85,000; in New
Haven, Buffalo, Washington, Cincinnati, Kansas City, Den-
ver, Ottawa, and elsewhere, either openly or under cover. By
1890, 93 per cent of the business came from outside New
Orleans, and two-thirds of the working time of the New
Orleans post-office employees was consumed in attending to
lottery mail.

As the lottery's income grew, so did its interests and its
power. This incredible enterprise, which by 1889 was showing a gross annual profit of $13,000,000, had to keep many
irons hot. As allies, the lottery counted some of the leading
banks which dominated the reserve capital of the state. Many
businessmen and planters were therefore afraid to criticize
for fear of being denied credit. Even when the federal government finally got around to curtailing the lottery's activities, the New Orleans National Bank, through its president,
Albert Baldwin, became the declared recipient of the lottery's
mail.

The lottery cornucopia supported the colorful French
Opera House, furnished capital for cotton mills, and even
built a large plant to relieve the cane planters of the trouble
of manufacturing their sugar. The octopus became the father
of a cemetery, because Charles Howard, piqued at being
denied membership in a swank racing club, vowed he would
eventually turn the grounds into a cemetery. He did.

The lottery's "reserve fund" handled most of its extra-
curricular enterprises. Hundreds of Louisianians, particularly
the poor relations of influential citizens, were on its pension
list. It controlled scores of jobs in its suboffices and attendant
policy business, and applicants for these positions had to be
recommended by two members of the legislature or equally
potent benefactors. The monopoly also had as supporters
many small, unknown stockholders as well as hundreds of

small businessmen who sold tickets from 25 cents to $50 at a 15 per cent commission.

❦ ❦

The average lottery-playing citizen of Louisiana gave scant thought to the spreading tentacles in those halcyon years from 1880 to 1890 when the lottery was building a $30,000,000 annual business. They were more concerned with the hundreds of provocative advertisements which the lottery generously distributed to the newspapers. Here is one:

LUCKY CORNER
TO BUY LOUISIANA STATE LOTTERY TICKETS

April 15 Drawing sold 59 Prizes

E. J. Lannes

Cor. Camp and Girod Streets, N. O.

Mr. Lannes also advertised:

See That E. J. Lannes Selects Your Tickets
As He Has a Lucky Hand

Illustrated limericks proclaimed that fingers get burned if money is invested in stocks, bankers abscond with savings, prices go down, and Jay Gould would nail a man to a fence— but:

> A sensible man full of pluck
> Ye lotterie ventured to buck;
> To his joyful surprise
> He drew a great prize
> And no longer is down on his luck.

Superstitions grew around almost any number. If you saw a stray dog, you should play No. 6. A drunken man meant No. 14; a naked leg belonging to neither wife nor mistress meant 11; a dead woman with gray hair, 49. To dream of a fish meant that 13 should be played. Catholics brought their tickets to be blessed by their priests until the archbishop banned the practice. As Morris and Howard raked in millions, savings accounts in New Orleans dropped from $2,000,000 in 1880 to only $915,000 in 1890.

The ritualistic procedure of the lottery was fascinating to the players. The tickets were placed in a large glass wheel in the sumptuous Lottery Building where nearly a hundred clerks were kept busy. In another wheel were deposited the descriptions of prizes to which each winning number was entitled. Under the military scrutiny of Generals Beauregard and Early in the monthly drawings, and three reputable citizens in the daily events, a blindfolded boy drew the tickets from the first wheel. Another boy drew the tickets on which the amounts of the prizes were printed, until all the prizes were drawn.

By 1890, the lottery's monthly income was more than $2,000,000, of which $1,054,800 went in prizes. The rest was the company's. The monthly capital prize was $300,000, and tickets for this event were sold all over the country. The daily drawings, at which the chances of winning were roughly 1 in 76,000, brought an average sale of $60 a day each in the 108 New Orleans policy shops alone.

In the beginning of its career as big business the lottery met an unexpected challenge which was to contribute greatly to its final undoing. A certain Colonel A. K. McClure, editor of the Philadelphia *Times*, strongly disapproved of lotteries. So, when in 1883 his newspaper was offered four times its usual advertising rate for a lottery notice, the colonel refused and started an investigation of lottery advertising. Soon he discovered that the lotteries were spending $50,000 a year for advertising in Philadelphia alone, though such advertising was illegal under state law. Whereupon the embattled colonel started a campaign to force state legislation which would fine a publisher who accepted advertising from lotteries.

When the Pennsylvania legislature passed such a law, the lottery decided that it was time to scare off such reformers. It filed suit for libel against the *Times,* and appealed the legislation to the United States Supreme Court, knowing that probably three years would elapse before a decision would be handed down.

A *Times* demurrer to the libel suit was sustained on the grounds that lotteries were illegal in Pennsylvania. Then, perhaps by coincidence, the editor of the New Orleans *Times-Democrat*—stanch supporter of the lottery—invited Colonel McClure to attend the great New Orleans Exposition. The unsuspecting colonel arrived, but even before he stepped off the train, he was served with a United States District Court writ in which the lottery claimed $100,000 damages for libel.

The issuing judge was Edward Coke Billings, a lottery henchman, who was thenceforth known as "Midnight Order" Billings. McClure hastily returned to Philadelphia, then angrily enlisted the aid of the United States attorney general in an effort to have the Supreme Court consider the lottery case early—on the grounds that lotteries were interfering with the administration of the postal laws. The lottery gave ground, and begged McClure to withdraw his charges. He did so, but his friends carried on a fight which eventually resulted in the barring of the lotteries from the mails through enactment of stricter postal laws. But all that lay ahead.

The bitter lottery war in Louisiana itself did not begin in earnest until 1890, almost five years before its original state charter was to expire. It was precipitated in April, 1890, by the publication of an open letter from John Morris in which he said that he would seek a 25-year renewal of the charter. In return for the extension, Morris wrote, the lottery would raise its original $40,000 a year payment to the state to $1,250,000 a year for charitable and educational purposes, pensions for invalid Confederates, levee building, and schooling. Actually it was a cheap price. The lottery paid no taxes, and would not pay anything but the sum offered by Morris.

The lottery people were confident that the charter would be renewed. They controlled every newspaper in New Orleans and four-fifths of those published in the state. In the fight that would follow, the staid *Picayune* would not indulge in prolottery panegyrics, but the *Times-Democrat* went overboard for the lottery, with long and fulsome editorials. This newspaper represented a merger in 1879 of the *Times* and the *Democrat*. Up to two days before the convention of 1879, the *Democrat* had fought the lottery. The *Times* bought it, and the combination became the lottery's mouthpiece from then on.

Not only the press was subservient. For a decade the lottery had contributed lavishly to charities and asylums, to relief funds in yellow fever epidemics, and to many other outstretched hands in Louisiana. Further to strengthen itself prior to the campaign for renewal of the charter, it had given $200,000 to aid several Louisiana river parishes which had been inundated in the spring. At the same time it had donated $65,000 to New Orleans for levee building, and $30,000 to the Auxiliary Sanitary Committee to establish public baths and to flush the gutters. In his presentation of the check to Edward Fenner, head of the Sanitary Association, Dr. Dauphin, the lottery president, said unctuously that "no greater service can be rendered the people of this city than providing the means to flush our gutters with pure water and to give the multitude an opportunity to take a refreshing bath at will and without cost."

Yet there were signs of moral indignation. The archbishop of Louisiana refused to permit a diocese debt to be paid off by the lottery; and several members of the Sanitary Board resigned, saying that they "could not endorse the lottery as a charity institution to the children of New Orleans for $30,000." The governor refused an offer of $100,000 for flood-control purposes. The lottery immediately parceled out this sum to the flooded parishes; and only one parish returned the money, although the lottery had never before aided in time of flood.

The antilottery people began their fight under the spur of an aroused ministry and indignant secular leaders. On May 12th, the day the all-important legislature convened, they came out with a newspaper of their own, the *New Delta*, with Harrison Parker and John C. Wickliffe as editors and a brilliant journalist, Frank McGloin, as its principal lasher of the public conscience. The *New Delta* soon began giving the *Picayune* and *Times-Democrat* a run for public attention if not for their revenue. Behind the newspaper and the entire antilottery movement stood a new and increasingly influential organization, the Antilottery League.

The legislative session of 1890 was a harbinger of similar travesties which the state would endure forty years later under Huey Long. Morris, austerely dignified, set up headquarters in Baton Rouge, to which he would summon complaisant legislators. At first, an unofficial survey indicated that a majority of the House was against Morris's proposition. Neugass of London also had a bid in for a charter. Morris raised his ante. Then a majority of the members of both Houses signed a pledge not to vote for the lottery. The pledge stated that if any of the signers did support it, their signatures would be evidence that they had been bribed.

Three times the bill started through the House. Its supporters were fervent in their praises. Representative Robert H. Snyder of Tensas almost wept as he pleaded that the lotteries would build the levees, educate the children, care for the insane and indigent.

"If it is not maintained here," he warned, "other lotteries will take the money from the state, whose asylums had been loaned money without interest or thought of repayment."

The fervent solon even dragged in white supremacy.

"The Democratic party, so recently back in control of the state, cannot afford to split over a question like the lottery," he shouted. "To bring it in is to put white supremacy in jeopardy."

The speech of the gentleman from Tensas was less blunt than the words of a Captain Weeks, who a few days earlier had declared at an antilottery meeting that "those who intended to vote against the lottery would rather see their mothers delivered of bastards than to vote for it." Above a disapproving report of this speech, the *Times-Democrat* wrote a headline: "A SHOCKING SENTIMENT RECEIVED WITH APPLAUSE."

But apparently a great many pledged legislators changed their minds about the evils of illegitimacy as well as bribery, even though lottery opponents proved that ordinary taxation of the lottery would net the state $1,772,000 more than Morris's offer. The lottery presented other arguments. This was a free country. The lottery does much good. Its drawings are fair, and a lot of people win prizes. What more could one ask?

A legislative majority asked no more. On the third attempt, the bill extending the lottery was passed. The state capitol was struck by lightning just as Representative S. O. Shattuck, who had introduced the measure, voted for it.

After numerous delays, the Senate also passed the bill. It was in the form of an amendment to the constitution, to be ratified by the people.

And then the lottery ran afoul of a snag. Governor Francis T. Nicholls, an old Confederate who had lost his left arm while leading his brigade at Chancellorsville, refused to sign.

"Should I affix my signature to this bill," he said, "I should be ashamed to let my left hand know what my right hand had done."

The lottery interests were afraid that they couldn't line up the two-thirds majority necessary to repass the bill over the governor's veto. In their canvass to line up the vote, there occurred a grimly amusing incident indicative of the bitterness of the fight. One enthusiastic lottery legislator had celebrated the original passage so vigorously in New Orleans that he went down with delirium tremens in his hotel. Physicians warned that he would die if moved, but his wife was willing to have him brought to Baton Rouge, where it was arranged for the legislature to meet in his sickroom. While the antis protested that such procedure would be illegal, the harassed celebrant up and died. Not a wealthy man, he was discovered to have a money belt holding $18,000.

So, instead of attempting to secure a two-thirds majority vote, the lottery forces rushed through a resolution declaring that Governor Nicholls had no right to veto a constitutional amendment. The bill was ordered sent to the secretary of state for promulgation, and the legislature adjourned. It was then discovered that all constitutional provisions had not been complied with. Whereupon, the secretary of the Senate, the clerk of the House, and a lottery senator returned to Baton Rouge, had the inappropriate printed forms destroyed, and the type forms changed to conform.

The secretary of state refused to promulgate or advertise the act, on the grounds that it had not been passed as the law required. Morris brought suit to compel him to do so. In April, 1891, the State Supreme Court decided by a 3 to 2 vote that the governor had no right to veto the amendment, and that the officers of both houses had the right to change the records after adjournment. By another of those coincidences, one of the affirmative judges, Samuel D. McEnery,

became the prolottery candidate for governor in the forth-
coming election of 1892.

The opposing forces took determinedly to the hustings,
for the governor's race and the amendment, so tightly linked,
meant life or death for the lottery. The Antilottery League
joined with the State Farmers' Alliance, a powerful rural
political organization opposed to the lottery. The octopus
itself organized the "Progressive League," endowed it with
near-limitless funds, and sent orators under its auspices
throughout the state. The ward bosses of New Orleans and
the professional politicians of the hinterland threw their
weight behind the lottery and its money bags.

Falling back on that old reliable, white supremacy, the
lotteryites sang:

> Hurrah, Hurrah,
> McEnery is the man,
> To lead our people brave and free,
> The Democratic clan.

They pointed to the lottery's benevolence, its honesty,
the impeccable character of Morris. Their backstage campaigning also was effective; and many sincere citizens supported the lottery on the grounds that it would provide the
impoverished state with badly needed revenues. Prolottery
petitions gained thousands of signers.

The antilottery movement, however, had the fanaticism
of zealots determined to reform their state. One powerful
pamphlet they used was a shocker published by the Reverend
Carradine of New Orleans, entitled *The Louisiana Lottery
Company, Examined—Exposed*. It consisted of two of his
addresses and additional thoughts on the subject. One cartoon
portrayed the church as a dead woman, her ears stuffed with
bank notes, silver dollars on her dead eyes, her lips sewed
with golden thread. Among his choicer descriptive phrases
were "the Great Finance Cancer," "the Great Incorporated

Rat Hole," "the Bloated Financial Monster." Ministers thundered, women volunteers cajoled, the rock-ribbed Protestants of rural Louisiana went to meetings chanting "Onward, Christian Soldiers." The fight became almost a Holy War. But if its opponents had the religion, the lottery had the money. Morris and his associates were not worried over much.

And then in the early stages of the campaign the United States government dealt almost a knockout blow to the lottery. The Louisiana quarrel had become a national issue. The influential press of Chicago, New York, Cincinnati, and elsewhere, and such national organs as the *Forum, Review of Reviews,* and the *American Law Review* excoriated the lottery in almost every issue. In September, 1890, Congress had enacted a law—shades of Colonel McClure—making it possible for the government to prosecute lotteries for posting of lottery tickets or for advertising through the mails. Since 1888, the Post Office Department had tried to secure convictions under the postal laws of 1876, but prosecution could be initiated only at the mailing point. The United States District Court in New Orleans, hand in glove with the lottery, had thwarted every effort.

With national interest high, President Harrison in 1890 sent a message to Congress, pointing out that the government was "an unwilling partner in a nefarious business" and recommending "severe and effective legislation." Congress immediately enacted a law, and the government instituted a test case against newspapers in New Orleans and Mobile which carried lottery advertising.

The Supreme Court was not to render a decision upholding the law until February, 1892, but the lottery's mail business fell off. In the ten days prior to the law's passage, the company received 30,000 letters and the New Orleans National Bank 8,464 registered letters. By July, 1891, the lottery received only 534 letters and the banks only 11 letters for the lottery in ten days. The business had been switched to the express companies.

In January, 1892, even before the Supreme Court ruling, the company ran this advertisement:

Important

Send your money by Express at our expense in sums not less than Five Dollars.

Congress having lately passed laws prohibiting the use of the mails to all Lotteries, we use the Express Company in answering correspondents and sending lists of prizes, until the Courts shall decide OUR RIGHTS AS A FREE INSTITUTION. The Postal Authorities, however, will continue to deliver all ordinary letters addressed to Paul Conrad [who had succeeded Dr. Dauphin as manager of the Company] but will not deliver registered letters to him.

The prizes grew bigger. The monthly capital prize in 1891 was $300,000, a whole ticket selling for $20 and the smallest fraction for $1. Other tickets, or monthly drawings for a $75,000 prize, also were broken into fractions as small as 25 cents, and whole tickets $5. The great semiannual capital prize was $600,000. It was a heady twilight.

But headier still were the voices of the lottery's opponents. One of them was that of the aging Benjamin Morgan Palmer, Confederate veteran and philippic-tongued pastor of the First Presbyterian Church of New Orleans. In 1891 he thundered that "if this Lottery cannot be destroyed by forces of law, it must unquestionably be destroyed by actual revolution. It is not competent to any isolated community to live against the moral convictions of the world."

Observers at that meeting, presided over by Colonel William Preston Johnston, chancellor of Tulane University and son of General Albert Sidney Johnston, reported that

"that night Dr. Palmer could have led the people as a mob to destroy the lottery offices and stands."

No mob was needed. Thousands of Louisianians had caught the crusade's contagion. Volunteer men and women swarmed over the state, demanding the destruction of the golden octopus that had corrupted and controlled Louisiana's government, that had defied the United States, that had smirked behind sanctimonious charity while it gathered its millions. They said, irrefutably, that the lottery had violated its covenant of 1879 by asking for an extension of its charter. It was a gambling enterprise of the worst sort, preying upon children, needy mothers, and improvident fathers. It was subject to no state supervision. Its gross profits were too high. And if Louisiana is so poor, she should run her own lottery instead of leaving it to Morris.

So spoke the crusaders. Against them the lottery's millions and the social prestige and political power of Morris could not prevail. In March, 1892, the voters of Louisiana rejected the lottery amendment and the candidate of the octopus. No longer would Louisiana be the river Monaco of the American Union.

Immediately after his defeat, Morris published a letter in the *Picayune*, withdrawing his offer of $1,250,000 a year —the lottery still had almost three years to go—and stating that he had made the proposal because he thought all the people of Louisiana were in favor of the lottery. Had he known there was to be opposition, he said, he would never have made his charitable offer. A not too graceful farewell from a graceful, cultured man who had amassed on the Lower Mississippi perhaps the greatest personal fortune in its history.

Even less gracious was the editorial requiem of the *Picayune*. Caustically—and in all truth—it remarked that legislative positions were no longer lucrative since the lottery had ceased to be politically lucrative. Nor would the post of legislator be really lucrative again on the river until the Kingfish of Louisiana found that a majority of the state's lawmakers could be bought "like sacks of potatoes."

The lottery continued to operate until its charter expired on December 31, 1895. And the final epitaph of the octopus appeared in a front page advertisement in the *Times-Democrat*. It read:

From and after January 1 my address will be

PAUL CONRAD

PUERTO CORTEZ, HONDURAS, C.A.

care Central American Express, Port Tampa City, Fla., U.S.A.

And in steaming, hopeful little Honduras the lottery died.

PART FIVE

Unsolved River

CHAPTER 23

Water Over the Levee

If THE Mississippi River could write its autobiography, I suspect there'd be a resentful reference to Seguine Allen, who for more than fifty years has been combating its flood-time possessiveness. Those fifty-odd years represent two-thirds of Seguine Allen's life. They also represent almost one-fourth of the total period of the white man's efforts to keep the Mississippi between its banks.

Seguine Allen is a ruddy-cheeked, keen-eyed little man who is ready to down a toddy or debate fine points of flood control with any man who shows the slightest interest in high water. He is the chief engineer of the Lower Yazoo-Mississippi Levee District which includes seven valuable and vulnerable river counties in the state of Mississippi. He is almost equally versed in flood-fighting tactics and Washington politics, which are the two requisites for his job.

Political shrewdness has been important because of the immemorial refusal of national, state, and local governments to treat the river as a nonpartisan menace. A great deal more might be written on this topic, but not here.

Now for the reasons why Seguine Allen and many another riverman must be skilled flood fighters. Before the days of the levees, the river's natural flow-way was some forty miles wide. During high water the river simply spread out. The first levees, which the French built, were erected principally on the east bank in the vicinity of New Orleans, so the river could still rage westward in its spring fury. Then the levees began to top the west bank, until the Lower Mississippi's flow was confined abnormally to an extreme width of from one and a half to ten miles. The inevitable result of this narrowing of the flow-way has been a steady rise in the flood plane, amounting to some eight or nine feet in the last fifty years alone.

As Seguine Allen can tell you, the Mississippi River is not one to take confinement lying down. And one wonders at man's temerity and partial success in the unending effort. For the Mississippi, together with its tributaries, drains a total area of about 1,224,000 square miles. At its most easterly point, the divide of this watershed is within 250 miles of the Atlantic, and its western limits extend to within 500 miles of the Pacific. In high water and low the Lower Mississippi receives the discharges of the Ohio, the Upper Mississippi, the Missouri, the Tennessee, the Cumberland, the White, the Arkansas, and the Red. The vast watershed is divided into six principal basins, any one of which may be in flood in any given year. And, conceivably, all of them may.

That's a lot of water to try to keep between artificial banks. The obvious observation is that no one should have tried to do it. But, just as obviously, men have kept trying because the fertile earth beside the river is a prize worth withholding from overflow.

❦   ❦

Attempts to restrain the Mississippi began almost simultaneously with the first white settlement thereon, when Le Blond de la Tour, Bienville's brilliant engineer, directed "a dike or levee to be raised in front [of New Orleans] more effectively to preserve the city from overflow."

By 1727 the New Orleans levee was almost a mile long, the handiwork of the land-grant planters who were required by the crown to build an embankment and a link in the public road along their own stretches of river front. Eight years later the levee or levees extended on both banks from twelve miles below New Orleans to thirty miles above, and the landed aristocracy began to reap profits from the protected acres.

When Seguine Allen's grandfather received his 3,000-acre Spanish grant in the 1790's and built his home, Nanache Hall, 19 miles below Vicksburg on the Big Black, there had been practically no change in the system of levee building. The levees were still small embankments erected where cultivation of land or the establishment of settlements made them advantageous. It was a haphazard business, and the principal object was simply to keep high water away from the immediate area of the levees. The planters were chiefly interested in passing the waters on downstream, with no thought of protection of the neighbor below. Through gaps in the series of individual dikes, the floodwaters escaped into the unprotected, unoccupied sections of the valley, without particular disturbance to anyone.

But by the turn of the century, thousands of new settlers were clearing lands and building levees where once the spring overflow had spread unhindered across the lowlands. As they threw up the protective dikes, and joined them in almost unending procession, the flood heights gradually increased; for the higher and more continuous the levees, the higher rose the river in its narrowing flow-way.

Eventually, the riparian landowners could not individually bear the expense, for the levees were growing in length, breadth and height—and in cost—and the areas which could be disregarded without menacing near-by plantations were rapidly diminishing. So flood control by legislative action had its beginnings.

The first compulsory levee-building laws were enacted by the river counties in the 1830's. These laws made levee construction and repair compulsory, levied taxes and provided for levee inspectors. Typical of the county legislation was an act passed by Warren County, Mississippi, in 1846. It provided for the taxation of back lands as well as riparian holdings when such back lands would be benefited by the erection of levees. But we would not recognize those low dikes as the forerunners of the great, 50-foot embankments of today. The dimensions of the levees of 1846 were prescribed as follows:

Be it further enacted that every levee, erected within the provisions of this act, shall be at least one foot above the highest water mark; and if under *two feet high* it shall contain five feet base for every foot of height, and if over two feet high then it shall contain six feet base for every foot in height; and the dirt used in making such levees shall be taken from the side next the river, at least twenty feet from the base of the levee.

In 1850, Washington County, Mississippi, prescribed that, during high water, levee inspectors must examine the levees at least twice a week. They were given authority to "call out all slaves, men and women, within five miles of the levee" to work on the river front, and "to kill hogs running at large within two miles of the levee."

By the beginning of the Civil War, the natural transition from highly localized flood fighting to district-wide co-operation had been completed. Throughout the lower valley levee districts had been organized, composed of groups of river counties charged with maintaining a uniform levee system along their river borders. In the strictest sense, however, this was still a patchwork system on a district instead of a plantation or county scale.

The higher the levees rose, the worse the floods when the river broke through. The years 1849 and 1850 were black ones for the valley. Again in 1858 tremendous damage resulted from the spring rise, and in 1859 thirty-two crevasses, or breaks in the levees, were recorded.

The Civil War interrupted the slow development of unified flood fighting. The untended embankments sloughed off into the river or were frequently destroyed by the opposing armies. And when the war was ended, carpetbag administration in the river counties took over the levee boards with more scandal than success. Yet despite this period of demoralization, successive levee boards were organized until by 1880 flood fighting along the entire lower river from its mouth to St. Louis was under the jurisdiction of an unbroken chain of organized districts.

The task was still too great for these underfinanced, localized groups to handle. By 1878 hundreds of miles of main levees had been abandoned or washed away. The citizens of the Lower Mississippi were simply unable to protect themselves financially from the river. Even if they had been able, the river was becoming too strong a foe to be dealt with by uncorrelated effort.

So these planters began to reason that, since navigation was as important to the shipping interests as levees were to themselves, they should have outside help. The earliest cry for federal flood control had come years before, in the 1840's, in the very name of navigation improvement. And it had come from such otherwise diverse political leaders as Abraham Lincoln, John C. Calhoun, Horace Greeley, and Thomas Hart Benton and at the wide intervals at which their careers flowered.

Such agitation met some success. After the floods of 1849 and 1850, Congress passed the Swamp Acts, which granted to the states all unsold swamp and overflowed lands within their limits. Under the Swamp Acts, the states were to apply funds acquired from the sale of these lands for drainage, flood-control, and reclamation projects. But the program was not effective, for the states and the levee districts failed to co-operate. The Swamp Acts fell short of their purpose.

The river people persisted in their efforts to have the federal government share responsibility for the river that drained a continent. At last, in 1879, a reluctant Congress created the Mississippi River Commission, a seven-man body appointed by the President. The act prescribed that the president of the commission should be selected from the Engineer Corps of the army. The commission was charged with the preparation of plans to protect the riverbanks, improve the channel and navigation, prevent destructive floods, and "promote and facilitate commerce and the Postal Service."

The first appropriation, made in 1881 under the Rivers and Harbors Act, was only $1,000,000. Today the government spends an average of $40,000,000 a year on the river. Levee work, under the commission's supervision, was started in 1882; but its activities were hampered, and would continue to be hampered for nearly half a century, because of insufficient funds. Levee construction and repairs were restricted for the most part to such work as could be justified as navigation improvement. The driblets of cash allocated to the various districts helped, but not enough. The lower valley continued to battle almost alone, and with little success, to hold back the floodwaters of the nation.

In these forbidding years when the South was emerging from Reconstruction, the river seemed to conspire against the people of the valley. Major floods inundated the lowlands in 1882, 1884, 1890, 1891, 1897, and 1898. In the great flood of 1882 alone, 284 crevasses were counted, and 224 in 1884. The 1897 overflow covered 20,000 square miles.

Yet buoyed after 1879 by the hope that the government would share responsibility, the people of the Lower Mississippi clung to the river, cleared thousands of additional acres, opened vast new areas to cultivation. Taxing themselves to their financial limits, they raised their levees a little at a time, praying that eventually they would be safe behind them, and that their lands would justify taxation through increased value. They drained the rich, low-lying alluvial soil, built roads, turned river landings into growing towns and growing towns into cities.

But the valley had found no security even by the turn of the century. The river struck hard in 1903, again in 1912 when $40,000,000 property damage was suffered, and in 1913. By now the Mississippi's ravages were beginning to stir the nation's conscience. In 1917 Congress passed what is known as the First Flood Control Act, authorizing the expenditure of $45,000,000 by the commission. Not more than $10,000,000 could be spent in any one year. The act required the local districts to contribute one-third of the cost of the work and to furnish all rights of way and maintenance. It actually amounted to a fifty-fifty split of the costs of flood control.

Another serious flood came in 1922. In its wake, Congress enacted a new flood-control law in 1923, called the Second Flood Control Act, authorizing $60,000,000 to be spent at the theoretical rate of one-sixth a year.

Then in 1927, O' Man River went wild. In Seguine Allen's district in the Yazoo-Mississippi Delta, 1,400,000 acres of land were flooded from two to eighteen feet for from seventy to ninety days. The Delta's towns and villages were submerged, its roads torn apart. A hundred thousand white and black refugees, many of them camped upon the levees, became temporary dependents upon the Red Cross. Many men and women and children were trapped by the floodwaters and drowned. And New Orleans was saved only by the dynamiting of the levee below the city, releasing the raging, pent-up waters upon the sparsely inhabited and comparatively valueless area below the city. The lower valley counted its physical loss at $236,000,000.

Now the United States was convinced at last that control of the Mississippi must be undertaken on a scale hitherto undreamed of. On May 15, 1928, Congress enacted what might be described as the flood emancipation act for the Mississippi Valley. An expenditure of $325,000,000 within ten years was authorized. The flood-control program adopted was that proposed by Major General Edwin Jadwin, then chief of engineers. The essential elements of the Jadwin plan, as modified from time to time by succeeding legislation, are:

Construction, extension and repair of the levees between Cape Girardeau, Missouri, and Head of Passes, Louisiana.

Improvement and regularization of the Mississippi by works designed to increase its flood-carrying capacity and to improve navigation, through the maintenance of a channel 300 feet wide and 9 feet deep at all stages.

Protection of the valley of the St. Francis River in Missouri and Arkansas from headwater floods.

Construction of a backwater levee at the mouth of the White River in Arkansas, to be used as an emergency reservoir when necessary to protect main-line levees from excessive stages.

Protection of the Yazoo Delta in Mississippi from headwater floods from the Yazoo River, through a system of dams and reservoirs in the state of Mississippi.

Provision of floodways to carry water in excess of the safe capacity of the leveed channel of the Mississippi. Floodways were designated for (1) a point opposite Cairo, Illinois; (2) in the vicinity of Eudora, Arkansas; (3), in the Morganza, Louisiana, area; (4) along the Atchafalaya River, a distributary of the Lower Mississippi, in Louisiana, and (5) at Bonnet Carré, above New Orleans, where the overflow could be channeled into Lake Pontchartrain and thence into the Gulf of Mexico.

Maintenance of a system of gauges; measurement of the discharge of the Mississippi and its tributaries; preparation and publication of maps and other physical data; and the making of surveys and investigations necessary for channel improvements and flood control.

Establishment of a hydraulics laboratory.

Establishment of an emergency fund for use in rescue work or repair or maintenance of any flood-control work on any tributaries of the Mississippi River threatened or destroyed by floods.

With the enactment of the Jadwin plan, flood control came almost exclusively under the direction of the United States engineers. And of immense significance to the valley which had spent its own wealth by the millions to hold back the river was the government's recognition of this long burden and the decision to give considerable relief from it. Section 2 of the Act of 1928 read in part:

... it is hereby declared to be the sense of Congress that the principle of local contribution toward the cost of flood control work, which has been incorporated in all previous legislation on the subject, is sound, as recognizing the special interest of the local population in its own protection, and as a means of preventing inordinate requests for unjustified items of work having no material national interest. (But) in view of the great expenditure estimated at *approximately $292,000,000 heretofore made by the local interests in the alluvial valley of the Mississippi River for protection against the floods of that river;* in view of the extent of national concern in the control of these floods in the interests of national prosperity, the flow of interstate commerce, and the movement of the United States mail; and in view of the gigantic scale of the project, involving flood waters of a volume and flowing from a drainage area largely outside the states most affected, and far exceeding those of any other

river in the United States, *no local contribution to the project herein adopted is required.*

This was salvation, although the bill required the local interests to provide all necessary rights of way and to maintain the works after completion. The enormity of even this contribution is apparent in the sum of $62,616,371 which the levee boards expended from 1928 to 1938 on rights of way and maintenance.

The Flood Control Act of 1928 was without doubt the greatest contribution to the valley's welfare in all its history. There have been high-water periods since then. In 1937 a considerable area was flooded. But, although the volume of floodwater in the river was greater even than in 1927, the area affected was but a fraction of that of 1927. The gov'-ment engineers and gov'ment money stand now in the gap that once the river people filled alone.

These are simply the dry—or wet—figures and facts which Seguine Allen gave me in his Levee Board office in the shadow of the levee at Greenville. He quoted dates, sums, and historic fact almost entirely from memory, pausing only now and then to verify statements through recourse to his files. I have put them down, almost as he gave them to me, for they are informative. But to those who know Mr. Allen and his fellow fighters on the river they are simply statistical addenda to impress the outsider with what they have been up against.

The river is much more than a statistical fountainhead to Seguine Allen, who was born on its Big Black tributary at the end of the Civil War. It is his alma mater; for there was no college education for the youngster who was one of seven children in a Reconstruction-scarred family. When Seguine was twenty he set out on his own. Learning his engineering the hard way, he was first a rodman in the construction of the Tupelo-Birmingham Railroad. From Birmingham he headed for eastern Kentucky, where the railroaders were laying tracks from Richmond to Beattyville. By now he had progressed from rodman to instrument man, and then to engineer; and when the Kentucky venture was "nearly busted" he came to Greenville, Mississippi, where he had friends and relatives. There he went to work for the Levee Board.

The river was naturally in his blood. As a boy he had learned early that men along the Mississippi judged each other by their courage and enterprise in a high-water fight. He could remember the dark nights when the river sloshed against tiny embankments, and white men drove convicts and their former slaves in desperate, backbreaking counterattack. He knew the old river fighters, personally or by reputation; men like Ben Humphreys, Colonel Green Clay, Merritt Williams, and the elder William A. Percy. In that valley boyhood, high water was something to keep away from your land and your neighbors', and to hell with what happened across the river in Louisiana and Arkansas or fifty miles up- or downstream. Sod and sandbags for your own stretch, and a prayer that if the break came it would come somewhere else than in your district—that was flood fighting three-quarters of a century ago. He could repeat the sinister stories of dynamiting raids through which the unscrupulous sought to protect their own property by forcing a break elsewhere; and the anecdotes of volunteer guards who patrolled and shot to keep away the shadowy figures who crossed the river in skiffs to blow up the levees. When he was a youngster he must have heard his father and his father's friends talking of the new Mississippi River Commission. Perhaps its formation might mean that the remote and unfriendly Washington government was realizing that the river could not be repelled except by the might and wealth of the entire nation. And he must have sensed the agricultural and commercial promise of the Lower Mississippi if only the river could be kept away.

In 1890 Seguine Allen was a levee inspector, whose job it was to repair the breaks in the district. There were plenty of these breaks, for Greenville was itself underwater before the summer. In 1891 the River Commission began spending a little money, and offered Seguine Allen a job. He took it, and remained with the commission until 1902.

From his memory of those years he draws some of his most colorful reminiscences. Did you ever hear of the Irish levee builders? Until 1865 slaves with homemade implements built the levees. From 1865 to 1890 the Negro was superseded, or reinforced, by thousands of Irish immigrant laborers.

"They were known as station men, or muckers," Seguine says. "They subletted from the levee contractor from one to five stations, or hundred-foot stretches of levee. They were the same two-fisted Micks who built the railroads.

"They were a delight to the engineer and to the contractor. Armed only with their fists, they went into the dark corners of the country, sustained only by their indomitable energy, their happy dispositions, and their almost reverential respect for constituted authority. Their unknown and unmarked graves dot the rights of way of all our early railroads and levee lines. And they passed to give way to the machine age."

That's just how Seguine Allen put it. If I were an Irishman, I'd like that eulogy even more than I do now.

The Irish worked usually in pairs, and lived in shanties which they threw up behind their sections. Seguine bossed hundreds of them. After he tested the solidity of their earthen walls, he would pay them off. And from payday until the hour their $50 to $100 paychecks, the earnings of many weeks, were exhausted, the majority of the Irishmen would forget "constituted authority." Into the river towns they'd stride with the clay thick on their brogans and their thirst thick in their mouths. Across the nearest bar they'd thrust their money, most of them, and drink until the sum was exhausted.

Devoted to their levee-building partners, their comradeship sometimes went to odd extremes. Seguine Allen remembers the death of one Irishman in his "log pigpen." His partner was told that he was dead. Instead of removing the body or sleeping elsewhere, he spent the night on his pallet beside his dead associate.

"I've lived and worked four years with old Terence," he said. "He wouldn't want me to leave him the first night he's gone."

And now all the Irish are gone from the levees. Some of their descendants remain on the river. But, except for that inherited pugnaciousness and loyalty, they are indistinguishable from the rest of the river folk.

After the Irishman and his wheelbarrow came the drag scrapers and the wheel scrapers, and the mule-drawn dump wagons which held one and a quarter cubic yards of earth and were pulled by twelve to sixteen mules. And on the heels of the first World War, the caterpillar tractor and dragline machines were perfected, and manual levee building was a thing of the lost past. Today, if you ask a Negro levee worker where his foreman is, he might answer: "He's out Fresno-in' with a tumblebug cat"—which means that he is using a small caterpillar tractor to drag a Fresno scraping machine.

There were no tumblebug cats in 1897 when Seguine Allen stood guard over twelve miles of imperiled levee at the upper end of his district. The river lapped at the sandbags piled two and a half feet on the levee. In three days he had directed the filling of fifty to sixty sloughs, where the levee had been washed away in miniature landslides. At four o'clock in the afternoon, a foreman reported the worst slough of the fight. On a long stretch the levee had fallen in so badly that the river was two feet over the top and spreading to a depth of three feet on the land side. In places on the land side the water had reached eight feet.

"The fight looked hopeless," Seguine recalls. "We summoned all available hands from the plantations, and put the women to sewing sacks. We had no timber and no lights. But about a block away was a four-room Negro cabin.

"I told my men to tear down the house and burn it a plank at a time. The manager of the plantation, which belonged to Governor Parker of Louisiana, was willing. By nine the next morning, after working through the night by the light of those cabin planks we had the break down to a spurt the size of your finger. But we wouldn't have been saved even then if the levee in the White River basin across from us in Arkansas hadn't given way."

"And the house?"

"I asked the manager what sort of settlement he wanted for the cabin. He could have just about named his price. He said 'Well, you saved the plantation, so just give us some old levee topping planks. We'll build another.'"

Later, in that same bleak spring, Seguine Allen locked horns with a less tractable planter. Along their own fronts the landowners were all-powerful autocrats. This planter demanded that the entire levee in front of his holdings be sacked with sandbags. Seguine told him it would be impossible. The planter wired the chief of engineers, who immediately backed up Seguine. So when the levee sloughed in three places in front of the plantation, Seguine Allen found he couldn't get any workers from the plantation to help in the fight.

"The next morning I saw sixty men plowing his land back of the river. I got mad. I sent word for him to come see me. He came down in a skiff. I asked him how about sending me his Negroes.

"'They're doing very well where they are,' he said.

"I knew this man had a mean reputation. But I had a pistol in my pocket and I knew I couldn't back down.

"'I can only say this,' I told him. 'If this levee breaks, every man and woman is going to know why. And I don't care what happens to any son of a bitch on this place.'

"'You use harsh words,' he said.

"'Shall I repeat them?' I asked, talking a lot brasher than I felt.

"'No,' he said after a couple of seconds. 'I'll send you all my men this morning.'

"He did. We saved the levee, and later he and I became pretty good friends."

⚜   ⚜

This complete domination of the planter over the activities of his tenants was typical of the South of that period. Nowhere was the dominance more apparent or put to more imperative use than in the high-water fights. The planter simply ordered his tenants to the levees; and buoyed by an occasional drink of cheap, straight Bourbon whisky, and plenty of hot coffee and food, they worked night and day.

The tenants who worked on the levees were paid by the Mississippi River Commission or by the Levee Districts, and paid well according to the standards of the day. But they did not always receive the $2 to $3 daily wages which they had earned. Sometimes the less scrupulous landlords, acting as paymasters for the commission or the district boards, would apply these not inconsiderable sums to the commissary accounts or other indebtedness of the tenants. Some of these debts were real enough; others were not. In any event, the denial of this pay, the Negro's best chance to earn cash money between crops, was a prerogative, and once an often abused one, of the planter.

This arbitrary power to commandeer labor in a flood emergency extended beyond the limits of the plantations. Convicts were brought out as soon as a high-water fight began. They still are. Many a time have white and black men in stripes, working under armed guards, saved stretches of levee that otherwise might have gone under. In some crises, however, the convict and tenant levies were insufficient. In desperation, the sheriffs of the river counties would round up loiterers in every town and crossroads store, charge them with vagrancy, and force them to the levees.

Once Seguine Allen caught a corvée of Tartars in such a crew. A sheriff had arrested every Negro he could find in the county and brought them to the levee. The zealous official's dragnet had also caught a half dozen white shanty boatmen. Resentful at being drafted for unaccustomed toil, these shantyboaters converged after nightfall upon Seguine Allen, complaining threateningly of bad food, hard work, and the lack of sleeping quarters. Then they asked the lone engineer what he intended to do about it.

Seguine Allen thought fast. He knew he couldn't afford to lose face, but he also knew he couldn't cow the menacing group. Whatever happened must appear to be the result of his own decision.

"You all been arrested?" he asked.

They answered in angrily affirmative chorus.

"Well, I don't want you around"—which was true; "you sons of bitches light out and don't let me see you again."

It was a diplomatic ending, says Seguine Allen, and one which was highly satisfactory to both sides.

Seguine has many similar stories over which he chuckles; and they are amusing enough now, though not humorous when they occurred. For in his fifty years of flood service there have been uncounted days and nights of weary, rain- and river-soaked sleeplessness, with wet death surging against the sandbags; days and lights when the vigil and toil of exhausted Negroes and their desperate leaders were unavailing; days and nights when the hoarse cry "She's breaking!" sent men scattering to rowboats, to trees, or to a section of levee of hoped-for firmness. Few of Seguine Allen's stories concern himself, for he shares fully the reverence of the river folk for the legion of great flood fighters. It is a homage strange only to those who don't know what the fight is like.

That reverence explains why Will Whittington, the Yazoo-Mississippi Delta's congressman, never has opposition. He is chairman of the Flood Control Committee, which to his people is the most important job in Washington. They keep able, outspoken Will Whittington—a prosperous planter and lawyer, but no politician—in Washington because he has fought indefatigably for flood control and with intimate knowledge of its need. It explains why Major General Harley B. Ferguson, retired, is sworn by in the valley. General Ferguson was until 1939 the president of the Mississippi River Commission, and director of the army engineers' manifold river activities. He fought for a system of cutoffs, which would shorten the river and eliminate the dangerous, curving channels that increased the flood threat in high water. In 1937 his cutoffs received much of the credit for averting a major flood.

❧ ❧

The levees were higher in 1937, and the cutoffs were meeting their first great test. Everyone felt that the river would be held, and it was. Even so, I could look from my newspaper office window in Greenville and see the gray Coast Guard cutters seemingly perched upon the levee. The river lapped at the levee top, and the cutters, on hand to aid in rescue work if needed, were moored twenty feet above the ground level of our street.

And one morning during that threatening February I drove for sixty miles along the ridge of the levee with Mr. Charlie Williams and Gervys Lusk. Like his fabled planter father, Mr. Charlie is a capable flood fighter, and one of Seguine Allen's right-hand volunteers in a crisis. Gervys, like myself, was along for the excitement, for Mr. Charlie was making an inspection trip. Rain fell continually. The crest of the levee was a slippery mud roadway, scarcely wide enough for two cars to pass. On our left side, driving north, the river sloshed two feet below the wheels of our automobile. And for miles the land side was a leaky morass; the river had worked under the levee in places, and had bubbled to the surface.

These leaks, known as sand boils, were a constant threat. They had to be spotted early and circled with sandbags. When the seepage inside these sandbagged areas reaches the level of the weak area of penetration on the river side, equalized pressure arrests the disintegrative, hidden flow. If the boils are not discovered in time, the levee can be eaten away deep inside its bowels.

Mr. Charlie explained these and other matters with gusto. To fortify ourselves against the damp cold, he had brought along a jug of his famed potable, the Chattahoochie, which is a mixture of lemon juice, sugar, Bourbon whisky, and possibly a stick of dynamite. At frequent intervals we tipped the jug, and after each sip Mr. Charlie, who was driving, became more articulate—not only vocally but with his hands. He'd gesture riverward, skyward, earthward, and the car would slither nervously toward the watery Scylla or the slick, precipitous Charybodis.

"God Almighty, Mr. Charlie," yells Gervys. "Hold onto that wheel!"

Mr. Charlie grins.

"You're right, son. Like the darky says, 'dat buckshot dirt is slicky.'"

And on we'd skid, with more gestures.

At intervals we lunged down the levee to a camp where engineers, inspectors, planters on volunteer patrol service, and scores of Negroes were swarming. Mr. Charlie knew everyone, and everyone knew him. At each camp we ducked into the cook tent, to drink black coffee, eat thick sandwiches, and discuss the outlook. Nobody seemed excited, though the threat was grave. After a few yarns and a second cup of coffee, up the levee we'd grind in low gear, and off to the next camp.

It was my first experience at close quarters with serious flood fighting. I had been too young in 1922, and I was too far away in 1927. And what I saw was simply the relaxed moments of a battle that had not and would not become intense. The river was not so fearsome in 1937, for the Engineers had been working for nine years and there was enough money and equipment to fight back.

❧   ❧

In 1902, when Seguine Allen quit the commission, there was neither enough equipment nor enough money. Nor was there enough for the next twenty years, in which he practiced his profession in Greenville, privately and as city engineer. In both capacities he participated in every high-water fight that came along.

They kept the water out of most of the district in 1922. The river overlapped the levees from an inch to a foot and a half, but they stemmed it with millions of sandbags, rushed by special trains from the North to Vicksburg. The bags were old trench sandbags, saved from the World War, and they were to be used again, but ineffectively, in 1927.

After the successful fight in 1922, Seguine Allen was

elected chief engineer of the Levee Board. Five years later he directed the hopeless battle of the lower delta against the mammoth flood of 1927. That spring the Mississippi hammered at the levees with a volume of two million feet per second, until the great embankments gave way.

"It mighty near crushed me to lose that fight," he says. To hear him say it you would think that he felt personally responsible for what happened.

The 1927 overflow proved an indirect blessing to the valley. First a shocked, generous nation rushed food and clothing and money to the stricken river people. Then the nation began asking questions. Why should the valley pay the costs of a nation's drainage? Why shouldn't flood control be as much a federal responsibility as navigation?

So came the Jadwin plan, and the beginning of more nearly adequate governmental expenditures. But these gains were not secured overnight. The river's leaders had to fight the Mississippi as hard in Washington as at home, for they faced blind, sectional-minded little men who twisted the doctrine of states' rights to challenge national interest.

Seguine Allen participated in the Delta's fight in Washington, lobbying, cajoling, debating, testifying, offering endless statistics to skeptical men who knew nothing of the river. He was no stranger in Washington, for almost every year since he became chief engineer he had attended the annual meetings of the Mississippi River Flood Control Association. There, practically hat in hand, he had begged year after year for the full appropriations which were authorized in the earlier acts. In 1923 a statement he made to the Flood Control Committee of the House played no small part in winning approval of the Second Flood Control Act: "In 1882 my district was 186 miles long, and at the present time, forty years having elapsed, it is still 186 miles long. But in that intervening time we have lost to the Mississippi River

220 miles of the main line of our levee, or about 115 per cent."

Now, in 1927, after the flood waters had receded, Seguine Allen is in Washington again, one of many Southerners pleading the cause of adequate flood control. He is making his most impassioned statement of his people's case. To the Flood Control Committee of the House and the Commerce Committee of the Senate he describes his district. It embraces 1,750,066 acres, of which 701,346 are cleared. The district has been organized since 1865 as a flood-fighting unit, maintaining a levee nearly 190 miles long. He tells of the taxation, the half century of hope that the government would help these people. He recounts the successive disasters and their meaning in dollars and cents. Since 1882 his district has spent $24,000,000 for levee protection. Its mortgages and outstanding bonds represent a levy of $75 an acre against all cleared lands.

Does not the government accept responsibility for navigation? Does it not build revetments to restrain the low-water channel so that ships can always move on the river? Why, then, does it not maintain the levees which restrain the high water?

"When revetments and levees are jointly necessary, each practically useless without the other, why say that it is the duty of the government to maintain revetment and the duty of the riparian owner to bear part of the cost of the levees? The equity is not there, any more than to say to the owner of land near some great dam or the landowner or merchant in some great seaport, 'You must bear part of the cost of the work because you know that this great channel and this great harbor will enable the commerce of this nation to flow freely at less cost.'

"The Levee Board can no longer continue to pay; and unless the government will assume full responsibility for protecting its own interest and that of its people against the ravages of its own waterway, then the valley will prove a canker upon the heart of the nation because its agriculture cannot bear the burden."

The river people continue to pay directly a part of the costs. Yet in Washington in 1927 and 1928 they won most of their long fight.

"Since 1927 I've just been sitting here," says Seguine. Which is a considerable understatement. The Levee Board still has a job to do, for the local interests continue to provide rights of way and maintain the works after they are completed. From the office of this board, and of the others along the river, the engineers cover their districts, maintaining the vigilance that pays dividends when the unpredictable river seeks openings in the valley's earthen armor. The people of the valley still pay taxes for flood control. Seguine Allen's work is not done.

But things are far different now from that spring of 1890 when young Seguine Allen battled his first flood. Today the United States engineers, and the proofs of their handiwork, are everywhere on the river. Today Cairo drowses behind a giant floodwall. Today the river in front of Greenville is no longer a river but a horseshoe lake, which is the fruit of one of the cutoffs which detach the river from the old dangerously curving beds.

The lower end of this lake, which is named for General Ferguson, joins the river four miles below the city. Its upper end is separated from the Mississippi by a dike; and the river flows today in a new, straight channel which the engineers dug and into which they diverted the Mississippi.

The speedy airboats of the engineers skim upon the river, collecting physical data for experimentation and control. The Mississippi's banks are held back by their willow fascines and the concrete and asphalt mattress which prevent crumbling, channel filling, and the scouring of new channels, and thus aid navigation.

Since 1928 the engineers have dumped about eight hundred million cubic yards of earth, more than twice the yardage excavated in building the Panama Canal, upon more than two thousand miles of levees. Perhaps the ghosts of grimy shanty Irish hover near the huge dragline machines, the government dredge boats, the hydraulic pipe lines, and the towers, wondering how men with wheelbarrows ever dared to challenge the floods.

The activities of the engineers are continuous and intricate, for flood control and maintenance of navigation are no more static than the river itself.

If you visit Vicksburg, center of the engineers' activities, you may be taken to the Waterways Experiment Station, which is under the direct supervision of the Mississippi River Commission. Here the army engineers, and their civilian associates, solve the complex problems of waterways and harbors by observing miniature, exact replicas. Nor are these problems simply those of the Mississippi. They come from all over the nation, and from foreign countries. At the station, models are built in conformity to the particular river area under study, and measured quantities of water, proportionate to the actual flow, are discharged through it. From the reaction on the model, the engineers determine the probable reaction of the river itself to the proposed works or improvements constructed on the minute scale.

And driving to New Orleans, you will see another monument to the army engineers. The Bonnet Carré Spillway was constructed to protect New Orleans from floods and to lower flood heights by discharging floodwaters into Lake Pontchartrain and thence into the Gulf of Mexico. Such a diversion plan had been dreamed of for a hundred years. The engineers made it a reality in 1931. And it met its first great test in 1937, when 285 of its 350 bays were opened.

Through them rushed enough water to cover 1,250,000 acres to a depth of ten feet. As a result, the river stages were lowered for more than a hundred miles, and New Orleans was relieved of all threat of flood.

This is only a glimpse of what the army engineers have done on the river. There are floodways on the Atchafalaya in Louisiana, and another near New Madrid, in Missouri. On reservoirs, revetments, and troublesome channels the engineers have been busy for fifteen years. And always there is more to do.

And there is much for Seguine Allen to accomplish also even now. The hill people of northern Mississippi, from where the Coldwater and Tallahatchie rivers pour into the Yazoo and flood it before it empties into the Mississippi, have little in common with their brothers of the Delta. They must continually be persuaded that reservoirs, already built or planned for, aid not only the river people but themselves. They must be reminded that a flood-free Delta, whose 17 counties pay one-third of the taxes of Mississippi's 82 counties, can prosper and pay those taxes only if they are kept dry. The Arkansans across the river also must be reasoned with. They smart under the two-foot levee height differential allowed the Deltans who started their levees first, maintained them alone longer, and who have developed their territory the most. The Arkansans, says Seguine Allen, have had their levees built high enough by the government to withstand a flood of the proportions of 1927. Why should not the more highly developed Delta be permitted the levee height supremacy which it started and principally paid for? And the Louisianians have staved off the construction of the Eudora Spillway, which would siphon the floodwaters across Arkansas and Louisiana lowlands—properly paid for by the government—and thence into the Red river for subsequent discharge again into the Mississippi far below.

Seguine frets over these obstructions to a nearly foolproof flood control. He has tried to keep his district dry for fifty years. He knows, as do the United States engineers, that levees alone cannot withstand the greatest conceivable flood. That task requires a combined system of cutoffs, diversions such as the Eudora, reservoirs, and stronger and higher levees.

After fifty years of struggle, Seguine Allen does not believe that the all-embracing flood-control program is progressing fast enough. He fumes at the local and state interests that obstruct the program of the army engineers. He wants them to have the completely free hand which is still denied them.

"This valley is an integral whole," he explains. "The only way to handle it is through a central authority. That authority should be the engineers. Their record is clean. They can keep clear of politics, and they are our ablest river engineers. It would be a sad day if the Mississippi Valley ever becomes a monumental kind of TVA civilian authority.

"But the engineers won't force an improvement on anybody. Because of the diversity of interests, they have never assumed complete responsibility. They are pulled from one side to another. I think that the Engineers Corps should develop a plan it believes will take care of all floods, and that the states and levee boards should accept it. That's the only way you can get rid of the political pulling and hauling of the thirty-five levee boards in Louisiana, Arkansas, Tennessee, Kentucky, Mississippi, and Missouri."

He worries a great deal about this pulling and hauling that keeps the four-point program of the engineers from complete fruition. Behind his worry is the fear of a monstrous Something that he has never seen in his seventy-five years. It is something he calls a superflood, that will fall upon the valley some raging spring when the Ohio, the White, the Upper Mississippi, the Missouri, the Red, and the Yazoo will be simultaneously in flood. If that happens, the valley will be fighting against a volume of four million cubic feet of water passing any given point each second. Two million such cubic feet precipitated the 1927 flood; and even in 1937, when the levees were higher, and the cutoffs were in operation, the levees were hard pressed to hold the less than three billion which the Ohio and the Upper Mississippi contributed. Four million cubic feet would mean a potential overflow sixteen feet higher than the present highest levees, if levees were the only obstacle.

And what is the defense against such a flood?

"God, diversions, and stronger levees," says Seguine Allen. "And one of these days we'll have to face it, as sure as you're born."

That gives a man something to think about, especially an old man who has spent his life combating the swollen Mississippi. You can't dally with the Mississippi. When she rampages, she doesn't give a damn for the conflicting interests of states and districts.

Which, if there had been states and districts two hundred years ago, the Choctaws and the Chickasaws could also have told you.

CHAPTER 24

Mound Bayou

Some two million Negroes live within overflow distance of the Lower Mississippi, but only one thousand of them populate Mound Bayou, Mississippi, the lone all-Negro town in the valley.

Despite this singularly insignificant ratio, the shabby little settlement has a mystic importance to the Negroes of the river, though as you drive through Mound Bayou, a hundred miles below Memphis, you would not consider it either singular or important. The side streets bisecting Highway 61 are dusty or muddy, depending on the season, and unpaved. A scattering of rusty-looking one- and two-story mercantile buildings line its two-block business section. In ill-defined squares covering some twenty acres, that merge with the surrounding cotton fields, are sprinkled about a hundred and fifty cottages, some neat, some dilapidated. Only the churches stand out.

Probably you will not slow down enough to notice the two large brick churches or the rambling, three-story residence which are the most imposing structures in Mound Bayou. You usually do not slow down much because Mound Bayou has no sign warning you to observe speed laws or be arrested. Such a sign would not be considered proper.

Mound Bayou was far less prepossessing in 1887, the year of its founding. In the early eighties what is now the Yazoo and Mississippi Valley Railroad had completed its Memphis to New Orleans line, which roughly paralleled the river. Along the right of way lay millions of acres of yet undeveloped land. So the railroad began to exploit this wilderness, and particularly a million-acre tract in the alluvial Delta. It was then generally believed that the Negro was better able to survive in this undrained, fever-ridden area, so it was to the Negro that the railroad beckoned.

The first man whom the railroad interested was Jim Hill, the Negro Republican leader of Vicksburg. Hill put the road's agent in touch with Isaiah T. Montgomery, also of Vicksburg, who before the war had been a house slave in the Jefferson Davis family at Natchez. Montgomery, a dignified, self-educated Negro, was impressed with the idea of an all-Negro colony. Journeying to Bolivar County, Mississippi, about midway between Memphis and Vicksburg, he selected a site for the town-to-be. On his return, he persuaded a young cousin, Benjamin T. Green, who ran a store in Newton, Mississippi, to join him in sponsoring the colony.

Together the two pioneers purchased 840 acres of land. By the end of the year another 700 acres had been bought in small tracts by a number of their friends, and a hundred black settlers were clearing the forest and building cabins for their families.

In 1887 this area was still a low wilderness of cane-brakes and giant cypresses. Its virgin state was understandable, for until the railroads knifed through the Delta, the towns and plantations hugged the river, their surest means of travel, trade, and communication. Twenty, even ten, miles back from the river, new lands awaited settlers, who were slow in coming. This was wild land and hard to open, land in which the bear and panther, the wildcat and wolf still prowled, land that was swamp-dotted and sun-hidden beneath its thick growth.

This was the land to which the black settlers came. They had cleared forests before, but not many of them had

swung the ax and pulled the crosscut saw for themselves.
Now they labored for a tenure of their own.

One of these first comers, A. P. Hood, told of his
pioneering in a pamphlet *The Negro at Mound Bayou,* published in 1909. This is his story:

I came to Mound Bayou in 1887 and purchased from
the L. N. O. and T. Railroad Company forty acres of
land on the terms fixed by them for such purchases. [Usu-
ally seven dollars per acre, one dollar per acre down and
the balance in five equal annual payments.] In 1888 I cut
timber from this land and built a log house on it and into
this house I moved my family whom I had brought up
from Vicksburg in February of the same year. When I
started to Mound Bayou I had $175 in total cash assets.
Out of this amount I paid my transportation. I also paid
the initial or entrance fee on my forty acres of land, and
after the purchase of provisions and other items of pressing
necessity, I had left only ten dollars.

I bethought myself now as to the best steps to be taken
when this little surplus of resources should be gone. I proceeded to clear off a small plot of ground and planted a
garden. About this time I was employed by Messrs. Montgomery and Green to clear up the land, about five acres
where the town site is, at four dollars per acre. I do not
need to say that I appreciated this opportunity to earn a
few very urgently needed dollars. I set my wife and children
about this employment while I, myself, went into the woods
and engaged in getting out stave boards at six dollars per
cord, as there was at this time no land open that we could
work. In the fall of the same year, most of the women
and children of the neighborhood went to Shelby and picked
cotton at fifty cents per hundred. I succeeded this year in
clearing up and planting in corn about one-fourth of an

acre. The following year I planted cane and made some molasses, and also planted some rice.

In 1889 I took my children and went about thirteen miles west of Mound Bayou and picked cotton for Messrs. Blanchard Bros., white planters, at seventy-five cents per hundred. Following this work I was able to earn from forty to fifty dollars per month and this enabled me to keep the wolf from my door and in the meantime to pay for the forty acres of land I had bought.

The general outlook from here at this time, however, was somewhat less than encouraging. A prominent white planter in conversation with me one day when we had casually chanced to meet, remarked: "Uncle, I can't see what Montgomery and Green brought you all up here for unless they brought you up here to starve."

I replied: "Mr. Blank, our forefathers wrought in the opening of the United States for settlement and occupation, and with a far greater measure of personal interest we are determined to work out the development of Mound Bayou."

I rolled logs at night and burned them and made staves in the day for my own support and that of my family. When the cotton chopping season came, my wife and children would go and chop cotton for people round about, thus materially adding to the support fund.

In 1890 I contracted with Mr. J. C. Lauderdale [white] to cultivate for him four acres of land on the share system. . . . I have Mr. Lauderdale's word for the remarkable yield of these four acres—seven full weight bales of cotton.

There can be no greater mistake than to get the notion in this everyday life that we cannot get along without this thing and the other thing. For many times we had only bread to eat and water to drink. Grease for use in the preparation of our scanty meals, at times we did not have except for a little lard; and meat, well it was a rarity and we often made along without it sometimes for two and three months in succession.

On one occasion I was out with some other gentlemen, John Montgomery, Morgan Thurston, and Alex Wilbert in search of a hog which I owned and which was missing, when we were brought face to face with a large she-bear and two small cubs. We dispatched the mother bear after a stubborn resistance and then easily succeeded in making captives of the cubs. By many people bear's flesh is regarded as a delicacy, even when other meats are obtainable, so in our circumstances it may be easily imagined that the capture of our animals was a most gratifying contribution to our larders.

Multiply this tale and you have the story of all the black pioneers of Mound Bayou; a story whose dignity lies in their toil, whose excitement lies in their survival, whose moral lies in the fact that they succeeded.

Soon Ben Green and M. R. Montgomery, a kinsman of the founder, established a general store, the first in the community. Within sight of this first business enterprise, the settlers felled oak, ash, gum, and cypress trees to hew into crossties for the railroads and thus pay for their lands. When the new fields were planted to cotton, the firm of Montgomery and Green built Mound Bayou's first cotton gin. In 1889 the townsite was laid out. A portion of the original 840 acres was divided into town lots and sold to the increasing settlers. In 1898 Mound Bayou was incorporated, with Isaiah T. Montgomery as its first mayor.

❦   ❦

Benjamin A. Green, who is Mound Bayou's mayor, its only lawyer—Harvard, 1912—and the first child born in the town which his father helped to found, told me much of this story when I met him there in 1940. He is a dark, small, hook-nosed man, and shrewd-looking, with a marked resemblance to Haile Selassie. First we talked in his law office, a one-story, two-room frame structure enhanced by a white-pillared gallery. Then we drove through Mound Bayou while I jotted down the figures and facts he offered.

". . . twenty-four stores . . . three groceries . . . the drugstore is the most successful business here . . . 34 telephones . . . one Chinese groceryman (the ubiquitous Chinese cover the Delta with their grocery stores) . . . a lawyer, a doctor, a dentist, a registered pharmacist . . . this is the new post office . . . old I. T. Montgomery's house has twenty-seven rooms (that's the biggest building in town, and it looks midwestern, not southern) . . . five churches . . . the high and grammar schools have 700 pupils . . . five teachers, who earn from $40 to $100 a month, mostly $40. . . ."

Some of the buildings and some of Ben Green's statistics have especial significance. Across the highway, in the northeast section of Mound Bayou, the Sir Knights and Daughters of Tabor were building a $50,000 forty-bed hospital. The Sir Knights and Daughters of Tabor is a 69-year-old, nationwide benevolent and fraternal organization for Negroes, which sells benefit policies for $1.35 a month. The hospital was being built by Negro labor, under the supervision of an imported Negro architect. Its staff are Negroes.

Here are the ruins of a tiny Carnegie Foundation library. It did not take with the citizens, and the last time it was used was in 1926, for a dance. But of the town's thousand inhabitants, no more than ten per cent are illiterate, and these are mostly the old-timers. In the Mound Bayou community area, which includes the surrounding farms as well as the town, perhaps twenty-five per cent cannot read or write. But forty years ago, the figure would have been nearer a hundred per cent.

The huge home of the dead patriarch, Isaiah Montgomery, is uninhabited. There is an unpleasant reason. The walls of an upper bedroom are pocked with holes and chippings from .45-caliber bullets. In 1939, Stella Montgomery, a daughter of the late leader, returned to Mound Bayou from Chicago, ensconced herself in the house, and defied her sister's husband, Eugene Booze, who had secured possession through tangled litigation. Stella Montgomery would not move out. So Booze appealed to the law, the white law, in Cleveland, a few miles away. A white marshal and the Negro broke in upon her in the big old house, when she was alone. They testified that she came at them with a butcher knife. And she died there in the upstairs bedroom, riddled with pistol slugs.

The white officer swore that he hadn't shot. Booze didn't talk, except to the grand jury, which exonerated both men. And a few weeks later Eugene Booze was shot to death from ambush, on a Mound Bayou street at dusk. His slayer has never been identified.

The two related killings were the first homicides in sixteen years in a black man's town which has no jail, and whose marshal goes unarmed.

Ben Green doesn't like this story. He liked Booze, whose widow is a Republican national committeewoman, even less. Throughout Booze's lifetime the two men battled for political supremacy. Booze never won.

"He always pretended he was a white man's nigger," says Ben Green.

I asked this Harvard lawyer, who in the First World War had served in France in the judge advocate general's department, why he returned to the unprofitable little town.

"Somebody has to stay here," he said. "I could have remained in Boston, or practiced in Greenville. But somebody has to stay."

As mayor, Ben Green conducts court in Mound Bayou. He has an explanation for its infrequency.

"I think we're consciously proud of having a town of our own, and that partly accounts for the small amount of lawlessness," he says. "I seldom fine anyone for a first offense. I just talk to him. You might laugh, but I try to appeal to his better side."

I don't laugh. But there are other questions which I want to ask and don't know just how. Ben Green senses this.

"You want to know whether we're like some other Negroes?"

I nod, uncomfortably.

"Well, legal marriages are the rule here instead of the exception. We don't condone concubinage. And I hope, and believe, it's dying out all around."

The ice is broken. What about the attitude of the white towns?

"Shelby and Cleveland [the two near-by white communities] have a pretty friendly attitude," Ben Green says. "Merigold isn't so good. Anything they can do to hurt us they do. They're just naturally hostile. Years back they had an officer who was very unfriendly. He used to beat our people with a whip.

"But the relations are better than they have been. The white people have taken a more sympathetic attitude. And the planters aren't as *strict*"—he put a meaningful emphasis on the word—"in a business sense. Probably because under some of the old methods they were losing their best tenants."

And the opportunity which a Negro lawyer has?

"I have appeared many times before white juries. I have never had a case where a white jury deliberately put me out of court. And the white lawyers give me the greatest co-operation. They are jealous of each other, not me." Ben Green laughs soundlessly when he says this.

But he doesn't laugh when he adds: "I've never been

conscious of walking a chalk line. But we spend a lot of time figuring out the white man, because we've got to get along.

"There's been a change on both sides. The Negro hasn't as much of an inferiority complex anymore. And the white man hasn't as much hatred and he's trying to find out more about the Negro. I think education has had a softening effect, because you don't meet just the master and servant type any more.

"I guess I'm more of an optimist than a pessimist about race relations."

What about Mound Bayou's future?

"I believe Negro towns should be encouraged. I wouldn't advocate towns as large as Greenville"—which is 21,000—"because we haven't had enough governmental experience yet, and wouldn't get along. And the all-Negro town isn't the ideal setup. The ideal is where all live under constitutional equality. But we can't have it, so I think a Negro town is a benefit to us.

"Mound Bayou is going to prove something. When a Negro has a stake, he makes a better citizen. Right here, seventy-five per cent of the Negroes in this area either own or are buying their homes in towns or their farms outside. Landownership is vital. So is a better school system, and better health facilities. That's a state problem. No, it's a national problem. Our greatest handicap is lack of finances, and we can't scrape up the money ourselves."

You wonder whether Ben Green has told you all that he really thinks; whether he is speaking for Mound Bayou or just for himself. While he goes into the other room, to confer with a client, you flip the pages of the bright yellow-backed Souvenir Program of the 1887-1937 celebration which he has given you.

In it appears all the history which Mound Bayou has

preserved. Here too are smudgy, badly reproduced pictures
. . . court being held in Mound Bayou in the open air in
1890 . . . a group of Negroes in shirt sleeves standing beside
an enormous felled tree . . . placid black men and women,
attired in the leg of mutton sleeves, the bowler hats, the
frock coats of an earlier generation . . . picture after picture of Mound Bayou's first citizens and their descendants,
tucked between advertisements inserted by "our white
friends" whose contributions largely made the booklet and
the celebration possible. And, at the back of the souvenir
program, this:

The citizens of Mound Bayou dwell in security. They
are the heirs of freedom and feel that they are part of a
great nation. They contribute to its well-being by their
toil, their hopes, their aspirations, and will forever look
with disdain on acts of tyranny.

As for the future, we have faith. Materially, we rise
and fall with the favor of King Cotton. We feel, however,
that we have something vastly more important than material
gain to offer to the Negroes of America, and that is freedom from petty prejudices and insults, and an opportunity
for the dark skinned citizens of America to develop without
restraints imposed because of race, into the highest type
of manhood and womanhood. On this principle we stake
our future, and on this principle we invite the Negroes of
America to join us.

Yet even if Mound Bayou offers the happiest solution
to the grievous problem of the Negro, it can solve that
problem only for a handful. It would be difficult to establish
an appreciable number of all-Negro towns. For one thing,
to create a town, you need strategically located land, and
such land comes high. Moreover, the same roads on which
the Negro farmer travels to Mound Bayou take him also

to Memphis and Clarksdale and Greenville, where the glitter
of the dime stores, the diggity-dawg of the western movies,
the catfish lure of the short-order lunchrooms in the Negro
sections, and the back-door honky-tonks have for many
a more powerful appeal than Mound Bayou's stark invitation
to self-government and prideful racial isolation. Nor is it
probable that the white South would assist in the establishment of many Mound Bayous. It would find the resultant
economic adjustment difficult indeed.

In this last meeting with the Negro in the story of
the Lower Mississippi I have not attempted to answer the
still unanswerable questions propounded by the Negro's presence here. Nor have I tried to analyze the character of the
descendant of the slave who came to the river almost as
early as did the white man. I do not believe that any true
blanket analysis exists. I have tried only to tell of a little
Negro town, and what a little Negro lawyer who lives
there told me. Therefore many questions remain unanswered.

Ben Green worries about the answers, and so do some
others on our river, both white men and black. But we
are a minority, among Mound Bayou's thousand citizens
and among the river's hundreds of thousands.

At one extreme of the two million Negroes of the river
stands Ben Green. At the other lounges the conjure man.
Neither is representative. I am not sure how to identify
the representative Negro. And I'll not try.

Suppose we forsake the presently insoluble and smile
for a space. It is something that the Negro has taught us
to do along the river. Remember, we are not smiling at
or smiling against.

In my small newspaper plant on the Mississippi, we print
a weekly Negro newspaper. For its editor I have great respect; and I read and frequently reprint his editorials. I also
read copy on his and another Negro paper's contents, and

on the assortment of circulars, business cards, pamphlets and other material which Delta Negroes, from Mound Bayou to Rolling Fork, bring to our plant for printing. And I want you to look with me at a casual selection of the printed matter which we turn out for an amiable, lost people with a happy faculty for living in the present, and a God-sent humor, conscious and unconscious, that makes their life passable.

I think you will laugh too, but not maliciously.

Here is a wedding invitation:

Mr. and Mrs. Henry Walters
Request the Honor Of Your Presence
At the Marriage of their Daughter
Miss Ethel May
to
Mr. De Grasse J. Culpepper
at
Rosewood Plantation
Sunday, April 16, 1940
twelve noon
P.S. THE GROOM IS FROM DETROIT

And here is a strictly business card.

PROFESSOR JAMES LEGION
Occult Mysteries - General Charmings
I Can Fix Your Man or Woman

This biologically convincing announcement heralded the formation of the Royal Funeral System of Clarksdale, Mississippi.

Born in the light of a new day, under the candelescent rays of the rising sun of knowledge, ushered on by the Century of Progress, the Royal Funeral System was born.

The fecundity of fertile brain, suffering intercourse of thought and action, impregnated the minds of two men, and with careful consideration gave birth to an organization as a result of experience of the once medieval days of oppression in the profession of proper care for the deceased loved ones of friends and families.

These are social items:

Water Valley—Mr. Jack Hall was hit by a train last Saturday near the South end trestle. Physicians say he will recover. Lucky Jack. His rabbit's foot won out.

Duncan—Rev. J. R. Keys received a spider bite which has given him much pain and no end of worry.

Merigold—Miss [sic] Essa Nichols and her sweet little daughter were charming visitors here Friday.

Boyle—Mrs. Buckingham, who is confined to city jail for shooting to death her brother-in-law two weeks ago, was visited by Mrs. O. C. Davis who journeyed here to see her godmother and to speak a word of cheer.

Renova—The "toe touching" party sponsored by the 4-H club last Wednesday night was full of fun and jollity. Games were played, toes touched, and delicious refreshments served.

And one last excerpt, this a news story:

Greenville—A great tragedy descended upon this fair city last Tuesday when Miss Etta Lou Holladay, housekeeper for Mr. Henry Partridge, was shot to death with a .45 by Mr. Partridge's one-time wife, Mrs. Mary McNab.

Some months ago, Mr. and Mrs. Partridge decided to part, and Mr. Partridge took unto himself a housekeeper, to sweep his floors and keep his premises in order. Last Tuesday night, Mrs. Partridge entered the house and shot Miss Holladay four times, Alas, she has swept her last floor and housekept her last house. Mrs. Partridge is resting in county jail.

In these quotations you may have discerned something of the saving humor of a basically humorless relationship. We laugh at their foibles, and they laugh at ours, and usually amiably. Except for the infrequent understanding of men of good will, such laughter is the only common denominator of the two dissimilar races that people the river. I wish I could say otherwise.

CHAPTER 25

Redneck on the River

LUKE WHITLEY is a new pioneer on the Lower Mississippi, and a great many of the sons of earlier pioneers don't want him here. I picked him up outside of Lake Village, Arkansas, whither he was walking from his farm.

He was dressed then, and probably is now, in overalls, an open-throated khaki shirt, a shapeless felt hat, and a pair of worn brogans. He was a lean man who didn't sweat easily, and his eyes were a dullish blue, fenced by the crow's-feet lines that identify the white man who works in the southern sun. His laugh, which was infrequent, showed several gold teeth and as many cavities.

Luke Whitley looks almost exactly like a hundred or a thousand others whom I have seen walking along southern highways, or loitering on courthouse steps on Saturday afternoons. They are men quick with a Barlow knife and a Biblical quotation, men who deified Huey Long in Louisiana, who vote consistently for Theodore Bilbo of Mississippi, and who cherish the widow lady who is Senator Hattie Caraway of Arkansas.

As a small farm owner Luke would have been a novelty thirty years ago in the river plantation counties of Arkansas and Mississippi. In those days the landowners prided themselves that their part of the country was populated only by "white folks and niggers," the niggers being niggers, and the white folks being the planter and professional gentility, and the genteel who once were landowners, and the respectful and respected tradesman fringe. Luke is none of these. He is what is known variously as a poor white, a peckerwood, and a redneck.

Of his kind, a great many unpleasant things have been said, especially by the planters of the river, and much of what they say is true. In their native habitats in the eroded, wasted lands of the South, Luke's similarly eroded kinsmen provide William Faulkner and Erskine Caldwell with characters from life, the Association for the Advancement of Colored People with lynching statistics, and the planters of the river with a feeling of impending doom.

Today, the rednecks are beginning to take over the cotton lands of the river. They have come to it for the same reasons that drew the sons of Virginia's and Kentucky's and Georgia's upper classes—its lands are richer and it offers a fresh start. But there is a great difference in the manner of their coming. In defining this difference I have no wish to belittle those early, adventurous gentry who opened up the river lands. They were usually resourceful, courageous men, and they went through hell and high water with an impenetrable assurance which is the strength of many of their descendants today. Yet most of them came with slaves and land grants or deeds, with household goods and some cash money, to settle and clear their lands. They had at least a toe hold on the wilderness. Others who did not come to the river with land waiting for them had degrees in law or medicine or engineering or the ministry, and the ramrodded conviction that they had something to live up to. And still others who came years ago to the river with peddlers' packs on their backs had their wares and the ancient knowledge that their people had survived by their wits and tenacity in a hundred nations and for two thousand years. Even the Negro, himself a pioneer though without choice, had security as a slave, and as a freeman the well-founded belief that from love, pity, self-gratification, or economic necessity the white man would after a fashion take care of him.

Not so fortified was the poor white on the Mississippi. He has come, since the turn of the century, only with empty hands, his towheaded kids, and his worn wife. First he was recruited to replace or augment the Negro share-croppers on plantations whose owners defied local prejudice against white croppers. This animosity of white planter for peckerwood is, and long has been, a very real thing. And it works both ways. The redneck is politically unmanage-able. He is frequently shiftless, uneducated, and vicious; and few stop to balance these failings against generations of malnourishment and hopelessness. The average planter mis-trusts him, and he mistrusts the average planter.

This clash between the landless and the landed white men in the South is historic. Some ascribe the difference to heredity, others to physical geography and to politics. I have also heard that the poor white is a persistent, predestined drag on civilization. I don't think so. Most of us were poor whites in the Middle Ages, in the Renaissance, and in the Merrie England that spewed its outcasts to the New World.

But it is unnecessary to go back that far to explain or to find hope for Luke Whitley's kind of people. Return only to the beginnings of the conflict between farm and plantation which is almost as old as southern agriculture itself. The planter in the virgin lands along the Mississippi defeated the small farmer just as he had done along the seaboard. This doesn't mean that the small farmer always remained a small farmer; but if he did so, he usually be-came a poor white in a few generations. In the expansionist days of cotton, the small white had three alternatives. If he could borrow or otherwise lay his hands on some money, he could turn planter himself. Many who were the brothers and cousins of the seedy ancestors of today's peckerwoods did just that, for there was no caste barrier to becoming a planter. Clerks, overseers, tradesmen became landowners if they had the price. Nor is there any barrier now. In the Yazoo-Mississippi Delta, Jews, Syrians and Italians, immigrants or the sons of immigrants, are large and prudent landholders. But almost inevitably the new planter, then and now, adopts the political-economic attitude of the older landowning aristocracy.

Yet only a minority of these earlier Southerners could thus escape the small man's dilemma. Another alternative was to sell one's land to the encroaching planter, and to settle near by on less fertile and even smaller acres. Out of this gradual agricultural degeneration emerged the poor white.

The third alternative was for the little man to sell his land and migrate to new territory. From the Piedmont spread a great migratory stock to the Midwest, where its descendants are held up today as models for its decayed collaterals of the burnt stump lands of the South.

The mistake of the small southern farmer, as he was pushed to less fertile ground, was that he refused to forsake the one-crop system for self-contained, subsistence farming. Burning with the cotton fever as hotly as the man with ten thousand acres, he tried to compete against the plantation. He couldn't win. The planter acquired the best soil, exhausted it, and moved southwestward to new land, for cotton demanded fresh earth, slave labor, and expansion. In his wake, the squatter and the poor white settled on the exhausted land, to burn it and himself further to ashy uselessness.

❦   ❦

Luke Whitley and I didn't talk about such matters on our ride to Lake Village. I have introduced them now only to explain in part the poor white class to which Luke belongs.

Or I should say, belonged. For Luke Whitley is on his way up, or believes he is; and this is the story of the past ten years of his life, as he told it to me along an Arkansas highway and later when I returned to visit his farm.

His father was first a sharecropper and then a sawmill worker in a Mississippi timber town a long way from the river. Luke was one of six children, and while the mill was running the family lived in a four-room milltown house. He left school at fourteen, with a sixth-grade education to work in the sawmill beside his father.

"It didn't last more than a year longer," says Luke. "They cut the timber out and the mill shut down. So the family moved to near Eudora, Arkansas, where my daddy went back to sharecropping."

By the time Luke was twenty-four, which was in 1934, four of his brothers and sisters had married and moved away from the three-room tenant house. That year, the elder Whitley and Luke made out pretty well. After the settlement the family had more than $400 in cash. So Luke, who had waited longer than most fellows, asked 16-year-old Nerva Hopkins to marry him. That fall, after the settlement, they were wed, and shortly thereafter moved to another cabin, to sharecrop on their own. Luke had hopes of another big year. But in 1935 they barely broke even.

In 1936 and 1937, unpredictable cotton was kind, though they had been scared to death by the threat of overflow.

"We hung on to our money," Luke told me. "Didn't buy a old car like most of them, especially the niggers. Don't have one yet. But I did have more'n two hundred dollars put by in 1937, and a fellow told me about the Farm Security Administration. So I asked 'em for a loan and got it. Five hundred dollars."

With this loan they leased a tiny farm. Its log cabin

was even less comfortable than their cropper cabin; but it was more like something of their own. In 1938 Nerva watched a baby girl crawling on the splintery floor. The family lived on slim rations, but a garden patch helped out.

For two hard, hungry years they struggled to prove to the FSA their honesty and their ability. They were playing for the biggest stakes in their lives. Never had they wanted anything so badly as one of the new FSA farms.

"We would walk up and down the road before them, imagining what it would be like to have one. We'd a done anything but steal to get one."

He did do almost everything else. During the winter he dug ditches to drain other men's fields, and worked on the levees that protected those fields and on the roads that bordered them. And God and the Security people must have both been watching him, he says, because on May 2, 1940, the government performed its miracle. On that day they moved into their trim, four-room FSA home, on a farm of their own.

The government had loaned Luke and Nerva $5,000. The government people had picked out an 80-acre plot of Arkansas Delta land and timber. On it they had built the house, a barn and a smokehouse, and a chicken house. They had put up fences, provided a mule and chickens and a cow and tools, all for that $5,000 they had loaned Luke and Nerva Whitley.

It's a sort of supervised life they lead, Luke admits. The government helps them plan their planting and their living. And the government will continue to do so until Luke and Nerva have repaid the money they borrowed. That was part of the bargain, and Luke isn't complaining. A government that gave them a start has a right to supervise them, he says. But he wants to pay out as quickly as he can; and he hopes to use something called the Variable

Payment plan which will make him complete owner in far less than the forty years he is allowed.

As a matter of fact, Luke rather likes the supervision. For one thing, it has taught him to keep a strict record of his earnings and expenditures.

"If I buy a penny of candy for the babies"—there's a little boy now, born in 1940—"it goes into our record books. I sell my own cotton and when I get my money I put it in the bank. When the season is over I go down and pay the loan on my farm and the advance they gave me to make the crop."

Luke finished his first season in good condition. He ended 1940 with his yearly payment made in full, and with cotton and corn seed aplenty for 1941. On the kitchen shelves there are more than 300 cans of vegetables which Nerva canned. They have 31 laying hens, three cows, two mules, and two baby calves. There were three hogs earlier, but they died of cholera. Luke is going to buy more when he is able. At the end of 1941 he was hoping to buy several hundred baby chicks.

And just as soon as the Rural Electrification Association or the power company extends its lines into Luke's neighborhood, he is going to wire his home. He will put in an electric pump and Nerva will have running water in the house. Now they have to carry water from their two yard wells.

Nerva likes everything. But Luke says that what pleases her most is the house itself. At last she has floors on which her babies can play without running splinters into hands and feet. And they have milk, all the milk the babies can drink, fresh from their own cows.

I sat on the steps of Luke Whitley's FSA house while he finished his story. And I liked it. I'll admit the ready charge that Luke has justified the government's faith to a greater extent than perhaps a majority of the sharecroppers to whom the government has given a new start on the river. The expense has been overly great, and many of the unqualified beneficiaries will return to tenancy.

But this much is true. Luke Whitley is no different in ancestry or in background from those who fail. Moreover, the money that is considered as wasted in the failure is but a fraction of what has been plowed beneath the earth of the South, to the endless destruction of men and soil. And Luke Whitley is escaping that.

There are too few Lukes, I know; and there are also too few places on the river for them to go. For thousands who talk and dress and look like him, there is no present hope. Perhaps some are past reclaiming: the river rats, for instance, who live in hovels and ragged tents and lean-tos of signboard tin, and in dilapidated houseboats. They send their barefoot, pregnant wives to town to beg; they poach upon the commercial fishermen's trotlines, and make vile whisky, and steal and kill and do everything but work. From the swamps of the lower coast to the Cairo river front, the Lower Mississippi has been cluttered with such human refuse since the beginning; and most of us are so accustomed to them that they live and breed, break our laws, and die unnoticed.

It is unjust to group the poor white with these who are even lower in the human scale and who superficially resemble them. It is also unjust to damn wholesale the tenant system under which most of the peckerwoods of the river and of the whole South live. Tenancy, as an agricultural expediency, can be justified. At its best, there is much to be said for it. The landowner offers a house, wood for fuel, space for truck gardens, poultry, hogs and a cow, and credit for provisions in exchange for labor. The landlord directs the cropper and sells the crop. After advances have been deducted, the profits on the season are split evenly. If the season is a failure, the planter takes the loss—and eventually, the banks may take the planter. As the spokesmen for tenancy point out, in no other enterprise is unskilled labor offered such a deal.

But the other side of the picture, the side which Luke Whitley remembers, is not so comforting. Nearly seventy per cent of all the cotton land of the South, and more than ninety per cent of the river's acreage, is worked by landless white men and black. Most of them live in wretched dwellings, in a status which nurtures neither initiative nor independence. The tenant farms a crop which must be produced by cheap labor or not at all, and which in most years offers him little more than bare subsistence. And his complete dependence upon the reckoning of the landowner is a temptation to the unscrupulous.

The situation is not blamable either upon the degradation of the river's peasantry or upon the rapacity of the river planter. Both are victims of a system they inherited, a system from which Luke Whitley is trying to escape.

You sit with Luke Whitley on the steps of a white cottage, tucked in the forefront of the eighty acres that may some day be his. The farm is doing well now. By and by the oldest child will be going to school. The school bus will pick him up and bring him home. He'll eat a hot lunch in the cafeteria, and at night he'll have decent light to read by. The public health nurse will examine the teeth that have a better chance of staying in his mouth than his father's teeth had. When Luke and Nerva finish paying for those eighty acres, there may be another eighty acres they can buy. And maybe, says Luke, the kids will go to one of those colleges some day.

Bright dreams, haltingly described; not the first that have been dreamed along the river, nor the most grandiose. But they are as ambitious to Luke Whitley, whose kind is not yet welcomed here, as were the dreams of his predecessors who counted their acres by the thousands.

"It's pretty nice," says Luke.

And all of this story is true except the names I have used.

CHAPTER 26

Will Percy

WILLIAM ALEXANDER PERCY lived in a great brown house that was never locked. Except to go to far places he seldom quit his paneled, book-littered study and his color-choked garden. He had position and breeding and fame and an assured income, and his was a tradition which some call feudal and some patriarchal, and some by less scholarly names. The Negroes of his Tralake plantation will tell you that he got and gave away a million dollars every Saturday night, a statement not precisely accurate as to figures but otherwise revealing.

In Washington County, which earlier generations of Percys led in habilitation and war and Reconstruction, Will Percy was not a leader in a popular, political sense. This is partly because he did not seek that kind of leadership, and mostly because the river people have broken away from the tradition which Will Percy and his predecessors represented. Which is presently unfortunate for Will Percy's Washington County and that part of the valley which is called the Yazoo-Mississippi Delta. Perhaps, when a sure sub-substitute has been found, it will not always be unfortunate.

Already I feel uneasy in trying to tell the story of Will Percy, who lived in his own adaptation of a disregarded tradition. For he has written his story, which is called *Lanterns on the Levee* and which has been read by his own people and many others. And if so many things are left untold in that book, what can be accomplished in a single chapter by another? But any story of the Lower Mississippi without such a chapter would be lacking; for he was a product of the river and I know of none other like him. This truth was as recognizable to his enemies as to his friends, and these are easily catalogued. He was loved by all who wanted nothing of him except his friendship, and by some who wanted whatever he would give them. He was disliked by many of those to whom he gave what they asked, and by all to whom an assured place and nonconformity within it were objectionable.

On some essentials of description most of them would agree. Will Percy was a small, fragile man, past fifty, with thick, silvery hair and a finely molded, beautiful face. One remembered that tired, sensitive face above the open, pastel-soft shirt because it reflected a composite of the trouble and happiness of all who brought their grief and joy to him. And especially did one remember the searching blue eyes; for if otherwise the face might have seemed wanting in granite, the eyes of a fighter in a poet's face disproved the lack.

A great many people can add more to this description, and each will make a different contribution. Creative folk, for instance, like Malvina Hoffman and Gerstle Mack and the dead Vachel Lindsay and so many others who were the friends of Will Percy, the humanist and lyric poet. And if you read poetry you can find more about him in the slim volumes whose songs welled from a spring that is now spent.

But perhaps you shy from poems and poets, as do most of those who live in Will Percy's town. So you might ask such a one as Gervys Lusk, the forthright, direct actionist of Greenville, who went to war as the town's buckaroo and came home a man with more solid ideas. Gervys Lusk returned with three medals, three wounds, and a captaincy, and Will Percy with a captaincy too, and decorated, and they had been together in France. They were together later, the little man and the big one who could twist him apart, in other raw, dangerous crises; and hard-fisted Gervys Lusk will tell you that he would rather have had Will Percy beside him in a tough spot than any other man he knows. And Emmet Harty, the hot-tempered Irishman turned ascetic judge, will describe out of the corner of his mouth how Will Percy kept at it in officers' training camp even though at the end of a march he had to be held up by his fellow officers-to-be. These men and others could tell later tales too, tales of the tense, threat-filled year when Will Percy and his father and their friends fought the white-sheeted hoodlums of the Ku-Klux Klan to a standstill while intolerance and hypocrisy rode violently through the Delta.

Herbert Hoover also could recall young Will Percy, member of the Belgian Relief Commission in 1916, who could look down any Prussian who tried to interfere with him. Eleven years later, in 1927, when the Mississippi submerged Greenville under eight feet of water, Will Percy directed the gallant fight which the little city made to save its thousands of refugees and to feed and clothe them. Mr. Hoover, inspecting the flood area, crossed swords with the Percys and fared no better than the Germans had.

Other facets gleam in the sunlight of inspection. The Negroes of the Delta have their own memories of Mr. Will Percy, the fabulous provider to whom they came for money and advice and sometimes for protection. He stood between black men and violent death, defended them in court against injustice. Once, in the 1927 flood, when restless, angry Negroes plotted revenge for the slaying of an unruly malingerer by a policeman, Will Percy walked alone and unarmed into a packed Negro hall where his and other lives were being threatened, and ended the impending racial clash. He was accused of being a Negrophile, but his ministry to them was in that vanishing spirit of pity and conscience and obligation which is called noblesse oblige.

There are others, as nearly underprivileged as the black man, who could also describe Will Percy—the mothers of cripples and convicts, the refuse with which even our small city abounds, men and women in need or pretended need who came to him again and again. And those with talent and little else but hope knew him as the first to spur their creative urging. In Greenville's Art Center, scores of men and women and children fashion in clay and oils because Will Percy, almost singlehanded, established it as a federal art project. Leon Koury, the young Syrian grocer whose sculpture is authentic, brought his poetry to Will Percy, decorated with marginal drawings. With both advice and tools furnished, he turned to clay instead. And a roll call that would provide a complete picture would include every social and racial and moral group in the central Delta.

Not all the stories would dovetail, for there are many who did not like the little man in the big house who was strangely fey and aloof, and raised flowers and played the piano and wrote poetry. He would stand up for a Negro against a white man, and he ran his plantation in challenging answer to dishonesty. He was not always satisfied with the Delta, but had to run off now and then to the South Seas or the Caribbean, or in happier days to Italy and the south of France, and usually alone. He made and was gulled by discreditable friends, and he embarrassed politicians and others with direct and uncomplimentary comments upon their activities. They could not classify him or touch him, and that in itself is reason for mistrust.

I am one of those whom he befriended, but I do not write of him simply because of that. He was responsible for my coming to his town, which is now my home. He wanted there a newspaper which would be a more active community force than the one which had been published for fifty years. Throughout the competitive struggle between the old-established daily and the newcomer he stood beside us with money and encouragement and advice, rallying as partisans all who were his friends. We won out. But not once in the first two years that ended in triumph or in the last three of monopoly did he seek to impose his own beliefs upon our editorial viewpoints. We differed, and on occasion each was wrong, and it caused no change. As any other in Greenville who loved him and was in trouble, I went to him in time of personal despair; and likewise I brought my little victories to share with him.

And in so doing I saw Will Percy's work at first hand. In his kitchen on a Sunday night I have eaten sandwiches with a boy just out of the state penal farm and seeking a new starting point. I have sat tensely in his study while our chief of police took up with him a dynamite-laden race morals case; and I have been joined there a half hour later by a documented stranger from the Rockefeller Foundation. The procession through the unlocked doors was unending— fresh-faced youngsters from England and the Dominions on tour, writers, tramps, men and women of worldly reputation, derelicts from the next block, all without rule of precedence, with no passkey except their own stories and with no common denominator save the man they came to see. Staying there when my own family was absent, I have nodded at breakfast to faces which weren't at the table the night before, and not even Will Percy would be sure just when or why they arrived. Sometimes the house was filled with the friends of his three adopted sons, who were the sons of another Percy, his cousin. They are grown now, and one is a surgeon, and one is married and the manager of the Percy's Tralake plantation, and one is an Annapolis graduate at sea; and they and Will Percy were together only infrequently. But always there were people in the big house, radiating from Will Percy like wheel spokes, and they were there because each found a different satisfaction in knowing him.

Now Will Percy is dead in the land which his father dominated and which his grandfather led back to political freedom. He was not happy before he died, for it was not the same privileged and quiet land of his Creole mother and his father, that earthy, brilliant man who once represented Mississippi in the Senate. Will Percy knew this. He was still the master of many acres, cultured, honorable, talented, and he was an anachronism on a river which had once been governed by his kind. From New Orleans to Memphis, on both sides of the river, lay the great plantations, and those who owned them were the law. The planters ruled, and so few of them ruled well. They were crushed by the Civil War, and they came back; but they could not maintain their political control against the upsurge of the poor whites. Some have battled the changing order, and in areas comparatively untouched by the influx of class-conscious, landless men the planter class still leads, as it led until recently in the Misissippi Delta.

It does not have control now even there, and I think this decline contributed much to the doubting which distressed Will Percy. Contemptuous of the Vardamans and Bilbos who toppled his father and the surviving statesmen-aristocrats of the Mississippi, he was as mistrustful of the lesser shadows who follow in their pattern and of the mass whose votes perpetuate them and their fantastic promises. Ever since the poor white began swarming into the Delta, Will Percy was unsure of the future. He did not want our town to grow, and it has grown in ten years from fourteen to twenty-one thousand. He wanted no new industries to attract still more strangers, and the bankers and the Chamber of Commerce worked overtime to persuade men with money to locate their plants along the river. So Will Percy was out of tune with our tuneless times. Yet I do not be-

lieve that his head-on clash with those who interpret growth
as progress deeply embittered him; nor do I believe that he
could have become bitter as long as there was one among
the newcomers or the black men or the dislocated residue
of his own kind whom he could individually aid. And at
the last his concern with his river town was overshadowed
by what was happening in the outside world which he knew
as well. Once he fought against Germany, and he never
after doubted that the fight was justifiable. Two years ago
he offered himself again, to Canada and to the United States,
but there was no place for a man with more courage and
purposefulness than vigor. The world that he loved—the
world that still had something of beauty and gentility and
kindliness and leisure—was crumbling beneath a brutal force-
fulness, and he could not tilt against it.

We talked of this frightful disorder time and again,
and of the impotence which paralyzed those who protest
it most. And once, in a troubled moment, I asked Will
Percy what he thought anyone could do in such a time.

"You can't do anything on the grand scale," he said.
"But you can work for your own people, in your own town.
It isn't national leaders we need so much as men of good
will in each of the little towns of America. Try to keep
Greenville a decent place by being a correct citizen yourself.
The total of all the Greenvilles can make the kind of country
we want or don't want."

Perhaps this is as worth while an objective as can be
devised today. It may be provincial. It may have been Will
Percy's wishful adaptation of the feudal spirit of the river
plantation, an entity no better or worse than its master.
Yet there is something comforting in this challenge to create
good cells in the disordered hive. The river country fumbles
leaderless. It has discarded an old order, but it has not
come upon a new one to guide it through the morass of
racial and economic readjustments. Few of us along the river

have any brief for those whose unawareness and ineptness and decadence hastened the discard. But we are concerned, if only selfishly, with the thoughtless substitution.

A silver-haired, gently imperious man, whose half century measured the span between the river valley's certainty and doubt, was disregarded by the deciding mass in the reshuffle. By any gauge except that of uncomprehending suspicion he was fine and brave and devoted. He loved passionately this broad flat land of cotton field and cypress brake. He was of those who first made it habitable and safe. And it is not so much his tragedy as it is the tragedy of the transition that his voice was not a commanding one.

CHAPTER 27

Out of the Current

O F ALL the people who have journeyed upon the Lower Mississippi, there are three whom I would have preferred most to accompany on their travels and to have had as living companions on our own. They are Mark Twain and James J. Audubon and old Zadok Cramer the navigator.

With Mark Twain, we would have come to know so well the people of the river. The shambling genius, Audubon, would have taught untrained eyes to discover and revel in the beauty of wild bird and beast and by means of his art and shy charm gain entrance for us through many unopened doors. And river-wise Zadok Cramer might have badgered us into charting the idiosyncrasies of the great highway itself, noting its waywardness, the peculiarities of its strength, the habits and superstitions of its challengers.

Yet none of these three saw and loved the same Mississippi. It is too long, too old, and too devious a river for any one narrator to capture; and in turn it captivates each in a different way. I have found in the Mississippi a tale of a mighty, persistent struggle of men against violent, heart-numbing opposition. In telling this story I have passed over settlements where persistence failed or violence touched but lightly. I have telescoped long years and wide areas. It leaves a sense of frustration. I can hear Sam Clemens drawling that in a tangled bend ahead we can find shanty-boat men and squatters whose yarns would be worth this whole book; and Audubon warning us to fall on our bellies to creep through a cypress brake snowy with heron; and Zadok Cramer, fussily nursing the wheel, asking us why this turn, this shallow, this river-born geographical jest had not been recorded.

To those who are not enviable shadows but present critics, I also apologize. The Lower Mississippi touches upon seven states: Illinois, at whose southern extremity it mates with the Ohio; briefly, Kentucky; Tennessee, for which it draws a short, western boundary; the southeast appendix of Missouri; still undeveloped eastern Arkansas; and encompassingly, Mississippi and Louisiana. Of them all, only Louisiana, Mississippi, and Tennessee have shared greatly in this story.

The anwer is that I have tried to steer a course in the main currents of the river's history. Arkansas and the west bank of Louisiana failed to participate in this history for a topographical reason. A glance at the map will show you that from Missouri's Cape Girardeau to the Gulf of Mexico there were no bluffs on the west bank to guarantee the early permanence of a Memphis, a Vicksburg, a Baton Rouge. The Illinois of the lower river's beginnings is notable only for Cairo, wedged between the junction point of the two great marauding streams. Memphis is Tennessee's only significant contribution to river history, as is New Madrid in the plantation appendage of Missouri. Kentucky's story is the Ohio's, even though it fringes for a short stretch upon the father of American waters.

And Arkansas. I don't know what to do about Arkansas. In the day of the Mississippi's conquest, the fertile territory was simply the wrong side of Jordan. When the pioneer reached the western bank he either kept going or took his chances with low wilderness and high water. Perhaps I shouldn't tell this libelous story. But they say that in the days of the southwestern rush a sign was posted across the river from northern Mississippi. Pointing to the southwest it read: "Texas this Way." All who could read followed the sign. The rest stayed in Arkansas.

River Arkansas has had its boosters since the earliest days. Ever hear of the Big Bear of Arkansaw? He was the first of Arkansas' unquenchable boosters. His great sales talk was reported by T. B. Thorpe of Louisiana, whose sketches of the backwoods were widely read in the 1850's.

Thorpe tells of his meeting with the Big Bear. He was taking a trip upriver from New Orleans on the "high-pressure-and-beat-everything" steamboat *Invincible*, when suddenly from the social hall, or bar, came a loud Indian whoop, followed by loud crowing. And from the bar into the cabin was thrust the head of a man who hallooed loudly: "Hurrah for the Big Bear of Arkansaw!"

Then into the cabin walked the stranger, "took a chair, put his feet on the stove, and looking back over his shoulder, passed the general and familiar salute—'Strangers, how are you?' " The stranger immediately started a conversation on hunting and announced that where he comes from only turkeys weighing forty pounds or more are shot.

"A wild turkey weighing 40 pounds!" exclaimed twenty voices in the cabin at once.

"Where did all that happen?" asked a cynical-looking Hoosier.

"Happen! happened in Arkansaw: where else could it have happened, but in the creation state, the finishing-up country—a State where the *sile* runs down to the centre of the 'arth, and government gives you a title to every inch of it? Then its airs—just breathe them, and they will make you snort like a horse. It's a state without a fault, it is."

"Excepting mosquitoes," cried the Hoosier.

"Well, stranger, except them; for it *ar* a fact that they are rather *enormous*, and do push themselves in somewhat troublesome. But, stranger, they never stick twice in the same place; and give them a fair chance for a few months, and you will get as much above noticing them as an alligator. They can't hurt my feelings, for they lay under the skin; and I never knew but one case of injury resulting from them, and that was to a Yankee: and they take worse to foreigners, anyhow, than they do to natives. . . .

"But mosquitoes is natur, and I never find fault with her. If they are large, Arkansaw is large, her varmints ar large, her trees ar large, her rivers ar large, and a small mosquitoe would be of no more use in Arkansaw than preaching in a cane-brake."

Then the Big Bear tells of the time he planted beets and potatoes and went to Kentucky for three months. While he was gone a man dropped in to look at his land with an eye to buying it. But the buyer decides not to buy, the "bottom land ain't worth the first red cent."

"Why?" said I.

" 'Cause," said he.

" 'Cause what," said I.

" 'Cause it's full of cedar stumps and Indian mounds, and *can't be cleared*."

"Lord!" said I, "them ar 'cedar stumps' is beets, and them ar 'Indian mounds' tater hills!" As I had expected, the crop was overgrown and useless: the sile is too rich, *and planting in Arkansaw is dangerous.*

"I had a good-sized sow killed in that same bottom-land. The old thief stole an ear of corn, and took it down to eat where she slept at night. Well, she left a grain or two on the ground and lay down on them: before morning the corn shot up, and the percussion killed her dead. I don't plant any more: natur intended Arkansaw for a hunting ground, and I go according to natur."

That was Arkansas.

Undeniably, Mississippi, east bank Louisiana, and the Memphis area provided the true thread of the narrative. Yet, at its end, we would like to begin a new tale. For there are challenges too in the plantation-fed towns of Arkansas—Helena, Arkansas City, Lake Village, Osceola—marketing their cotton, defying the floods, building obscurely yet surely in the third century of struggle. On the western bank in Louisiana, slumbering towns likewise stir the imagination; placid Old World French settlements like Plaquemines and Donaldsonville, each so untroubled by the present. And again on the east bank Baton Rouge, rich and raucous, where the round, squat Standard Oil tanks hem in the city from the north, and a movie-set university that once was a dictator's plaything glistens at its southern extreme; and rising from its heart a towering skyscraper of a capitol that looms in warning against politicians who would follow its boss-builder's footsteps.

And the countless people of yesterday and every day whose stories should be told. Only a little while ago, on a cold and rainy fall day, a sunburned young couple tied their canoe to the converted quarterboat which serves our town as a yacht club. Both newspaper reporters and not long married, the boy and girl had started out eight months before from the far northwest partly as a newspaper stunt and partly for adventure. The river was no place for the girl to be, in that November weather, for she was to become a mother in another two or three months. But they had started out together, had reached the source of the Mississippi together, and now so near New Orleans they wanted to finish together. Until the weather cleared, they were our delightful guests. Then, one Saturday, they paddled away. A sudden storm that afternoon overturned their canoe, and drove them drenched and shivering onto a sand bar, twenty miles or so below Greenville. They rescued their canoe and most of their belongings and spent the night on the shelterless shore, beneath their soggy pup tent. The next day they telephoned from a near-by plantation. Bob and Louise Lynd didn't want to give up, but we persuaded them that Louise should rest awhile with us. It was arranged that he would telephone when he reached Baton Rouge, and we would drive down so that she could join him for the last lap of a hundred-odd miles, to New Orleans. A week passed, and no word from Bob. So, somewhat uneasy, we drove to my father's home near Baton Rouge, where Louise was to wait until we heard of Bob's whereabouts. Several days later he turned up in Baton Rouge, with a wound in his side. A bull had gored him on the riverbank one afternoon, and he had lain wounded and alone until he could proceed. They finished the trip together.

I think the Lynds provide a present link with the olden courreur de bois, the flatboatmen, and first steamboaters who also dared the unknown. In telling their story, perhaps I make amends to the nameless legions who have traveled the perilous highway.

And to make amends likewise to the river whose story is without end or prediction of end, and to the overlooked settlements along its banks, I will tell two more tales, each of which may be considered a parable.

The first is about Reelfoot Lake in Tennessee, three miles east of the Mississippi. Now a fish and game preserve, Reelfoot Lake is a wandering body of water 18 miles long by 2½ miles wide, and only 2 to 9 feet deep. Its surrounding state-owned lands are dark with vine-matted forests of cypress, oak, and cottonwood. Green, iridescent seed moss chokes the cypress knees in the shallows and decaying snags of walnut, oak, willow, and cypress trees break its dark surface. Water lilies line its shores, ringed with the tender grasses and wild rice so esteemed by waterfowl.

The people of Reelfoot Lake catch the crappie, bass, bream, and spoonbill catfish for pleasure and profit, and net the huge alligator gar because it destroys the food fish. Sportsmen come from everywhere to cast in Reelfoot Lake, and to shoot the limit in mallard and pintail and Canadian goose. The purple gallinule and the blue heron and the wood ibis watch the intruders anxiously; and in the tangled forest the bald eagle preys on the fox, the squirrel, and the swamp rabbit. The elk, the bear, and the deer have disappeared from Reelfoot, but the preserve abounds with corn, opossum, mink, and muskrat. And underfoot, at the water's edge, glide the evil cottonmouth moccasin and the giant loggerhead terrapin.

Reelfoot Lake would not have seemed out of place in the Paleozoic age. Yet it is only 130 years old, and it owes its very being to the Mississippi. From mid-December, 1811, to the end of March, 1812, a tremendous earthquake series rocked this region. High bluffs disappeared, riverbanks were swallowed, entire islands caved out of sight into the river. Great forests crackled like splinters to the ground as the earthquake swelled across the breast of the valley. Into the cavity it created, the Mississippi, its current reversed, swept hungrily to fill the twisted fissure which is Reelfoot Lake.

The other story is of New Madrid, Missouri, an unprepossessing small town that once held as great a promise as any along the river. New Madrid is not now located on its first site, for floods and the shifting channel have forced the town to move four times. In 1783 two Canadian trappers, François and Joseph Le Sieur, located a fur trading post on the original site. It became known as L'Anse à la Graise and to the Americans as Greasy Bend or Fertile Cave.

When the Americans began straining at the river's confining limits, following the Revolution, Colonel George Morgan, a veteran of the war, suggested that Spain create a buffer colony in the region of the trading post. He would control the fifteen million acre colony. Settlers would receive liberal land grants, religious freedom, and self-government; and New Madrid, its capital-to-be, would be established as a port of entry so greatly in demand by the Westerners who otherwise had to flatboat their goods to New Orleans. Spain tentatively agreed to the proposal. Colonel Morgan laid out his town in a four-mile rectangle along the river, providing sites for schools, churches, and market places. Unusually visionary, he decreed that game must be protected and forbade the cutting down of trees along the unsettled streets or in the parks of the town.

The venture swiftly drew settlers. But Morgan's scheme ran afoul of the dreams of Spanish Governor Estevan Miro and of General James Wilkinson who, history indicates, were plotting a Mississippi Valley empire for Spain. On Wilkinson's advice, Miro halted the project. Settlers who had already taken up their grants were allowed to retain them and New Madrid persisted as a trading village. Many settlers left but others came and the New Madrid area boomed again after the Louisiana Purchase; then in December, 1811, the same earthquake movement that created Reelfoot Lake put an end to New Madrid's hope of rivaling New Orleans. For two years the earth shocks continued, making the river hazardous and turning settlers in fear from New Madrid. And, for fifty years more, development of the territory was retarded. Never again was New Madrid to dream of splendor.

Thus was a lake fashioned and a town doomed. I think the parables are obvious, for the river and nature are one, and they offer no certainty to men:

Above the sagging mantel where the patch
Of lighter brown betrays, a portrait hung.
Beneath it lay a saber. Both were his,
The last male Comtois, slain when he was young,
Deep in the Wilderness. The ragweeds snatch
At the white columns marked by flood and grime;
The windows gape, the gallery stairway is
Scratched by complacent hens, stained with their lime.

Mose Turner, Negro tenant, and his spawn
Work the thin fields in fief to state and bank.
Theirs is the broken house, the harrowed lawn;
And theirs the privilege to scrape and thank
When shouting tourists toss a dime and share
With ghosts they cannot see the humbled stair.

CHAPTER 28

River's End

O<small>N THE</small> evening of December 6, 1882, the leading citizens of New Orleans, and Captain James B. Eads, their bald, thin-bearded guest of honor, looked approvingly upon this menu in the ballroom of the St. Charles Hotel:

Little Neck Clams
Château Yquem

POTAGES
Bisque of Clam   Consommé Chatelaine
Amontillado

HORS D'OEUVRES
Radishes   Pelitier Croustades à la Pelissier   Olives

POISSON
Pompano grillé à la Royal   Fresh Codfish, Oyster Sauce
Potatoes en Surprise   Cucumbers
Liebfraumilch

RELEVÉS
Tenderloin of Beef à la Rothschild
Saddle of Lamb à la Chancelieu
Tomatoes la Reine
G. H. Mumms Extra Dry

ENTREES
Sweetbreads braised à la Moderne
Suprême of Chicken à la Toulouse
Fresh Lobster Cutlets à la Victoire
Cauliflower   New Green Peas
Veuve Clicquot Ponsardin Dry

SORBET
Au vin de Champagne

GAME
Canvasback Duck   Quail Truffle   English Snipe sur Canapé
Salade Assortée
Château Lafitte

GLACÉ
Pudding à la Coburgh   Bavarois Rubane   Gelée Danzig
Biscuit Tortoni

DESSERT
Fromages de Roquefort et Brie   Fruits de Saison
Café   Liqueurs

By this banquet the food-wise Orleanians were making amends to Captain Eads whom for two distinct reasons they had frequently anathematized in the past twenty years. The aging little engineer must have chuckled at the contrast. Less than five years earlier the Orleanians had still ridiculed his proposal to keep open the mouth of the river by means of jetties. They had accused him even of conspiracy with the railroads to defeat their own project, a ship canal from New Orleans eastward to the Gulf of Mexico, as the only means to save the city's—and the valley's—maritime commerce.

Twenty years earlier, the older men among his hosts had hated Captain Eads for another reason. At the beginning of the Civil War, Eads the engineer had built seven unbeatable ironclad gunboats for the Union. He had constructed six others, wholly of iron, in 1862 and 1863, and invented a method of steam-handling their heavy 11- and 15-inch guns. The Eads gunboats had swept the Mississippi from Cairo to Vicksburg, while Farragut closed in from the south.

But this night in the St. Charles Hotel the Orleanians had forgotten their wartime resentment and their peacetime disbelief in Eads's genius. This Indiana Hoosier's skill and persistence had assured the security of the port of New Orleans from closure of the river's mouth to seagoing vessels.

Never before had there been such assurance. At its mouth, the Mississippi had played for many years a final sardonic trick upon the human beings who tried to master it. Until it neared the gulf, the river maintained a natural depth of several hundred feet. The gulf itself, a few miles off South Pass, was 600 feet deep, and this increased to 3,000 feet twenty-five miles out. These were depths enough for any vessel, and to spare. But along the three channels into which the Mississippi divided before it reached the gulf, the river flowed sluggishly and shallowly over the ever-extending shoals built up for centuries by the silt it carried. When the sediment-laden river reached the true land's end and spread over these shoals and submerged banks, it lost its velocity. And since the amount of earth scourings it could carry in suspension depended upon the velocity of its current, it was forever dropping more sediment. Thus freed from the narrower confines of its previous channel, the river formed the treacherous sand bars that had baffled everyone before Eads.

The French had tackled the river's mouth with iron harrows which they dragged over the bars to deepen the outlet to the sea. By 1837, the United States Army engineers were unsuccessfully using bucket dredging. In 1852 a weird proposal to scrape the river's bottom so that its silt would be washed out into the gulf was entertained. Jetties also were proposed then but the idea was abandoned as unsound. Then in 1868 a steam-propelled dredge, built at a cost of $350,000, was used for three years to stir the mud to the surface so that the current would carry it away. But dredging was a losing contest.

Vexing even in the colonial days of shallow-draft sailing ships, the problem of channel maintenance had become a nightmare by the 1870's. The valley must have a year-round outlet to the sea. Yet it did not have such an outlet, and the increases in the size and drafts of oceangoing vessels made the crossing of the bars progressively more hazardous. Between 1872 and 1877, 417 vessels grounded and were held up for a total of 12,467 hours, with tremendous losses of cargo.

During these latter years the government made its most strenuous efforts to keep the channel open. It had made no progress in 1873 when Captain James B. Eads, already famed as a construction engineer, declared for a system of parallel jetties.

The army engineers scoffed. Their solution was the construction of a ship canal from New Orleans to the gulf, and in this they were enthusiastically seconded by the Orleanians. Jetties would be undermined at their sea ends, the engineers said; their foundations would be too unstable, their presence would greatly accelerate the advance of the bar. The Orleanians said even more. Hysterically, the city's newspapers hinted that Eads was conspiring with the railroads to destroy forever the city's water-borne commerce.

Almost alone James Eads persisted. He had one great ally, his reputation, and like himself it was unshakable. The self-educated farm boy had made his elders blink in 1842 when as a 22-year-old embryonic engineer he had constructed a foolproof diving bell for recovering cargoes from sunken steamers. In 1845 he had built the first glassworks west of the Mississippi. During the war he had designed and constructed the unbeatable ironclads. And afterward, at St. Louis, he had built the first bridge across the Mississippi, a marvel for visitors from all over the world.

He had been doubted in all these undertakings. So not even the army engineers and an equally skeptical Congress could brush him aside in 1873 when he advocated jetties. To back up his conviction, Eads offered to open the mouth of the river by making a jetty-guaranteed channel 28 feet deep between Southwest Pass and the gulf at his own risk. If he succeeded, his fee would be ten million dollars. He proposed that he would get no money until a 20-foot channel had been secured. At 28 feet he would receive a million dollars for the first 20 feet and a million for each additional two feet up to 28. The last five million would be paid in installments, contingent upon the permanence of the channel.

Despite this offer, the national House of Representatives passed an eight million dollar ship canal bill. But the Senate decided to investigate Europe's jetties. As a result of this investigation, the army engineers reluctantly reported in January, 1875, that jetties would work. They recommended South Pass for the experiment, instead of Southwest Pass where Eads wanted to build his jetties.

On June 12, 1875, a steam tug set out for South Pass. It towed a floating steam pile driver and three flatboats, one to board the workmen and the other two loaded with materials to build quarters and warehouses. Soon afterward a steamboat arrived from St. Louis towing a barge loaded with coal and machinery. Below the Head of Passes, where the river separated into its three channels, construction was begun.

Eads was handicapped by official hostility and high interest rates; his men by yellow fever, which took many lives in 1878. The final financial agreement was harsh. A half million dollars was to be paid after the jetties and auxiliary works had scoured the channel to a width of 200 feet and a depth of 20. At 22 feet, another half million would be paid, and so on to 28 feet. Eads agreed to extend and maintain the jetties in case the bar re-formed ahead of them, pledging $90,000 a year for ten years. As guarantee of a 30-foot channel, he allowed the government to retain a million dollars. Thus, he staked not only his reputation but his fortune on the efficacy of willow mattresses, piling, and stone, sunk in perpendicular walls to make a permanent bank.

And Eads won. On July 8, 1879, the army engineers

reported that a 30-foot channel existed at the mouth of the Mississippi. Three and a half years later, when the citizens of New Orleans tendered their dinner to Captain Eads, the jetties still maintained the 30-foot minimum. They do today.

🎖 🎖

With as much justification, another group of Louisianians might have given a jubilee dinner for Captain Eads. They were the bar pilots, the continuance of whose arduous calling the success of the jetties had assured. And if the bar pilots dined as well in 1882 as they do now in their houses on stilts at land's end, Captain Eads would have left their table as fully fed if not as fancifully.

Perhaps someday you may be the guests of the bar pilots, as we have been. Don't refuse an invitation. We owe ours to Captain R. J. McBride, the father of a boyhood friend and superintendent of the tightly knit, co-operative organization known as the Crescent City Bar Pilots' Association. Its members have only one thing in common with the roistering, swashbuckling rivermen who guided the old sailing ships across the bar a hundred years ago. That common denominator is uncanny skill in navigation.

If you have our luck, Captain McBride will ask you to meet him on the New Orleans river front to make the entire trip downriver on the pilots' pride, the *Jennie Wilson*. If it is your first visit to the water front, it will be worth your while to arrive early. For here, the second port of the United States girds the Mississippi's east bank in a great crescent. Across its docks, and into the holds of indomitable freighters, pass cotton and grain from an inexhaustible valley, and armaments for the beleaguered enemies of Nazism. Here, until the outbreak of war, entered lumber fom Scandinavia, spices from Java, the industrial products of England and Europe. Here still arrive Brazil's coffee, bauxite from the

West Indies, bananas from Central America, cargoes from a hundred ports of which Bienville never dreamed. Here youngsters from your own town may be filing up the gang-planks of army transports, bound for the fighting fronts of the world.

And while you wait for Captain McBride, look back at this sprawling metropolis. Above this river and its lower valley, many flags have flown. De Soto brought the castles and rampant lions of Leon and Castile; and above La Salle and the brothers Le Moyne floated the golden lilies of France. Here O'Reilly raised the standard of Bourbon Spain above that of Bourbon France; and the encompassing banner of Great Britain waved over West Florida, and once, briefly, before the eyes of Jackson's riflemen. For twenty days the tricolor of Napoleon's crashing empire fluttered above the wreckage of Louisiana Frenchmen's hopes, to be replaced on December 20, 1803, with the 15-striped flag of the infant United States. The brief glory of the West Florida Republic fluttered in the Lone Star emblem. For a few days in 1861 Louisiana's state banner, a single star and thirteen stripes, waved before it gladly made way for the Stars and Bars of the Confederacy. And only since 1862, when Farragut's landing party hauled up the banner of the Union, has there been no challenge.

Captain and Mrs. McBride and one of their sons are making this trip, as are half a dozen other pilots and mem-bers of their families. When you meet these bronzed, assured Americans and their children, to whom the journey is a familiar pleasure jaunt, you will realize how great is the change of a hundred years in the river and its people. Here are youngsters with college degrees or the intention to acquire them, mothers who talk of garden clubs and bridge, pilots whose homes in New Orleans and upcountry are those of men of substance and achievement. And little more than a hundred years ago their predecessors were a wild, carousing lot, whose now abandoned base of operations, the Balize, was a swampy den of piratical lechers.

We look riverward, for the *Jennie Wilson* is headed for the dock. Our own voyage is an especially eventful one, for it is the *Jennie Wilson's* first journey downriver since she was remodeled. For sixty-four years she has been meeting the vessels of all nations; yet until this overhauling she carried her original engine. Now, Diesel powered, her lines trimly altered, and her hull, her deck and superstructure freshly painted, the *Jennie Wilson* is a beautiful craft.

We go aboard, and inspect the new innards, under the proud eye of Captain McBride who had drawn the new design. Soon she is underway, giving three answering toots to the applauding blasts with which a score of familiar ships hail her maiden reconditioned voyage.

The river front is crowded. An English ship is listing at her moorings, and French and Italian freighters, soon to be seized, rest idly in mid-river. Catfish fishermen and scavengers paddle downstream, incurious of the great ships above them, and on the banks below the city the willows and live oaks and cypresses stand seemingly as thickly as in the days of the first white men.

As the *Jennie Wilson* puts mile after mile behind us, an oddly contrasting panorama unfolds. For here, on the last surge of the Mississippi to the gulf, have been discovered the treasures which Law's settlers sought so vainly. At Port Sulphur, the earth's largest sulphur mine and shipping point, the yellow, noisome mineral is pumped in liquid form from a dome a thousand feet below, and loaded onto reeking freighters. Under the shallow floor of the gulf, just out of sight, lie vast oil deposits for which man is hungrily reaching. From these swamps behind the river come much of the pelts which make Louisiana's fur production greater than

that of all the rest of the nation's, greater even than Alaska's
and Canada's. The trappers take more than two and a half
million skins annually, principally from muskrat; but the
mink, the raccoon, the otter, and the skunk also contribute
to what is a $5,000,000 annual business for the marsh
trappers.

Diverse are the gifts of the river as it nears its journey's
end. On these banks and along the bordering gulf and its
tidal bays, Manilamen, Chinese, Malays, and Yugoslav fishermen trawl for the gray, delectable shrimp; the oyster luggers
chug to the unfailing beds; and along this last wild stretch
of the Mississippi, farmers of French and German and Italian
ancestry harvest the Louisiana orange, and press out its juice
for a sweet and heady wine.

❧ ❧

It is more than a hundred miles from New Orleans to
the pilot station at South Pass, where we are visiting Captain
McBride. But we stop only once, at Pilottown, where the
river separates into its two navigable passes to the gulf and a
third which no longer is open to seagoing vessels. Pilottown
is a tiny village, existing almost entirely for the pilots. At the
stanchly timbered station house, the pilots rest between trips,
awaiting their next turns in the shuttle system under which
they work. The next ship may be a freighter southbound
from New Orleans to a Texas port. A river pilot takes her
downstream as far as Pilottown. Here the bar pilot whose
shingle hangs at the top of a board in the station hall goes
aboard and takes her down Southwest Pass and into the gulf.
He transfers offshore to one of the pilots' tugs and returns
to the little station at the mouth of the pass. He hangs his
shingle at the bottom of the board there, and remains at this
station until his shingle has moved to the top. Then it is his
turn to take the next ship upriver.

Most of us aboard the *Jennie Wilson* are bound for South Pass. Below Pilottown a mist blots out the thin land line between sky and river, merging the low willows of the horizon with the dark river and the gray sky. It was here that Captain Eads began building the jetties, now strengthened and extended on this pass, and duplicated in Southwest Pass. It is difficult now, as the *Jennie Wilson* comes to a stop, to discern the low rim of land on each side of us, or the river beneath us or the marshes beyond. So we are not aware that we have reached land's end. An hour later, with the renewed sun, we know.

❦   ❦

There are no orange groves or oil derricks or sulphur mines at South Pass station, where the *Jennie Wilson* ends her 117-mile journey from New Orleans. The two-story pilot station and the handful of cottages belonging to the pilots are perched on pilings sunk deep in the narrow, uncertain spit of land behind the western jetty, and are connected by raised plank walks. Just below, the Mississippi streaks like a dark avenue into the blue gulf. Above us lurch the ugly, lumbering pelicans and wheeling gulls, and in the reedy marshes behind the cottages white herons rise. Out in the gulf the whistling of the buoy mocks the shrill cries of the scavenging sea birds.

Here at the river's mouth lurk unfriendly neighbors. Distant alligators slither through the mud and rozo grass, and under the runways on which we idle water moccasins are gliding. Huge mottled spiders scurry across the oyster-shell fillings on the bank. When the wind comes east from Texas, swarms of mosquitoes besiege the well-screened cottages. The stingaree and the devilfish and the gar plague these warm waters whose surface is so placidly broken now by fat, untroubled porpoises.

Yet domestic ducks paddle beneath the boardwalk, and a sleek tabby cat is nursing three puppies whose mother was killed by a moccasin. And at this outpost of a continent the bar pilots have made a habitation so pleasant that their families and their friends come here gladly for weekends.

There is much we can do besides laze in the gulf sunshine and listen to the pilots tell of the seven seas. If we like to fish, the tarpon is shining silver in the sun and the redfish and the sunfish are ready for our bait; or, more indolently, we can net crabs and seine for shrimp. And if we want to exercise our legs and our lungs, we might accompany one of the youngsters who are trudging out to inspect the muskrat traps they have set in the marshes. In the little recreation cottage we can join the pilots and their friends as they play pool, and listen to the radio, and read or talk.

And perhaps most of all we enjoy the food that is routine to the pilots: seafood gumbos, broiled and fried fish of many kinds, chicken and steak, highly seasoned salad, vegetables, pickles, ice cream, and strong coffee. Each meal is a feast, and one so varied that we regret the limitations which make us stop our gorging.

But for the visitor who has caught the spirit of these people of the river's mouth, the most enjoyable of pastimes is meeting the ships which the pilots will take up the pass to Pilottown.

Out in the gulf, beyond the bar, a freighter signals for a pilot. Everyone piles aboard the *Jennie Wilson*. In ten or fifteen minutes we have reached the incoming ship. An apprentice pilot lowers a tiny dinghy, and rows the pilot to the ship's side, the dinghy bobbing alongside as the pilot climbs up the ship's ladder. Back to the *Jennie Wilson* rows the apprentice in his cockleshell, and back we race to the station with the freighter or liner behind us.

The pilots are ritualistic in this business of going aboard. Between ships, they lounge about in pajamas and an old straw hat. But when they climb the ladder they are dressed neatly in a dark business suit, felt or crisp straw hat, and white shirt and necktie; and this is a carry-over from earlier times when the bar pilots, emerging from their rollicking period, dressed decorously in frock coats before boarding the ships.

To the spectator, it seems so easy to bring the boats across the bar. They enter the pass almost noiselessly, and thrust upstream so close to us ashore that we could almost throw a rope aboard; for here the jetties are much closer together than are the natural banks of the river farther upstream. The pilots tell us, diffidently, that they can navigate blindfolded, guided only by the sound of the buoy outside the bar, and by timing the echo of a ship's bell against the riverbanks. And this uncanny ability is needed on the foggy days and black, tempestuous nights when the gulf is whipped into ecstatic frenzy and the bars and shallows reach for the unwary hull.

But they will talk very little about such times, and less on another topic, the only subject about which they are sensitive. These capable, solid men do not like to be linked with their harum-scarum predecessors. Nor do they have any kinship with the pilots of two centuries and even a century ago except this common profession and a common knowledge of the bar and the passes.

But the contrast between the bar pilots of today and the freebooters of the old Balize provides a story of which they should be proud; for it is the story of determined and successful effort to bring dignity and worth to a calling which was not always honored on the Lower Mississippi.

To learn that story we must go back more than two hundred years ago when the French built the Balize—which is an ancient Gallic word for beacon.

The Balize was located on a little island which was then

at the river's mouth, eighteen miles below present Pilottown, and some ten miles northeast of Port Eads. Now the submerged relics of the Balize lie six miles above Southeast Pass. The river has extended its banks that far since the days of the Frenchman's beacon.

The earth of the Balize was a long, narrow, and marshy strip, deposited centuries ago; and now it is useless to pilots, and the site of the Balize is only a part of the great Pass à l'Outre hunting grounds of Louisiana.

The Balize was the first fort at the river's mouth. So low was the land on which it was situated that it could be located from the gulf only by the new rough buildings and the flagstaff which were landmarks to the incoming sailing ships. Here the pilots awaited the cargo vessels and troopships of France to steer them on the tortuous trip upriver to New Orleans, a voyage which required three to four days in favorable weather, and at other times from two to three weeks.

After Spain acquired Louisiana, exclusive piloting rights were given to one Jean Ronquillo, who maintained a force of twenty pilots at the entry point. Ronquillo had not altogether a happy time there. In 1795 a French privateer, *La Parisienne*, mounting six guns, took possession of the post and held it for eight days. Then hearing that the Spaniards were descending the river, the privateersmen retired after destroying everything they couldn't take away.

The pilot system—if it could be called such—at first degenerated after the American occupation. Under Spain, Ronquillo had been the sole branch pilot. He was replaced by two Americans, named Johnson and Bradish, who farmed out the actual jobs of piloting to "deputies," who were sailors picked up at the lowest possible cost. In 1805, however, the governor of Louisiana was empowered to appoint "two or more branch pilots," a maneuver which ended the monopoly of Messrs. Johnson and Bradish, but which did not improve the quality of the pilots.

For the next twenty years the pilot service was negligently performed, and the pilots were principally a reckless and desperate gang of seafarers. The Balize took on the aspect of a bordello, with drunken debauches, brawlings, and slayings as commonplace occurrences. Upon the swampy prairie, most of it covered at the gulf's high tide, ramshackle bars and stews on stilts gave riotous welcome to seamen, oyster pirates, and ship deserters and their women.

In 1837 the governor of Louisiana was authorized to appoint not more than fifty branch pilots, who must be citizens of the United States with two years' residence in Louisiana. Each pilot had to post a $1,000 bond. The system of employing deputy pilots was outlawed, and pilotage prices were fixed.

The results were near-miraculous. The pilots selected were principally men of substance. They built a public school at the Balize for their children, installed a reading room, and employed policemen to keep the little settlement in order. In spare time they joined their wives in beautifying the bleak island, constructing an embankment for horticulture and planting trees and shrubs. They kept a pilot boat at Southwest Pass, which cruised southward and eastward, and four others at Northeast Pass. The boats had to remain at sea until all ships approaching the river had been boarded.

By 1847, the population of the Balize was almost 350, with 70 more at Southwest Pass. Sober New England skippers and mates left their clippers to become pilots and to build homes at the once cheerless and desolate mouth of the river. Then, in 1860, a crevasse silted up Bayou Balize. The old channel became unnavigable. So the settlement, then a thriving community of perhaps a thousand people, was abandoned.

But the mission of the newer pilots had been fulfilled. The Pilots' Association, forerunner of today's Crescent City

Pilots' Association, made piloting an honorable and trust-worthy profession. And at the site of the Balize, a crumbling iron tomb hidden in the rozo cane reminds the explorer of the gentleness of the newer Balize of the 1850's. The inscription reads:

Joseph

Son of Captain Joseph and Jemima Preble

Died Sept. 2, 1852

Aged 8 Months and 25 Days

Death should come gently

To one of gentle mould like thee,

As light winds wandering through groves of bloom

Detach the delicate blossoms from the tree.

Death came less gently in the earlier days of the Balize, which now also is dead. And gone too are the swarthy knife fighters of a hundred ports and the rigid men of Marblehead. But the river whose waywardness remained to be tamed at its ship-trap mouth by Captain Eads still draws the sea-borne commerce of the world.

CHAPTER 29

Return Trail

THIS IS the backtracking of the trail that led to an American challenge: De Soto's trail westward, on which Americans return because of a challenge to America. Along that trail through the sandy lowlands of Florida's training camps slog men from the Lower Mississippi, shouldering rifles, fumbling with unaccustomed fingers the tools of war.

Under their feet the long peninsula along which De Soto's men stumbled for gold points as a finger points, toward the sea lanes of the Caribbean, and the Hispanic-American lands. It is a warning finger, not leveled at the countries once pillaged and infused by Spain, but at those who might launch galleons by ocean or sky against the Americas. And to give authority to that warning the river's men came to Florida, intently swarming, so that the long promise may not again be successfully threatened. They came as soldiers from the sensuous city which was once the pestilent isle of Orleans, from Vicksburg and Natchez and Baton Rouge, and a score of lesser towns of the valley.

There are names to snare the imagination among these boys of the river valley, and faces to bring the past to life. With O'Reilly to New Orleans sailed the Diaz and Mendozas and Garcias, and on the rolls of the Louisiana companies are Diaz and Mendozas and Garcias again. The Creoles who joined Jackson are dead, but the lean, dark Landrys and Perraults wear today the olive drab and the work denim. The Highlanders who hewed the cypress below Baton Rouge

433

have left their red hair and their clan names among the
McNabs and Campbells; and the restless men who struck out
by land and river from Kentucky and Virginia to the Yazoo-
Mississippi Delta would find their children's grandchildren
here.

Chapter by chapter this story of the Lower Mississippi
could be told again in their genealogy, for the most part
forgotten by those who are the present proof. And the forgetting of the episodic descent is as well. For this valley which
was the first racial crucible of the Americas has this
important distinction from the later. The lines of Spain and
England and France and Germany go back so far into the
American past as to be disregarded save for unembittered
pride. There is no rankling link with an older, forlorn world
whose hatreds roll against, and in places inside, the American
barrier. To put abused words to better use, the foreigners
were here before the Americans. The alien men of Europe
became American long ago in the conquest of a wilderness,
and in common cause against the river which was the enemy-
friend. And these boys in a Florida army camp are of their
sinews. Whether they think of it or not, the spirit of combat
survives in them strongly, for it has been inescapable as far
back as their first deep-rooting in the valley's soil. The prospect of conflict and the preparation for it are accepted without introspection or debate. The river towns called few men
to fill by mandatory service their established quotas, for the
men did not wait. And only a few here think of this with
prideful marveling.

I have been one of these so self-consciously proud
through a rainy winter in the scrub pines and palmettos and
moss-dripping oaks of our encampment; and the contemplation of what I believe to be true has provided an obvious, if
unended, conclusion to this story of a river valley's challenge.

The ending is like the beginning, a defiance of man and
nature's violence. Only they don't put it that way here. They

laugh on a cheerless Christmas, with the rain sifting through the tents' eyelets, and the soggy sand outside a deceptive bog. The boys from the Mississippi make loud and uncomplimentary remarks about the liquid sunshine of Florida, and bend to the spades that dig the rain-water channels along the company streets. And when the rains cease, they become even more boisterously critical of everything that is not like the river. They brag of the Mississippi's mud, and the Mississippi's girls, and mock the Florida flounder with reminiscence of the river's golden fried catfish. In the tents of the New Orleans troops and those from the older settlements of Bienville's Biloxi and Mobile, swarthy, small fishermen sing French obscenities that have been chanted on the gulf and at the river's mouth for two hundred years. I have listened night after night with others who understand them better and some who understand them not at all; and outside, in the star-sprinkled night, it is difficult to realize that anything has changed.

And sometimes I have talked with the men, sweating after the hardening-up marches, and the lake-shore artillery practices, and the jabbing and cover-taking of the infantrymen. Conversation comes easily until we get around to why we are here. Then it is difficult, for this isn't a generation of phrase makers or phrase users. But inevitably the answer, spiced profusely with goddamns, is directed at the men who lead beneath the swastika, together with a blasphemous hope that they get a crack at the bastards. I am sure that they mean this. For what they are saying is simply what their fathers have said whenever in the past two hundred years their homes and their holdings and their preferential ways have been menaced. The rivermen of many bloods have been alike in this, as the empires of France and Spain and Great Britain and the union of the United States record. And nothing I have seen or heard in the months of preparation has made me fear that the old reaction is slower or confused by doubting.

There are malingerers and homesick boys, and men who will prove to be cowards, but in no greater proportion than before. They do not count against the whole.

Should the story of the brawling, buffeted people of the Lower Mississippi end here, in a Florida encampment, and in this manner? I think so. For we are gripped now by other brawlings. The blows which until now have hindered our upsurge may seem puny in the historical perspective of another hundred years, or even of a decade. The river valleys of America are not so far today from the empire makers with an old formula and a new concept of gold; and this is a challenge to all who believe their valleys are the greenest and the dearest.

So we are here, Cajun and Mississippi redneck, sons of planters and sharecroppers and shopkeepers, the landless and the landed; and in our heavy shoes grinds the white sand which once clung to the jackboots of Cordova. Sightseeing along hard-surfaced miles by weekend, we look wonderingly into the bright, transparent lakes where the stubborn Ocala swam to escape the lances of De Soto's mailed horsemen. And through the weeks we explore the complexities of today's mechanized soldiering so that the people of our river will never have to pit naked bodies against a conqueror's army.

And thus living, it is difficult to contemplate that future which lies beyond the pressing immediacies. Yet some of us still have dreams for our river, and for an Eden's promise fulfilled through the free cooperation of free men. This day will come to a valley whose earth can feed and clothe a nation, but does not yet satisfy the hungry and the shelterless and the unclothed who are cast up along its thousand river miles. The sureness of this directed change has kinship with the sureness of the men in keelboats and adventuring caravans who looked upon a river's wilderness and saw the tilled field and the laden ship and the ordered street. And this certainty is only an extension into the future of the provable, upward-moving past.

From that past threads an indestructible procession: tough, leather-shirted Canadians, aloof Spaniards, wayward Gauls; earth-fondling Germans of the Palatinate and uprooted peasants of Acadia, solid, free Englishmen and the roistering red-shirted boatmen of the river. The oxcarts and the deadly, questing horsemen of Virginia and Kentucky wind with them, and sweating black bodies break the trail ahead. And in their ears and ours throbs the 300-year diapason of the river: death wail of the Natchez and the shrieking of scalped children, the sullen bellow of a breaking levee and the high lilt of Forrest's bugles. Listen, and you will hear the warning of mute voices to drag out the yellow fever dead, the crackling of muskets on the hills of Vicksburg, and the thoughtless tinkle of a girl's voice in a high-ceilinged white room.

And other notes, cacophonous now, will blend with the symphony of the river. I can hear them in the coughing of artillery trucks, scrubbed clean of the mud of the Mississippi, and in the banter of the lads of the valley, playing poker in their tents at night. If these sounds are a part of a tragic cycle of conflict we are not disturbed by it here; for conflict has since the beginning been inextricably a part of the Lower Mississippi's progress. I believe only that Eden is still attainable, though not easily; that the Mississippi, great sewer, father of waters, master and slave of its self-created earth, is destined to become the true artery of a nation's impregnable heart.

Acknowledgments

I T IS no more possible to encase the history and spirit of the Lower Mississippi between the covers of a single book than to restrict its flow always with the high slopes of its levees. Nor can one learn even the partial story upon its banks alone. I have heard new tales about the Mississippi in places and from persons far removed from the river.

This is as much of the story as there is space to tell it in. Many people and many records have helped me to put it down. In so doing, I have discovered regretfully that a paragraph should become a chapter, a chapter a book, and a book only one of the many that remain to be written about the Lower Mississippi and its people.

I particularly want to thank two persons: my wife, Betty Carter, who persuaded the editors and myself that I could write this book, and who worked with me throughout its preparation; and Dr. William Ransom Hogan, associate archivist of the State Department of Archives, Louisiana State University, to whom I am indebted for suggestions and sources that led to a number of chapters.

The extensive use made of certain special studies demands confession beyond mere bibliographical listing. Among these are the essay on Bennet H. Barrow by Dr. Edwin Adams Davis, archivist of the State Department of Archives, Louisiana State University; the monographs on the Kemper brothers and the West Florida rebellion, by Stanley Clisby Arthur, director of the Louisiana State Museum; the articles on Natchez houses, by Mrs. Edith Wyatt Moore; and the book on Memphis by Professor Gerald M. Capers, Jr.

I also acknowledge especially and with gratitude the direct or indirect assistance of the following:

Robert J. Usher, librarian of Howard-Tilton Memorial Library, and Mrs. Philip Werlein, both of New Orleans.

Two other members of the staff of the State Department of Archives, Louisiana State University: Beatrice Carlton, registrar of manuscripts, and Sue Lyles Eakin, research assistant; and Hart Bynum, of Baton Rouge.

Mrs. Mary Berkeley Finke, of New York City, and David Brush, of Greenwich, Connecticut.

Dean Paul Buck, of Harvard University.

The late William A. Percy, Howard Hyde, Mrs. Stephenson Finlay, J. Seguine Allen, John Boatner Carter, and the Reverend H. H. Humes, editor of the *Delta Leader* (Negro), Greenville, Mississippi.

Mayor Benjamin Green of Mound Bayou, Mississippi.

Captain R. J. McBride of Hammond, Louisiana.

Mrs. Shirley A. Boatner of Natchez, Mississippi.

Jennie B. Gardner and Robert Snowden of Memphis.

Dewey A. Somdal of Shreveport, Louisiana.

John and Catherine Marshall and Elizabeth Knower of Jacksonville, Florida.

THE OLD CABIN HOME

(From "Songs of the Rivers of America" edited by Carl Carmer with music arranged by Dr. Albert Sirmay)

Selected Bibliography

This is a list of the books, pamphlets, manuscripts, periodicals, theses, and newspapers, which were found to be most useful and interesting as source material for the story of the Lower Mississippi.

Books and Pamphlets

AIME, VALCOUR, *Plantation Diary.* New Orleans, 1878.

ANTHONY, IRVIN, *Paddle Wheels and Pistols.* Philadelphia, 1929.

ARTHUR, STANLEY CLISBY, *Old New Orleans.* New Orleans, 1936.

——— *The Story of the Kemper Brothers.* St. Francisville, La., 1934.

——— *The Story of the West Florida Rebellion.* St. Francisville, La., 1935.

ASBURY, HERBERT, *The French Quarter.* New York, 1938.

ASHE, THOMAS, *Travels in America.* London, 1809.

BAIRD, ROBERT (RICHARD BACHE), *View of the Valley of the Mississippi.* Philadelphia, 1834.

BALDWIN, J. G., *The Flush Times of Alabama and Mississippi.* San Francisco, 1899.

BAMORIS, AMANDA, *The Female Land Pirate.* Cincinnati, 1847.

BARTRAM, WILLIAM, *Travels Through North and South Carolina, Georgia, East and West Florida, the Cherokee Country, the Extensive Territories of the Creek Confederacy, and the Country of the Choctaws.* Philadelphia, 1791.

BASSO, HAMILTON, *Beauregard, the Great Creole.* New York, 1933.

Biographical and Historical Memories of Louisiana. Chicago, 1892.

BOWERS, CLAUDE G., *The Tragic Era.* New York, 1929.

BRACKENRIDGE, H. M., *Views of Louisiana.* Pittsburgh, 1814.

BUNNER, E., *History of Louisiana from its First Discovery to the Present Time.* New York, 1842.

BURKE, EDMUND, *An Account of the European Settlements in America.* London, 1765.

CAPERS, GERALD M., JR., *The Biography of a River Town: Memphis.* Chapel Hill, N. C., 1939.

CARRADINE, REV. B., *The Louisiana State Lottery Company Examined and Exposed*. New Orleans, 1890.

CAUGHEY, JOHN WALTON, *Bernardo de Galvez in Louisiana, 1776-1783*. Berkeley, Calif., 1934.

CHAMBERS, HENRY E., *A History of Louisiana*. Chicago, 1925.
——— *Mississippi Valley Beginnings*. New York, 1922.

CHAMPIGNY, JEAN, *État-présent de la Louisiane*. La Haye, 1776.

CHARLEVOIX, FATHER FRANÇOIS X. DE, *Letters to the Duchess of Lesdiguiere*, London, 1763.
——— *Journal of a Voyage to North America*. London, 1761.

CHITTENDEN, HIRAM M., *History of Early Steamboat Navigation on the Missouri River*. New York, 1903.

CLAIBORNE, J. F. H., *Mississippi as a Province, Territory and State*. Jackson, Miss., 1880.

CLAPP, THEODORE, *Autobiographical Sketches and Recollections*. Boston, 1857.

COATES, ROBERT M., *The Outlaw Years*. New York, 1930.

COHN, DAVID L., *God Shakes Creation*. New York, 1935.

COLLOT, VICTOR (Introduction and translation by J. Christian Bay), *A Journey in North America*. Firenze, 1924.

CONRAD, PAUL (ed.), *Tips*. New Orleans, 1891.

CORNING, HOWARD (ed.), *Journal of John James Audubon*. Boston, 1929.

Cornucopia of Old—the Lottery Wheel of the New—The Generous and Tender Hand-Maiden of All the Virtues, By A Louisianian, The. New Orleans, 1877.

COX, ISAAC JOSLIN (ed.), *The Journeys of La Salle*. New York, 1905.

CRAMER, ZADOK, *The Navigator*. Pittsburgh, 1806.

CUMMINGS, SAMUEL, *The Western Pilot*. Cincinnati, 1848.

DAWSON, SARAH MORGAN, *A Confederate Girl's Diary*, Boston, 1913.

DAYTON, FRED E., *Steamboat Days*. New York, 1939.

Dictionary of American Biography (20 vols. and index). New York, 1928-1937.

DIXON, FRANK HAIGH, *A Traffic History of the Mississippi River*. Washington, 1909.

DORSEY, FLORENCE L., *Master of the Mississippi; Henry Shreve and the Conquest of the Mississippi*. Boston, 1941.

DROMGOOLE, J. P., *Yellow Fever Heroes, Heroines and Horrors of 1878*. Louisville, 1879.

DU BOIS, WILLIAM E. B., *Black Reconstruction*. New York, 1933.

DUNBAR, SEYMOUR, *A History of Travel in America*. Indianapolis, 1915.

DUTRÔNE, JACQUES-FRANÇOIS, *Histoire de la Canne et Précis sur les Moyens de la Cultiver et d'en Estraire le Sucre*. Paris, 1801.

ELLICOTT, ANDREW, *The Journal of Andrew Ellicott*. Philadelphia, 1803.

ESKEW, GARNETT L., *The Pageant of the Packets*. New York, 1929.

Famous American Race Horses. Philadelphia, 1877.

Federal Writers Project, *Mississippi, A Guide to the Magnolia State*. New York, 1938.

—— *Missouri, A Guide to the "Show Me" State*. New York, 1941.

—— *New Orleans City Guide*. Boston, 1938.

—— *Tennessee, A Guide to the State*. New York, 1939.

FERTIG, JAMES W., *The Secession and Reconstruction of Tennessee*. Chicago, 1898.

Final Report of the U. S. De Soto Expedition Commission. Seventy-sixth Congress, First Session, House of Representatives, House Document No. 711. Washington, 1939.

FORTIER, ALCÉE, *Louisiana Studies*. New Orleans, 1894.

FRENCH, B. F., *Historical Memoirs of Louisiana From the First Settlement of the Colony to the Departure of Governor O'Reilly in 1770*. New York, 1853.

GARNER, JAMES W., *Reconstruction in Mississippi*. New York, 1901.

GAYARRÉ, CHARLES, *History of Louisiana*. New Orleans, 1885.

GOULD, EMERSON W., *Fifty Years on the Mississippi*. St. Louis, 1889.

GREEN, FRANCIS VINTON, *Campaigns of the Civil War* (Vol. 8, *The Mississippi*). New York, 1882.

Guide Book to the City of New Orleans. New Orleans, 1895.

HAKLUYT, RICHARD, *Divers Voyages Touching the Discovery of America and the Islands Adjacent*. London, 1850.

HALL, JAMES, *Notes on the Western States*. Philadelphia, 1838.

HERBERT, HENRY WILLIAM, *Frank Forester's Horse and Horsemanship of the U.S. and British Provinces of North America* (Vol. 1). New York, 1857.

Historical Sketch Book and Guide to New Orleans and Environs. New York, 1885.

HORN, STANLEY F., *Invisible Empire*. Boston, 1939.

HOWARD, H. R. (comp.), *The History of Virgil A. Stewart.* New York, 1939.

HULBERT, ARCHER B., *The Paths of Inland Commerce.* New Haven, 1920.

HUTCHINS, THOMAS, *An Historical Narrative and Topographical Description of Louisiana and West-Florida.* Philadelphia, 1784.

IMLAY, GILBERT, *A Topographical Description of the Western Territory of North America.* London, 1797.

INGRAHAM, J. H., *The Sunny South.* Philadelphia, 1860.

JAMES, JAMES ALTON, *Oliver Pollock, The Life and Times of an Unknown Patriot.* New York, 1937.

JEWELL, EDWIN L. (ed. and comp.), *Crescent City Illustrated, The Commercial, Social, Political and General History of New Orleans.* New Orleans, 1873.

JOHNSON, THOMAS C., *The Life and Letters of Benjamin Morgan Palmer.* Richmond, 1906.

KEATING, J. M., *History of Memphis.* Syracuse, 1886.

——— *History of the Yellow Fever.* Memphis, 1887.

KENDALL, JOHN S., *History of New Orleans.* Chicago, 1922.

KING, GRACE, *Creole Families of New Orleans.* New York, 1921.

——— *Sieur de Bienville.* New York, 1892.

LANMAN, CHARLES, *Adventures in the Wilds of the United States* (2 vols.). Philadelphia, 1856.

Mafia in New Orleans, The. Collection of pamphlets in the Howard-Tilton Memorial Library, New Orleans.

MARBOIS, BARBÉ, *The History of Louisiana, Particularly of the Cession of That Colony to the U.S.A.* Philadelphia, 1830.

MARGRY, PIERRE, *Découvertes et Établissements des Français.* Paris, 1876-1886.

——— *Mémoires et Documents pour Servir à l'Histoire des Origines Françaises des Pays d'Outre-Mer.* Paris, 1879.

MARSHALL, THEODORA BRITTON, and EVANS, GLADYS CRAIL, *They Found It in Natchez.* New Orleans, 1939.

MARTIN, F. X., *The History of Louisiana from the Earliest Period.* New Orleans, 1829.

MATHEWS, CATHERINE VAN CORTLANDT, *Andrew Ellicott, His Life and Letters.* New York, 1908.

McNEILY, J. S., *War and Reconstruction in Mississippi.* Publications of the Mississippi Historical Society, Jackson, Miss., 1908.

MERCIER, LOUIS SEBASTIAN, *Memoirs of the Year Two Thousand Five Hundred.* Liverpool, 1802.

Mississippi River, The. Mississippi River Commission, Vicksburg, 1940.

MONETTE, JOHN W., *History of the Discovery and Settlement of the Valley of the Mississippi.* New York, 1848.

New Orleans as It Is. New Orleans, 1850.

NOLTE, VINCENT O., *Fifty Years in Both Hemispheres* (translated from German). New York, 1854.

PARKMAN, FRANCIS, *La Salle and the Discovery of the West.* Boston, 1907.

PERCY, WILLIAM A., *Lanterns on the Levee.* New York, 1941.

PHILLIPS, ULRICH B., *Life and Labor in the Old South.* New York, 1929.

PICKETT, ALBERT J., *Eight Days in New Orleans.* Montgomery, Ala., 1847.

PITTMAN, PHILIP, *The Present State of the European Settlements on the Mississippi.* London, 1770.

PRENTISS, GEORGE L., *A Memoir of S. S. Prentiss.* New York, 1886.

QUICK, HERBERT and EDWARD, *Mississippi Steamboatin'.* New York, 1926.

QUINN, DENIS A., *Heroes and Heroines of Memphis.* Providence, 1887.

RAND, CLAYTON, *Men of Spine in Mississippi.* Gulfport, Miss., 1940.

RAVEN-HART, ROWLAND, *Down the Mississippi.* Boston, 1938.

REED, WILLIAM, *History of Sugar and Sugar Yielding Plants.* London, 1866.

RICCIUTI, ITALIO W., *New Orleans and Its Environs; the Domestic Architecture.* New York, 1918.

ROBERTSON, JAMES ALEXANDER, *Louisiana Under the Rule of Spain, France and the United States, 1785-1807.* Cleveland, 1911.

ROOSEVELT, THEODORE, *Louisiana and Aaron Burr (The Winning of the West).* New York, 1896.

ROURKE, CONSTANCE, *Audubon.* New York, 1936.

ROWLAND, DUNBAR (ed.), *English Dominion Letters and Enclosures to the Secretary of State from Major Robert Farmer and Governor George Johnstone.* Nashville, 1911.

———— *History of Mississippi, the Heart of the South.* Chicago, 1925.

———— (ed.), *Official Letterbooks of W. C. C. Claiborne.* Jackson, Miss., 1917.

ROWLAND, DUNBAR (ed.), *A Symposium on the Place of Discovery of the Mississippi River by Hernando de Soto*. Mississippi Historical Society, Jackson, Miss., 1927.

ROWLAND, MRS. DUNBAR, *Life, Letters and Papers of William Dunbar*. Jackson, Miss., 1930.

SAXON, LYLE, *Fabulous New Orleans*. New York, 1928.

—— *Father Mississippi*. New York, 1927.

—— *Lafitte the Pirate*. New York, 1930.

—— *Old Louisiana*. New York, 1929.

SCHULTZ, CHRISTIAN, *Travels on an Inland Voyage Through the State of New York*. New York, 1810.

SEIFERT, SHIRLEY, *River Out of Eden*. New York, 1940.

SHEA, JOHN D. G., *Early Voyages Up and Down the Mississippi*. Albany, 1861.

SHIELDS, JOSEPH DUNBAR, *Natchez, Its Early History* (edited by Elizabeth D. Shields). Louisville, 1930.

South in the Building of the Nation (12 vols.). Richmond, 1909.

SOUTHWOOD, MARION, *Beauty and Booty, the Watchword of New Orleans*. New York, 1867.

Souvenir Program of the 50th Anniversary of Mound Bayou, Mississippi. Greenville, Miss., 1937.

SPRATLING, WILLIAM, and SCOTT, NATALIE, *Old Plantation Houses in Louisiana*. New York, 1927.

STAHL (?), (GEORGE M. WHARTON), *The New Orleans Sketch Book*, Philadelphia, 1853.

STAPLES, THOMAS S., *Reconstruction in Arkansas*. New York, 1923.

Status of Flood Control Legislation and Works. Hearings before the Committee on Flood Control, House of Representatives, Seventy-sixth Congress, First Session. Washington, May, 1939.

STEELE, MAJOR MATTHEW FORNEY, *American Campaigns*. Washington, 1909.

STODDARD, AMOS, *Sketches of Louisiana*. Philadelphia, 1812.

TAYLOR, RICHARD, *Destruction and Reconstruction*, New York, 1879.

THORPE, T. B., *The Hive of the Bee Hunter*. New York, 1854.

TINKER, EDWARD, L., *Pens, Pills and Pistols*. Franco-American Pamphlet Series, New York, 1931.

TONTI, HENRI DE, *Relation of Henri de Tonti Concerning the Explorations of La Salle from 1678 to 1883* (translated from French). Chicago, 1898.

TROLLOPE, FRANCES, *Domestic Manners of the Americans*. London, 1832.

TWAIN, MARK, *Life on the Mississippi*. New York, 1908.

Vue de la Colonie Espagnole du Mississippi ou des Provinces de Louisiane et Florida Occidentale en l'Année 1802. Paris, 1803.

WALTON, AUGUSTUS Q., *A History of the Detection, Life and Designs of John A. Murel*. Athens, Tenn., 1835.

WARDEN, D. B., *A Statistical, Political, and Historical Account of the United States of North America* (3 vols.). Edinburgh, 1819.

WARMOTH, HENRY CLAY, *War, Politics and Reconstruction*. New York, 1930.

WAUGH, WILLIAM F., *The Houseboat Book*. Chicago, 1904.

WHITTINGTON, WILLIAM M., *Flood Control and State's Rights*. Washington, 1939.

WILLIAMSON, FREDERICK W., *Yesterday and Today in Louisiana Agriculture*. Baton Rouge, 1940.

WISSLER, CLARK, *Indians of the United States—Four Centuries of Their History and Culture*. New York, 1940.

Manuscripts

Archives of the Spanish Government of West Florida, 19th Judicial District Court, Baton Rouge, La., Vol. 8. Transcribed by Survey of Federal Archives in Louisiana, Works Progress Administration.

JENNINGS, NEEDLER R., and HENNEN, ALFRED, Family Papers, 1796-1901. A. W. Spiller Collection, Hammond, La.

JOHNSON, WILLIAM T., and FAMILY, Memorial Collection. Department of Archives, Louisiana State University, Baton Rouge, La.

MANDEVILLE, HENRY D., and FAMILY, Papers. Department of Archives, Louisiana State University, Baton Rouge, La.

MARKHAM, THOMAS and WILLIAM, Papers. Department of Archives, Louisiana State University, Baton Rouge, La.

MINOR, WILLIAM J., and FAMILY, Papers. Department of Archives, Louisiana State University, Baton Rouge, La.

Periodicals

BRYCE, JAMES, "Legal and Constitutional Aspects of the Lynching at New Orleans," *New Review*, May, 1891.

BUEL, C. C., "The Degradation of a State; or the Charitable Career of the Louisiana Lottery," *Century Magazine*, February, 1892.

CRAVEN, AVERY, " 'The Turner Theories' and the South," *Journal of Southern History*, 1939.

DAVIS, EDWIN A., "Bennet H. Barrow, Ante-Bellum Planter of the Felicianas," *Journal of Southern History*, November, 1939.

De Bow's Review, New Orleans, 1846-1880.

DIMITRY, CHARLES, "Zamba's Plot, A Chapter in the History of New Orleans," *Magazine of American History*, December, 1884.

GAYARRÉ, CHARLES, "A Louisiana Sugar Plantation of the Old Regime," *Harper's New Monthly Magazine*, December, 1886–May, 1887.

Louisiana Historical Quarterly, New Orleans, 1917–.

MARR, ROBERT H., JR., "The New Orleans Mafia Case," *American Law Review*, May–June, 1891.

McGLOIN, FRANK, "Shall the Lottery's Charter Be Renewed?" *Forum*, January, 1892.

SCRAMUZZA, V. M., "Galveztown, A Spanish Settlement of Colonial Louisiana," *Louisiana Historical Quarterly*, October, 1930.

STEPHENSON, WENDELL H., "A Quarter-Century of a Mississippi Plantation: Eli J. Capell of 'Pleasant Hill,' " *Mississippi Valley Historical Review*, 1936.

STUBBS, W. C., "Origin and Development of the Sugar Industry of Louisiana," *Louisiana Sugar Planter and Sugar Manufacturer*, June 2, 1923.

SWEARINGEN, MACK, "Thirty Years of a Mississippi Plantation: Charles Whitmore of 'Montpelier,' " *Journal of Southern History*, 1935.

WICKLIFFE, JOHN C., "The Louisiana Lottery: A History of the Company," *Forum*, January, 1892.

Theses

SINGLETARY, MATTIE BELL CAWTHON, "Louisiana's Mysterious Manchac." M.A., Louisiana State University, 1931.

WHITE, JOHN T., "The History of the Louisiana Lottery." M.A., Tulane University, 1939.

Miscellaneous

BUCK, PAUL, Southern history lectures at Harvard University, 1940.

Newspapers

The files of the Natchez (Miss.) *Democrat*, Natchez *Semi-Weekly Courier*, New Orleans *Daily Delta*, New Orleans *Daily Picayune*, New Orleans *Item*, New Orleans *Item-Tribune*, New Orleans *Moniteur de la Louisiane*, New Orleans *The New Delta*, New Orleans *Times-Democrat*, New York *Spirit of the Times*, Memphis *Commercial Appeal*, Memphis *Appeal*, Greenville (Miss.) *Times* and *Democrat-Times*, Baton Rouge *State-Times*, and Vicksburg *Herald*.

Index

453